DICKENS AND CRIME

DICKENS AND CRIME

BY

PHILIP COLLINS

INDIANA UNIVERSITY PRESS
BLOOMINGTON   LONDON

CONTENTS

An ardent desire to understand and explain his works is, to the honour of the present age, so much increased within the last forty years, that more has been done towards their elucidation, during that period, than in a century before. . . . The meanest books have been carefully examined, only because they were of the age in which he lived, and might happily throw a light on some forgotten custom, or obsolete phraseology; and, this object being still kept in view, the toil of wading through *all such reading as was never read* has been cheerfully endured. . . . Almost every circumstance that tradition or history has preserved relative to him or his works, has been investigated, and laid before the publick. . . .

EDMUND MALONE
'*An attempt to Ascertain the Order in which the Plays of Shakespeare were Written*', *1790*

"PROBABLY no other writer in English literature offers himself to such a variety of approaches as does Dickens," remarked Professor J. Hillis Miller in a symposium on *Dickens Criticism: Past, Present and Future Directions* held (and published) in Boston in 1962. Professor Miller, while acknowledging that most approaches had their usefulness, was worried about the tendency to seek in Dickens and his literary contemporaries too much "what can somehow be melted into the general context of Victorianism" instead of paying attention to what was likely to provide a richer interest, those parts of Victorian novels and poems which transcend their age. He was answered by Professor George H. Ford, who suggested that a knowledge of the historical context was anything but detrimental to the significant work of literature, however much it might tend to reduce the secondary work to a mere historical phenomenon; and he saw as one "future direction" in Dickens criticism a fuller exploration of cultural history:

> How profitable it has been to discover in what respects Dickens is like Kafka or like William Faulkner or like Angus Wilson—as he is. But may we not have reached a stage where it would be equally profitable to remind ourselves that he is like Carlyle, like Thackeray, like Browning—as he is? . . . The reader of Dickens who has been intimately familiar with the critical theories of Henry James or with the writings of Proust or Gide or Joyce has had obvious advantages in assessing his novels. But we shall also need scholarly readers who are equally intimately familiar with the writings of Ruskin, Arnold, Thackeray, and even such minor novelists as G. W. M. Reynolds; familiar also with the Victorian newspapers and magazines, for Dickens read them, and with Victorian sermons, for Dickens listened to them. A gap, that is, exists in our studies of Dickens which needs to be closed over.

The present book, and its later companion-volume *Dickens and Education,* are attempts to close parts of this gap: and I am surprised that, in the present boom in Dickens studies (on both sides of the Atlantic, and outside the English-speaking world too) comparatively little has been done to reduce this gap from other directions. Humphry House's *The Dickens World* (1941), the study which most influenced my approach, is, though very suggestive, a short book which

necessarily leaves unexamined many areas of so large a world as
Dickens reflects in his novels; and we have the advantage over House
of a quarter of a century's further detailed scholarship on Dickens
and on the Victorian period. My work does not, of course, stand alone
as a successor to House's or an answer to Professor Ford's plea: Professor Ford's own book on Dickens's critical reception and reputation,
and various books and essays by Professors Kathleen Tillotson, John
Butt, K. J. Fielding, Ada Nisbet, and Monroe Engel (among others)
have clarified further aspects of his relationship with his times. But
much remains to be done, and some of the most stimulating of recent
critical work on Dickens could (as I think) have been the more convincing if more continuously informed by a sense of the Victorian
implications of his writings.

Thus, when I find myself dissenting from some of the arguments
in Professor Hillis Miller's brilliant and influential book, *Charles
Dickens: The World of his Novels* (1958), it is often because he strikes
me as misapprehending passages from the novels, through failing to
control his reactions to them by an historical awareness of what they
could have meant to their author and his original readers. Certainly,
as Professor Miller said in the symposium, Dickens matters because
he transcends his age (and because in his concerns he speaks with
peculiar urgency and relevance to ours); but, at more points and more
fully than almost any other English writer, he participates in and
starts from the features of his own period, and if we ignore (or are
ignorant of) this fact, we risk re-creating his novels as twentieth-
century works, or as American or Russian or German rather than
essentially English ones. It may be less exciting, but it is safer and
juster, to try to read them faithfully as what they are; and my book
will, I trust, help this process and will at least not hinder understanding by imagining a Dickens that never was.

Professor Fielding, reviewing my book, suggested that "many of its
profounder critical implications still remain to be drawn." I hope indeed that my readers will be stimulated to further awareness that I
lacked the space (or the wit) to discuss. In my Preface to the Second
Edition, I acknowledge that I would now write some things differ-
ently and would give more attention to some matters which I insufficiently explored, and I mentioned some later studies of Dickens which
would have supplemented or modified my views. It may be useful if I
now mention some more recent books that further advance our knowledge or interpretation, in this area of his work.

Felix Aylmer's *The Drood Case* (1964) is an ingenious attempt to solve the mystery; I cannot accept his case, but it deserves examination. Three general studies of Dickens contain arguments I would certainly discuss, if I were now rewriting the present book: Steven Marcus's *Dickens from "Pickwick" to "Dombey"* (1965), particularly on *Martin Chuzzlewit;* Taylor Stoehr's *Dickens: The Dreamer's Stance* (1965), and Ross H. Dabney's *Love and Property in the Novels of Dickens* (1967). On *Great Expectations,* a novel I discussed insufficiently, there are useful new studies by R. George Thomas (1964) and John Barnes (1966), and a handy collection of comments, *Assessing Great Expectations,* edited by Richard Lettis and William E. Morris (1960). The Clarendon Edition of *Oliver Twist* (1966), edited by Kathleen Tillotson, contains a wealth of detail about the composition and reception of the novel, and a useful glossary of thieves' slang, as well as establishing a more accurate text and recording the variants (which are often significant).

The book I most regret not having been able to draw upon, however, is J. J. Tobias's *Crime and Industrial Society in the 19th Century* (1967). Based on a great deal of new research, this is much the most convenient and learned survey that I know of criminals and their treatment in the Dickens period. It would have greatly amplified and enriched the background of my book: and it provides useful and convincing confirmation both of the substantial accuracy of Dickens's presentments of this part of his society, and of my arguments about the degree of his typicality on matters of opinion.

P.A.W. C.

The University of Leicester
April 1968

DICKENS AND CRIME

I

DICKENS AND HIS AGE

'WHAT he liked to talk about was the latest new piece at the theatres, the latest exciting trial or police case, the latest social craze or social swindle, and especially the latest murder and the newest thing in ghosts': thus George Augustus Sala described the conversation of his friend and master Charles Dickens.[1]* These are common tastes, and Dickens was, of all great writers, the closest in outlook to the common man of his day and of ours; he was not ashamed to avow these tastes, for he never assumed the airs of social or intellectual superiority. Not that these tastes were frowned upon at this time: even the *Annual Register* then devoted a generous amount of space to the year's most notable criminal trials. His interest in the more spectacular aspects of crime was, in the first place, that ordinary ghoulish delight which has made the fortunes, over the centuries, of the proprietors of *The Newgate Calendar*, *The Police Gazette*, broadsheet 'Last Confessions', *The News of the World*, and their like.

His concern with crime was, however, more persistent and more serious than most men's. Extraordinary in character as well as in literary skill, he had strong and conflicting feelings about criminals. He readily identified himself, in imagination, with their aggressive activities, but would also strongly repudiate this sympathy by extolling their adversaries, the police, and by demanding severe punishment for offenders against the law. At one period he even contemplated becoming a paid Metropolitan Magistrate. This ambition came to nothing, for he lacked the necessary qualifications, but anyway he already had another kind of professional pre-occupation with crime. The literary tradition in which he chose to write — the 'Sensation Novel', related both to Gothic fiction and stage melodrama — was rich in violence, villainy and mystery. Sinister strangers lurk in the background; there are secrets — long-lost wills or heirs, or undetected misdemeanours — which

---

* Notes are printed at the end of the book. When the superior numeral in the text is italicised it indicates that the Note to which it refers contains additional information or discussion.

I

the wicked characters seek to maintain; crimes are committed, flights and pursuits ensue. Dickens's commercial interest in sensational excitement is seen at its simplest level in such a letter as this, to Wilkie Collins, who was collaborating with him on a story:

> I have a general idea which I hope will supply the kind of interest we want. Let us arrange to culminate in a wintry flight and pursuit across the Alps, under lonely circumstances, and against warnings. Let us get into all the horrors and dangers of such an adventure under the most terrific circumstances, either escaping from or trying to overtake (the latter, the latter I think) someone, on escaping from or overtaking whom the love, prosperity, and Nemesis of the story depend. There we can get Ghostly interest, picturesque interest, breathless interest of time and circumstance, and force the design up to any powerful climax we please. If you will keep this in your mind as I will in mine, urging the story towards it as we go along, we shall get a very Avalanche of power out of it, and thunder it down on the readers' heads.[2]

Later he and Collins devised a suitable pursuer and pursued, and endowed the latter with an ample achievement in crime. For Dickens inclined more to the criminal regulars of sensational fiction — thieves, swindlers, and murderers — than to such favourite civil offenders as heartless seducers, rapacious landlords, and greedy money-lenders. Few of his novels are without one or two of the grosser offences against property or the person; few closing chapters lack the operation of justice, human or divine, against the offenders — prison, the gallows, disgrace, or providential sudden death.

There was a further reason why, inevitably, he gave so much attention to this topic. Crime, then as now, was not merely the morbid concern of the newspaper addict, and the great stand-by of popular story-tellers: it was an inescapable social problem, and Dickens is of course conspicuous among great novelists for his passion for dramatising and commenting upon the outstanding topical issues of his day. Particularly in his earlier years, crime was formidably common and unchecked; pocket-picking, for instance, was then a highly-organised major industry. On this ground alone, the Gaol and the Gallows were bound to occupy him, along with the School, the Workhouse, and other such central social institutions. This was the more likely, because his lifetime coincided with the greatest period of legal and penal reform in our history. In

1837, the year which saw the completion of his first novel (*Pickwick Papers*), Queen Victoria made her first speech to Parliament, a month after her accession. 'I perceive with satisfaction,' she said, 'that you have brought to maturity some useful measures among which I regard with peculiar interest the amendment of the Criminal Code and the reduction of the number of Capital Punishments. I hail this mitigation of the severity of the law as an auspicious commencement of my reign.'[3] The movement for reform had been active for two decades, and by the middle of Victoria's reign almost every aspect of the social treatment of crime had been overhauled, and many had been radically altered: the criminal law and its administration in the courts, the police system, the prisons and other forms of detention, and the scope and operation of capital and other such physical punishments.

When Dickens died, in 1870, the system for dealing with criminals was recognisably the one we have inherited; the system that obtained in his boyhood belongs to another world, at least as much akin to the sixteenth century as to the twentieth. Exactly what the changes were, how they came about, and how Dickens regarded them, will appear more fully in later chapters, but it may be useful here to sketch the background of these momentous years, so that the nature of Dickens's interest in these matters may be more apparent.

Dickens was born in 1812, only four years after Sir Samuel Romilly had begun his Parliamentary campaign to reduce the savagery of the law. In 1810, Romilly said that 'there is probably no other country in the world in which so many and so great a variety of human actions is punishable with loss of life as in England'. Twenty years later, after the passage of many Acts, the Home Secretary, Robert Peel, could still justly tell the House of Commons that 'capital punishments are more frequent and the criminal law more severe on the whole in this country than in any country in the world'.[4] Under the 'Bloody Code', over two hundred offences were capital; indeed, the Home Office return for persons committed for trial in 1817 showed that a majority of the 13,932 persons accused of crimes were liable to be punished by death.[5] Very few of those found guilty were actually executed, however, and many offenders had escaped detection or prosecution altogether, because the police system was so inefficient, or because their victims were reluctant to prosecute when such a savage penalty might be exacted for a relatively trivial offence. The existing court-procedure, too, in some ways favoured the criminal, while juries often quite blatantly reduced the charge on which the prisoner was found guilty, to remove him from danger of the gallows — if, indeed, they did not altogether refuse to convict. Indeed, the most telling argument for reform of these laws was not the humane impulse of Romilly and his followers but the spate of Petitions from property-owners and business-houses, begging that Parliament would reduce the penalties for offences against property, from death to some punishment which juries would be willing to countenance; at the moment, they complained, their interests were unprotected because offenders could reckon on escaping any penalty, through the soft-heartedness of juries. Some offenders guessed wrong, of course: a jury might commit an accused man, through detestation of his crime or in the expectation that he would be reprieved, and the reprieve might not be granted. But even in the first decade of the century, only one in seven of persons capitally committed was actually hanged.[6]

Like many other aspects of the criminal and judicial system of the early nineteenth century, the possibility of incurring execution was very much a lottery, and thus the law, for all its savagery, was demonstrably ineffective as a deterrent. The chances of escaping detection, prosecution, and conviction were all very high; so was the chance of a reprieve, if the sentence was capital. Prison, according to the luck of the locality where one was convicted, and depending also on one's physical and financial resources, could be very comfortable, even profitable, or it could be almost bestially unpleasant and degrading. As an experienced prison-official wrote of the 1820s, when he began his duties: 'Useless severity was strangely combined with the most pernicious laxity.'[7] Some trivial or venial offenders were hanged; at Chelmsford, for instance, a man was hanged in 1814 for cutting down a cherry-tree, and a boy aged nine in 1831 for setting fire to a house. From 1832 onwards, however, murder was virtually the only crime for which capital punishment was exacted; from the 1820s onwards, one crime after another became non-capital, until in 1861 the Offences against the Person Act defined the system which remained basically unchanged until the Homicide Act of 1957 — only four capital offences remained, namely murder, treason, piracy, and setting fire to dockyards and arsenals. During Dickens's lifetime, too, the adjuncts and circumstances of capital punishment took on their present form. In 1820 occurred the last beheading after hanging, and in 1832 the last gibbeting; in 1832 also the Anatomy Act ended the barbarous custom of publicly dissecting the bodies of certain hanged persons. Most important was the Capital Punishment Amendment Act of 1868, which at last made executions private (though for another twenty years they were witnessed by newspaper men and other 'privileged' guests of the Sheriff). Dickens had urged this reform, twenty years earlier, and has often been given a good share of the credit for its eventual adoption. Other barbarous public punishments had been abolished back in the 1820s and 1830s. As late as 1810, a newspaper could report without indignation the pillorying of four men, who were blinded and unconscious, and one of them not expected to live, after the missiles and blows they had received from the crowd.[8] This punishment was abolished in 1816, and so a few years later were public whippings, while the frequency and severity of flogging inside the prison walls were also greatly reduced. If the punishments that were still exacted in 1870 seem harsh by the standards of nearly a century later, they were much more humane, and more rationally adjusted to the offences that earned them, than they had been in 1812.

During the same period, there was a notable change in the prisons. It is significant that the word 'penology' was invented in 1838, and by an American author; America was, at this time, the international leader in penal matters, and punishment was just beginning to be regarded scientifically. It is equally significant that the allied word 'criminology' arrived much later — in 1885, and from Italy — for the belief in the efficacy of a science of punishment was strong in the 1830s and 1840s, and it was the gradual disillusion of this belief that led to a deeper study of the individual criminal, and of his physical and psychological characteristics.[9] The criminal prisons of England were generally in a shocking state when Dickens was a boy — inefficient, corrupt, and lacking in any defined purpose. With the exception of a few Crown establishments — the Tower of London, the Hulks, and Millbank Penitentiary — they came under the control of local county and civic authorities, and therefore varied enormously, according to the diligence, good sense, and policy of the local Visiting Magistrates. Various Prisons Acts existed, but there was only the most nominal enforcement, so they were ignored widely and with impunity. Howard's work in the late eighteenth century had effected some temporary good, and some of his admirers had built, and continued to administer, prisons of a better type, under his inspiration, but, as the Victorian penal reformer, Matthew Davenport Hill, said: 'With the exception of those changes which approve themselves to the common instincts of benevolence, such as cleanliness, ventilation, drainage, &c, the seed sown by Howard fell in stony places. Whatever required the faintest tincture of philosophy for its appreciation was lost, and had to be refound, and in many cases it has been reinvented.'[10] Few prisons of the first three decades of the century could even boast of much cleanliness, ventilation or drainage, while most kinds of barbarity, laxity and mal-administration flourished. As was noted above, a prisoner's fate depended largely on the luck of where he was committed, how strong was his arm, and how deep his purse. Many gaolers and turnkeys were open to bribery; they sold various privileges, sometimes connived at escapes, and regularly trafficked at great profit in the large stores of illicit goods entering their prisons. Male and female prisoners were often in the same prison, sometimes in the same building or room, and the officials did not always strive to promote propriety; they were, indeed, often involved financially and otherwise in the systematic debauchery of the female prisoners. Work might be non-existent in a prison, or it might take the form of the treadmill (invented in 1818) or of that perennial favourite of prison-governors, oakum-picking. Some prisons, on the other hand, taught trades or were highly-organised factories, either with a view to the permanent benefit of the prisoners or to relieve the Rates by making a profit from their work.

This haphazard system was transformed by a series of Prison Acts, of which those of 1823 and 1835 were the most important. The 1823 Act was the first general prison-reform measure framed and enacted by a Government (Peel was Home Secretary), but though its provisions were a great improvement on existing practice it was largely ineffective, being limited in scope and still providing no adequate machinery for inspection and enforcement. As a magistrate had said back in 1793, 'It is not so much for want of good laws, as from their inexecution, that the state of the prisons is so bad.'[11] This fault was remedied in 1835, when the Home Secretary was empowered to appoint Prison Inspectors, who soon made their presence felt throughout the country. Four years later, special institutions began to be provided for juvenile and lunatic offenders. Subsequent legislation followed a familiar Victorian pattern, in two respects: firstly, it progressively increased the power of the central government over local authorities, until in 1877 all prisons became vested in the government; secondly, a series of Acts, permissive and then mandatory, regulated various aspects of the architecture, organisation, functions and discipline of prisons. Behind these organisational changes there was a long and heated debate about the fundamentals of prison-discipline. The old gaolers had been little more than the agents of detention; this aim was now seen to be inadequate, and much discussion and experiment were devoted to the question whether reformation or deterrence should be the primary purpose of imprisonment, and which of several rival systems of prison-government best promoted one or other or both of these ends.

The abolition of imprisonment for debt, in the 1860s, relieved the prisons of one large group of inmates, but this hardly compensated for the continued increase in criminal prisoners due to the final ending of transportation in the same decade. Under the Bloody Code, transportation to the colonies had been the main substitute for the death penalty. Strongly criticised by the 1837 Select Committee, the system was modified in the following years, but the vociferous refusal of one colony after another to accept any more transports brought about the virtual end of transportation by 1852; the last convict-ship left England in 1867, and the Gibraltar convict prison, the last refuge of the system, was closed in 1874. The last of the Hulks had closed in 1858. To replace these receptacles for the criminal population, the penal servitude system was devised and a number of great convict-prisons were established, some of which, such as Dartmoor, are still familiar names. Most of our existing prisons, indeed, date from the mid-nineteenth century, the great age of prison-building — not only the convict-prisons but the local prisons (as they then were) such as Wandsworth, Brixton, Holloway, Strangeways and Wakefield. Nor was the money skimped on those monuments to Victorian penology. Reading Gaol, completed in 1844, was reckoned the finest building in Berkshire except Windsor Castle; its architecture, wrote its proud Chaplain, symbolised its twin aims, for 'With the castellated it combines a collegiate appearance'.[12] The frequency of Royal Commissions and Select Committees into one aspect or another of the treatment of crime, and the series of Prisons Acts and Penal Servitude Acts, likewise show an urgent, if confused, official interest in these large problems. By the end of Dickens's life, the penal system had settled in the form which it kept until the twentieth century. The Penal Servitude Acts of 1853 and 1857, the Prison Act of 1865, and the Habitual Criminals Act of 1869, established a severe regime for the serious, and even the trivial, offender; remission could be earned by good conduct, while recidivists could receive long sentences of preventive detention. During his sentence, a prisoner passed through Progressive Stages, with increasing, though never generous, privileges.

One other major development in the treatment of crime during this period must be noted: the notable improvement in the police forces. In Dickens's boyhood, England was still the worst-policed nation of the civilised world. The ramshackle system of parish-constables and watchmen, inherited from Tudor times, had only been modified, since the mid-eighteenth century, by a few more efficient local units such as the Bow Street Runners and Patroles, and the Thames River Police. The situation was gradually and remarkably transformed after Peel's momentous 1829 Act establishing the Metropolitan Police. The Metropolitan force extended its area of responsibility during the next few years, and, from being a mocked and hated body of men, became quite soon an accepted and then a respected part of the London scene. The *doyen* of English constabularies, it soon also became their model, for again legislation followed the familiar pattern: permissive Acts for establishing municipal and county police forces were followed by compulsory Acts, with the Government gaining fuller control through an Inspectorate backed by financial sanctions. By 1856, the whole country was policed by full-time paid forces on the new model. Jokes about Bobbies and their partiality for cooks and their kitchens had begun their long career, and some old fogies continued to lament the passing of the Bow Street Runners, whom they considered superior to the Metropolitan force, but there was general agreement that the New Police were more efficient and diligent, and less corrupt, than their predecessors. The early decades of Scotland Yard were, indeed, remarkably free from serious and sustainable charges of corruption; it was not until 1877 that public confidence in the police was badly shaken, when the 'de Goncourt case' proved that most of the senior members of the Detective Department were involved in a fraudulent race-gang. This Department, which became the CID in 1878, had been established in 1842, and though it remained very small in numbers throughout this period it soon had earned a record of creditable achievement. By the 1850s, the popular prestige and mystique of the Detective had become established.

'The primary object of an efficient police force is the prevention of crime:' so ran the first of the nine Principles of Police devised by Peel and the two Metropolitan Commissioners in 1829.[13] Many other ideas about the Prevention of Crime were being discussed and tried out, however. 'Which is best, — to pay for the policeman or the schoolmaster, — the prison or the school?' asked one pamphleteer, and mottoes to the effect that the teacher was 'the cheapest policeman', and that 'a penny spent in teaching will save a pound in punishing', were common. 'What is crime? Ignorance — in action,' ran the epigraph of one leading book on London's prisons.[14] Many books and essays, ranging from the impressionistic and rhetorical to the doggedly statistical, traced the relation between crime and its 'cause' or 'causes', and undoubtedly the favourite explanation was Ignorance. The remedy was clear — more and better schools, with compulsory attendance. Another factor often mentioned was bad housing; better standards of social responsibility, it was argued, would emerge if such foul rookeries were destroyed as the notorious criminal areas of London's Seven Dials, Jacob's Island and Saffron Hill. Not in England alone, the study of 'criminal ecology' was beginning, though it was still at a pre-scientific, or quasi-scientific, stage.[15] A fine example of this study of crime as a social phenomenon is Henry Mayhew's fourth, supplementary, volume of *London Labour and the London Post*, entitled *Those that will not Work* (1862), and the sections on the causes of crime in his *Criminal Prisons of London*, published in the same year. Many other 'causes of crime' were being canvassed by various investigators or speculative pamphleteers — drunkenness, vagrancy, laziness inborn or acquired, religious unbelief or ignorance, over-population. Some authors blamed everything on one factor; others, more cautious, listed a number. Frederic Hill, for instance, a former Prison Inspector, named six — bad training and ignorance; drunkenness and other profligacy; poverty; habits of violating the laws, engendered by the creation of artificial offences; other unjust, unnecessary and vexatious laws; and the probability of escaping detection, or of receiving only a light punishment.[16]

While many such observers were trying to define, and then to eradicate, the causes of crime, other philanthropists were making great efforts to reclaim offenders, particularly juveniles, or to save those who were on the brink of a criminal career. Dickens's age is the great period of the foundation of such charitable organisations. The Ragged School movement began in the 1840s, the Reformatory School movement in the 1850s: under the pressure of these voluntary organisations, Parliament passed the 1847 Juvenile Offenders Act, the 1854 Reformatory School Act ('the Magna Carta of the neglected child') and the 1857 Industrial School Act, which provided special institutions for the training and correction of delinquent or neglected children. As a prison-chaplain remarked, with reference to Lord Shaftesbury's invaluable work for the Ragged and Reformatory Schools: 'Our age has more need of an Ashley than a Howard.'[17] The '40s and '50s also saw the establishment of many Asylums and Refuges for incipient or repentant prostitutes, in an attempt to cure 'the Great Social Evil'. Adult male offenders were a less dramatic, and doubtless a less promising, field for philanthropic work, but from the 1850s onwards there was a steady growth in local Discharged Prisoners' Aid Societies, aimed at helping them too to settle down to an honest way of life.

Dickens's lifetime, then, spanned a period of remarkable developments in the criminal law and its administration, in the scale and spirit of punishment, in police organisation and techniques, in the study of the causes of crime, and in attempts to remove or reduce these causes. Most of these developments occurred most strikingly, too, during his adult working life — from 1836, when his first books appeared, to 1870 when he died. A man so alert to the most dramatic social problems and changes of his day inevitably found occasion to dramatise these issues, and, as my reminder about the nature of his novel-tradition showed, his plots often provided opportunities for crime to occur in one form or another. Dr Walter Phillips, in his book *Dickens, Reade and Collins: Sensation Novelists*, argues that Dickens popularised this tradition, though Bulwer Lytton began it. The earlier novels of Lytton are much concerned with criminal psychology and the social causes and treatment of crime, especially *Pelham* (1828), *Paul Clifford* (1830), *Eugene Aram* (1832), and *Night and Morning* (1841). Dickens admired Lytton, and learned from him, as Mr Jack Lindsay has shown. Harrison Ainsworth's vastly popular *Jack Sheppard* (1839) was the most important item in what reviewers identified as 'the Newgate School' of fiction. Dickens was often included in this 'School', to his great annoyance, on the strength of *Oliver Twist* and perhaps also because *Jack Sheppard* had begun its serial run in

Bentley's Miscellany before Dickens handed over its editorship to Ainsworth. Later it was in Dickens's own periodical *All the Year Round* that Wilkie Collins's great mysteries *The Woman in White* (1859–60) and *The Moonstone* (1868) first appeared; Charles Reade was another of his contributors, though Reade's indignant novel on the scandals of prison-discipline, *It is never too late to mend* (1856), appeared elsewhere.

Collins's novels are generally reckoned the first English detective-stories, but this new form of fiction was of course arising independently elsewhere: Poe in America and Balzac in France are two obvious names. Indeed, a similar concatenation of literary and social forces was producing in several countries a new kind of interest in crime as a fictional subject. The penological debate of the late 1820s and the 1830s was international, spreading from America to Britain, France, the Low Countries, Scandinavia and Prussia at about the same time; at this period, too, all these nations were devising more scientific methods of detective work and police organisation. The fictional possibilities of these social questions and developments were manifest; the 'novel with a purpose', the 'social novel', the detective-story and the sensational thriller could all avail themselves of one or another of these new slants on a perennial literary theme. Thus, much of what M. Savey-Casard writes in *Le Crime et la Peine dans l'œuvre de Victor Hugo* may be applied to Dickens. 'Les questions qui se rattachent au crime et à la peine ont été à l'ordre du jour durant l'époque romantique,' he begins, and he goes on to show how this interest flourished at the level both of popular entertainment and of serious philosophical and psychological exploration, and how it derived both from morbid curiosity and from pity for the suffering and oppressed. 'Victor Hugo, qui fut l'écho de son siècle, a été attiré d'un bout à l'autre de sa carrière par ces questions de droit pénal qui passionaient ses contemporains' — Dickens's name could clearly be substituted for Hugo's here. One other great novelist from this period might be mentioned, as a reminder of how widespread was the criminal theme and at what various depths it could operate: Dostoyevsky's *Letters from a Dead House*, about his Siberian prison-experience, appeared in 1861–2, *Crime and Punishment* in 1866, *The Possessed* in 1871, and *The Brothers Karamazov* in 1880; and Dostoyevsky was a great admirer and professed imitator of Dickens.[18]

Dickens was not only a novelist, however. As several references

have already reminded us, he was also a leading editor and
journalist. Early in his career he edited, but did not own, *Bentley's
Miscellany* (1837-9) and the *Daily News* (1846). During the last
twenty years of his life he was editing, or 'conducting', his own
weekly magazines (*Household Words* from 1850, and *All the Year
Round* from 1859). These contained, along with fiction and light
essays, many articles on social questions such as crime and punishment. Dickens wrote some of these — articles, for instance, on the
Pentonville penal experiment, on juvenile delinquency and street
ruffianism, on the Detective Police, and on the criminal law and
its administration. In the years before *Household Words*, he had
written also some notable letters to the Press on capital punishment. His colleagues on his weekly periodicals wrote many more
articles on penology, sometimes at his suggestion and according to
his instructions, and always subject to his power of veto. For all the
contents of his journals were anonymous (except for the main
serial stories, and some of his own essays), and he vehemently
insisted that his contributors should express, or at least not con-
tradict, his own opinions on social issues.[19] Later chapters will contain some illuminating examples of his obtaining conformity from
writers on penological matters, and will refer to other articles in
his periodicals which may be taken as, at least, being in consonance
with his ideas.

For Dickens had very decided opinions on most issues to do with
crime — opinions based on a fair amount of observation, reading,
and discussion with officials from the prisons and the police. He
witnessed several executions, though he was not (as some recent
commentators have averred) a morbid devotee of these ceremonies; he abhorred them. He was, however, an avid follower of
murder-trials. As for prisons, his testimony on this subject, said the
reviewer of *American Notes* in the *Edinburgh Review* of January 1843,
'is really of great value. Prisons and madhouses have always had
strong attractions for him; he went out [to America] with the
advantage of a very extensive acquaintance with establishments of
this kind in England . . . Mr Dickens's observations [on American
prisons] will be read with great interest . . . [and we] highly . . .
esteem his opinion in such a matter.' About 1840, says his biographer John Forster, he made a circuit of nearly all the London
prisons, and in later years he visited many more in Britain,
Europe and America. The chapter in *American Notes* condemning
the world-famous Philadelphia system of prison-government was

widely noticed, and bitterly disputed, at the time, and half a century after its publication its facts and arguments were again challenged in a pamphlet issued by the Howard Association (a forerunner of the Howard League for Penal Reform) and written by its Secretary, William Tallack. Penal progress, as Tallack and his Association viewed it, was lamentably slow, one of the hindrances being 'the still lingering influence, upon the popular mind, of the fictitious description of the Philadelphian system of prison separation, written more than fifty years ago, by Charles Dickens'.[20] Whether Tallack or Dickens was nearer the truth on these matters must be discussed later; I mention this episode now, only as a striking piece of evidence of the influence Dickens had, or was thought to have, not only during his lifetime but also in the decades after his death. As well as visiting prisons, he was friendly with several important Prison Governors, both because he was interested in their work and because he was active in several good causes affecting their clients. He was the most prominent literary supporter of the Ragged Schools during their early years, and between 1846 and 1858 he devised and virtually ran a 'Home for Fallen Women' and for other young delinquent girls.

His activities on behalf of Ragged Schools and other such bodies are described in my book (complementary to this one), *Dickens and Education*, where I also discuss his adherence to the view that Ignorance causes Crime and his support therefore for a State System of education. I shall, in my present book, refer to these discussions but shall not, of course, repeat them. Both here and in *Dickens and Education*, I try to show the fluctuating relation between his fiction and the facts (at least, as he knew them). His interest in crime and its treatment is in many respects akin to his concern for education, for both were important contemporary issues involving questions of social efficiency and social justice. But in both cases there operated a deeper emotional force than simply the good conscience (or the news-sense) of a topically-minded publicist. It is a commonplace that his sympathy for suffering and neglected children, which lies at the root of his educational concern, drew much of its strength from the traumatic experience of his own childhood - the period, about his twelfth year, when the family was in financial straits, his father was in the Marshalsea Prison, and he was left alone in the world, working at the hated blacking-warehouse. The 'little boy lost' situation is, however, only the most obvious emotional derivative from this period. In an article with the significant title 'Where we stopped Growing', he recalls various childhood experiences and memories which have become a part of himself; among these, 'We have never outgrown the rugged walls of Newgate, or any other prison on the outside. All within, is the same blank of remorse and misery.'[21] The prison, like Wordsworth's sounding cataract, 'haunted him like a passion'; the novels keep reverting both to the Debtors' Prisons (the Marshalsea and King's Bench and Fleet) and to Newgate and other great criminal prisons. In those sad early years in London, he developed 'a profound attraction of repulsion to St Giles's', and would beg anybody who took him out to go through the Seven Dials area. 'Good heaven!' he would later exclaim, 'what wild visions of prodigies of wickedness, want, and beggary, arose in my mind out of that place!'[22] It was the same 'attraction of repulsion' that he felt for prisons and their denizens.

Mr Edmund Wilson, in his notable essay 'Dickens: the Two Scrooges', published in 1941, drew upon modern psychological theory and recent discoveries about Dickens's origins and life, to extend very greatly the interpretation of the blacking-warehouse period which had been traditional since Forster's *Life* of 1872-4. Thus — 'For the man of spirit whose childhood has been crushed by the cruelty of organised society, one of two attitudes is natural: that of the criminal or that of the rebel. Charles Dickens, in imagination, was to play the roles of both, and to continue up to his death to put into them all that was most passionate in his feeling.' Mr Wilson then surveys the range and nature of Dickens's preoccupation with prisons, executions, thieves, murderers and rebels; eighty pages later, his essay ends with a discussion of Dickens's last and uncompleted novel, *Edwin Drood* (1870), in which, he argues, the murderer John Jasper presents 'an insoluble moral problem which is identified with his own'.[23] This concern with the criminal, not as a social problem so much as a psychological case that engaged Dickens's most intimate penetration, occurs early as well as late in his career. *Pickwick Papers*, his first novel (1836-7),[24] was commissioned (and to some extent devised) by the publishers, but even there — as has often been noted — the action moves towards a prison, where several of the major characters are reunited. The criminal theme is much clearer, however, in his next novel, *Oliver Twist* (1837-9). In his Introduction to that novel, Humphry House expands on Mr Wilson's thesis, and shows admirably the connection between the 'little boy lost' theme of

Oliver himself and the criminal theme which has its climax in Bill Sikes's murder of Nancy and his subsequent flight and death.

The psychological condition of a rebel-reformer is in many ways similar to that of a criminal, and may have the same origins. A feeling of being outside the ordinary organization of group life: a feeling of being an outcast, a misfit or a victim of circumstance; a feeling of bitter loneliness, isolation, ostracism or irrevocable disgrace — any one or any combination of such feelings may turn a man against organized society, and his opposition may express itself in what is technically crime or what is technically politics: treason, sedition, and armed rebellion manage to be both. Dickens's childhood had been such that all these feelings, at different times in different degrees, had been his: he knew no security and no tenderness: the family home was for a time the Marshalsea prison, and for six months Dickens himself was a wretched drudge in a blacking-factory. These two experiences, and others similar, lie behind the loneliness, disgrace and outlawry which pervade all his novels. These were always his leading psychological themes. *Oliver Twist* reveals them in an early stage, not fully developed, certainly not analysed, but very clear.[25]

Mr Wilson, House and their successors have devoted much more attention than earlier critics and biographers to the violent, necrophilic and morally ambiguous elements in Dickens's personality and writings. They have found it more prominent, and have valued its literary quality more highly, than their predecessors did; for some years now, the 'dark' Dickens has been outstripping the traditional comic Dickens in critical interest and esteem. As House said in 1947, 'The present lively interest in Dickens has in it an element never before prominent in all his hundred years of popularity — an interest in his mastery of the macabre and terrible in scene and character.' Noting some of those newly-discovered features of his life and character that caused Professor Edgar Johnson, a few years later, to entitle his great biography *Charles Dickens: his Tragedy and Triumph*, House remarks also that 'It is clear from the evidence of the novels alone that Dickens's acquaintance with evil was not just acquired *ab extra*, by reading the police-court reports (much as he loved them) and wandering about Seven Dials and the Waterside by night; it was acquired also by introspection'.[26] From this new point of view, such fictional episodes as the crimes and flights of Bill Sikes and Jonas Chuzzlewit have loomed larger; speculation about the psychology of John Jasper has replaced the concern of former critics about just how he was to have been convicted of the murder of Edwin Drood, had Dickens lived to finish the book; there has been much discussion about the significance of Dickens's fatal addiction to giving his Public Reading of the Murder of Nancy, which certainly was thought to have hastened his death. The recurrence of prisons in the novels has been seen, not primarily as a likely ingredient in the paraphernalia of a melodramatic plot, nor the chosen theme of a social reformer, but rather as a constant reminder of the shame of his own boyhood and as a symbol of some of his maturest intuitions about the nature of human existence. Anyone familiar with recent Dickensiana will be able to extend this sample of the new lines in Dickens-criticism, and further examples will be discussed later in this book.

I owe a great deal to these critics, and would not have written my book without the impulse they provided. Many of their arguments will be incorporated into mine, but I shall at points wish to contest the tenour and some of the details of this now-accepted view of Dickens. House and Wilson are two of the three critics who, writing independently of one another around 1940, started the modern re-assessment of Dickens. The third is George Orwell, and whereas the other two stress Dickens's imaginative projection into the criminal mind, Orwell argues that he 'shows less understanding of criminals than one would expect'. He continues: 'Although he is well aware of the social and economic causes of crime, he often seems to feel that when a man has once broken the law he has put himself outside human society. . . . As soon as he comes up against crime or the worst depths of poverty, he shows traces of the "I've always kept myself respectable" habit of mind.'[27] There is a good deal of truth in this, which must be reconciled with the important truth also present in the Wilson-House account. My estimate of the literary quality of 'the macabre Dickens' is, moreover, not always as favourable as theirs, and I think also that their account of his development is incomplete. Wilson particularly, and his American inheritors, have noted the increasingly 'dark' tone of his novels in the '50s and '60s, and have seen this as betokening a more severe — and thus, by implication, a more comprehensive and just — judgment on contemporary society. My interpretation will differ, and an account of Dickens's views on penology seems particularly relevant to this issue. For this is one of the few social questions over which he displays a fairly marked change of opinion.

In *Great Expectations* (1860–1) he describes Pip's visit to Newgate, supposedly about 1830. 'At that time,' he writes, 'gaols were much neglected, and the period of exaggerated reaction consequent on all public wrong-doing — and which is always its heaviest and longest punishment — was still far off. So, felons were not lodged and fed better than soldiers (to say nothing of paupers), and seldom set fire to their prisons with the excusable object of improving the flavour of their soup.'[28] It is sad to find Pip and Dickens speaking in the tone of the Mr Bounderby of *Hard Times* — who, it will be remembered, accused any of his employees who were not quite satisfied, of expecting 'to be set up in a coach and six, and to be fed on turtle soup and venison, with a gold spoon'.[29] In the 1840s Dickens's opinions on prison-discipline had been, on the whole, enlightened; by the '50s and '60s he was running level with, or even behind, public opinion, let alone progressive opinion, in this field. In the '40s, too, he had advocated the abolition of capital punishment; by 1859, he was threatening to hang any Home Secretary who stepped in between one particular 'black scoundrel' and the gallows. 'I doubt the whipping panacea gravely,' he wrote in 1852 during a wave of brutal assaults; sixteen years later, during a similar outbreak, he writes of the street ruffian — 'I would have his back scarified often and deep.'[30] These developments in his ideas about punishment must be traced in fuller detail, and related not only to other aspects of his life and works but also to changes in his society.

For there was a general reaction in public opinion on these issues, akin to that which Dickens displays. As Dr Max Grünhut says at the end of the historical survey in his book, *Penal Reform*: 'Prison history is a history of "ideals and errors" . . . Prison discipline seems to be in a permanent state of reform . . . It is a general experience of social and legal history that every institutional form has its specific manner of decay. . . . This makes a periodical swinging of the pendulum almost inevitable.'[31] An illuminating example is the reception of Carlyle's *Latter Day Pamphlet*, 'Model Prisons', published in March 1850. It was the culmination, and the extremest statement, of a reactionary mood in popular thought about prisons, which had been mounting for the past two years, but even the less enlightened of Carlyle's readers were taken aback by his savagery. *Punch*, which was itself becoming reactionary on penal questions by this time, deplored the 'barking and froth' of this pamphlet, and in its 'trial' of Mr

Carlyle reported a witness as saying that it was not consistent with
public safety that, 'in his present temper, the accused be trusted
with pen-and-ink . . . *Mr Punch* observed, this was a melancholy
case. . . . It is believed that if the accused again offend, the whole
body of publishers will insist upon his compulsory silence.' *The
Athenæum* declared that it was almost ashamed to deal with 'Model
Prisons' at all, and Crabb Robinson recorded in his diary: 'I perceive that he has now disgusted readers in general. . . . His derision
of the Philanthropists is not altogether unfounded, but in spirit
very offensive.'[32] (Dickens, however, as we shall see, still took a
more favourable view of Carlyle than most readers and journalists.)
There is a significant retrospective comment on this episode by
Carlyle's friend and biographer, J. A. Froude, writing in 1884:
'He did not expect that his protests [against current penology]
would be attended to then, but in twenty years' time he thought
there might be more agreement with him. This, like many other
prophecies of his, has proved true. We hang and flog now with
small outcry and small compunction.'[33]

On the whole, the earlier decades of Dickens's working life were
a period of penal reform and idealism. The faults of the old unreformed prisons, as of the Bloody Code of criminal law, were gross
and manifest, and many legislators and publicists hoped not only
to remedy these faults but also at the same time to effect a wonderful transformation in the treatment of offenders, which would
result in a high rate of reformation among them. Back in 1791,
Bentham had enthusiastically described his projected Model
Prison, the Panopticon, as 'a mill grinding rogues honest and idle
men industrious'. The plan would be equally effective either for a
workhouse or a gaol, he maintained: 'Morals reformed, health
preserved, industry invigorated, instruction diffused, public
burdens lightened, economy seated, as it were, upon a rock, the
Gordian knot of the Poor Laws not cut, but untied, — all by a
simple idea of Architecture!'[34] Bentham even obtained Government support for his wonder-working 'simple idea', though for
various reasons the Panopticon Penitentiary was never actually
built, and this particular Benthamite nostrum had no permanent
embodiment in England. But, especially during the 1830s and
'40s, other zealots put forward other 'simple ideas' as penological
panaceas, with scarcely less confidence than Bentham.

This period of penal reform was characterised, as all its historians
have noted, by the 'rationalistic error' of expecting far too much

from a mere change of system, organisation, or architecture. Enthusiastic system-mongers tended to forget that prison governors and officers, and prisoners, were all individuals, and that talking about '*the* system' and '*the* prisoner' concealed the actualities of the situation. The reformers of the 1830s were, no doubt, also the more euphoric because of the spate of important legislation during that decade; the rapid succession of such measures as the Reform Act, the 1833 Factory Act, the Municipal Corporation Act and the Poor Law Amendment Act must have suggested that faulty social institutions would be amended more radically, speedily and successfully than proved to be the case. As Morley wrote in his *Life of Cobden*, the hopes and disappointments of the 1832 Reform Bill aroused 'such a degree of fresh and independent activity among all the better minds of the time, that the succeeding generation, say from 1840 to 1870, practically lived upon the thought and sentiment of the seven or eight years immediately preceding the close of the Liberal reign in 1841. . . . It was now the day of ideals in every camp. The general restlessness was as intense among reflecting Conservatives as among reflecting Liberals; and those who looked to the past agreed with those who looked to the future, in energetic dissatisfaction with a sterile present. . . . With all of them the aim to be attained was social renovation.'[35] Penal reformers were a conspicuous example of this restlessness and idealism.

A reaction was inevitable. The reforms were less extensive, and their results less dramatically successful, than had been hoped, and the idealism of the early years of Victoria's reign gave ground before the relative complacency which, unfairly, we are apt to think characteristically Victorian. The widespread conviction of the '30s and '40s that prisons should aim at reforming their inmates was not new, of course, nor was it unchallenged during these decades, nor did it ever die; but, after several fluctuations, there was a general return by the '60s to the view that prisons should deter through severity instead of making futile attempts to alter prisoners' character through humane treatment, secular and religious education, and trade-training. The historic Carnarvon Committee — the House of Lords Committee on the Present State of Discipline in Gaols and Houses of Correction — was established after the panic of the garotting outbreak of 1862. Its fire-and-brimstone Report, of 1863, 'a landmark in the movement of opinion on penal questions,' noted the general impression that British prisons were 'not of a sufficiently penal character', but, having acknowledged that this impression was erroneous, it went on to propose an even harsher and drearier regime. It rejected the view that the treadmill and crank degraded or demoralised the prisoner, and that industrial occupation should replace these 'more strictly penal elements' in the discipline: these were 'the chief means of effecting a deterrent influence', and should therefore hold first place in convict discipline.[36] The Committee's main proposals were accepted by Parliament, with hardly any opposition, and were embodied in the 1865 Prison Act which, with further Acts of 1874 and 1877, established the harsh regime — 'hard labour, hard fare, and a hard bed' — which lasted until 1898 (and in many respects later than that). The more hopeful and sympathetic proposals of earlier Parliamentary Committees, of 1850 and 1856, were disregarded. It is characteristic that the Separate, or Cellular, System of prison-discipline, commended by idealists and Prison Inspectors in the 1830s and 1840s as humane and reformatory, though criticised by some observers (including Dickens) as being a subtle form of cruelty, was now applauded by the Carnarvon Committee because it 'seems to be regarded with great dislike by most [convicts], and especially by those who are criminals by profession'. As a later survey, the Gladstone Committee of 1895, pointed out, the original intention of this System was lost sight of, within about fifteen years of its introduction into English prisons: 'the main object of the separate confinement had come to be deterrence.'[37] And so, writes Sir Lionel Fox of the 1865–1877 Acts, 'in the English prison system, the lights that had been lit in Newgate by Elizabeth Fry, on Norfolk Island by Captain Maconochie, and at Portland by Colonel Jebb, went out; for twenty years our prisons presented the pattern of deterrence by severity of punishment, uniformly, rigidly, and efficiently applied. For death itself the system had substituted a living death. It became legendary . . . even in Russia.'[38]

Dickens, as we saw, wrote ironically in 1861 about prisoners' 'setting fire to their prisons with the excusable object of improving the flavour of their soup'. He was alluding to the great riots at Chatham Convict Prison two months earlier, which had been provoked mainly by a sudden reduction in the prison diet.[39] A few years later, a tough young army officer, Major Arthur Griffiths, went to Chatham as Deputy-Governor. 'I have seen men at Chatham greedily devour the railway grease used in the traffic of the trucks,' he later recalled; men ate their candles, and even such live frogs and worms as they could capture when at work outdoors. There was much strong flogging, and men would often throw themselves under the moving trucks, preferring the amputation of a limb to having to endure more of this terrible daily life. Not that this desperate expedient saved them from being flogged again; as the Governor told the Royal Commission of 1879, 'There was no reason why they should not be flogged because they had only mutilated an arm or a leg.' What makes all this the more tragic is that the Governor was acting quite legally inside the official prison-regulations of his time; he cannot be written off as a sadist exceeding his powers, like the Governor of Birmingham Gaol who was imprisoned for an abuse of regulations in 1854. The system itself was, as a recent historian has said, designedly 'a massive machine for the promotion of misery'. Major Griffiths had been in charge of the Gibraltar Convict Establishment, but he was shocked by the conditions that he found in Chatham. He writes:

> I could not help commiserating the convicts, yet I was powerless to mitigate their sufferings. The prison system of those days cannot well be defended. It was rigorous and relentless, formed by men who thought most of deterrence through enforcing a rigid, almost barbarous, rule, from which all solace and alleviation were scrupulously eliminated. . . . There was no light in the lot of the Chatham convicts, no horizon to which they could look for coming relief. . . . No creature comforts, no ease, no treats, hardly the gratification to the palate of a sufficiency of food.[40]

Dickens of course was living a few miles from this prison, but I have no evidence of his having visited it during this period; had he seen these enormities, he would doubtless have found them repulsive. But there is little in the letter or spirit of his later pronouncements on prison discipline that contradicts the ideas which had their logical and dreadful outcome in this reign of terror. He was, in his later years, a less frequent visitor to prisons, but during his American Reading Tour of 1867–8 he did see one which embodied ideas more current in the 1960s (if still imperfectly carried into practice) than in the English prisons of the 1860s. The Governor of the Maryland Penitentiary, knowing his interest in penology, invited him round as this was 'regarded as the model prison of the States'. The prisoners were working busily at their trades, with little supervision, in warm comfortable workshops; the proceeds from their work were divided into three equal parts, one going to the prison expenses, one to the prisoner's family, and one into his bank-account. The food was excellent, especially for the long-term inmates. 'The governor was desirous of knowing how his establishment compared with the prisons in England, and was surprised to find that nothing of the kind was in existence there. Mr Dickens remarked at the same time that the Maryland Penitentiary was more like a "huge hydropathic establishment, without the privilege of going out for a walk".' Immune to Dickens's irony, the Governor was delighted by this 'tribute', and sent some handsome souvenirs, made in the prison, to his hotel.[41] As these instances suggest, Dickens did not transcend the outlook of his society on such issues, at least in his later years and during the general reaction against the hopes and ideals of the previous generation.

I am not arguing that Dickens, close though he generally was to public opinion, was merely its echo or reflector. He was not, I think, immune to the common tendency of mankind to be radical and reformist when young, and to become more conservative or reactionary in middle and later life. It is, of course, possible to be strongly radical in general outlook and at the same time reactionary on some particular social issue such as penology, but this capitulation to the retrograde popular, and official, ideas on prison-discipline, together with the abandonment of his earlier opposition to flogging and hanging, consorts ill with the picture of the mature Dickens presented by Mr Wilson and Professor Johnson and so many other commentators — a Dickens increasingly clear-sighted in his radical opposition to the structure and ideology of his society. There is a further apparent paradox, which my book must attempt to explore. In these later years, when he displays in his comments on public affairs an increasing, and sometimes very distressing, severity towards criminal offenders, he exhibits, in his novels, an ever-increasing intimacy with the criminal mind. His later criminals are more fully understood, and more fully and realistically presented, than his earlier ones, and they are closer to Dickens himself in social position and in character. The early villains are, typically, outsiders — obvious professional criminals, grotesques and rogues, such as Sikes and Fagin, Quilp and Jonas Chuzzlewit. The murderers in his two final novels are middle-class — the painfully respectable schoolmaster Bradley Headstone, and the cathedral organist John Jasper. Evil is no longer associated with an immediately identifiable out-group of social enemies and misfits.

Sir Winston Churchill, as Home Secretary in 1910, made a speech to the House of Commons which has often been quoted:

> The mood and temper of the public in regard to the treatment of crime and criminals is one of the unfailing tests of any country. A calm, dispassionate recognition of the rights of the accused, and even of the convicted criminal, against the State — a constant heart-searching by all charged with the duty of punishment — a desire and eagerness to rehabilitate in the world of industry those who have paid their due in the hard coinage of punishment: tireless efforts towards the discovery of curative and regenerative processes: unfailing faith that there is a treasure, if you can only find it, in the heart of every man. These are the symbols, which, in the treatment of crime and criminal, mark and measure the stored up strength of a nation, and are sign and proof of the living virtue within it.[42]

Churchill's test applies to the individual as well as to a nation. Much can be deduced from a man's views on crime and its treatment: his moral and social standards, his emotional temperament, his psychological insight, his resources of sympathy and good will, and his intellectual reach. For this perennial social problem raises a host of questions, which still largely baffle professional criminologists who have the advantage over Dickens of a century more of inherited experience — a century, too, which has revolutionised our understanding of the human mind. With all these benefits, the best informed and most experienced of present-day criminologists would not claim, in their wiser moments, to give categorical answers to the questions Dickens and his generation had to face and to tackle; and even where our wisest contemporaries are generally agreed on at least a provisional solution, they find it difficult to carry lay, and thus political, opinion with them and thus to obtain the resources to put their ideas into operation. Modern criminologists, moreover, are not immune to the errors we have noticed, and shall notice, in their forbears of a century ago — as they were reminded, at the 1960 United Nations congress on crime prevention and the treatment of offenders. The Director of the Cambridge Institute of Criminology was reported as having put in its right perspective

> criminology, in its infinite variety of subdivisions (criminal anthropology, penology, prison pedagogy, or even criminal prophylaxis, to give but a few of the variants) ... Professor Radzinowicz gave his colleagues a warning against what he termed crusading zeal, dogmatic beliefs, and narrow expertise. Research material in these

fields was tainted by mannerisms and deformities. Conspicuous in the welter of published matter were jargon, padding, overelaborated statistical data, hunting for far-fetched hypotheses, pretentiousness, and repetitiveness. These were criminologists' deadly sins.[43]

When, therefore, we find Dickens's notions inadequate, or even plain wrong, we must hesitate before too roundly condemning, or patronising, him and his contemporaries. What he says must, of course, be compared with the lay and the professional opinion, and the actual practice, of his age, and he will not always appear obtuse or unsympathetic by these standards. Many of the most striking of his pronouncements that I have so far quoted are, certainly, unimpressive or deplorable as comments on these tragic situations. I have given this emphasis, in this introductory chapter, because Dickens has always enjoyed the reputation of a reformer, and is still generally assumed (without inspection) to be on the side of the angels on any issue about which his commentators happen to feel strongly. As we shall see, he is given an honourable mention in almost all the standard histories and textbooks on penal history, and I have referred to the widespread recent interest in and respect for his presentation of criminal characters. Both these claims require some modification, I think, but neither of them should be dismissed altogether.

For there is one trend in modern studies of Dickens's life and art that I can more wholeheartedly accept and shall hope to illustrate in this examination of a single strand in his huge creative work: this is, the contention that he is more complex and ambivalent that earlier critics have recognised. This applies at the level of his character, which was — as one of his acutest critics has said, when discussing his behaviour at the crisis of his unhappy marriage — 'so extraordinary that it is difficult for the ordinary person to understand the power of the driving-force which took control of him at this time and allowed him neither rest nor recreation. . . . Anyone can offer to analyse him, but the stress under which he lived is almost impossible for the ordinary person to imagine.'[44] His daughter Katey, recalling this episode, exclaimed, 'What could you expect from such an uncanny genius?' On another occasion she described her father as 'a wicked man — a very wicked man.'[45] The kindest of men, as so many friends and acquaintances have witnessed, he could indeed be intolerably aggressive. A charming and humorous companion, he had moods of morose indifference. The novelist most warmly associated with the domestic bliss of hearth and home, he dismissed his wife with great *éclat*, lived with an actress less than half his age, and proposed to replace *Household Words* with a similar magazine which was to be called *Household Harmony* (he suggested this title, 'quite delighted to have got hold of it,' without a glint of irony or humour, and when Forster demurred — for obvious reasons — he 'was at first reluctant even to admit the objection').[46] The greatest of English humorists, his sense of humour could, clearly, desert him disastrously on some occasions. His novels, too, present a remarkable mixture, of hilarious comedy, uninhibited pathos, moral earnestness, and melodramatic violence, to which few critics have done justice; they have tended to focus their attention on only one or two of these elements and to give their admiration to them alone. Those recent critics who have been obsessed with the dark Dickens are no improvement on, though they are a useful supplement to, their predecessors who saw and hailed only the comic Christmassy Dickens, or the novelist of homely pathos, or the noble reformer. The complexity of Dickens appears, further, in his opinions on public issues. Sometimes there is a development over the years, sometimes a simple inconsistency; anyway, it is rarely safe to take a single statement or dramatisation as fully representing his views on a matter which engaged his attention more than momentarily. Nor is it even safe to take the novels as a whole, or the journalistic essays as a whole, or the letters and speeches as a whole, and to assume that one of these modes of his pronouncements will by itself contain the essence of his thought on a social topic. One must read and accept the lot, taking and trying to explain the developments or inconsistencies as they come.

In his excellent Introduction to *Oliver Twist* to which I have already referred, Humphry House refers to Dickens's Preface, with its social analysis of the origins and circumstances of crime in the London slums, but then points out that his most revealing comment on *Oliver* was not in the Preface but, implicitly, in that Public Reading of the murder of Nancy to which he gave himself with such reckless abandon in the last eighteen months of his life. He insisted on giving it, as often as three nights out of four, though his health was failing and his doctors were alarmed by the effect it demonstrably had on him as well as on his terrified audiences. Later he confessed to his Manager, who had tried hard to dissuade him from repeating this performance, that 'it was madness ever to have given the "Murder" Reading, under the conditions of a travelling life, and worse than madness to have given it with such frequency'.[47] House's comment on this episode is, for me, one of the seminal remarks in modern Dickens-criticism: 'How utterly remote are these scenes and this state of mind from the earnest moralities of the Preface! To understand the conjunction of such different moods and qualities in a single man is the beginning of serious criticism of Dickens.'[48] It is a hint, and a challenge, which my choice of subject forces upon me.

II

NEWGATE

IN the autumn of 1835, Dickens (then aged twenty-three) was excitedly planning his first book, *Sketches by Boz*, which appeared the following February. It consisted mainly of essays and stories contributed to various journals over the previous two years, but, as he explained to his publisher, Macrone, he would add a few pieces to fill out the two volumes. In particular, he was seeking permission to go over Newgate — 'I have long projected sketching its Interior, and I think it would tell extremely well.' Three weeks later, he had finished writing 'a long paper' on this subject, entitled 'A Visit to Newgate', and was very anxious for Macrone to see a corrected proof of it, for two experienced journalists had already praised it highly, assuring him that 'it would "make" any book'. Further letters written before the book was published refer to his gratification at Macrone's and Harrison Ainsworth's opinions of this piece, and then the critics kindly reiterated in public the view that this was 'the most remarkable paper in the book. . . . It is written throughout in a tone of high moral feeling, and with great eloquence, and must leave a deep and lasting impression on the mind of every reader'.[1] The sketch remained popular, too: half a century later it was reprinted in a Penny Library, with a gruesome Appendix about some of the more notorious episodes and characters in the prison's history.[2] Newgate was probably the first criminal prison Dickens ever visited; about the same time he went over another prominent London prison, Coldbath Fields, intending to make it the subject of a further new item for *Sketches by Boz* (though he dropped this idea). A few months later, *Pickwick Papers* began to appear; its basically farcical tone did not give Dickens much occasion for social commentary nor for criminal deeds, but the civil prison which is a prominent scene of the later part of the book is presented so grimly as to dash even Mr Pickwick's spirits. 'I have seen enough,' he says after touring the Fleet. 'My head aches with these scenes, and my heart too. Henceforth I will be a prisoner in my own room.'[3] But already, in 1836, Dickens was planning another novel in which Newgate was to be a central feature, *Gabriel Vardon, the Locksmith of London*, though for various reasons it did not appear until 1841, under the title *Barnaby Rudge*.[4] Meanwhile, of course, *Oliver Twist* had appeared (1837–9), which culminates in the condemned cell at Newgate — 'Fagin's Last Night alive.'

Dickens's last and uncompleted novel, *Edwin Drood* (1870) was also to have ended in a condemned cell. Dickens was planning to take his illustrator, Luke Fildes, to see the one at Maidstone Gaol, the handiest prison from Gad's Hill and the appropriate place for a murderer from 'Cloisterham' or Rochester.[5] Many of the murderers in intervening novels had escaped imprisonment and execution, having died in some other way, but prisons had nevertheless appeared quite often. Sometimes the references were brief and incidental — Kit Nubbles's separate confinement, for instance, as a first offender (on a trumped-up charge), or George Rouncewell's when he is suspected of killing Mr Tulkinghorn, or Pip's visit to Newgate on Mr Wemmick's genial invitation.[6] The prisons best remembered from the novels are, no doubt, the debtors' prisons described at such length and from painful personal memory — the Fleet in *Pickwick Papers*, the King's Bench in *David Copperfield* (1849–50) and the Marshalsea in *Little Dorrit* (1855–7) — but the two latter novels contain criminal prisons as well. David Copperfield visits the 'Model Prison' of which his former school-master Mr Creakle, now a magistrate, is so proud; *Little Dorrit* begins in the common gaol of Marseilles, and, as Professor Trilling has shown in detail, prisons actual and metaphorical recur throughout the novel as its central symbol. The novel which follows *Little Dorrit* (and is closely related to it) is *A Tale of Two Cities* (1859), where Dr Manette's sufferings in the Bastille are powerfully expressed, and Darnay is imprisoned in both cities — in Newgate and in La Force. 'Buried Alive,' the phrase first used about Manette, is applied — like the prison-image in *Little Dorrit* — to other characters and circumstances later in the book, and was the theme of the Public Reading from this novel which Dickens devised and published, though he never actually delivered it.[7]

Crime and punishment were, moreover, a frequent subject in his non-fictional work, often with reference to prisons he had visited for charitable activities he had undertaken. 'The Falls of Niagara and your Penitentiary are two objects I might almost say I most wish to see in America,' he is reported as saying to the officials of the world-famous prison at Philadelphia in 1842, and the book he wrote on his return home, *American Notes*, contains a celebrated account of this prison, and briefer descriptions of half-a-dozen more.[8] Four years later he was founding-editor of the *Daily News*; his main contributions to it, during and immediately after his brief tenure of this office, were 'Crime and Education' and 'Capital Punishment', in the first of which he claimed to 'know the prisons of London well', and to have 'visited the largest of them more times than I could count'.[9] After another four years, he established his own weekly periodical, *Household Words*, and in its second issue he began his attack on the Pentonville experiment with a few sentences, expanded three weeks later into a long article entitled 'Pet Prisoners'.[10] Two of the London prisons — Coldbath Fields and Tothill Fields — he knew particularly well; his friendship with their Governors, and his opinion of the system they espoused, will be discussed in the next chapter. Often too, when on holiday or on Reading-tours, he inspected the local prisons not only in England, but in Scotland, France, Switzerland, Italy, and in America during his second visit of 1867–8; his comments sometimes appear in his essays, more often in his private letters (which are many, substantial and vivid). He always had a journalistic flair for seeing and interviewing, instead of reading, speculating, or cogitating; as he wrote typically in his first prison-piece 'A Visit to Newgate' — 'We saw the prison, and saw the prisoners; and what we did see, and what we thought, we will tell at once in our own way.'[11]

Not that he was unread in the subject. Neither an omnivorous nor a nicely selective reader, he did read fairly widely, if indiscriminately, on the social topics which engaged his interest.[12] His articles on penology, for instance, discuss and quote from Gibbon Wakefield's *Facts relating to the Punishment of Death* (1831), Joseph Adshead's *Prisons and Prisoners* (1845), the Reverend John Field's *Prison Discipline* (1848), and the Reverend Joseph Kingsmill's *Prisons and Prisoners* (1849). His letters refer to C. P. Measor's *The Convict Service* (1861), Frederic Hill's *Crime: its Amount, Causes, and Remedies* (1853), and various pamphlets by the notable penological reformer Captain Alexander Maconochie. Three of these pamphlets were in the Gad's Hill Library, as was Wakefield's book; so were Hepworth Dixon's *John Howard* and *The London Prisons* (both of 1850), Dr W. C. Ward's *Criminal Lunatics* (1854), 'A Prison Matron's' *Female Life in Prison* (1862), a Report on the influential Mettray 'Colonie Agricole' for delinquent boys (1846), and many pamphlets about Newgate.[13] Two of his favourite authors, Sydney

Smith and Carlyle, made striking pronouncements on penology, which — as we shall see — chimed with his own views at several points, while the novelists who most clearly influenced his work — the eighteenth-century masters whom he read in his childhood — had often included prison-scenes in their stories, with comments which doubtless helped to form his opinions on these matters. Henry Fielding, an energetic and experienced magistrate himself, often portrayed and remarked upon the administration of the law, and his heroes' misadventures generally include a spell in prison: Joseph Andrews narrowly escapes it, but Tom Jones, Jonathan Wild, and William Booth do not. Smollett's Peregrine Pickle and Humphry Clinker similarly manage to land in gaol, and so do Goldsmith's Dr Primrose and his son George; Dr Primrose improves the occasion by discoursing on prison-discipline, and setting about the reform of his fellow-prisoners.[14]

Dickens's preoccupation with prisons sprang, I have suggested, from several roots: the aching private memory of his own boyhood, the widespread topical interest in penological questions, and the novel-tradition of rogues and villains which he espoused. Moreover, prisons were a 'fine subject' for a writer of his temperament; he uses this phrase about the subject of another essay he projected for *Sketches by Boz*, Bedlam, which also aroused his melodramatic taste for powerful emotions. He had abandoned his intention of writing about Coldbath Fields in *Sketches by Boz* because, he told his publisher, 'You cannot throw the interest over a year's imprisonment, however severe, that you can cast around the punishment of death. The Tread-Mill will not take the hold on men's feelings that the gallows does.'[15] Dickens was, among other things, a conscious manipulator of his readers' and hearers' emotions (though not an insincere one).

But, one should add, prisons dominated the urban, and particularly the Metropolitan, scene much more in Dickens's time than in ours. As he wrote in *Nicholas Nickleby*: 'There, at the very core of London, in the heart of its business and animation, in the midst of a whirl of noise and motion: stemming as it were the giant currents of life that flow ceaselessly on from different quarters and meet beneath its walls: stands Newgate. . . .'[16] A glance at Henry Mayhew's 'Map Illustrative of the Locality of the Several Prisons of the Metropolis' shows a number of major prisons within a couple of miles of Charing Cross — Coldbath Fields, the Clerkenwell House of Detention, Whitecross Street, Tothill Fields, Millbank, the

Queen's Bench, and Horsemonger Lane, as well as Newgate. Insets in the corners of the map are needed for the prisons of the future — Pentonville, Brixton and Holloway, built on the outskirts of London in the 1840s and 1850s, which have survived long after the old central-London prisons have been demolished.[17] Many town-dwellers of today never see a prison, and can remain as oblivious of their existence as, proverbially, the Germans were of Hitler's concentration-camps. This was impossible in Dickens's London. The most central, the most awesome and the most historic of the prisons was Newgate, which held pride of place among its companions in the celebrity of its inmates both in the past and the present. It was inevitable that Dickens's prison-writing should start there, and that it recurs more often in the novels than any other prison: so it is with Newgate that our more detailed examination of his prison fiction and journalism must begin.

I have quoted already the comments Dickens puts into Pip's mouth, about the contrast between the Newgate he visited about 1830, when 'gaols were much neglected', and the prisons of 1861 which had, through a process of 'exaggerated reaction', gone too far the other way.[18] Dickens never doubted that the old unreformed gaols were a shocking scandal. The Newgate of the late eighteenth century appears in both his historical novels, *Barnaby Rudge* and *A Tale of Two Cities*. The Gordon Riots, he said in the former, were supported mainly by 'the very scum and refuse of London, whose growth was fostered by bad criminal laws, bad prison regulations, and the worst conceivable police'.[19] The trial of Charles Darnay at the Old Bailey is prefaced by a similar attack on criminal law and penal system of the 1770s; Newgate, he says, 'was a vile place, in which most kinds of debauchery and villainy were practised, and where dire diseases were bred. . . .'[20] Half the crimes committed in and about London, wrote Howard of the Newgate of that period, were planned in the prison itself: and it was long after Howard's death before the authorities did much to prevent this. By the time Dickens first visited it, in 1835, some reforms had been partially introduced: more attention was now paid to hygiene, and a rudimentary system of classification was in operation, so that prisoners tried and untried, of all ages, both sexes, and every degree of depravity, were no longer all herded together. But classification was never satisfactory at this period, when criminal records were virtually non-existent: a vicious habitual criminal might be convicted on a trivial charge, and could — if unrecognised by the magistrates or turnkeys — easily pass himself off as a first offender. Newgate in 1835, and for long after, remained one of the worst prisons in England. Indeed, the three Metropolitan prison-authorities — the City of London, and the Counties of Middlesex and Surrey — were, right up to the '50s and '60s, the worst laggards in prison-reform, continually chivvied by the Prison Inspectors but recalcitrant to their advice. It was only in 1856 that some radical reforms were introduced at Newgate, and later than that before the necessary reconstruction of its interior was begun.

There are, fortunately, two long and trustworthy accounts of Newgate about the time of Dickens's *Sketch*. In 1826, Edward Gibbon Wakefield (later famous for his work in colonizing New Zealand) was sentenced to three years' imprisonment for abducting an heiress; he described his time in Newgate in *Facts relating to the Punishment of Death* (1831), which Dickens certainly knew later, for he quoted it extensively in his *Daily News* letters of 1846. The inside of Newgate, Wakefield wrote, was a *terra incognita*, where he had witnessed scenes he would have found incredible had he not seen them himself; far from being reformative, it was 'the greatest *Nursery* of crime'.[21] Four years later, the principal turnkey at Newgate affirmed to a Parliamentary Committee that the chances of a man's leaving the prison better than he was on entering it were 'very small indeed'.[22] In 1836, the Prison Inspectors opened their First Report with a long and devastating account of this prison, stressing 'the earnestness with which we deem it our duty to mark the evils of the system, now for a long period in disastrous operation in the gaol of Newgate'. The classification-system, in their view, was totally ineffective: 'The Association of Prisoners of all ages, and of every shade of guilt, in one indiscriminate mass, is a frightful feature of the system which prevails here; the first in magnitude, and the most pernicious in effect. . . . Another feature . . . is the utter absence of all employment for the prisoners.' The Inspectors proposed a total change of system, which would involve rebuilding the prison; they enclosed an architect's plan, but nothing much was done until 1858–61.[23] According to one observer, it was still, in 1850, 'one of the worst hot-beds of vice and moral disease in London,' with little or no employment or instruction, and the untried still consorting with the convicted.[24]

'I have been today over Newgate, and the House of Correction,'

wrote Dickens to his fiancée when he was collecting material for
the *Sketches*, 'and have lots of anecdotes to tell you of both places
when I see you tomorrow — some of them rather amusing: at
least to me, for I was intensely interested in everything I saw.'[25]
It was the interest of a casual observer, or a journalist, not of a
penologist. In his 'Visit to Newgate', Dickens prefaces his description by referring to the current scientific and official investigations
into prison-discipline, but firmly takes the other way: '. . . we do
not intend to fatigue the reader with any statistical accounts of the
prison; they will be found at length in numerous reports of numerous committees, and a variety of authorities of equal weight. We
took no notes, made no memoranda, measured none of the yards,
ascertained the exact number of inches in no particular room: are
unable even to report of how many apartments the gaol is composed.'[26] As his penological opponents of later years complained,
his accounts of the prisons he visited were dangerously impressionistic, because of this disregard for statistics and other such dry but
necessary details. He may often be defended, however, for doing as
perceptively as he could what he was best equipped to do: statistics, memoranda, and measurements were not his line, and many
lesser men could and did provide those in plenty. A more striking
deficiency in this early *Sketch*, compared with his later prison passages, is the absence of a penological point of view. He scarcely
notices the features of prison-discipline discussed by Wakefield
and the Inspectors, and has no formed opinions by which to judge,
commend or criticise. The original text of the *Sketch* was even less
positive than that in later reprints (as Professors Butt and Tillotson
have pointed out). For instance, Dickens originally described the
young pickpockets in Newgate as 'irreclaimable wretches', but in
1850 changed this to 'creatures of neglect'; this and other revisions
in *Sketches by Boz*, as they remark, show 'the substitution of practical social reform for ironic defiance'.[27]

Even ironic defiance is rarely present in 'A Visit to Newgate',
much of which is a straightforward and quite effective account of
what Dickens sees on his way round the prison. He expresses compassion for some of the prisoners, and horror at the depravity
patent in others, but most of the description is non-committal and
without comment. Thus, at one point he adds a footnote in the
1839 edition: 'The regulations of the prison relative to the confinement of prisoners during the day, their sleeping at night, their
taking their meals, and other matters of gaol economy, have been

all altered — greatly for the better — since this sketch was first published. Even the construction of the prison itself has been changed.' This footnote seems, however, to record a change in Dickens's views as much as in the prison regime, for the passage in the essay to which it refers hardly suggests that he was critical of the arrangements he was describing. If he was critical, he did not very aptly convey this feeling. The sentences immediately leading up to the asterisk are in a neutral tone —

> In every ward on the female side, a wardswoman is appointed to preserve order, and a similar regulation is adopted among the males. The wardsmen and wardswomen are all prisoners, selected for good conduct. They alone are allowed the privilege of sleeping on bedsteads; a small stump bedstead being placed in every ward for that purpose. On both sides of the gaol is a small receiving-room, to which prisoners are conducted on their first reception, and whence they cannot be removed until they have been examined by the surgeon of the prison.

The use of prisoners as disciplinary officers was obviously an invitation to bullying and corruption (it finally became illegal by the 1865 Prisons Act), but this passage does not suggest that Dickens was aware of the problem. Nor had he been critical in his account of what he saw 'of the confinement of prisoners during the day, their sleeping at night, and their taking their meals'. He describes the female ward — 'a spacious, bare, whitewashed apartment, lighted, of course, by windows looking into the interior of the prison, but far more light and airy than one could reasonably expect to find in such a situation.' The women were sitting on wooden forms around a large fire, eating their dinners; on the walls hung their sleeping-mats, and on the shelves were their rugs and blankets. Their food, of sufficient quantity, was served in pewter dishes, 'which are kept perfectly bright, and displayed on shelves in great order and regularity when they are not in use.' The women themselves were 'all cleanly — many of them decently — attired, and there was nothing peculiar, either in their appearance or demeanour'. Several were engaged at needlework. Though it was a cheerless scene, it was an orderly one, and Dickens expresses no sense either of its deficiencies as a penal system or of its being so great an improvement on the terrible Bedlam it had been until Mrs Fry and her companions began their work in Newgate in 1817. He certainly knew of Mrs Fry, and briefly expressed his respect for her in another of the *Sketches*, but he did not mention her work in 'A Visit to Newgate', though during their visit to the prison, as he reminded Macrone, 'I saw a quakeress in the office, and turning round to you in jest said — "Mrs Fry"; but whether it was really her, or some other good quakeress of whom there are numbers, God only knows — I am not even sure she's alive. . . .'[28]

The description of the male wards, which no Elizabeth Fry had tackled, is less favourable, though Dickens does not suggest what should be done to them. The only very striking difference between these and the female wards, he says, is 'the utter absence of any employment'. The men, 'all alike in one respect, all idle and list-less', sat huddled around the fire or were 'sauntering moodily about, lounging in the window, or leaning against the wall, vacantly swinging their bodies to and fro'. A similar vagueness appears in his reference to the custom, only recently discontinued, of making men awaiting execution sit next to their coffins during the last Sunday service before their deaths. This, he says, 'may seem incredible, but it is true. Let us hope that the increased spirit of civilisation and humanity which abolished this frightful and de-grading custom, may extend itself to other usages equally bar-barous; usages which have not even the plea of utility in their defence, as every year's experience has shown them to be more and more inefficacious.' But he does not specify, either here or else-where in the essay, the barbarous usages he deplores. Nor, in this passage about the twenty-five or thirty prisoners under sentence of death, does he draw the conclusion he would later have insisted upon (it was a commonplace among law-reformers of this period) — 'There was very little anxiety or mental suffering depicted in the countenance of any of the men; — they had all been sentenced to death, it is true, and the recorder's report had not yet been made; but we question whether there was a man among them, notwithstanding, who did not *know* that although he had undergone the ceremony, it never was intended that his life should be sacrificed.' It was, clearly, both barbarous and ineffective to inflict the death-sentence on so many criminals who would not in fact be hanged; the chances of a reprieve for any offence short of murder were so high that the penalty was no deterrent. In the *Daily News* letters of 1846, Dickens quoted Gibbon Wakefield's conversation with a Newgate convict who had been 'within an ace of being hanged'; he had often seen other men hanged, he said, but the spectacle had not frightened him — 'Why should it?' He and his fellow-criminals were prepared to take their chance of the very small risk of being hanged, for none of them ever thought that *he* would be the unlucky victim in the lottery of the law.[29]

Though some of Dickens's phrases suggest that he had more reserves about Newgate than he actually expresses, his account of the prison is in fact the least critical of any that I have seen from this period. There are, certainly, many limitations in the penological wisdom of the Prison Inspectors (Home District) whose Report for 1835–6 begins with eighty scathing pages about Newgate, but their account shows not only a professional insight which the young Dickens could not be expected to possess, but also a moral revulsion at the prison's laxity, inefficiency and corruption which the more confident Dickens of a year or so later would certainly have expressed. He conveys, of course, a sense of the stark hopelessness of the prison atmosphere, but with the implication that this is how prisons necessarily are, and should be. As a young journalist making his first visit to a prison, and being taken on a two-hours' conducted tour, he naturally failed to see any of the features which excited the wrath of the Prison Inspectors: he was doubtless steered clear, for instance, of the frequent scenes of intoxication which occurred because beer was so freely admitted into the prison, and, though he gives a brilliant description of the visitors he saw talking with some of the female prisoners, he probably did not discover how scandalously lax were the arrangements for such visits. A stream of prostitutes, receivers of stolen goods, and professional criminals were in and out of Newgate daily, to comfort their imprisoned friends and arrange for their future criminal careers. Only the very experienced and perceptive amateur observer, of course, can escape being bamboozled about such deficiencies in any institution, whether it be a prison, a school, or an army camp.

In later visits to prisons, Dickens is more perceptive and more confident (if sometimes imprudently hasty) in his judgments. He was, of course, very young when he wrote *Sketches by Boz* and *Pickwick*, and 'awoke and found himself famous': and he developed rapidly in general outlook as in literary skill. G. H. Lewes recalls his disappointment on meeting the 'marvellous Boz', just after *Pickwick* — 'I came away more impressed with the fullness of life and energy than with any sense of distinction.' Two years elapsed before they met again, and by then Dickens 'had remarkably developed. His conversation turned on graver subjects than theatres and actors, periodicals and London life. His interest in public affairs, especially in social questions, was keener. . . . The vivacity and sagacity which gave a charm to intercourse with him had become weighted with a seriousness which from that time forward became more and more prominent in his conversation and his writing.'[29a]

As one would expect, he is particularly moved by the spectacle of the young prisoners in Newgate, and more compassionate towards the girls than the boys. He describes two girls, one receiving a visit from her mother, and the other visiting hers. The former was 'a good-looking robust female', perfectly unmoved by the terrible anguish of her wretched old mother; the latter was thinly-clad and shaking with the cold.

> Some ordinary word of recognition passed between her and her mother when she appeared at the grating, but neither hope, condolence, regret, nor affection was expressed on either side. The mother whispered her instructions, and the girl received them with her pinched-up half-starved features twisted into an expression of careful cunning. It was some scheme for the woman's defence that she was disclosing, perhaps; and a sullen smile came over the girl's face for an instant, as if she were pleased: not so much at the probability of her mother's liberation, as at the chance of her 'getting off' in spite of her prosecutors.

He comments upon the second girl, who is not a prisoner herself at the moment but is obviously likely to be, or become, a street-walker or some other kind of petty delinquent.

> The girl belonged to a class — unhappily but too extensive — the very existence of which should make men's hearts bleed. Barely past her childhood, it required but a glance to discover that she was one of those children, born and bred in neglect and vice, who have never known what childhood is: who have never been taught to love and court a parent's smile, or to dread a parent's frown. The thousand nameless endearments of childhood, its gaiety and its innocence, are alike unknown to them. They have entered at once upon the stern realities and miseries of life, and to their better nature it is almost hopeless to appeal in after-times, by any of the references which will awaken, if it be only for a moment, some good feeling in ordinary bosoms, however corrupt they may have become. Talk to *them* of parental solicitude, the happy days of childhood, and the merry games of infancy! Tell them of hunger and the streets, beggary and stripes, the gin-shop, the station-house, and the pawnbroker's, and they will understand you.

This paragraph clearly foreshadows such characters as Nancy in *Oliver Twist*, and the other 'fallen women' in the novels; it is connected also with his many orphan and oppressed children, such as Oliver Twist and Little Nell, 'who have never known what childhood is;' and it is the pity and indignation expressed here which helped to provide the impetus for his splendidly energetic and intelligent work for the young prostitutes and other delinquent girls in Urania Cottage, the 'Home for Fallen Women'.

It is always easier for men who look round prisons to muster some sympathy for the girls and women than for the boys and men. Females, admittedly, are by general consent more difficult to manage in prisons than males, but their crimes are less numerous and less serious, and their sex evokes a chivalric impulse (to put it at its best) from male observers. Dickens's account of the boys charged with pocket-picking lacks the understanding and pity which he displays over the girls, nor has it the relish at the irrepressible cheekiness of these cocky *gamins* which appears in another of the *Sketches*, 'Criminal Courts', and in the Artful Dodger's conduct at his trial in *Oliver Twist*.[30] It is a grim description of the illkempt lads he sees in the prison 'school', to which boys under fourteen awaiting trial were committed.

> . . . fourteen such terrible little faces we never beheld. — There was not one redeeming feature among them — not a glance of honesty — not a wink expressive of anything but the gallows and the hulks, in the whole collection. As to anything like shame or contrition, that was entirely out of the question. They were evidently quite gratified at being thought worth the trouble of looking at; their idea appeared to be, that we had come to see Newgate as a grand affair, and that they were an indispensable part of the show; and every boy as he 'fell in' to the line, actually seemed as pleased and important as if he had done something excessively meritorious in getting there at all. We never looked upon a more disagreeable sight, because we never saw fourteen such hopeless creatures of neglect, before.

This final phrase, 'creatures of neglect', had originally (it will be remembered) been the more hopeless 'irreclaimable wretches'. The change of phrase suggests Dickens's growing preoccupation with the need for increased State and voluntary activity over education; and, as the passage about the girls foreshadows Urania Cottage and the 'fallen women' in the novels, so also this paragraph about boys reminds one of the terrible children, Ignorance and Want, in *A Christmas Carol*, Jo in *Bleak House*, and Dickens's writings and activities about the Ragged Schools — episodes in his life and art which I have discussed more fully elsewhere.[31]

After visiting the female and male sides of Newgate, Dickens enters the prison chapel, where one object 'rivets the attention and fascinates the gaze, . . . *the condemned pew*'. Here sat the prisoners on the last Sunday before their execution, to hear the 'condemned sermon' and to join in the responses to their own burial service. Dickens straightway identifies himself with them on this macabre occasion: 'Imagine what have been the feelings of the men whom that fearful pew has enclosed, and of whom, between the gallows and the knife, no mortal remnant may now remain! Think of the hopeless clinging to life to the last, and the wild despair, far exceeding in anguish the felon's death itself, by which they have heard the certainty of their speedy transmission to another world, with all their crimes upon their heads, rung into their ears by the officiating clergyman!' He then moves to the condemned ward, where the twenty-five or thirty men await the confirmation or reprieve of their death-sentences, and then to the press-room which contains three more men under sentence of death, 'the nature of whose offence rendered it necessary to separate them even from their companions in guilt.' (Mr W. J. Carlton has identified them and their crimes: two were hanged on 27 November 1835 for an unnatural offence, and the third, guilty of robbery with menaces, was reprieved.)[32] The two who were later executed — they were already, said the turnkey, 'dead men' — attracted Dickens's special attention: one was stooping over the fire, with his head buried in his hand, the other looked ghastly with 'pale, haggard face, and disordered hair, . . . and his eyes wildly staring before him, he seemed to be unconsciously intent on counting the chinks in the opposite wall.' The third man, hopeful of reprieve, walked jauntily up and down, but the other two were still in the same position, 'motionless as statues,' when Dickens passed through their room again later in his tour.

This fascination with the appearance and imagined feelings of men condemned to death is the sort of passage often pointed to by biographers who maintain that Dickens was morbidly given to indulging his suppressed aggressive instincts, or his latent criminality, by projecting himself into such characters and circumstances. Before agreeing to this interpretation, we should, however, recognise the degree to which Dickens here, as so often elsewhere, is speaking for Everyman. Who, being conducted round a prison

and seeing men whose execution was imminent, would fail to give
them a second glance and speculate about their feelings? And who,
seeing such appurtenances of death as the condemned pew, would
not be more fascinated by this than by the ordinary pews or 'the
bare and scanty pulpit' and 'the tottering little table at the altar'?
Gibbon Wakefield gives a long and unsensational account of the
Sunday 'condemned service' and other preliminaries to capital
punishment; and all other volumes of prison-memoirs, from his
time and from ours, mention such murderers and executions as
have come within the experience of the erstwhile prisoner or
prison-official. Moreover, murders, even in 1835, provided the
majority of the clients for the scaffold, and they are, surely, the
criminals with whom ordinary peace-loving citizens can most
readily identify themselves. Dickens is not uniquely depraved
here. As newspaper men have always known, a good murder is
worth a dozen thefts or swindles any day. 'Depend upon it, Sir,'
said Johnson to Boswell, 'when a man knows he is to be hanged in
a fortnight, it concentrates his mind wonderfully.'[33] One may dis-
agree with Johnson's judgment here, but many people, innocent of
any crime or criminal intent, must have speculated about how
murderers face their execution, or how they themselves would
behave in the circumstances. 'Condemned to death! These five
weeks have I dwelt with the idea' — so begins Victor Hugo's *Last
Days of a Condemned*, written seven years before Dickens's 'Visit to
Newgate'.[34] The theme is obviously a promising one for any
writer interested in extreme sensations. It is Dickens's literary skill
and imaginative power, more than the fact of his being attracted
to the subject, that marks him off from other men and writers.

He manifestly realised the literary potentialities of the situation,
and the two closing pages of the essay, prompted by his inspection
of the condemned cells, are the most dramatic and emotional in
the whole book. 'Conceive the situation of a man, spending his last
night on earth in this cell,' he begins, and soon his rhetoric quickens
with his excitement.

Buoyed up with some vague and undefined hope of reprieve, he knew
not why — indulging in some wild and visionary idea of escaping, he
knew not how — hour after hour of the three preceding days allowed
him for preparation, has fled with a speed which no man living would
deem possible, for none but this dying man can know . . . and, now
that the illusion is at last dispelled, now that eternity is before him and
guilt behind, now that his fears of death amount almost to madness,

and an overwhelming sense of his helpless, hopeless state rushes upon him, he is lost and stupefied, and has neither thoughts to turn to, nor power to call upon, the Almighty Being, from whom alone he can seek mercy and forgiveness, and before whom his repentance can alone avail.

Hours have glided by and still he sits upon the same stone bench with folded arms, heedless alike of the fast decreasing time before him, and the urgent entreaties of the good man at his side. The feeble light is wasting gradually, and the deathlike stillness of the street without, broken only by the rumbling of some passing vehicle which echoes mournfully through the empty yards, warns him that the night is waning fast away. The deep bell of St Paul's strikes — one! He heard it; it has roused him. Seven hours left! He paces the narrow limits of his cell with rapid strides, cold drops of terror starting on his forehead, and every muscle of his frame quivering with agony. Seven hours! . . . Hush! what sound was that? He starts upon his feet. It cannot be two yet. Hark! Two quarters have struck; — the third — the fourth. It is! Six hours left. Tell him not of repentance! Six hours' repentance for eight times six years of guilt and sin! He buries his face in his hands, and throws himself on the bench.

Worn with watching and excitement, he sleeps, and the same unsettled state of mind pursues him in his dreams. . . . The scene suddenly changes. He is on his trial again. . . . How full the court is — what a sea of heads — with a gallows, too, and a scaffold — and how all the people stare at *him*! Verdict, 'Guilty.' No matter; he will escape.

— and he dreams of running out of the prison, and sleeping soundly in the country, having thrown off his pursuers. 'He wakes, cold and wretched': it is the prison cell after all, 'and in two hours more he will be dead.'

It is a magnificent *tour de force*, but it is surpassed by the closely similar passage written only three years later, 'Fagin's Last Night alive.' This chapter in *Oliver Twist*, written by a less-hurried Dickens, who had meanwhile grown rapidly in literary skill and in judgment of public affairs, shows a nicer insight into the criminal's mind and a greater readiness to comment on judicial and penal processes. It opens with the scene at the Old Bailey: the 'sea of heads' of *Sketches by Boz* reappears in this sentence — 'The court was paved, from floor to roof, with human faces . . . all looks were fixed upon one man — Fagin . . . he seemed to stand surrounded by a firmament, all bright with gleaming eyes.'[35] There follows a fine passage about Fagin's state of mind as he awaits the return of the jury.

He looked up into the gallery again. Some of the people were eating, and some fanning themselves with handkerchiefs; for the crowded place was very hot. There was one young man sketching his face in a little note-book. He wondered whether it was like, and looked on when the artist broke his pencil-point, and made another with his knife, as any idle spectator might have done.

In the same way, when he turned his eyes towards the judge, his mind began to busy itself with the fashion of his dress, and what it cost, and how he put it on. There was an old fat gentleman on the bench, too, who had gone out, some half an hour before, and now come back. He wondered within himself whether this man had been to get his dinner, what he had had, and where he had had it; and pursued this train of careless thought until some new object caught his eye and roused another.

Not that, all this time, his mind was, for an instant, free from one oppressive overwhelming sense of the grave that opened at his feet; it was ever present to him, but in a vague and general way, and he could not fix his thoughts upon it. Thus, even while he trembled, and turned burning hot at the idea of speedy death, he fell to counting the iron spikes before him, and wondering how the head of one had been broken off, and whether they would mend it, or leave it as it was. Then, he thought of all the horrors of the gallows and the scaffold — and stopped to watch a man sprinkling the floor to cool it — and then went on to think again.

Fagin is pronounced guilty, sentenced, and taken to the condemned cell, but not until the Sunday night before the execution (held, by tradition, on Monday morning) is he 'able to consider more than the dim probability of dying so soon'. The hours pass, marked by the chimes of the clock, as in 'A Visit to Newgate'. Fagin begins to collapse — first into 'a paroxysm of fear and wrath', then into a distracted wandering and muttering about his old life, which renders him oblivious to the presence of his visitors, Mr Brownlow and Oliver Twist. 'Those dreadful walls of Newgate,' Dickens comments, 'which have hidden so much misery and such unspeakable anguish, not only from the eyes, but, too often, and too long, from the thoughts, of men, never held so dread a spectacle as that.' Unrepentant, and anxious only to cheat the gallows, Fagin whispers to Oliver a mad scheme of escape. And the chapter ends —

The men laid hands upon him, and disengaging Oliver from his grasp, held him back. He struggled with the power of desperation, for an instant; and then sent up cry upon cry that penetrated even those massive walls, and rang in their ears until they reached the open yard. . . .

Day was dawning when they again emerged. A great multitude had already assembled; the windows were filled with people, smoking and playing cards to beguile the time; the crowd were pushing, quarrelling, joking. Everything told of life and animation, but one dark cluster of objects in the centre of all — the black stage, the crossbeam, the rope, and all the hideous apparatus of death.

The treatment of Fagin's last days is longer, and pitched higher, than the corresponding passage in *Sketches by Boz*; it also shows more insight into the character of the condemned man; and, as the final paragraph about the scaffold instances, the effect is more complex. It is interesting to speculate how, over thirty years later, John Jasper would have been shown spending his last days in the condemned cell, had Dickens lived to complete *Edwin Drood*.

Dickens often returned to Newgate, personally and in his fiction. In 1837 he was planning an expedition there (probably because *Gabriel Vardon* was on his mind again), and it was no doubt this projected visit which the actor Macready describes in his diary for 27 June 1837. Macready had called at Dickens's house, and was directed to Coldbath Fields Prison, where he found Dickens with Forster and other friends. They went on together to Newgate, where in one room they saw a man reading, and were startled (as Forster recalls) by a sudden tragic cry from Macready — 'My God! there's Wainewright!' Twenty years later, Dickens was to write a short-story, 'Hunted Down,' about this notorious artist-murderer.[36] It was presumably these visits to Newgate in the 1830s that provided the memories on which Pip's tour of Newgate was based. It is noteworthy that, although the *Great Expectations* passage deplores the luxury of the prisons of the 1860s, it is much more critical of old Newgate than *Sketches by Boz* had been. 'A potman was going his rounds with beer,' says Pip; 'and the prisoners, behind bars in yards, were buying beer, and talking to friends; and a frowsy, ugly, disorderly, depressing scene it was.' When Pip emerges from the gaol he feels tainted, contaminated, soiled: 'I beat the prison dust off my feet as I sauntered to and fro, and I shook it out of my dress, and I exhaled its air from my lungs.' Earlier in the book, he had seen, just after arriving in London for the first time, 'the great black dome of St Paul's bulging at me from behind a grim stone building which a bystander said was

Newgate Prison.' As he looked about him, 'an exceedingly dirty and partially drunk minister of justice' insisted on showing him the yard where the gallows was kept and where offenders were publicly whipped, and the door out of which culprits came to be hanged — 'heightening the interest of that dreadful portal by giving me to understand that "four on 'em" would come out of that door the day after tomorrow at eight in the morning, to be killed in a row. This was horrible, and gave me a sickening idea of London.'[37] Dickens clearly shares, and expects the reader to share, Pip's revulsion.

How mixed were his feelings about Newgate and prisons appears in *Barnaby Rudge* (1841). The moral of this story about the Gordon Riots is expressed in its Preface thus: '. . . these shameful tumults, while they reflect indelible disgrace upon the time in which they occurred, and all who had act or part in them, teach a good lesson,' namely that 'what we falsely call a religious cry, is easily raised by men who have no religion; . . . that it is senseless, besotted, inveterate, and unmerciful. . . .' But as Mr Edmund Wilson nicely puts it, 'the historical episode, the contemporary moral, and the author's emotional pattern do not always coincide very well'; and on his equivocal handling of the episode which marks the culmination of the Riots — the storming and burning of Newgate — Mr Wilson comments, 'The satisfaction he obviously feels in demolishing the sinister old prison, which, rebuilt, had oppressed him in childhood, completely obliterates the effect of his right-minded references in his preface to "those shameful tumults". . . .'[38] *Barnaby Rudge* is, as Professors Butt and Tillotson point out, peculiar among Dickens's early novels, in having the long gestation period of five years — it should have been his first published novel, not his fifth — and the fact that Dickens proved so tenacious of this plot, when he had so many other projects in mind, shows how strongly it had seized his imagination. Probably, as they argue, it was the burning of Newgate that had first engaged his interest in the subject (again, the Preface gives only a superficial explanation — 'No account of the Gordon Riots having been to my knowledge introduced into any Work of Fiction, and the subject presenting very extraordinary and remarkable features, I was led to project this Tale.') Certainly it was this ultimate sacrilege against the stronghold of society that most struck the writers of Dickens's sources. As Professors Butt and Tillotson remark: 'In contemporary accounts, the burning of Newgate appears more terrifying than all the attacks upon Catholic chapels and property in its expression of the lawlessness of the mob; and to the next generation it carried the shadow of a far greater historical event, the fall of the Bastille.'[39] It is significant that Dickens's only other historical novel, *A Tale of Two Cities*, deals with exactly that event.

Dickens's overt intentions about the Riots would have been even clearer, had not Forster persuaded him of the 'unsoundness' of his original plan to make the leaders three escaped Bedlamites. ('Where is the unsoundness of this?' wrote Wilkie Collins in his copy of Forster. 'I call it a fine idea. New, powerful, highly drama-tic, and well within the limits of truth to nature. It would have greatly improved the weakest book that Dickens ever wrote.')[40] The mob-leaders Dickens did employ suggest a wider range of social irrationality and resentment; as several critics have pointed out, this choice is almost allegorical — the crazy Lord Gordon, the idiot Barnaby Rudge, the 'mere animal' Hugh the Bastard (son of a dissolute gentleman and a gipsy woman hanged for passing forged notes), the exhibitionist apprentice Simon Tappertit, and the sadistic hangman Ned Dennis with his slogan of 'Down with everybody, down with everything!' The recurrent imagery by which the mob is described is, moreover, that of devils, savages, animals, the sea, and of irrational, insane, diseased and feverish creatures.[41] But Dickens's much-quoted letters to Forster, about his progress in writing the novel, show at least an imaginative sympathy with the mob: 'I have just burnt into Newgate, and am going in the next number to tear the prisoners out by the hair of their heads.' 'I have let all the prisoners out of Newgate, burnt down Lord Mansfield's, and played the very devil. Another num-ber will finish the fires . . . I feel quite smoky when I am at work.'[42] Not for nothing had he written to another friend a few months earlier, declining the loan of further books about Lord George Gordon: 'As to the riot, I am going to try if I can't make a better one than he did.'[43]

One should not, of course, make too much of the novelist's absorption in his work, or his determination to create a striking effect. But it is noteworthy that he chose this subject (and later the French Revolution), and that, while disapproving of the mob's activities and doing little to excuse them on the grounds of their being ignorant or oppressed, he 'follows' the mob and not their victims or opponents. The Newgate chapters in *Barnaby Rudge* are not much concerned with penological questions, nor with criminal psychology (though his picture of Mr Rudge in custody, reminiscent of the 'Fagin's Last Night alive', is a striking piece of work). The episode is more interesting for its presentation of mob-psychology, and for its revelation of Dickens's attitude to authority, and it is on these aspects that I shall concentrate.

Like other artists, of course, he found wicked or roguish characters easier to dramatise than virtuous ones: he was unlike other writers only in finding the task of creating the virtuous characters so congenial, and in feeling such complacency about the results, abysmal though they generally were. But good people threatened by a vicious mob are much more promising material than good people simply being good, and the brave and resolute defenders of law and order are also a good strong subject. Thus when the Indian Mutiny broke out, Dickens's moral, political and imaginative allegiances were all at one, wholly on the side of beleaguered white men; he wrote a story, 'The Perils of Certain English Prisoners,' on the theme for the next Christmas Number of *Household Words*, and its simple heart-whole attitude to insurrection is represented by Captain Carton's retort to the civil servant who warned him that 'Government requires you to treat the enemy with great delicacy, consideration, clemency, and forbearance' —

> 'Sir,' says Captain Carton, 'I am an English officer, commanding English Men, and I hope I am not likely to disappoint the Government's just expectations. But, I presume you know that these villains under their black flag have despoiled our countrymen of their property, burnt their homes, barbarously murdered them and their little children, and worse than murdered their wives and daughters? . . . Believing that I hold my commission by the allowance of God, and not that I have received it direct from the Devil, I shall certainly use it, with all avoidance of unnecessary suffering and with all merciful swiftness of execution, to exterminate these people from the face of the earth. Let me recommend you to go home, Sir, and to keep out of the night-air.'[44]

Dickens had himself used almost identical language about the rebellious Indians, and what he would do to them, in a letter to Miss Burdett Coutts.[45] As Professor Ford has remarked, with reference to Dickens's equally ruthless and single-minded reaction to another episode of colonial bloodshed, Governor Eyre's 'firm' treatment of the Jamaicans in 1864: 'It is sometimes forgotten that Dickens was not so much the friend of the common man as the friend of the common Englishman.'[46]

His reaction to the Indian and Jamaican troubles shows that his imaginative interest, let alone his moral sympathies, did not always belong to the mob. It is the more illuminating, then, that in *Barnaby Rudge* he finds it quite impossible to identify himself with the authorities who had to restore law and order. He was, of course, engaged in the congenial task of making gibes against the feebleness and inefficiency of Governments, Lord Mayors, and magistrates, and his allegations about the authorities of 1780 were — like much of the novel — sound enough historically. The actual Lord Mayor of London in office during the Riots was fined £1,000 for dereliction of duty. Dickens had no such bias, here or elsewhere, against the military, who effectively put an end to the Riots. The army, indeed, is the only official body that comes out well in his story — from General Conway and Colonel Gordon, to Sergeant Joe Willet who, like Edward Chester, is given a good showing (as befits a man destined to become a bridegroom in the final chapter). The military party which captures Barnaby Rudge and has to march him into custody is praised not only for its efficiency but also for its officers' wisdom — 'humanely anxious . . . a merciful prudence . . . this wise proceeding. . . .'⁴⁷ But Dickens is otherwise little interested in the problem of quelling the Riots, as it appeared to the civil or military authorities, or in the process whereby they eventually succeeded. There is none of that imaginative relish here, that appears in his portrayal of the mob themselves. 'By this Friday night,' he announces without much explanation, '. . . the disturbances were entirely quelled, and peace and order were restored to the affrighted city. . . . In a word, the crowd was utterly routed.'⁴⁸

This inability to sympathise with established authority — with the conspicuous exceptions of the New Police and, overseas, of those who resolutely disciplined the turbulent natives — should not be mistaken (as sometimes it has been) for a fundamental hostility towards established authority in a Parliamentary regime, or a tendency towards anarchism or political revolution. Dickens hated mobs and their violence, even if he could not imaginatively approve of their rulers. Nor did he deny the necessity for firm government: as he comments on the early stages of the Riots: 'Hot and drunken though [the rioters] were, they had not yet broken all bounds and set all law and government at defiance. Something of their habitual deference to the authority erected by society for its own preservation yet remained among them. . . .'⁴⁹ But it was not only because history recorded a bad verdict on the authorities of 1780, that Dickens gives them such scant attention, let alone respect, in *Barnaby Rudge*. Despite the authoritarian strain in his character, he could rarely identify himself with the Establishment in its exercise of judicial and administrative functions. Some reasons for this inability will be discussed in a later chapter.

Dickens's attitude to the storming of Newgate is expressed, in parody-form, by that complex figure, Dennis the hangman. Dennis had been among the leaders of assault, and when the gates had been burned down he 'stood in the lobby, directing some to go this way, some that, and some the other; and . . . materially assisted in bringing about the wonderful rapidity with which the release of the prisoners was effected' (though he tried to prevent the mob's finding and rescuing the men he was due to hang).[50] But he 'played his cards throughout, with great care' (as he reflected at a later stage of the Riots) — he 'had changed sides at the very nick of time; had delivered up two of the most notorious rioters, and a distinguished felon to boot; and was quite at his ease'.[51] (The rioters were Barnaby and Hugh, and the felon was Mr Rudge.) It was not only prudence that had caused this hedging of his bets, but resentment against Hugh's having released the four men awaiting execution. 'Don't you know they're left for death on Thursday?' he had remonstrated at the time. 'Don't you respect the law — the constitootion — nothing?'[52] And when the soldiers had arrested Hugh and his companions, Dennis turned to him, 'in a tone of resignation,' and said: 'I'm sorry for it, brother; but you've brought it on yourself; you forced me to do it; you wouldn't respect the soundest constitootional principles, you know; you went and wiolated the wery framework of society.'[53] For Dennis's interpretation of the Constitution, as existing chiefly to provide ample fodder for the gallows, Dickens has of course no sympathy, and he later stresses that the rioters who were eventually hanged 'were for the most part the weakest, meanest, and most miserable among them'.[54] Indeed, as Dr Folland has argued in a recent article, 'The controlling theme of *Barnaby Rudge* is the deceptive and complex relationships between the doer and the deed, deeds and their consequences, and the doer's responsibility. . . . The organising ethical theme . . . is really the evil of action divorced from responsibility; its world is one in which evil flourishes because its true connections and causes are hidden and must be gradually searched out.'[55] But, while the *éminences grises* behind the violence,

Gashford and Chester, escape prosecution, Dickens does have the less culpable leaders of the crowd punished. Dennis and Hugh are hanged, Barnaby is reprieved only at the last moment, Tappertit's 'graceful limbs' are crushed and amputated, and Gordon, after various vicissitudes, dies in gaol (history here, of course, gave Dickens no option). Dickens realised the justice, as well as the inevitability, of punishing those who thus attacked the central symbol of law and order, but his description of their assault had displayed a fascinated interest, as well as horror and disgust. Mr Akerman the head gaoler, like the other representatives of legitimacy, is a shadowy and momentary figure; the mob's actions and emotions are followed intricately.

'They howled like wolves,' they 'thirsted, like wild animals' for blood, their 'savage faces' glared upon their victims.[56] They were mad, sub-human, as appeared in their crazy attempt to batter down the walls of the prison.

> And now the strokes began to fall like hail upon the gate and on the strong building; for those who could not reach the door spent their fierce rage on anything — even on the great blocks of stone, which shivered their weapons into fragments, and made their hands and arms to tingle as if the walls were active in their stout resistance and dealt them back their blows. The clash of iron ringing upon iron mingled with the deafening tumult, and sounded high above it, as the great sledge-hammers rattled on the nailed and plated door; the sparks flew off in showers; men worked in gangs, and at short intervals relieved each other, that all their strength might be devoted to the work: but there stood the portal still, as grim and dark and strong as ever, and, saving for the dints upon its battered surface, quite unchanged.[57]

Baffled in this attempt, they decide instead to burn their way in, and gleefully watch the flames: 'the mob began to join the whirl, and with loud yells, and shouts, and clamour, such as happily is seldom heard, bestirred themselves to feed the fire, and keep it at its height.'[58]

> Now, now, the door was down. Now they came rushing through the gaol, calling to each other in the vaulted passages, clashing the iron gates dividing yard from yard, beating at the doors of cells and wards, wrenching off bolts and locks and bars, tearing down the door-posts to get men out, endeavouring to drag them by main force through gaps and windows where a child could scarcely pass, whooping and yelling without a moment's rest, and running through the heat and

flames as if they were cased in metal. By their legs, their arms, the hair upon their heads, they dragged the prisoners out. Some threw themselves upon the captives as they got towards the door, and tried to file away their irons; some danced about them with a frenzied joy, and rent their clothes, and were ready, as it seemed, to tear them limb from limb. Now a party of a dozen men came darting through the yard into which the murderer cast fearful glances from his darkened window, dragging a prisoner along the ground, whose dress they had nearly torn from his body in their mad eagerness to set him free, and who was bleeding and senseless in their hands.[59]

It is an orgiastic scene only surpassed in this novel by the description of the fire at the Vintner's house — 'as though the last day had come and the whole universe were burning . . . it seemed as if the face of Heaven were blotted out.' That episode made a fitting climax to the Riots, and like the attack on Newgate it was described often in the very words of contemporary references.[60]

Newgate was not the only gaol destroyed. 'Not that gaol alone,' cried Hugh, when a man in the crowd urged them to march on Newgate to rescue their comrades, 'but every gaol in London.'[61] In the four days of rioting, Dickens notes later, four strong gaols were destroyed; and about the prisoners released from Newgate and Fleet he makes an interesting observation which he was to amplify in later years. In the historical accounts of the Riots he had read that some of the released prisoners returned voluntarily to gaol.[62] Two years earlier he had described a similar phenomenon, in *Nicholas Nickleby*. When Dotheboys Hall finally 'broke up', there were 'a few timid young children, who, miserable as they had been, and many as were the tears they had shed in the wretched school, still knew no other home, and had formed for it a sort of attachment which made them weep when the bolder spirits fled, and cling to it as a refuge.'[63] When Newgate was breached, Dickens describes one prisoner leaving it slowly and sadly, 'because that gaol, his house, was burning.'[64] Similarly, when the gaolers at the Fleet and the King's Bench released their prisoners because the prisons were threatened with a like fate,

There were some broken men among these debtors who had been in gaol so long, and were so miserable and destitute of friends, so dead to the world, and utterly forgotten and uncared for, that they implored their gaolers not to set them free, and to send them, if need were, to some other place of custody. . . .

Even of the three hundred prisoners who had escaped from

Newgate, there were some — a few, but there were some — who sought their gaolers out and delivered themselves up, preferring imprisonment and punishment to the horrors of such another night as the last. Many of the convicts, drawn back to their old place of captivity by some indescribable attraction, or by a desire to exult over it in its downfall and glut their revenge by seeing it in ashes, actually went back in broad noon, and loitered about the cells. Fifty were retaken at one time on this next day within the prison walls; but their fate did not deter others, for there they went in spite of everything, and there they were taken in twos and threes, twice or thrice a day, all through the week. Of the fifty just mentioned, some were occupied in endeavouring to rekindle the fire; but in general they seemed to have no object in view but to prowl and lounge about the old place, being often found asleep in the ruins, or sitting talking there, or even eating and drinking, as in a choice retreat.[65]

If Dickens was ambivalent towards prisons, he was also aware that prisoners too had mixed feelings about their 'home'. In this passage, we see the germ of several important episodes in later novels — Mr Micawber never so carefree and confident as when in the King's Bench, Mr Dorrit relapsing into memories of his grandeur as the Father of the Marshalsea, Dr Manette suddenly reverting to being 'One Hundred and Five, North Tower' of the Bastille, and anguished because he cannot find his cobbler's bench and tools —

> 'Come, come!' said he, in a whimpering, miserable way; 'let me get to work. Give me my work.'
> Receiving no answer, he tore his hair, and beat his feet upon the ground, like a distracted child.
> 'Don't torture a poor forlorn wretch,' he implored them, with a dreadful cry; 'but give me my work! . . .'[66]

The defenders of the Philadelphia Penitentiary, whose system Dickens had stigmatised as 'cruel and wrong, . . . torture and agony', later hailed as convincing proof that he was wrong, the fact that the German on whom he had expended so much sympathy ('My heart bled for him; and . . . the tears ran down his cheeks . . .') served eight further sentences there, and in 1884 actually rang the bell on the prison gate and begged to be allowed to come inside to die.[67] Dickens would not have been surprised, nor would he have regarded this wretched career as a vindication of the prison's regime.

III

THE SILENT SYSTEM —
COLDBATH FIELDS PRISON

NEWGATE remained for most of Dickens's lifetime, and in all his writings about it, an old-style prison barely touched by the new reforms. There were, however, two London prisons which he knew much more intimately and continuously, and which had emerged from a state of chaos and corruption even worse than Newgate's into the leading English exemplars of one of the great rival systems of prison-discipline. The Middlesex House of Correction, Coldbath Fields, and the Westminster Bridewell, Tothill Fields, were both reorganised in the 1830s on the Silent System, and Dickens became a close friend and admirer of their Governors — Captain George Laval Chesterton, Governor of the former from 1829 to 1854, and Lieutenant Augustus Frederick Tracey, RN, Governor of the latter from 1834 to 1855. The histories of these two prisons were much the same, as were the reformist policies adopted by their Governors and Visiting Magistrates, so I shall fully describe only the events at Coldbath Fields; these are much better documented, partly because Chesterton wrote two books — an autobiography, *Peace, War, and Adventure* (1853), and a book of memoirs and reflections, *Revelations of Prison Life: with an Enquiry into Prison Discipline and Secondary Punishments* (1856). Moreover Coldbath Fields was the more famous and important of the two prisons, both because Chesterton enforced the common system more intelligently and comprehensively, and because this prison then had the additional distinction of being the largest in Britain or, perhaps, in the world.

Unfortunately Dickens never wrote a full-scale description and assessment of either of these prisons, comparable to his accounts of Newgate, which we have examined, or of Pentonville, which will be discussed in a later chapter. He had intended to write an account of Coldbath Fields for *Sketches by Boz*, as a companion-piece to 'A Visit to Newgate', but then (it will be remembered) he decided that this essay had already stolen all the thunder which the prison-theme could produce.[1] In later years, he often warmly commended the two Middlesex prisons, their Governors, and the disciplinary system which they adopted — but only briefly and in general terms. When he was in America in 1842, and had begun examining its famous penitentiaries, he sent his first impressions to Forster: 'I am confident that the writers who have the most lustily lauded the American prisons, have never seen Chesterton's domain or Tracey's. There is no more comparison between those two prisons of ours, and any I have seen here YET, than there is between the keepers here and those two gentlemen.'[2] Visits to further American prisons only confirmed this judgment, which he repeated in *American Notes*, saying that two London prisons were 'in all respects equal, and in some decidedly superior' to any he had seen or heard of in America. Their Governors, Chesterton and Tracey, were 'enlightened and superior men: and it would be as difficult to find persons better qualified for the functions they discharge with firmness, zeal, intelligence, and humanity, as it would be to exceed the perfect order and arrangement of the institutions they govern'. Four years later, he repeated this testimonial in the *Daily News*: it would, he said, be 'hard, if not impossible' to find prison-governors 'more intelligent and humane'.[3] His published works contain other passing references to these Governors and their prisons, and there are many more in his letters. Dickens never disagrees with them on the fundamentals of prison-discipline, and only rarely on the details.

A description of Coldbath Fields, then, and of its Governor's outlook, will provide us with a detailed picture of the prison ideas which Dickens approved — the more useful, because his penological writings are mainly devoted to attacking prison systems, which, for one reason or another, he deplores. For this reason, my account of Coldbath Fields will be fairly lengthy. Moreover, when Chesterton arrived there in 1829, it was typical of the unreformed prisons all over the country, the inefficient squalor of which provoked those great penological campaigns and debates of the second quarter of the century, that form the background to Dickens's writings on this topic. The earlier part of this chapter will, therefore, be a convenient point at which to describe the two main rival disciplinary systems then introduced — the Silent System, which included among its supporters Chesterton and Tracey and Dickens, and the Separate System. Some account of the state of public opinion on these issues will also be given here, so that Dickens's relation to contemporary ideas may appear more clearly.

Coldbath Fields and Tothill Fields were both local prisons, under the control of the Middlesex Magistrates, and they catered for minor offenders with sentences ranging from one week to three years. The average sentence at Coldbath Fields in 1850 was six weeks. Coldbath Fields stood in Clerkenwell, reputed to be the most vicious part of London, with the highest murder-rate and the densest criminality: nearby were Saffron Hill and Field Lane, the Fagin area in *Oliver Twist*. Dickens was within half a mile of the prison during the 1830s, when he lived in Furnival's Inn and Doughty Street. Tothill Fields was in the 'Devil's Acre' — the moral plague-spot of the whole kingdom, as one of Dickens's colleagues called it — just behind the Houses of Parliament; it is Jenny Wren's area in *Our Mutual Friend*.[4] They were old-established prisons; their buildings dated from 1794 and 1836 respectively, though a Bridewell had stood in Tothill Fields since the seventeenth century.[5]

From its earliest years Coldbath Fields had enjoyed a terrible reputation. Coleridge's lines in 'The Devil's Thoughts' (1799) are often quoted —

> As he went through Cold-Bath Fields he saw
>   A solitary cell;
> And the Devil was pleased, for it gave him a hint
>   For improving his prisons in Hell.

Coleridge was referring to the scandals, Sir Francis Burdett's exposure of which had led to some temporary reforms.[6] The prison soon reverted to its bad ways, and generally lived up to its nickname of 'The Bastille' (abbreviated in criminal slang to 'The Steal'). But by the late 1820s it was more conspicuous for its inefficiency and corruption than for its toughness. Parliament was told in 1828 that the Middlesex gaols were actually increasing in iniquity, vilely overcrowded, grossly disorderly, and in a state of incredible filth.[7] It was in the following year that Chesterton became Governor of Coldbath Fields; the previous Governor, suspected, like several of his predecessors, of having connived at the escape of prisoners, had been forced to resign. 'I knew nothing of prisons,' wrote Chesterton later, recalling the time when he accepted this post: and, he adds, 'I was not then aware that, considering the prevailing mismanagement of that period, happy was he who did not.'[8]

For Coldbath Fields was entirely corrupt, unhealthy and un-comfortable, while its being so large made it even more difficult to reform than other prisons in a like condition. Chesterton had been appointed, as a former army-officer, to raise its moral and social tone; the Magistrates were looking for 'a gentleman' to replace the dismissed Governor, who like many at that period, had been 'a mere police officer' (from the pre-Metropolitan Police era, of course). Chesterton's judgment on his predecessors was severe, but justified. They had, he said, 'held that their primary obliga-tion consisted in feathering their own nests, and at the same time enriching their subordinates.'[9] Twenty-five shillings a day in perks was what one ordinary turnkey expected; Chesterton over-heard him boasting so in a pub (for he was driven to some very devious courses, to spy out abuses, with the whole staff implacably against him). The whole machinery of the prison, he wrote, 'betokened the most appalling abuse; and I found every thing around me stamped with iniquity and corruption. The best acquainted with the prison were utterly ignorant of the frightful extent of its demoralisation.' The officers conspired to maintain the iniquities of this 'sink of abomination' because they made a profit of seven or eight shillings in the pound on the vast illicit commerce which was conducted in the prison.[10] Most would-be reformers thought that only the grosser immoralities could be checked at all, since it would be dangerous to interfere very far with the criminal inmates, who certainly were of 'a brutality, daring and lawlessness which can scarcely be over-charged'.[11] The more powerful prisoners, of course, supported the turnkeys in resisting the reforms which would end their power, profit and comfort — for the criminal 'yardsmen' took a further two shillings in the pound on the goods which entered the prison, in addition to the turnkeys' large commission. The sinister effects of the 'tobacco barons', so familiar in modern prison memoirs, existed then, but on an infinitely larger scale. For every kind of contraband entered the prison, and was hidden in caches everywhere. Chesterton visited the Infirmary one night, and found the mattresses stuffed with merchandise, while the beds were occupied by able-bodied prisoners who paid half-a-crown a night for this extra comfort. An even more dramatic occasion was his bursting one afternoon into an attic, where the male and female prisoners were enjoying their daily reunion, with the connivance of the turnkeys; but even the blandishments of the females — many of whom were prostitutes by profession — failed to divert him from the course of duty.

Several years' unremitting work, and the wholesale replacement of the staff, were needed before these abuses were removed. His notable success in ending illegal trafficking was noted in 1830 by Bulwer Lytton, who visited the prison when seeking material for *Paul Clifford*, and described Chesterton as 'apparently a very intelligent and active man, every way fitted for this most arduous undertaking'.[12] Though in danger of reprisals by the angry turnkeys and prisoners, he was upheld by a few 'gentlemanly' prisoners, an excellent chief-turnkey he appointed from the Army, and the reforming Magistrates (prominent among whom was Samuel Hoare, the brother-in-law of Elizabeth Fry — a visitor whose memory Chesterton 'devoutly honoured').[13] His first task, of course, was to enforce common honesty, decency and efficiency in the prison, and he was justified (if immodest) in writing, after his retirement:

> It became my happy privilege to prove useful in the work of regeneration, where its need was a crying exigency, and I may be pardoned for looking back with honest pride upon exertions which public avowal has flatteringly confessed to have been fraught with benefit to society at large. My emphatic claim is to have been one of the humble instruments in . . . that onward and eventful movement, by whose civilising influence, the chief prison of the metropolitan county . . . was transformed from one of the worst specimens of corruption and mis-rule, into an establishment distinguished for industry, order, and impressive discipline.[14]

But what kind of industry and discipline did he establish, and to what ends? — for though the establishment of good order and probity was an essential first step, there remained the question, what should he do with the prisoners, once they were docile and well-managed?

One of the most thoughtful, and certainly the best-written, of mid-Victorian books on English prison history is the Reverend Walter Clay's *The Prison Chaplain* (1861). There it is stated that in the mid-1820s 'the prison-disciplinarians had branched off into three sects which still exist, their respective principles being: (1) to reform by industry (the Benthamites); (2) to reform by religion

(Mrs Fry's school); (3) to deter by punishment (Sydney Smith and all writers who trust to their "common-sense" and their ignorance). Of course each sect *partially* adopted the principles of the other two'.[15] As the Webbs further point out, what gave acrimony to the interminable controversy about prison-systems which started in the next few years, was less the conflict of evidence about the efficacy of the several systems, than 'the unavowed differences of opinion upon the relative importance to be attached, not merely to the maintenance of the prisoners in physical and mental health, but also to success in deterring, success in reforming, and success in economising public expenditure.'[16] The last of these items was very important, to Dickens among others, at a time when (even more than today) there were many competing claims on a very limited budget of public funds. For the systems varied a good deal in their costs, one being cheaper to establish and another cheaper to run. There was much controversy, too, about whether prisoners should engage in producing manufactured or hand-made goods — whether, indeed, prisons could or should be made self-supporting. Inevitably, therefore, there was much confusion, and angry debate, during these decades. The idea of making prisons purposive at all was relatively new; there was hardly any British experience to draw upon; reports from overseas were enthusiastic but contradictory; prison-reformers did not agree, anyway, about fundamentals and priorities. As the *Quarterly Review* remarked querulously in 1853: 'A sustained clamour has long existed as to punishment in general, and every kind of system enforcing it has been canvassed, adopted, and abandoned in turn. The hanging system, the hard-labour, the solitary, the silent, the separate, and the transportation systems, with their various modifications, have all been taken up and thrown down with such astonishing rapidity as to make one doubt whether there is anything called experience, or whether it is of any use.' (The writer might indeed also have mentioned the Marks System, and a year or so later he would certainly have mentioned the Irish System.) 'Some wholesome truths, however, do creep out from this weary rubbish,' he admitted — notably the general recognition that '*the* crying evil' of the unreformed prisons was Association, the liberty given to prisoners to talk together and thus to complete the corruption of any who were relatively innocent.[17] In the early 1830s, when Chesterton, having set his house in order, began to contemplate more radical reforms, and when Dickens started visiting prisons and writing about them, there were two main disciplinary systems in the field. Both aimed at eliminating the evils of Association, and both came from America. They were often known as the Philadelphia and the Auburn systems, after the famous prisons in the States of Pennsylvania and New York which had popularised them.

Under the Philadelphia System — also known as the Separate, the Solitary, or the Cellular System — prisoners occupied individual cells day and night. Usually they were given pious books to read, or handicraft to execute, but sometimes they were left without any employment to meditate on their sins and the baleful consequences thereof. They took exercise in separate individual yards, and did not even leave their cells for Divine Service; it was read in the corridors by the Chaplain, and the prisoners sat alone in their cells, reverently listening to it (or so it was claimed). Food could be pushed into the cells through hatches so designed that the warder could see the prisoners without being seen by them. Admirers of these prisons were always very annoyed when people carelessly or maliciously used the term 'solitary confinement' to describe the Separate System, but the distinction between separation and solitude must often have seemed academic to the prisoners themselves, who never saw or spoke with anyone except the officers and approved prison-visitors (and them not very often). Such, at least, was the strict Philadelphia version of the system; in the English modification of it, prisoners left their cells more often, for religious and secular instruction, but then had to wear masks or veils to prevent their even seeing the faces of their fellow-prisoners, whom they never met. In this way, it was hoped, another means of the corruption of prisoners would be eliminated: for it was notoriously difficult for a prisoner under the old system to go straight, on his release, if some of his erstwhile companions could recognise him and blackmail him into supporting their nefarious plans.[18] Under the Auburn — or Silent Associated — System, however, prisoners were allowed to work together, but under very strict supervision, for they were forbidden ever to speak, or otherwise communicate, with one another. Ideally, they should have slept in separate cells, but in many Silent System prisons, the prisoners continued to sleep in the old dormitories, as the Magistrates were unwilling to go to the expense of replacing them. Warders had to be with the prisoners, therefore, night and day, watching for any infringement of the rules.

The merits of these two systems were hotly, often angrily,

debated, with the devotees of each generally claiming every kind of incompatible virtue for his particular nostrum; it was healthier, more reformative, more deterrent, less cruel, less costly, and so on. On the whole, however, the Separatists tended to rely more on producing a change of heart in their prisoners through moral and religious influence, while the upholders of the Silent System believed rather in deterring criminals by a regime of 'wholesome severity'. De Tocqueville, one of the many distinguished European observers sent to look at the American prisons in the early 1830s, offered a plausible judgment. The Philadelphia System, he said, produced a more profound reformation when it succeeded at all, but the Auburn one was more effective in persuading its victims to avoid offending the police again — 'the Philadelphia system produces more honest men, and that of [Auburn] more obedient citizens.'[19] There were rival administrative advantages and disadvantages, too. The Silent System could be operated, more or less effectively, in most existing buildings, though a huge staff was necessary to prevent the rules from being flouted; moreover, work in Association was financially more profitable than work in separate cells. On the other hand, the Separate System was impossible without a cellular prison, so it required an expensive building programme, but once such a prison had been built, it needed a relatively small staff. Most British prisons needed re-building, anyway, both for greater security and better hygiene; one of the main reasons for the eventual triumph of the Separate System, as a later Chairman of the Prison Commission remarked, was its security and economy, though in its origins it had been 'essentially a religious movement'. Or, as a contemporary observer tartly commented: '. . . the officials like it; it gives them little trouble, so, without pretending to understand its complicated effects, moral or mental, they almost swear by it.'[20]

Coldbath Fields had very few separate cells, and partly for this reason Chesterton decided in favour of the Silent System; later experience confirmed him in his choice, and in his detestation of its rival. So, one day in 1834, he suddenly informed his prisoners that all inter-communication by word, gesture, or sign was henceforth prohibited, and throughout his remaining twenty years as Governor, the Silent System was enforced with unyielding strictness: 'Not one single known infringement of the rule was overlooked.' Somewhat humourlessly he added that 'The legitimate opportunities, nay, the demands, for the use of speech are numerous.

The daily responses in chapel, communication with the governor, the chaplain, the schoolmasters and various officers, all tend healthfully to employ the tongue'. It must be admitted, however, that Chesterton never equalled the superb achievement in unconscious humour of his successor, who adorned the walls of Coldbath Fields with the wriest prison joke I know — the text 'Behold how good and pleasant it is for brethren to dwell together in unity!'[21]

Chesterton had chosen unwisely, if he wanted to stand well in the opinion of officials and of penological pundits. As the next few years showed, it was chiefly laymen, and some economically-minded officials, who advocated the Silent System, while most of the professionals — the Prison Inspectors, the Home Office, and people apt to write books on prison-discipline — preferred its rival. Most of the Inspectors appointed under the 1835 Act were staunch Separate System men. Those who were responsible for London and the Home District included William Crawford, who had recommended the Philadelphia system in his report on his Government-sponsored visit *(Penitentiaries of the United States, 1834)*, and the Reverend Whitworth Russell who, as Chaplain of Millbank, had earlier introduced several features of the Separate System, including its religious bias. (As a later Millbank official said, 'the prayers, expositions, and genuflections were more in keeping with a monastery of monks than a gaol full of criminals.')[22] The advocates of the rival systems had little modesty, and were rarely disposed to recognise merit in their opponents, so Coldbath Fields came off badly in official publications. The Second and Third Reports of the Prison Inspectors (published in 1837 and 1838) were notably partisan documents, bent on proving the splendid potentialities of the Separate System (the only system 'adapted to the endless varieties of human character'), and equally on showing that the Silent System was 'cumbrous and intricate in its construction, inadequate to the purposes it contemplates, and dependent, for its successful working, upon circumstances which can neither be universally secured nor relied upon'. Coldbath Field naturally attracted the Inspectors' heaviest fire, on account of its size and its reputation as the best specimen of the Silent System.[23] Chesterton reviewed the historic Third Report in *The Monthly Law Magazine* (October and November 1838), arguing that it was very biassed, but he could not stem the tide. The Government accepted its Inspectors' arguments, and their 'Suggestions for the Construction of a Model Prison on the Separate

System (in or adjacent to the Metropolis)' were fulfilled when Pentonville was built a few years later.

Chesterton's opponents were, indeed, many and influential, and they often pointed out that, to enforce his system, he had to inflict numerous and severe punishments for infringements of prison regulations. Dickens was taken to task by one of these critics, for praising Coldbath Fields and Tothill Fields, which between them accounted for over one third of the total number of punishments inflicted in all the prisons of England and Wales.[24] But Chesterton's confidence remained unshaken, as did Dickens's. Chesterton accepted the need to punish his offenders lavishly (after all, he said, only three per cent of his charges were punished on any one day!) — certainly he thought this preferable to the yet more unnatural life and the 'fugitive and cloistered virtue' of the Separate System. Temptation was a part of life, and prison discipline should include it. Nor was he abashed when about one third of his prisoners returned to crime; he thought no system a cure-all. 'In the selection of a system of prison discipline, you have only a choice of evils,' he wrote. All he claimed for his system was that it would 'effect as much good as is derivable from any penal process'.[25] Asked by a Parliamentary Committee whether he considered a large proportion of prisoners irreclaimable, he replied, 'Yes, that is the point I wish to impress upon the Committee.'[26] The careers of the 'hopeless class' might conceivably be checked by 'wholesome severity' in prison, though the better hope was to catch them young, and train them to better things. He was, therefore, critical of the 'super-sensitive' reformers whose 'mawkish theories' would 'tend to strip imprisonment of much of its salutary terrors'.[27] While admitting that the tread-mill did not produce 'a state of mind . . . favourable to moral reformation' — words that were often quoted against him — he defended its use for most classes of prisoner, and used it throughout his career.[28] Though it was 'useless labour', it was healthy (if not inflicted to excess) and was suitably unpleasant — though, apparently, not as unpleasant as some of its alternatives, for, he said, many prisoners regarded it as 'calculated to vary the monotony of their confinement', and they 'shed tears of disappointment' when he denied their importunate requests to be given a turn. Not surprisingly, *Punch* reported this statement with irony.[29]

Coldbath Fields was much occupied by unproductive hard labour. There was shot-drill — that is, passing large cannon balls from man to man, putting them on the ground, and taking them up again. As Henry Mayhew remarked, 'It is impossible to imagine anything more *ingeniously useless* than this form of hard labour.'[30] Also there was the crank-machine, a contraption like a mangle or knife-cleaner, the handle of which had to be turned, say, ten thousand times a day in one's cell. Not all the work in Coldbath Fields was of this kind, however. Apart from the notorious oakum-picking rooms, there were workshops for mat-making, cobbling, and other handicrafts, and schoolrooms for the juveniles and illiterates. But Coldbath Fields was generally regarded as a severe prison. Even the labour was 'used as a *punishment*, rather than as a means of industrial training or of self-support among the prisoners themselves'.[31] A young pickpocket described his Metropolitan prison progress, from the unreformed City Bridewell at Blackfriars, in 1840, where he had excellent food, cigars, and easy hours, through his friends' bribing the turnkeys, *via* Tothill Fields, where he found the Silent System strictly enforced, and incurred many punishments, to Coldbath Fields — and, he said, 'if I thought Tothill Fields was bad, I found Coldbath Fields worse.'[32] Caroline Fox, visiting it in 1842, thought it 'on the whole the best of our Houses of Correction, though a severe one, as whipping and the tread-mill are still allowed. It was sad to see the poor exhausted women ever toiling upward without a chance of progress.'[33] Chesterton certainly did not pamper his prisoners. Their work tasks were tough, their punishments frequent and sharp, and their living conditions hardy (to say the least). He explained to a Parliamentary Committee in 1850 that his prisoners were locked up in their cells for twelve hours a day in all seasons; the cells were unlighted — which he agreed was objectionable — but he did not regret that they were unheated, too. There was no heating system in the prison — 'nor do I think it at all necessary,' he said; the opposite danger, of enervating the prisoners through over-heating them, was the greater. As Mayhew commented a few years later, 'Either the cells at Pentonville are wantonly luxurious, or those at Coldbath Fields are disgracefully defective.'[34] It must be acknowledged, however, that Chesterton's prisoners kept healthier than those in most English prisons at the time, and that he had only one suicide during his twenty-five years' service.

This good health record was creditable to Chesterton, and a telling argument for his system, since one of the major issues in the great debate was the allegation that the rival Separate System led to a disturbing incidence of suicide, madness, consumption, and

other physical complaints. These allegations were certainly justified, and the Pentonville regime was therefore continually being
modified, though the authorities were never candid about the extent or the causes of the damage being done to the prisoners. One
of the more ingenious official excuses, to account for the incidence
of morbid symptoms among the Pentonville convicts, was that they
had become over-excited by the 'somewhat sulphurous earnestness
of a too-vehement chaplain'.[35] As we shall see, the status and function of Prison Chaplains were another important issue in the
penological controversy, and one about which Dickens had strong
feelings. At Coldbath Fields, there were no such religious excesses
as in some other prisons of the period. Chesterton admired Elizabeth Fry, but she was not allowed to give her famous Bible-readings
in Coldbath Fields — 'owing to the High Church principles of the
directors and chaplains of the prison.'[36] Chesterton's chaplains
were self-consciously reticent about claiming any conversions
among their flock: as they said in one Annual Report, with a
glance at such rival chaplains as the Reverend John Field (who,
as we shall see, aroused Dickens's wrath and irony), their report
would contain

> ... but little of what too many in the present day may desire and
> look for. . . . The humbling confession, and the earnest promise of
> amendment (even were they more frequently realised in practice, and
> found worthy to be relied on, than their experience teaches them that
> they are,) form, in their judgment, no matter for records such as
> these. Moreover, from the very nature of their labours, their actual
> successes, whether many or few, are not always to be discovered or
> accurately traced. Their labours are registered elsewhere; their
> successes and their failures only another Day shall make known.[37]

It was a notable sign of Dickens's confidence in Coldbath Fields
that, prickly as he was about Prison Chaplains, he allowed one of
the two serving this prison to sit on the management committee of
Urania Cottage.[38]

Hepworth Dixon's survey, *The London Prisons* (1850), contains
much praise for Coldbath Fields and its 'courteous and communi-
cative governor'. Henry Mayhew, writing a dozen years later, was
much more critical of the prison, but admired Chesterton himself:
'This gentleman we have long known in private life, and known
only to esteem for the kindness of his heart and the soundness of
his views as well as for the fine integrity of his principles.' Chesterton was, indeed, an eminent and widely respected figure; even his

penological opponents praised his energy, ability, and character.[39] Dixon had nothing against the Silent System, but was distressed to see that Coldbath Fields still relied so heavily on the tread-mill, 'a mere relic of ignorance and barbarity,' and on such degrading and uninstructive work as oakum-picking. Otherwise, considering the short sentences served there and the disorderly character of its clients, and the inconvenience of the buildings Chesterton had to use, 'the cleanliness, order, and industry prevailing in it are highly meritorious to its governor and officers. In many important respects, it is the best of our metropolitan gaols.'[40]

Chesterton was, clearly, an admirable and a capable man. Upright, conscientious, and determined, he had effected some very necessary reforms, in the face of huge difficulties. An humane and hopeful man, too; he had discovered, he said, 'so many traits of excellence in countless apparently abandoned subjects,' that he entertained, perhaps, 'a superior opinion of human nature to most others. . . . By far the majority [of prisoners] exhibit many redeeming virtues, which compel you to pity their fallen condition.'[41] But sympathy for his charges did not often cause him to mitigate his severity. He defended flogging, as 'beneficial — nay, *indispensable*', as well as the tread-mill and other forms of useless hard labour. 'I know,' he wrote, 'that ethical writers enlarge upon the neglected condition of the criminal masses, and the moral corruption they have imbibed from vicious parents, and abandoned haunts — and they thence infer that pity, and not blame, should light upon them. That is a true proposition; but, like other salutary considerations, it must have a practical limitation.'[42] Chesterton must, indeed, be the prison-governor described in Carlyle's 'Model Prisons', since internal evidence points to Coldbath Fields as the only London prison fitting the description. This is how Carlyle describes him:

> The Captain of the place, a gentleman of ancient Military or Royal-Navy habits, was one of the most perfect governors; professionally and by nature zealous for cleanliness, punctuality, good order of every kind; a humane heart and yet a strong one; soft of speech and manner, yet with an inflexible rigour of command, so far as his limits went: 'iron hand in velvet glove,' as Napoleon defined it. A man of real worth, . . . A true '*aristos*', and commander of men . . . I looked with considerable admiration on this gentleman; and with considerable astonishment, the reverse of admiration, on the work he had here been set upon.

Rightly or wrongly, Carlyle detected in 'this excellent Captain' a continual though unexpressed protest against his Visiting Magistrates' abolition of the tread-wheel, and against other visitors' mawkish pity for 'his interesting scoundrel-subjects'.[43] There is nothing here which contradicts my understanding of Chesterton. His penological ideas, and his reformism, were indeed limited. He was not very imaginative, nor deeply reflective; rather, he was a Carlylean practical leader and driver of men — a good administrator and firm disciplinarian, but not a fundamental reformer. He could see how 'signally inhuman' was the 'refined torture' of the Separate System in its American form, and how unrealistic it was in its milder English form; in separate confinement, he said, the only practical lesson was that of patient endurance.[44] Later penologists would agree with him here, but would regard as almost equally artificial and cruel the Silent System, about which he was so complacent, though it was to his credit that, compared with many of his colleagues in the prison service, he made no sweeping claims for his disciplinary scheme. He was a moderate, common-sensible man, with an often-justified contempt for whole-hog system-ridden theorists, who were certainly more prominent among the Separatist zealots.

Much the same could be said of the other Middlesex prison-governor whom Dickens knew and admired, Lieutenant Tracey of Tothill Fields. It would seem that Tracey was a closer friend, very popular with the Dickens family, while Chesterton was the man whose prison Dickens knew better, and whom he consulted more often on penal matters. Chesterton was a more conspicuous figure in the prison world, but Tracey's policies were little different from his. Both were responsible to Visiting Justices elected from the same collection of eligible magistrates, and Tothill Fields was, if any-thing, a less go-ahead prison than Coldbath Fields. 'There is no part of the mere management of this gaol that is not admirable,' reported Hepworth Dixon in 1850; 'and this at the same time that, in construction and in some parts of the system, it is as faulty as can easily be conceived.' Like Coldbath Fields, it operated the Silent System, but it had none of the large manufactures used there for certain classes of its prisoners. 'No trades are taught — no kind of work. The only labour afforded, is the disgusting oakum-picking, and the still more disgusting tread-wheel. The annals of this prison furnish no examples of criminals instructed in honest handicrafts, and so brought back into the pale of society.' A decade later, Henry Mayhew found that a little tailoring, cobbling, carpentry and gardening had been introduced, but all work was still enforced 'as a matter of punishment rather than as the means of educating the young prisoners in some handicraft, or, indeed, inculcating in them the love of honest exertions. Of industrial training there is not a shadow, nor, to do the authorities justice, the *least pretence*'.[45] Another contemporary, protesting against 'the strong and injurious disposition to convert our gaols into institutions for inducing mere moral reformation, rather than penance', was able to praise the juvenile section of Tothill Fields highly, noting with satisfaction that eleven per cent of the boys were placed in the dark punishment cells during the year.[46] One wonders, indeed, what had been the relations between Tracey and his Deputy-Governor, Lieutenant William Austin, who left Tothill Fields for Birmingham gaol, where his over-lavish use of the punishment cells and of illegal punishments led to a boy's suicide, a Royal Commission, and Austin's serving a six months' sentence for these abuses.[47] Without making Tracey responsible for his former subordinate's misdeeds, one can fairly say that Austin must have been happier at Tothill Fields, where the regime was severe if not inhumane, than in his subordination at Birmingham to the Governor whom he soon ousted, the saintly reformist Captain Maconochie, who relied not on fear but on respect and affection, and whose primary and over-riding aim was the reform, not the crushing, of his prisoners.

Perhaps Dickens did not realise the distance between Maconochie's aims, and those of Tracey and Chesterton. Or perhaps, in the mid-1840s, he hoped to promote a useful compromise or cross-fertilisation. Certainly it was he who introduced and commended Maconochie to these two important prison governors. Dickens had met and admired Maconochie, who had recently returned from seven years in the colonies, bursting with new ideas about prison-discipline. We shall later discuss the extent of Dickens's acquaintance and sympathy with Maconochie. But he had certainly known Chesterton and Tracey longer, and more intimately, and had often praised their methods; it would, indeed, be interesting to know how far his opinions on penology, at this time and later, were influenced by his conversations with them, and by what he had seen at their prisons, and how far he independently came to similar conclusions. Unfortunately, he was never very explicit, nor very conscious, about his intellectual debts and processes, and Chesterton's books are almost silent about his connection with the novelist. It is, however, possible to indicate the coincidence of their views, and outline the course of their friendship and association. Again, I shall confine myself almost entirely to the relationship between Dickens and Chesterton, whom he knew over a longer period and about whom the available record is much fuller.

Dickens had first visited Coldbath Fields, as we saw, in 1835, when he was collecting materials for *Sketches by Boz*, and had been struck, like most visitors, by its severity and its tread-wheel routine. He became a frequent visitor, and a friend of the Governor.[48] In 1842 and 1846 occurred the published eulogies in *American Notes* and the *Daily News*, which have already been quoted, but it is from 1846 onwards that we have the most frequent references to his contact with Chesterton, and admiration for him. For Chesterton was his chief helper and adviser in establishing and running Urania Cottage.[49]

In his first long letter to Miss Coutts about this project, Dickens urged that they should seek the co-operation of Chesterton and Tracey, 'both of whom I know very well,' and subsequent letters contain many references to their activity over the Home.[50] Chesterton took the larger share, and Dickens often praises his energy and benevolence in the good cause. 'He may be implicitly relied upon. His experience is as great as any man's alive, on such subjects, and his humanity and good sense are equal to it. I know nothing of him but what is good.' 'I cannot tell you how much cause I have seen, and see daily, during the preparation of [Urania Cottage], to admire the goodness and devotion of Mr Chesterton, whose time is always at our command, and whose interest in the design cannot be surpassed.'[51] Sometimes he disagreed with Chesterton over details of policy, but much more often they worked in harmony, and several features of the Urania Cottage regime were probably copied from Coldbath Fields. Thus, the girls' past histories were officially kept a secret, even from the Matron and staff; this was the practice in many prisons, including Coldbath Fields, where Chesterton went even further in his attempt to cut his prisoners free from their past, for no names were ever used there, only prison Numbers, and 'Every kind of personality, that can possibly be sunk, is sunk'.[52] Moreover, Coldbath Fields was the main source of recruits during the first years of Urania Cottage, until in 1850 it was given over to adult male offenders, the females and juveniles being all transferred to Tothill Fields. For Coldbath Fields had been the regular place of punishment for London prostitutes, for whom the Home was originally intended.[53] Chesterton wrote an interesting account of his difficulties in finding suitable candidates for the Home — how the numerous young prostitutes in his charge would disdainfully reject his earnest invitation, and how, 'Strange to say, my good offices in that merciful object were impeded by a late magistrate, who perversely insisted . . . that Miss Coutts had no right to confer with prisoners within these walls, nor was it "to be tolerated that Mr Charles Dickens should walk into the prison whenever he pleased".' This magistrate, Benjamin Rotch, objected to Dickens's penology as well as to his presence. He 'attempted with much asperity, to depreciate the writings of Mr Dickens', explaining that his remarks on prisons in *American Notes* had been 'blown to the four winds of heaven, by the works of Mr Adshead!' (the author of a fiercely Separatist book) — a judgment which proved unacceptable to his fellow-magistrates, one of whom countered with heavy irony about the contrast between the obscure Mr Dickens and 'the immortal Adshead' of world-wide reputation.[54]

Rotch's animosity towards Dickens and Chesterton throws some light on Dickens's penological ideas, and it had (as I shall argue later) a curious literary result. For this antagonism was as much a matter of principles as of personalities.[55] As his invocation of Adshead suggests, Rotch was at loggerheads with most of his brother-magistrates, and their prison-governors, over prison-discipline. He enthusiastically admired the Separate System: they still preferred the Silent. He lacked restraint and wisdom in his advocacy, and Chesterton certainly suffered a good deal from him. Chesterton was not the first public man to be bothered by Rotch, who had once challenged the Lord Mayor of London to a duel; as this, and his behaviour at Coldbath Fields, showed, he was foolish and hot-tempered — often, too, gullible and unscrupulous. A zealous teetotaller, he wanted all prisoners to sign the pledge (in circumstances where the pledge was virtually meaningless), and he displayed notable favouritism towards those prisoners and officers who, at least nominally, supported his campaign. At length, writes Chesterton, 'in his converse with these men, he seemed to be absolutely bereft of ordinary penetration.' Making wild promises — which he could not fulfil — to obtain pardons for suitable men who would emigrate to Australia, he insisted on bringing live sheep into the prison, day after day, for demonstrations and practice in the art of shearing. As 'Drinkwater Rotch, the Sheep-shearing Magistrate', he became the object of 'universal ridicule' in the popular press. Chesterton, embarrassed by this sort of publicity about his prison, persuaded the other magistrates to restrain Rotch from activities which, in his view, betrayed 'the warped imagination and puerile designs . . . of an erratic mind' — whereupon Rotch became the bitter enemy of Chesterton and his prison, seizing every opportunity to attack and disparage them.[56]

Granted that Rotch was a difficult and intemperate man, he had nevertheless some good and humane ideas, and it is Dickens's derisive rejection of these which is most significant. Like other advocates of the Separate System, Rotch had more belief than Dickens and Chesterton in the corrigibility of criminals, through exhortation and through training in honest work. He tried to encourage domestic tendencies in the female prisoners by writing 'tracts in humble culinary occupations, and in economic cookery' which were distributed, on their discharge, to prisoners whose conduct has been irreproachable. Similarly, his pamphlet on *Juvenile Depravity* contained sensible proposals for reforming boys before they became confirmed criminals.[57] With much of this, certainly, Dickens would have agreed. But above all, Rotch wanted prison-work to be useful and not simply punitive; as Chairman of the Visiting Magistrates in 1848, he reported with great pleasure that all female prisoners now had industrial work instead of the tread-wheel, and he added his earnest hope that the Magistrates 'may yet see the day when the few remaining Tread-wheels in the male prison may be superseded by . . . Workshops'.[58] But when Rotch died, in 1854, Coldbath Fields had not abandoned its tread-wheels, and when Mayhew surveyed it a few years later it still had, and used, no less than six tread-wheel yards, containing twenty wheels.[59]

Here Dickens was vehemently opposed to Rotch. In 1849, the year when Rotch was ousted from the Visiting Magistrates, the new Chairman, Mr Wilks — a man much more to Dickens's taste — had reported the recent tendency 'to render confinement rather a boon than a punishment — and especially to multitudes of a juvenile and vagrant population, who have begun to prefer the Prison to the Work-house, and the cleanliness and comfort there enjoyed, to their own miserable homes'.[60] There had recently been some relaxation of the more penal aspects of the prison discipline, doubtless through the influence of Rotch and his supporters. Early in 1849, *Punch* had waxed satirical about 'the Chesterton Hotel'. A cartoon showed its inmates enjoying various luxuries (a Turkish bath, deep armchairs, pots of ale, cups of chocolate, pipes of tobacco); a page boy enquires of one, whether he would prefer some oakum-picking or tread-mill exercise, and he replies 'Oh, give my Compliments to the Guv'ner, and say I shan't come out today. I don't feel very well'. A prisoner writes to a friend, regretting that only two months of his six are left: 'We have our baths, and every luxury that could be desired.' The tread-wheel is being discontinued, he says, and trades or 'genteel businesses' are taught gratis. At a stormy meeting of the Magistrates, in March of this year, Wilks and others expressed alarm at the increasing number of prisoners. One magistrate attributed this to the comforts now available at 'the Chesterton Arms' and 'the Tracey Hotel', which should (he said) be barricaded on the outside, not the inside, for intrusions were now a greater danger than escapes. Another, the famous Sir Peter Laurie, attacked chaplains and other soft-hearted officials, and made fun of the activities of Mr Rotch, who there-upon defended himself at some length.[61] A reaction soon set in, to prevent the notion spreading that the Middlesex gaols were a home-from-home. Rotch having been ejected from control, his altera-tions at Coldbath Fields were short-lived. Wilks's Report stated that the Magistrates had recently lowered the diet, and introduced shot-drill as a substitute for other labour that was 'only nominally "*hard*" '. They could report with satisfaction that 'the benefit of the experiment has been already demonstrated'. Despite this strengthening of an already stern discipline, however, Dickens was complaining six months later that 'the Magistrates of Middlesex have almost abolished the tread-mill'.[62]

It is distressing evidence of Dickens's harsh ideas on penal discipline at this period, that he could think even the Middlesex Magistrates too soft. For Wilks was much more typical of Middlesex penology than Rotch, and Middlesex was generally regarded by penal reformers as one of the most retrograde of prison authorities. By 1847–8, writes Clay, 'The day of the Silent System was almost over, and it had now but few advocates.' Maconochie's 'Mark System' was now the real rival to the Separate System.[63] Dickens was attracted to the Marks System, but he thought that it should be combined with the Silent System. The Middlesex Magistrates remained one of the two or three county authorities still using the Silent System in the early 1860s, undaunted by the continuous onslaughts of the Prison Inspectors, whose Report for 1861, for instance, noted 'the reproach under which the metropolitan county had so long lain', for the inadequacy of its prisons, and for which it was 'still conspicuous'.[64] Their attachment to the tread-wheel — universally condemned by progressive opinion — was equally strong. Dickens supported them, except in their momentary diminution of the tread-wheel task; he ended his important article 'Pet Prisoners' (1850), which was mainly concerned to attack the Pentonville regime as being too soft —

> Under the separate system, the prisoners work at trades . . . Is it no part of the legitimate consideration of this important point of work, to discover what kind of work the people always filtering through the gaols of large towns — the pickpocket, the sturdy vagrant, the habitual drunkard, and the begging-letter impostor — like least, and to give them that work to do in preference to any other? It is out of fashion with the steeplechase riders we know; but we would have, for all such characters, a kind of work in gaols, badged and degraded as belonging to gaols only, and never done elsewhere. And we must avow that, in a country circumstanced as England is, with respect to labour and labourers, we have strong doubts of the propriety of bringing the results of prison labour into the overstocked market. On this subject some public remonstrances have recently been made by tradesmen; and we cannot shut our eyes to the fact that they are well founded.

Earlier in that article, he had defended the Silent System; though imperfect, it was much preferable to the Separate System as understood at Pentonville. It was severe, workable, and reasonably cheap. While preserving its prisoners from contamination, it allowed them to remain members of a society, not isolated beings. As for the objection that it involved a large number of punishments for breaches of prison discipline, this came ill (he said) from the supporters of the Separate System, who virtually removed their prisoners from all temptation and yet claimed that they were 'converted' by this so-called discipline.[65]

The distance between Dickens and the more fundamental prison-reformers of his age appeared yet more sharply three years later. One of the *Household Words* staff, Henry Morley, had written a laudatory review of a recent book, *Crime: its Amount, Causes and Remedies*, by Frederic Hill, who had recently retired from the Prison Inspectorate. Hill argued that prisons should aim to cure their inmates; harsh and vindictive treatment or useless hard labour would not do this; only a taste for steady useful work, and the skill to perform it, could fit a criminal for an honest life. Morley accepted these arguments, but Dickens insisted on re-writing his article. '*Impossible of insertion as it stands*,' he wrote to Wills, his assistant-editor. 'A mere puff for Hill, with all the difficult parts of the question blinked, and many statements utterly at variance with what I am known to have written. . . . Do they teach trades in work-houses, and try to fit *their* people (the worst part of them) for Society? Come with me to Tothill Fields Bridewell, or to Shepherd's Bush [Urania Cottage], and I will show you what a work-house girl is. . . . Mr Hill thinks prisons could be made self-supporting. Have you any idea of the difficulty that is found in disposing of Prison-Work? . . . I can never have any kind of prison discipline disquisition in *HW* that does not start from the first great principle I have laid down, and that does not protest against prisons being considered *per se*.' These and other points are made in the article, after Dickens's revisions, and presumably it was he who inserted — he certainly approved of — this deplorable passage, echoing and amplifying the points he had made in 'Pet Prisoners':

> I think it right and necessary that there should be in gaols some degraded kind of hard and irksome work, belonging only to gaols. I don't think Mr Hill's punishment of cleanliness and discipline, and no beer and no tobacco, half enough for the regular hands. I think it a question by no means to be left out of view, What kind of work does the determined thief, or the determined swindler, or the determined vagrant, most abhor? Find me that work; and to it, in preference to any other, I set that man relentlessly. Now I make bold to whisper in Mr Hill's ear, the enquiry whether the work best answering to that description is not almost invariably found to be useless work? And to such useless work, I plainly say, I desire to set that determined thief, swindler, or vagrant, *for his punishment.* I have not the least hesitation in avowing to Mr Hill that it is a satisfaction to me to see that determined thief, swindler, or vagrant, sweating profusely at the treadmill or the crank, and extremely galled to know that he is doing nothing all the time but undergoing *punishment.*[66]

Even Chesterton, severe though he was, had never written as fiercely, or as foolishly, as this.

Several points recur in these statements by Dickens on prison-discipline and in others he made about this time: the comparison between prisons and work-houses, the demand for penal hard labour, and the contention that it is unjust to teach prisoners trades, or to let their products compete with those of honest artisans. How did his opinions on these matters compare with lay and professional opinion at this period?

Dickens often repeated his conviction that prisoners fared better than paupers in work-houses and even than the honest poor in their own homes. We have met it, not only in the letters and articles just quoted, but also in *Great Expectations*; it recurs in *Bleak House* and *Our Mutual Friend* with reference to the poor outcasts Jo and Betty Higden.[67] Dickens was by no means alone in this opinion. *The Times*, in its leading article on the opening of Pentonville, noted with pleasure that the convicts would receive 'a daily supply of *sufficient wholesome food*', and it hoped that this humane principle would soon spread to other prisons — and to work-houses. Years later it made the same point, but with more asperity — 'to maintain Parkhurst and Pentonville on a scale of costly magnificence while honest labourers in Dorsetshire and Hampshire are earning eight shillings a week by hard work for large families, seems . . . wicked and . . . unwise.'[68] The topic provided many jokes good enough for *Punch*, which roguishly announced in 1849 that 'an alteration — severe, certainly, but wholesome' was to be made in prison-discipline. 'Henceforward it is intended to commit all convicts who may violate the gaol regulations to — the work-house.' This waggery appeared often, in verse, prose, and picture: one other example was *The Pauper's Song*, which began —

> A houseless, famish'd, desp'rate man,
>   A ragged wretch am I!
> And how, and when, and where I can,
>   I feed, and lodge, and lie.
> And I must to the Workhouse go,
>   *If* better may not be;
> Ay, *If*, indeed! The Workhouse? No! —
>   The Gaol, — the Gaol for me.

— and this refrain is repeated, as stanza after stanza records the nice clean easy conditions that prisoners enjoy.[69]

There was justice in this contention, as even convicts recognised. A poetical old lag at Portland, several decades later, compared his happy lot with that of the honest pauper —

> ... While they are fed on workhouse fare,
>   And grudged their scanty food,
> Three times a day my meals I get,
>   Sufficient, wholesome, good.
> Then to the British public health,
>   Who all our care relieves;
> And while they treat us as they do,
>   They'll never want for thieves.

A younger delinquent was reported as giving this explanation for his having smashed the windows of the Chelsea Workhouse: 'Because, please, they gives us four pounds of oakum to pick in the house in the day and it scrubs our fingers and we can't do it, and in the prison we only get two pounds and far better vittles.'[70] Less impressionistic were the statistics, such as those published in *The Times* in the early 1840s, showing that the official workhouse dietary for able-bodied men provided less than half the weight of food than was allowed to a convicted felon in the penitentiary, or the evidence given at the inquest on a Pentonville prisoner in 1843. The Prison Steward had formerly been Master of the St Marylebone Workhouse, where, he said, the inmates certainly did not live as well as his present charges — 'The paupers had twelve ounces of bread a day, and meat twice a week, when at work. Here the prisoners have sixteen ounces of bread daily, and meat five times a week.' It was not only popular journalists who protested against this disparity: the Law Amendment Society, too, was demanding in the 1840s a 'speedy remedy' to this abuse, by lowering the prison diet to a mere sufficiency of the coarsest possible food.[71]

The official answer to this criticism was that the rigours and nervous strain of separate confinement made a good diet necessary, if health was to be preserved. Tread-wheel labour, too, must have strained the constitution, but prisons where it was employed were generally tougher in their regulations and were rarely accused of over-feeding their inmates. But food was only one item in this comparison between the prisoner and the honest pauper — the most often mentioned, because it was the most easily measurable. Prison-officials were, indeed, in some difficulty here, for it was unrealistic to demand that all the living conditions of prisons or workhouses — diet, heat, and accommodation — should be kept below the level of the meanest honest man's, at a time when desperate poverty, filth, and deprivation remained so common. The demand came, of course, chiefly from people who believed in deterrence as the sole or main object of prison-discipline, and it is near-kin to the familiar device for blocking any particular proposal for spending public funds (build a National Theatre? — not until we've raised policemen's pay, or the Old Age Pension, or constructed more by-pass roads). Dickens, like most men of any generation, begrudged spending money on prisons and their wicked inhabitants, and there were certainly many other good causes starved of public money in his day. Education was the one Dickens and many of his contemporaries most often mentioned as having a much higher priority than building further palatial, or castellar, prisons. (Again, there was justice in the complaint that during the rebuilding craze of the 1840s some prisons were much more ambitious architecturally than was warranted by their functional needs, or by social justice.) But Dickens was plainly wrong in contending that the inmates of a prison should be 'worse off in every imaginable respect than the bulk of honest paupers and honest labouring men', and that — health and cleanliness ensured — their condition should 'in no particular, present a favourable comparison' with the poorest life outside the walls.[72] As a Commission of Medical Officers reported, in reply to such opinions, it was difficult to determine officially what *was* the ordinary diet of free labourers; and if it was badly chosen or cooked, should the prison authorities reproduce these errors? The quality and amount of prison food should be determined, they said, 'not by the standard of any class of labourers, but by the actual necessities arising out of the prisoners' altered circumstances.'[73] In their excellent discussion of this controversy in prison-discipline, the Webbs sensibly write: 'What was required was to make the conditions of prison as of workhouse life, less pleasurable, *taken as a whole*, than private employment, not necessarily less really advantageous to the inmate, or even less pleasurable in particular respects.'[74] Dickens and others speaking in like vein ignored the obvious fact that the inescapably unpleasant feature of all prisons, however warm and comfortable, is that they deprive the prisoner of his liberty: this is a sufficient punishment, except for the minority who enjoy such an escape from responsibility. The phrase had not yet been invented, but the thought was already current, that a man is 'sent to prison *as* a punishment, not *for* punishment'.

Dickens was, indeed, thoughtless and irresponsible on this matter. Several of his remarks quoted come from the late 1840s and early 1850s, the period which, as was noted in the first chapter, saw a reaction against 'soft' methods of prison-discipline. This reaction was, I said, expressed most fully and ruthlessly in Carlyle's *Latter Day Pamphlet* of 1850, and it was checked by the Birmingham atrocities of 1853, which made most people have second thoughts about their wisdom in having so vociferously demanded 'firm' treatment of criminals. Two judgments on this episode by calmer-minded contemporaries are worth quoting, the first being the *Edinburgh Review* comment on Carlyle's mischievous 'extravaganza'. No-one, it said, could seriously maintain that the State should fail to keep its prisoners clean, healthy, and reasonably fed, whatever the conditions of people outside prison might be; nor, though the State had done little to educate honest labourers, would it be tolerable that criminals should be denied such moral and religious and secular instruction as might prevent their returning to crime and thus to prison.

> Hence when cynical visitors contrast, for purposes of serious condemnation, the warmed and ventilated cell of the criminal in Pentonville, his comfortable hammock, his clean floor, his ingenious water-closet, his substantial and salutary meals, his Bible and his work for the solace of his solitude, and his bell to call the attention of his gaoler, if he need his services, — with the often cold, gloomy, close and dirty room or hut of the workman without the walls . . . , — they are finding fault with arrangements which, in their secret minds, they know perfectly well cannot and ought not to be altered. They are indulging themselves, at the expense of candour, justice, and public duty, in the prerogative of 'Her Majesty's opposition', — that of blaming while in exile the precise course of conduct which they themselves would find it necessary to pursue when in power.[75]

The *Edinburgh* was right, and it was such irresponsibility (for Dickens largely agreed with Carlyle) that increasingly discredited him with the more solid leaders of opinion, even when his heart was much nearer to being in the right place than it was on this particular issue.

The second comment comes from Walter Clay's *The Prison Chaplain*. Clay has a very interesting passage, which I shall quote in a later chapter, on Dickens's place in the penal reaction of 1847–53. It was a reaction not merely against 'soft' discipline but also, as Clay points out, against the idea of making prisons reformative rather than simply deterrent — and it 'led to issues singularly calamitous. These issues may, with some justice, be fathered on the able editors [of *The Times, Punch,* and other journals] and their allies; for though they would have vehemently repudiated the paternity, yet such results were the inevitable alternative of abandoning the principles they had so strenuously denounced'. (Clay is of course referring to the Birmingham scandal, and the very similar one at Leicester about the same time.) 'Able editors, pamphlet writers, and Members of Parliament, joined in one chorus of indignation against the unfortunate justices and gaolers, who had carried to their murderous (but strictly logical) consequences the principles which their critics themselves had preached only three years before.' Dickens, however, may be exonerated on this part of Clay's charge, I think, for I have not noticed his making any remarks at all about the Birmingham or Leicester tragedies. His news-digest, the *Household Narrative,* reported the cases, but neither there nor in *Household Words* did the editor or his contributors criticise the peccant authorities. At both prisons the legitimate 'hard labour' which had been used to excess (others had been used that were entirely illegal) was the crank-machine, which was generally replacing the tread-wheel as the Separate System replaced the Silent System: for the small crank-machine could be set up in every individual cell, whereas the huge tread-wheels involved prisoners leaving their cells. A scandal over the crank-machine was inevitable sooner or later, says Clay, though this device was 'the very thing which the public had been crying for; it satisfied the requirements of *Punch,* the able editors, and the justices. Among the latter the tread-mill was still widely regretted, and the substitute for it was hailed with eagerness'.[76] The Middlesex Magistrates whom Dickens admired had welcomed this new addition to their penal armoury — delighted, they said, with 'the ingenuity and efficacy, of a cheap and moveable machine, admirably calculated to correct the indolent and punish the refractory' and providing 'judicious and salutary means for healthful industry and punitive hard labour'.[77]

The tread-wheel, however, had never disappeared from the Middlesex gaols, and, though somewhat out of favour during the 1850s, it made a general re-appearance after the Carnarvon Committee of 1863 enthusiastically commended it. A note on its history and reputation is relevant here, for it was central to the deterrent conception of prison-discipline. Though legalised as a prison occupation by the 1779 Penitentiary Act, it had not become effective until Cubitt invented a simple form of it about 1818; in the next few years it was hailed as a godsend by many penal reformers on the lookout for a suitable substitute for the death penalty (though Peel thought its duration should be limited to fourteen years).[78] As Mayhew sadly commented:

> . . . to the present century belongs . . . the high philosophic honour of having contrived an apparatus like the tread-wheel, which combines the double moral absurdity of rendering prison labour not only more than usually irksome, but also more than usually profitless. If our forefathers were foolish enough to expect to cure idleness by rendering work a punishment (instead of endeavouring by industrial training to make it a pleasure), it remained for the sages of our own time to seek to impress lazy men with a sense of the beauty and value of industry, by the invention of an instrument which is especially adapted to render labour inordinately repulsive, by making it inordinately useless.[79]

The tread-wheel died, just within the nineteenth century: it was abolished, along with the crank-machine, by the Prisons Act of 1898.

Irksome and laborious it inevitably was, but not always quite useless. At some prisons it was made to grind corn, or raise water, or even provide power for a neighbouring contractor's machinery: not at Coldbath Fields, however, where during Chesterton's period of office it merely 'ground the air', turning a huge outdoor fan, the sole purpose of which was to provide a regulated resistance to the wheels. This suited Dickens, who preferred the useless version, as being the more hated and resented by the prisoner. The *Household Words* article, it will be recalled, expressed satisfaction at the thought of the old lag 'sweating profusely at the tread-mill or the crank, and extremely galled to know that he is doing nothing all the time but undergoing punishment'. The Carnarvon Committee spoke — alas — for Dickens, though a decade later: 'The Committee . . . do not consider that the moral reformation of the offender holds the primary place in the prison system; that mere industrial employment without wages is a sufficient punishment for many crimes; that punishment in itself is morally prejudicial to the criminal and useless to society, or that it is desirable to abolish both the crank and tread-wheel as soon as possible.'[80] As the tones of both *Household Words* and the Committee's Report suggest, it was not only for its allegedly deterrent effect that they admired the tread-wheel, but also from a feeling of retaliation; as the Webbs remark, 'an almost vindictive emphasis' characterises the

Committee's summing-up.[81] These penal devices of useless hard labour had, however, been much criticised by witnesses before the Committee, and by many observers, lay and professional, since their introduction.

The heyday of the tread-wheel had been in the 1820s, when it was 'regarded as the infallible panacea for larcenous propensities. . . . It was heresy . . . to question its reforming efficacy on convicts; the only point on which there existed any difference of opinion was as to the number of diurnal revolutions which yielded a maximum of reforming power'. Even then there had been the heretical objectors: notably James Mill, whose famous 1824 *Encyclopaedia Britannica* article on 'Prisons' protested against the severe modes of prison-government which had 'lately been most in repute' and proposed instead the Benthamite panacea of useful labour as the one salvation of all reformatory discipline.[82] There had been prisons, too, such as Preston, that closed their tread-mills and opened their workshops — a policy which evoked Sydney Smith's much-quoted contributions to the *Edinburgh Review* which, for nasty self-righteous brutality, would have equalled Carlyle's 'Model Prisons' if only Smith had more often commended God for agreeing with him on penological principles. (Carlyle, it hardly needs saying, was another diehard defender of the tread-mill.) Smith's tone may be judged from this sample:

> We would banish all the looms of Preston gaols, and substitute nothing but the tread-wheel, or the capstan, or some species of labour where the prisoner could not see the result of his toil, — where it was as monotonous, irksome, and dull as possible, — pulling and pushing, instead of reading and writing, — no share of the profits — not a single shilling. There should be no tea and sugar, — no assemblage of female felons round the washtub, — nothing but beating hemp, and pulling oakum, and pounding bricks, — no work but what was tedious, unusual, and unfeminine . . . Mrs Fry is an amiable excellent woman, . . . but hers is not the method to stop crimes. In prisons . . . there must be a great deal of solitude; coarse food; a dress of shame; hard, incessant, irksome, eternal labour; a planned and regulated and unrelenting exclusion of happiness and comfort.[83]

Dickens greatly admired both Sydney Smith and Carlyle, dedicating to them a son and a book respectively. His ideas on the ethics of punishment had, then, a long, if not a respectable, history — and a long future too, of course: one hears afar off the voices of

Lord Chief Justice Goddard, the *Daily Express*, and other such Mammons of Righteousness.

But Bentham and Mill and Mrs Fry also had — as they still have — their inheritors. In the more 'reformative' era of penal history, these included many of the 'able editors' and literary commentators; thus one finds Bulwer Lytton criticising the tread-wheel, if only for its inequality of punishment ('a strong man suffers no fatigue, and a weak one loses his health for life'), and *The Times* of 1842 demanding its total abolition, as 'a most objectionable' punishment. The Prison Inspectors rejected it, as did most of the early believers in the Separate System, since they relied much more on reformative than deterrent treatment, and even the defenders of the tread-wheel, such as Chesterton, acknowledged (as we saw) that 'the state of mind produced by the tread-wheel was [unfavourable] to moral reformation'. It was, inevitably, in Silent System prisons that the tread-wheel was most popular, though some supporters of that system deplored this adjunct of it.[84]

The opponents of the tread-wheel wanted a regime based either on moral and religious education, or on industrial training with inducements to work, or on some mixture of both. The Reverend John Field, Chaplain of Reading Gaol, and a representative of the extreme religious wing of the Separate System, remarks on how difficult it was, in the bad old days before his prison was re-organised, for his converts to learn their daily portions of Holy Scripture in the communal wards. Instead, 'they learnt during intervals of rest in the house of the tread-wheel.' Few prison officials even tried to effect this compromise between texts and tread-wheel: in the later reformed Reading, the magistrates noted, 'We have no tread-wheel, or anything approaching hard labour.' The prisoners 'pick a little oakum, and they learn to knit. But the great object with us is such study as may lead to reformation of character'. (It is surprising that Dickens, who wrote a brisk review of Field's fatuous book, missed this nice detail about the knitting.)[85] Reading was not typical, however, of local gaols: more of them approximated towards the Preston model, where a more judicious amount of religious and secular instruction was combined with some trade-training and industrial work. The idea of making prisoners produce saleable goods appealed, of course, to some authorities rather on economic than on therapeutic grounds.

Dickens, as we shall see, was extremely sceptical about the religious approach to prisoners, and he objected also to their doing useful work (at least if they were adult or habitual offenders). His objection was based, partly, of course, on his belief that useless work was nastier, and thus both satisfied society's desire for vengeance and made the infuriated criminal more likely to avoid committing further crimes which might land him back on the tread-wheel. But there were other notions of social justice which made him oppose trade-training and industrial work. 'Do they teach trades in work-houses?' he had asked Wills, when rejecting Morley's article on Frederic Hill. '. . . Whatever chance is given to a man in prison, must be given to a man in a refuge for distress.'[86] The implication here, as always when this type of argument is used, is that the first thing to do is to stop trade-training in prisons, not to start it in work-houses. Moreover, he thought it unfair that goods produced by prisoners should compete in the market with honest men's work. Back in 1842 he had made this point in *American Notes*, and it recurs in various articles and letters (we have already met it in 'Pet Prisoners'). Even in America, he remarked, which was a new and sparsely-populated country, the employment of prisoners in trades where they competed with free labour was becoming less and less acceptable; in Britain, where unemployment existed, the prejudice against this practice was 'naturally very strong, and almost unsurmountable'.[87] This problem is, to be sure, not solved yet; prisons still find it difficult to dispose of such manufactures as prisoners, especially those serving short sentences, can be expected to produce. Dickens, however, is as much impressed by the injustice of the attempt, as by the difficulty. A visitor to American prisons, seeing the prisoners at work on ordinary occupations, was less impressed than he would be had he found them engaged on 'some task, marked and degraded everywhere as belonging only to felons', he said.

> In an American state prison or house of correction, I found it difficult at first to persuade myself that I was really in a gaol: a place of ignominious punishment and endurance. And to this hour I very much question whether the humane boast that it is not like one, has its root in the true wisdom or philosophy of the matter.
>
> I hope I may not be misunderstood on this subject, for it is one in which I take a strong and deep interest. I incline as little to the sickly feeling which makes every canting lie or maudlin speech of a notorious criminal a subject of newspaper report and general sympathy, as I do to those good old customs of the good old times . . .[88]

He inclined little also (he might justly have said, going to the root of the matter) to any real sympathy for the adult criminal. That was why he shows no goodwill towards the idea of industrial work, or of other reformative devices, in prison.

For all his gaiety and high spirits, Dickens was not at bottom very optimistic about human nature. To adopt the reformative policy in prison discipline, obviously one must believe that at least a substantial number of prisoners are reclaimable; Dickens on the whole did not. Again, explaining to Wills his objections to Morley's article, he wrote: 'It is exactly because the great bulk of offences in a great number of places are committed by professed thieves, that it will not do to have Pet Prisoning advocated, without grave remonstrance and great care. That class of prisoner is not to be reformed.' Like his friend Chesterton, he supported the Silent System not because he thought it would work wonders but because it seemed the least objectionable of a number of devices, from none of which could much be hoped. In his novels, it will be remembered, there are few cases where his characters alter in outlook or behaviour. Mr Dombey, Mr Gradgrind, and Pip are the most ambitious exceptions that come to mind; Sydney Carton, indeed, shows unexpected reserves of fortitude, and Richard Carstone is a fairly successful minor study in deterioration. There is also of course the notoriously unconvincing change in Mr Micawber, from charming failure to complete success as a magistrate in Australia. The great majority of his characters, however, major and minor, are as virtuous, or as wicked, at the end of the action as at the beginning; Dickens was not much interested in character-change, because he did not strongly believe that it happened.

The classic discussion of the emotional pattern behind this attachment to 'flat' characters is, of course, Mr Wilson's essay 'Dickens: the two Scrooges', though his discussion arises in a different context from mine and makes a different point about Dickens's own temperament than I am now making (but one which will be relevant later) —

The world of the early Dickens is organised according to a dualism which is based — in its artistic derivation — on the values of melodrama: there are bad people and there are good people, there are comics and there are characters played straight. The only complexity of which Dickens is capable is to make one of the noxious characters become wholesome, one of his clowns turn into a serious person. . . . But the reform of Scrooge in *A Christmas Carol* shows the phenomenon in its purest form. . . . Scrooge represents a principle fundamental to the dynamics of Dickens' world and derived from his own emotional constitution. It was not merely that his passion for the theatre had given him a taste for melodramatic contrasts; it was rather that the lack of balance between the opposite impulses of his own nature had stimulated a taste for melodrama. For emotionally Dickens *was* unstable. Allowing for the English restraint, which masks what the Russian expressiveness indulges and perhaps over-expresses, and for the pretences of English biographers, he seems almost as unstable as Dostoevsky.[89]

Dickens's general incapacity for imagining and tracing the slow development of character is, indeed, apparent in much of his behaviour and outlook. I cannot, for instance, recall his ever acknowledging that he has changed his mind on a public issue (not that he often *did* change his mind). This inexperience, and disbelief, in change of character helped, then, I think, to reinforce his scepticism about reformative penology and thus to make him adhere to the deterrent policy. There were of course other reasons for his tending this way. Deterrence is the penal idea most obvious to thoughtless people, and Dickens was not much given to thinking. The deterrent idea appealed also to the aggressive side of his personality, while his acquaintance with evil, through introspection as well as observation (to recall Humphry House's words), further increased his doubts about the prospects of reforming criminals.

How completely he believed in the irreclaimable depravity of at least some criminals appears in a passage in *Little Dorrit* (1855-7), when a Swiss pastor is discussing the Rigaud murder with the simple Frenchwoman who is the landlady at the Break of Day Inn. The Swiss begs for a charitable attitude towards this sinner:

'. . . It may have been his unfortunate destiny. He may have been the child of circumstances. It is always possible that he had, and has, good in him if one did but know how to find it out. Philosophical philanthropy teaches —'. . .

'Hold there, you and your philanthropy,' cried the smiling landlady. . . . 'Listen then. I am a woman, I. I know nothing of philosophical philanthropy. But I know what I have seen, and what I have looked in the face, in this world here, where I find myself. And I tell you this, my friend, that there are people (men and women both, unfortunately) who have no good in them — none. That there are people whom it is necessary to detest without compromise. That there are people who must be dealt with as enemies of the human race. That there are people who have no human heart, and who must be crushed like savage beasts and cleared out of the way. They are but few, I hope; but I have seen (in this world here where I find myself, and even at the little Break of Day) that there are such people. And I do not doubt that this man — whatever they call him, I forget his name — is one of them.'

The landlady's lively speech was received with greater favor at the Break of Day, than it would have elicited from certain amiable white-washers of the class she so unreasonably objected to, nearer Great Britain.[90]

The ideas and phraseology are very reminiscent of Chesterton's contempt for the 'mawkish theories' of the 'super-sensitive' re-formers, 'displaying a spirit of humanity untempered by discre-tion', who wanted to abolish the tread-mill and the whip, and who argued that criminals should excite one's pity and charity since they so often came from 'vicious parents and abandoned haunts'.

For Dickens was not, I think, referring only to those criminals we have learnt to call psychopathic: he thought that a substantial proportion of at least the habitual criminals displayed gross psychological abnormality. As he comments in *Edwin Drood* (1870), when Rosa Bud is baffled in her attempt to understand John Jasper: 'what could she know of the criminal intellect, which its professed students perpetually misread, because they persist in trying to reconcile it with the average intellect of average men, instead of identifying it as a horrible wonder apart.'[91] He was not prepared to extend an Erewhonian charity towards such mentally-abnormal cases, nor towards criminals whose home and family backgrounds (as he often admitted) made their criminal careers almost inevitable; instead, he thought that the only sensible policy, once their criminal propensities had been formed, was to have them 'crushed like savage beasts and cleared out of the way'. He de-scribes this policy more precisely in a late essay, 'The Ruffian' (1868):

Why is a notorious Thief and Ruffian ever left at large? He never turns his liberty to any account but violence and plunder, he never did a day's work out of gaol, he never will do a day's work out of gaol. As a proved notorious Thief, he is always consignable to prison for three months. When he comes out, he is surely as notorious a Thief as he was when he went in. 'Just Heaven!' cries the Society for the protection of remonstrant Ruffians. 'This is equivalent to a sentence of perpetual imprisonment!' Precisely for that reason it has my advocacy. I demand to have the Ruffian kept out of my way, and out of the way of all decent people. I demand to have the Ruffian employed, perforce, in hewing wood and drawing water somewhere for the general service, instead of hewing at her Majesty's subjects, and drawing their watches out of their pockets. If this be termed an unreasonable demand, then the tax-gatherer's demand on me must be far more unreasonable, and cannot be otherwise than extortionate and unjust.

This essay, as Dr K. J. Fielding has pointed out, has been cited by several recent biographers as evidence of a striking change for the worse in Dickens's final years; but no one who had attentively read Dickens's novels and journalism over the previous thirty years should have been surprised. It was an opinion he had often expressed or implied, and it was repeated in many articles by contributors to his journals.[92] Perhaps it was this acceptance of the principle of perpetual imprisonment that allowed him to ignore, as he seems to have done, the embittered resentment which would inevitably result from his policy of making prisoners sweat on the tread-wheel, and the likely consequences of this embitterment once the prisoners were discharged. There was, of course, some plausibility in his belief that some criminals were incorrigible, and that society should recognise that its only protection against their depradations was perpetual imprisonment. Re-phrased 'preventive detention for recidivists', his proposal sounds quite respectable. Indeed, in his own day, Matthew Davenport Hill and various other reformers were suggesting the principle of the 'indeterminate sentence' — that is, the idea that criminals should not be released from prison until there is some assurance that they will be harmless. What is distasteful about Dickens's handling of the topic, however, is the entire absence of pity or regret in the tones in which he recommends it, and his desire that society should continue wreaking a spiteful lifelong revenge on its enemies ('. . . have the Ruffian employed, perforce, in hewing wood and drawing water . . .', 'crushed like savage beasts').

Dickens's penological attitude was not, however, entirely this blank and hopeless repressiveness. Though, as he told Wills, professed thieves were 'not to be reformed', something could be done: 'We must begin at the beginning and prevent by stringent education and supervision of wicked parents, that class of prisoner from being regularly supplied as if he were a human necessity.'[93] He was much more hopeful about preventing crime, and about reforming the young prisoner, than about any measures adopted for adult prisoners — and in this, of course, he was sensible. Here one naturally recalls his propaganda for more State activity in education, his practical help to Ragged Schools and other such stop-gaps, and his attacks on bad housing and sanitation, and other causes of demoralisation. 'Don't set Gaol, Gaol, Gaol, afore us, everywhere we turn,' appealed Will Fern to the gentlefolk, in *The Chimes*, urging them to take more positive action to prevent crime. Nicholas Nickleby on one occasion reflects at some length on 'how, in seeking, not a luxurious and splendid life, but the bare means of a most wretched and inadequate subsistence, there were women and children in that one town, divided into classes, numbered and estimated as regularly as the noble families and folks of high degree, and reared from infancy to drive most criminal and dreadful trades; how ignorance was punished and never taught; how gaol-doors gaped and gallows loomed, for thousands urged towards them by circumstances darkly curtaining their very cradles' heads. . . .' In 'A December Vision' at the end of the first year of *Household Words*, Dickens hears 'a low dull howl of Ignorance' and sees 'Thirty Thousand children, hunted, flogged, imprisoned, but not taught'; in the New Year, he recalls a recent case of two children 'whose heads scarcely reached the top of the dock' being sentenced to be whipped for stealing a loaf, and he exclaims 'Woe, woe! can the State devise no better sentence for its little children? Will it never sentence them to be taught!'[94] Dozens of other examples could be given, for he was 'continually protesting against the neglect of youth'. One of his colleagues recalled that 'the subject was one which at all times roused him to passionate indignation; at all seasons, at his own table, in private conversation, as well as on public occasions, he denounced the treatment of our unfortunate juveniles as inhuman and unnatural, a monstrous evil calling for immediate reform'.[95]

He did not, however, stop at advocating the prevention of crime through trying to ensure that all children had a decent start in life. For the young offender he felt a charity and optimism notably lacking in his attitude towards adult criminals. The Ragged Schools, which he supported, were partly preventive but also partly reformative institutions. He realised that prison was the worst possible solution for juvenile delinquency. As he made Rose Maylie say, when she pleads for their not giving up young Oliver Twist, who had been caught during the housebreaking operation: 'But even if he has been wicked, think how young he is; think that he may never have known a mother's love, or the comforts of a home; that ill-usage and blows, or the want of bread, may have driven him to herd with men who have forced him to guilt. Aunt, dear aunt, for mercy's sake, think of this, before you let them drag this sick child to a prison, which in any case must be the grave of all his chances of amendment. . . .' Even Bill Sikes is enlisted to make an improbable speech on how to cure the juvenile delinquency problem, as he ponders on his need for a small boy as a house-breaking assistant:

> 'Lord!' said Mr Sikes reflectively, 'if I'd only got that young boy of Ned, the chimbley-sweeper's! He kept him small on purpose, and let him out by the job. But the father gets lagged; and then the Juvenile Delinquent Society comes, and takes the boy away from a trade where he was arning money, teaches him to read and write, and in time makes a 'prentice of him. And so they go on,' said Mr Sikes, his wrath rising with the recollection of his wrongs, 'so they go on; and, if they'd got money enough (which it's a Providence they haven't), we shouldn't have half a dozen boys left in the whole trade, in a year or two.'[96]

Dickens was prepared to give to juveniles, even if they were convicted, that second chance, through re-training, that he was apt to deny to adult prisoners on the grounds of its injustice to the law-abiding poor. Thus he praised the Massachusetts system, whereby a young offender was sent, not to a common gaol, but to a home where he was taught a trade, after which he was apprenticed to a respectable master — so that his conviction, instead of being the prelude to a life of crime, would more likely lead to his becoming a worthy member of society.[97] Such, of course, was his own policy with the girls at Urania Cottage. He was neither sentimental over them, nor savagely resentful against them for their wickedness, as he too often was over adult male offenders. He himself was mainly responsible for selecting the girls, and Urania Cottage had such advantages as a generous staff-inmate ratio. But the projectors of the establishment, he explained in an anonymous article, 'had no romantic visions or extravagant expectations. They were prepared for many failures and disappointments, and to consider their enterprise rewarded, if they in time succeeded with one third or one half of the cases they received.'[98] It is striking that, emotional extremist though he was, he never expected a high rate of success, even when operating his own pet scheme with chosen young women. Here and elsewhere in his outlook on penology, he had at least the virtue of being realistic. It is saddening that, if anything, he underestimated the possibilities of success in reforming the delinquent, and that he so soon and so often reached the limits of his compassion for moral incurables.

Yet Dickens had, and has, the reputation of being a kindly and generous-minded man — as of course he very often was: 'perhaps the largest-hearted man I ever knew,' wrote his friend Thomas Adolphus Trollope. '. . . His benevolence, his active energising desire for good to all God's creatures, and restless anxiety to be in some way active for the achieving of it, were unceasing and busy in his heart ever and always.'[99] Nor, indeed, was the Reverend Sydney Smith a man of cold or mean mind, though his penological remarks display a disgraceful lack of Christian charity. The ease with which such good-hearted men can descend to such vulgar and unintelligent asperity on this subject is a sad reminder that we are all floggers and hangers not far under the skin, and that the slightest scratch, or threat, will suffice to make most of us quickly forget the need for patience, intelligence, and charity in dealing with criminals and other deviants from our norm. One hardly needs to explain Dickens's, or anyone else's, fierce demand for retributive punishment; this is the instinctive reaction of the stupid Old Adam, or original Lord Beaverbrook, in us all. It is the rarer occasions when Dickens, and others, have wiser second thoughts that call for explanation. Of course, there are people whose charity towards the evil-doer is excessive and indiscriminate — the 'amiable whitewashers' whom Dickens scorned. It is ironical, however, to note that Dickens himself was classed among them, by some of his contemporaries.

The point may be illustrated by a letter from Charles Kingsley to Sir Henry Taylor, praising his pamphlet *On Crime and its Punishment* (1868). He comments —

> As against any just and rational treatment of crime, two influences are at work now. 1. The effeminacy of the middle class, which never having in its life felt bodily pain (unless it has the tooth-ache) looks on such pain as the worst of all evils. . . . 2. The tendency of their speculations is more and more to the theory that man is not a responsible person, but a result of all the circumstances of his existence . . . a confusion which issues in this: The man is not responsible for his faults. They are to be imputed to circumstance. But he is responsible for, and therefore to be valued solely by, his virtues. They are to

be imputed to himself. An ethical theorem, which you may find largely illustrated in Dickens's books, at least as regards the lower and middle classes.

Kingsley's master, Carlyle, who was also admired by Dickens and friendly with him, makes a similar complaint —

> Dickens, he said, was a good little fellow, and one of the most cheery innocent natures he had ever encountered. But . . . his theory of life was entirely wrong. He thought men ought to be buttered up, and the world made soft and accommodating for them, and all sorts of fellows have turkey for their Christmas dinner. Commanding and controlling and punishing them he would give up without any misgivings in order to coax and soothe and delude them into doing right.[100]

Neither Kingsley nor Carlyle was a very subtle and patient observer of other men, to be sure; certainly, their ideas on 'commanding and controlling and punishing' men were severe, if not Draconic; still, they were not complete fools, nor are the later historians, who, as I have mentioned, have classed Dickens among the lay angels of nineteenth-century penology. If my interpretation and judgment of Dickens are correct (which imply that he should have satisfied Carlyle and Kingsley more, and the historians of penology less), I should nevertheless attempt to explain why their misapprehensions — as I regard them — arose. Of course, I have studied this aspect of his work more closely than they did, or could be expected to do, but the interesting question remains, why should their more superficial reading have been so misleading?

The answer, I think, lies partly in the fact that his reputation has often blinded his readers to the implications of what he actually wrote. He was 'the apostle of the people', 'the friend of the poor', 'the poet and prophet of Christmas', and so forth — and passages that did not correspond to these simple labels went unnoticed or were soon forgotten. Dickens, it should be remembered, too, became famous very young, with his first novel, and the reputation established by his earlier works dominated — as it still largely dominates — the popular notion of him. As recent critics have insisted, it is the earlier novels that most fully correspond to this inadequate image of Dickens, as simply a warm, jolly, tender-hearted, Christmassy figure — the Dickens of *Pickwick Papers*, *Nicholas Nickleby*, *The Old Curiosity Shop*, and *A Christmas Carol* — good stories, no doubt, but not the whole of Dickens, and arguably not the best. The later novels have more edge, and less fun. As his remarks on Coldbath Fields in the 1840s showed, he was not soft or sentimental about criminals even then, but it is in the second half of his career that he becomes both fiercer in his views and more explicit in expressing them. By then, however, the Christmassy-sentimental image of Dickens had been long established, and it was not substantially modified by the evidence of his later works.

Moreover, many of the quotations I have used to illustrate the harsher side of his attitude to criminals came not from the novels, but from his journalism (and from private correspondence which was not available to his contemporaries). The passages from *Little Dorrit* and *Great Expectations*, indeed, expressed clearly enough a reaction against penological reformism; but they seem to have been little noticed. The *David Copperfield* satire on Model Prisons, a few years earlier, was very funny, and many readers, perhaps, were too amused to see its full implications, which were certainly clearer in the articles appearing about the same time in *Household Words*. There are other passages in the novels which express or imply the same 'tough' view of prison-discipline, but in general this aspect of Dickens appears more fully in his anonymous journalism — which was inevitably more ephemeral, less impressive, and therefore more readily forgotten. (The *Miscellaneous Papers* volume containing 'Pet Prisoners' and other such pieces was compiled by B. W. Matz in 1908, and has not appeared in most sets of 'The Complete Works' since then; it is not very easy to come by, so its contents are unfamiliar except to Dickens specialists.) It is not only, of course, his penology that is more precise in his non-fictional writings: his other social ideas — some of them more thoroughly praiseworthy than his views on criminals — also tend to be vaguer in the novels, more positive in the journalism. This is what one would expect, both from the nature of fiction, and from Dickens's being so eminently a satirical artist. I treasure an exchange in Humphry House's *The Dickens World*. House quotes G. M. Young's epigram that Dickens was 'equally ready to denounce on the grounds of humanity all who left things alone, and on the grounds of liberty all who tried to make them better', and he comments — 'This is on the whole true of the novels, less true of the short stories, and hardly true at all of the occasional journalism and speeches.'[101] We shall see, in the next chapter, another instance, different in kind, of the disparity between the novels and the other areas of his writing and activities, which will confirm the justice of House's remark, and of this remark by one of House's inheritors, Dr K. J. Fielding. Introducing his recent edition of Dickens's *Speeches*, Dr Fielding pointed out that they 'give us what he was prepared to stand up and say in public, which was not always the same as what he expressed as his opinions to his correspondents, or what he published in the guise of fiction'. The difference is not mainly, nor significantly, due to any conscious suppression of facts or opinions which the reading public might find improper or unpalatable. As Dr Fielding says later, 'although he was deeply concerned about contemporary affairs in both his public life and his fiction, they never quite correspond. . . . Much of Dickens's public life and private philanthropy does not seem to be directly related to his imaginative writing.'[102] There were, simply, parts of his knowledge and experience which, for one reason or another, he could not easily use in his fiction.

Sometimes, the novels do discredit to his reputation as a reformer (resulting in such adverse judgments as G. M. Young's), but sometimes, where his ideas were not really humanitarian at all, the novels do more than justice to him, by largely concealing the fact. The aspects of penology we have so far examined are a case in point, for, the more precisely his views were expressed, the less could they sustain a reputation for humanity. One should, however, add a further reason why Kingsley and Carlyle, and others, basing their judgment mainly or wholly on the novels, remained unaware of Dickens's tougher side. There is, no doubt, exaggeration in the adage that 'Tout comprendre, c'est tout pardonner' but, insofar as an author understands, and makes his readers understand, a fictional character, this tends to make the character more sympathetic, and his faults more forgivable. A good example is the handling of the old lag Magwitch in *Great Expectations*: Dickens is interested in him, and wants us to share — indeed, to anticipate — Pip's later affection for him, after the terror and revulsion he had excited earlier; so Pip is made to ask him his life story.

'What were you brought up to be?'
'A warmint, dear boy.'
He answered quite seriously, and used the word as if it denoted some profession.

A little later, Magwich expands on the theme:

'In gaol and out of gaol, in gaol and out of gaol. There, you've got it.

That's *my* life pretty much, down to such times as I got shipped off . . . I first become aware of myself, down in Essex, a-thieving turnips for my living. Summun had run away from me — a man — a tinker — and he'd took the fire with him, and left me wery cold. . . .

'This is the way it was, that when I was a ragged little creetur as much to be pitied as ever I see . . . , I got the name of being hardened. "This is a terrible hardened one," they says to prison wisitors, picking out me. "May be said to live in gaols, this boy." Then they looked at me, and I looked at them, and they measured my head, some on 'em — they had better a-measured my stomach — and others on 'em give me tracts what I couldn't unnerstand. They always went on agen me about the Devil. But what the devil was I to do? I must put something into my stomach, mustn't I? . . .'[103]

Similarly, Nancy in *Oliver Twist* has 'never known a better life'; the alley and the gutter have been her cradle, and are likely to be her death bed too; her life has been spent 'in the midst of cold and hunger, and riot and drunkenness'.[104] Here one sees the type of explanation by exonerating circumstances which annoyed Kingsley. But Dickens has no consistent or thought-out view on these issues of free-will and determinism and moral responsibility; he alters the focus, according to the exigencies of his novel and his own prejudices. He is partial in his distribution of such pleas for sympathy. Doubtless Fagin and Bill Sikes could have told similar hard-luck stories; Compeyson, in *Great Expectations*, was admittedly a gentleman born, but he could have been endowed with an unfortunate childhood, had Dickens wanted to make us understand and forgive his delinquencies. And when Dickens leaves fiction for real life, and discourses about real convicts, he usually forgets such explanations, or regards them as irrelevant to the problem of what to do here and now. Again, he speaks for Everyman, who is prepared to allow greater weight to mitigating arguments of this type when the subject is imaginary or decently far away.

Dickens's charity could be aroused, then, when he came into close imaginative contact with some of the criminals he had invented, or indeed when he came face to face with actual convicts. Like many people inclined thoughtlessly to huff and puff against villainous criminals, he generally showed more understanding and tolerance when he met them as individuals. Late in his life, when he would breathe fire and slaughter whenever he wrote on the subject in *All the Year Round*, he happened to visit Stirling Gaol, while he was on one of the Reading Tours. 'Here and there,' recorded his companion, 'Mr Dickens said kind and comforting words to the prisoners, which seemed to be a relief to them in their miserable position.'[105] Years before that, he had shown remarkable tact, patience, and good heart in his almost daily dealings with the inmates of Urania Cottage — though not without a requisite degree of 'commanding and controlling and punishing' them (which might have surprised and cheered Carlyle). To this fascinating episode in his life I must now turn: and with pleasure, for here Dickens, in my opinion, shows up very well.

IV

THE HOME FOR HOMELESS WOMEN

WHEN Dr William Acton, the acknowledged authority of his age on prostitution, addressed the London Dialectical Society in 1868, he welcomed 'the change of tone that had occurred since he first began to write on this subject'. Now, he said, it was discussed with ladies present, but twenty years before almost everyone shied off it; even Lord Shaftesbury, when approached on the matter, 'had said that he knew little of it, and wished to know less.'[1] The 'forties and 'fifties had seen a growing concern over 'the Great Social Evil', a greater willingness to discuss and attack it, and a corresponding decrease in tolerance for the men who, as customers, promoted it.[2] This period saw also the establishment of many institutions and societies for reclaiming 'penitent females', and a surprising number of unlikely individuals made a hobby of addressing homilies to prostitutes on their beat, or of succouring them until they could be found an honest livelihood. Gladstone's well-known activities in this field had been earnestly cogitated while he was still at Oxford in the 'thirties — a pleasant undergraduate tradition which we find surviving fifty years later, when G. Lowes Dickinson at Cambridge was asking freshmen for subscriptions for the same benevolent purpose — while in the 'fifties (to name one other instance) the young Pre-Raphaelite Brotherhood, scouring the streets for models, took in their stride the Rescue of the Fallen.[3]

The Pre-Raphaelites produced, moreover, some notable paintings and poems on this theme, which had become a favourite one in the literature of the period, from the popular melodrama and street-ballad ('She was poor but she was honest') to the work of the most earnest and sophisticated of writers. Hood's 'Bridge of Sighs' and Mrs Gaskell's *Mary Barton*, in the 'forties, provide familiar examples of this concern for the Fallen Woman, which recurs in many novels of the period; Mrs Gaskell returned to the theme several times, and it was taken up by Kingsley, George Eliot, Wilkie Collins, Trollope and others, down to Hardy's defiant presentation of 'A Pure Woman' in the 1890s.[4] All these invited

94

the reader to regard with more understanding and forgiveness 'these tarnished and battered images of God'. Some of them indicated how the unfortunate girls might be restored to a decent place in society, usually through private rather than institutional benevolence (for Dickens was not alone in exhibiting some animus towards do-gooders, whether professional or amateur: Wilkie Collins, for instance, is sarcastic about Godfrey Ablewhite's preoccupation with various Ladies' Charities, including 'Magdalen societies for rescuing poor women').[5] The stereotype situation in fiction, verse, and melodrama is the country girl seduced by the local squire's son, then fleeing in shame to London, where she attempts to drown herself, sometimes in the Serpentine but usually in the Thames: 'Standing on the bridge at midnight . . .', 'In she plunged boldly, No matter how coldly The rough river ran. . . .'

The recurrence of these clichés should not prevent our recognising that they rested on some, though not all, of the notorious facts of the contemporary situation. Acton maintains that anyone acquainted with rural life knows that 'seduction of girls is a sport and a habit with vast numbers of men, married . . . and single, placed above the ranks of labour . . . , the farmer's son, farmer, first, second or third class, squire or squireen'; and Hood's 'Bridge of Sighs', however much over-written, was based on an actual case, which had evoked comment from Dickens and *The Times* among others (though for artistic reasons Hood had shifted the scene from the Regent's Canal to the Waterloo Bridge, a notorious favourite for suicides).[6] On the other hand, Acton and Mayhew and other investigators protested against some of these clichés, which were so misleading as to impede the efforts of workers practically involved with the problem: seduction, they argued, was only a minor cause of prostitution (low wages, and psychological instability, were more frequent causes), and fallen women, whether or not they became prostitutes, did not usually die a watery or a pauper's death, but lived out the normal span, generally re-entering more or less respectable society. These, said Acton, were the assumptions on which profitable social work must be based; and he stressed the point by using as his epigraph a sentence by Laman Blanchard: 'Had the poets to fable a new mythology, the Eros of the London streets would be not the offspring of Venus, but the child of SORROW and STARVATION.'[7]

Dickens of course was not behind his contemporaries in feeling an earnest concern over the Great Social Evil, or in showing this concern in his activities as well as his writings. There are several instances recorded of his unobtrusive charity towards such girls: his kindness towards the young infanticide whose case he attended as a juror, for example, or his giving sixty dollars to a New York chambermaid so that she could escape to California with her illegitimate child.[8] The concern appears early in his fiction. 'The girl is a prostitute,' he says of Nancy in the 1841 Preface to *Oliver Twist*, though (he adds) 'I endeavoured, while I painted [the truth] in all its fallen and degraded aspects, to banish from the lips of the lowest character I introduced, any expression that could by possibility offend. . . . In the case of the girl, in particular, I kept this intention constantly in view.' As several critics have remarked, Dickens concealed the truth all too well; Nancy's profession is suggested very obliquely, and her actions and sentiments, as well as her vocabulary, are improbably discreet; even the bluntly identifying phrase ('the girl is a prostitute') is cut from later editions of the Preface.[9] Dickens was proud of his achievement, however. 'I hope to do great things with Nancy,' he had told Forster, and later he defended his conception of her character (particularly her loyalty to the brutal Sikes) by referring to his years of observation of such girls and their environment: 'It is useless to discuss whether the conduct and character of the girl seems natural or unnatural, probable or improbable, right or wrong. IT IS TRUE.' On this point, of the loyalty of prostitutes to their ponces, recent research has confirmed his observation.[10] Nevertheless, many aspects of Nancy's conduct are implausible and cliché-ridden. She was of course stoically resigned to a watery death ('Look at that dark water. . . . I shall come to that at last'), though in fact she dies, less plausibly, holding up towards Heaven 'a white handkerchief — Rose Maylie's own'. Little is said about the cause or cure of her condition, beyond the usual plea for Christian forgiveness (' "Oh, lady! lady!" she said, clasping her hands passionately before her face, "if there was more like you, there would be fewer like me, there would — there would!" ')[11]

Nancy's premature and violent death at least saved Dickens from having to imagine a future life for her, in due consonance with the novel's happy ending and her state of repentance. Alice Marwood, ten years later, in *Dombey and Son*, is similarly obliging; she dies repentant, hearing the blessed story of Christ's ministry to 'the criminal, the woman stained with shame, the shunned of all our dainty clay'. Dickens is able to evade the problem again in his briefer references during the 1840s to the poorer outcast women of society (Edith Dombey, being better placed, had of course been able to retreat to Italy at Cousin Feenix's expense). The vision of Lilian Fern, oppressed by poverty and giving way to 'the dreadful thoughts that tempt me in my youth', thus 'falling very low' and dying with a broken heart, is (happily) averted; and The Haunted Man's encounter with 'the ruined Temple of God, so lately made, so soon disfigured' is as transitory as it is melodramatic.[12] It is in *David Copperfield* (1849–50) that he returns to a fuller treatment of the problem, Martha Endell and Little Emily both being alive — stained but repentant — at the end of the action. The treatment of Martha is in the most rhetorical tradition of melodrama.

> 'Oh, the river!' she cried passionately. 'Oh, the river! . . . . . . I know it's like me! . . . . . . I know that I belong to it. I know it's the natural company of such as I am! It comes from country places, where there was once no harm in it — and it creeps through the dismal streets, defiled and miserable — and it goes away, like my life, to a great sea, that is always troubled — and I feel that I must go with it!'
>
> . . . 'She is in a state of frenzy,' I whispered to [Mr Peggotty]. 'She will speak differently in a little time.'

Which she does; having been restrained from suicide and persuaded to search for Emily, she strikes an equally implausible note of nobility (her freedom from a Norfolk accent still remaining notable): 'It has been put into your hearts, perhaps, to save a wretched creature for repentance. I am afraid to think so; it seems too bold.' On proper occasion, however, she can revive her grand metaphorical style, as when she discovers and awakens Emily ('Rise up from worse than death, and come with me!') and defies the cravens who try to stop the rescue: 'Stand away from me, I am a ghost that calls her from beside her open grave!'[13] This shows no advance in realism or insight over Nancy or the other previous 'ruined Temples of God'. It was however Emily that represented Dickens's main effort and source of pride, in this aspect of the book. 'I feel a great hope,' he told Forster, 'that I shall be remembered by little Em'ly, a good many years to come.' And in a letter to another friend he referred to the cruel difficulties in the way of such girls' returning to virtue, and undertook in this novel to put this matter 'in a new and pathetic way, and perhaps to do some good'. He had, he said, been turning it over in his mind for some time.[14]

He had indeed been thinking over the problem, and not only

as a novelist, for several years. Since May 1846 he had been planning, and since November 1847 virtually running, Miss Coutts's 'Home for Homeless Women'. This is the title he gave it, in a long anonymous article about it in *Household Words* in 1853, but it had in fact been established specifically for Fallen Women. The letters to Miss Coutts are remarkably reticent about this fact; nearly four years after they had begun discussing the project, there is curious evidence of this, in a letter to her in which he refers, as in the letters quoted above, to his hopes that the Emily episode might 'bring people gently' to a consideration of the plight of fallen women. 'I shall be very glad indeed to talk with you,' he continues, 'on the sad subject to which you have — with a moral bravery which you must forgive my saying I cannot enough respect — directed your thoughts.' One wonders through just what delicate periphrases and ellipses their conversations about the Home had hitherto been conducted, for the leaflet which he wrote, to be handed to prospective candidates, was entitled *An Appeal to Fallen Women*, and described how their anonymous benefactress had been moved to compassion by seeing from the window of her house (in Piccadilly) 'such as you going past at night'.[15]

In the event, the Home did not restrict itself to prostitutes; there seems to have been a change of policy, unnoticed or unrecorded. Probably the reason was that there were not enough suitable ex-prostitutes applying for admittance. Chesterton, from whose prison most of the inmates were drawn in the earlier years, writes thus of his difficulties in recruiting girls of this kind:

> I derived some new light into that blind infatuation which impeded the corrigibility of the 'unfortunate' class. Although I had daily access to, at the lowest computation, 150 of those frail and suffering creatures within the prison walls, ... I soon found the impracticability of winning many over to accept so great a boon. Objections would be raised, conditions critically sifted, and disdainful rejections of the offer would ensue too frequently to prove encouraging to my mission. Some would appear gratefully to assent, but as their enlargement approached, a change of mind would arise, and some plausible pretext be advanced to give colour to the ultimate refusal. I even applied to a very intelligent inspector of police — whose duty led him into a neighbourhood suitable to the proposition — and he readily consented to extend his assistance. At length, however, he was compelled to proclaim the utter failure of his efforts, since he found all to shrink from the irksomeness of quiet domesticity, and the prospect of ex-

patriation. However, I succeeded in making a, perhaps, second-class selection, approved, after a personal examination into their frame of mind and general fitness by Mr Dickens, aided by the matron and myself. . . .

In the *Household Words* article, written when the Home had been open for five years, Dickens described its clientèle as having included

> starving needlewomen of good character, poor needlewomen who have robbed their furnished lodgings, violent girls committed to prison for disturbances in ill-conducted workhouses, poor girls from Ragged Schools, destitute girls who have applied at Police offices for relief, young women from the streets: young women of the same class taken from the prisons after undergoing punishment there as disorderly characters, or for shoplifting, or for thefts from the person: domestic servants who have been seduced, and two young women held to bail for attempting suicide. No class has been favoured more than another; and misfortune and distress are a sufficient introduction. It is not usual to receive women of more than five or six-and-twenty; the average age in the fifty-six cases would probably be about twenty. . . . Nearly all have been extremely ignorant.[16]

Many of them came straight from prisons or Police-courts, having been interviewed there by Dickens; others were passed on from other institutions, such as the Elizabeth Fry Refuge or the Magdalen; or by social workers, such as Sidney Herbert and Matthew Hill; or by officials such as Grey, the Home Secretary, or Jebb, the Inspector-General of Prisons. Dickens found some girls, too, by visiting Ragged Schools, or by speaking to them in the streets 'in the course of my nightly wanderings into strange places'.

Miss Coutts paid the bills, and it would seem that it was she who had originally decided on the project, but the planning and execution were almost wholly Dickens's. She often visited the Home on Saturdays, and sometimes attended its monthly Committee meetings; Dickens insisted on her seeing the Lady Superintendent, before he appointed her; but it was typical of their respective roles that he insisted she should not see the house at Shepherd's Bush, which he had leased and renamed Urania Cottage, until it was quite ready, and that he had to urge her several times to attend his interviews with candidates in prisons, where she could be a silent and unnoticed observer. Chesterton says that she only once visited Coldbath Fields, though Dickens (it will be recalled) was in and out of the prison so often that Mr Rotch the magistrate protested. On some points Dickens disagreed with Miss Coutts, but generally his views (which were more sensible) prevailed. Thus, she was very suspicious of brightness of dress, which she felt was the cause of much female delinquency; and he had to reiterate, again very much against her opinion, his contentions that girls should be offered the bait of eventual marriage as a reward for their repentance and re-education, and that in the later stages of their training they should not be protected against all temptations. The only major item over which he had to give way was her dismissal of a Deputy Superintendent who was discovered to be a Dissenter. This episode was, he told Miss Coutts, 'extremely painful to me, as it involves a point, on which, though I have no sympathy whatever with her private opinions, I have a very strong feeling indeed — which is not yours.'[17]

Miss Coutts devolved the responsibility for the administration on a committee 'composed of a few gentlemen of experience'; its effective members were Dickens, and the two prison-governors whom he had recommended, Chesterton and Tracey. The other members, who seem to have attended rarely, included the senior Chaplain from Coldbath Fields, two other clergymen, Miss Coutts's friend Dr William Brown, and the educationist Kay-Shuttleworth.[18] As we have seen, Dickens was enthusiastic in his gratitude to Chesterton in particular, whose experience and contacts proved invaluable in establishing the Home and finding suitable applicants,[19] but the guiding spirit behind the enterprise was, undoubtedly, Dickens himself. This is the only charitable activity and institution to which he gave his consistent attention over a prolonged period (some ten or twelve years), and as most of the ideas and their execution were of his devising, it is instructive to watch him at work on a long-term project of remedial education.

His first mention of it occurs in a letter, some two thousand words in length, to Miss Coutts, in which he outlines almost all the principles and policies which were in fact adopted. He concluded: 'I do not know whether you would be disposed to entrust me with any share in the supervision and direction of the Institution. But I need not say that I should enter on such a task with my whole heart and soul' — and, knowledgeable as ever, he offered meanwhile to examine every Institution of this kind in Paris, where he was then going, since 'I believe more valuable knowledge is to be got there, on such a subject, than anywhere else'.[20]

'A first-rate practical intellect': such, a friend had said, was the impression he made when one met him; and Urania Cottage offered a splendid field for its exercise. His earlier letters on the scheme show him devising its purpose (to prepare girls for emigration, and to arrange their voyage to and reception in the colony selected), the curriculum appropriate to this end, the spirit in which it should be operated, the means for recruiting suitable girls, and so on.[21] His absence abroad delayed for some time the purchase and opening of the Home, but he was able meanwhile to study similar institutions in Paris and London. 'Very little has yet been done in this respect,' he informed Miss Coutts; 'and if you could do no better than has been done already I really doubt the expediency of founding an entirely new establishment in preference to assisting in the endowment of an existing one.' He became confident that they could improve on existing methods (his criticisms of which will be noted later), and that they should achieve about fifty per cent success from the very beginning. As the project got under way, his energetic efficiency became obvious; his letters show him (sometimes with the help of one of the prison-governors) finding a suitable house in Shepherd's Bush, arranging for its renting and Income Tax payments, ordering furniture and books for it, writing the *Appeal to Fallen Women*, interviewing staff and possible inmates, laying in 'all the dresses and linen of every sort for the whole house', selecting and hanging up suitable texts in the living room, marking in the Prayer Book some passages for the twice-daily services, deciding on the hours of bedtime and such other matters of daily routine as 'the arrangements for washing and dressing, and putting away of clothes', organising music-lessons in simple choral singing, numbering and docketing and paying all the bills, and keeping in his own handwriting a case-book with full particulars of every girl. As he wrote to Miss Coutts (towards the end of another letter of nearly three thousand words) a few days before the Home eventually opened, in November 1847: 'I hope there is nothing whatever, in the business arrangement, which is not in working order. . . . I believe that nothing has been done without a reason.' During the years of his association with Urania Cottage from 1846 to 1858, he was also active in other charitable affairs, the size of his family rose from six to nine, he established and conducted *Household Words*, and he wrote five full-length novels as well as sundry articles and short-stories. As Humphry House says, 'This grind of charitable business would be astounding in any man: it is scarcely credible in the greatest English creative genius of his time.' No wonder that, as he confessed to Forster on one occasion, 'What with *Bleak House* and *Household Words* and *Child's History* and Miss Coutts's Home, and the invitations to feasts and festivals, I really feel as if my head would split like a fired shell if I remained here' — so he escaped to Boulogne for a rest.[22]

The Home held thirteen girls, and there were two Superintendents, usually one middle-aged and one younger lady. The staff were often a trial to him. 'Our friend Mrs Greaves is rather of a delicate gentility, I fear; and her aspect is sombre,' he discovered; moreover, her colleague Mrs Holdsworth was objecting to the instruction that she should 'get up on every alternate washing-day. . . . She . . . informed me, with a face of most portentous woe and intensity, that "she couldn't do it" '. Dickens's patience was strained: 'It is intolerable to be met with such mincing nonsense from those toiling and all-enduring dowagers.' Soon Mrs Greaves departed, to be replaced by Miss Cunliffe, who turned out to be 'a woman of an atrocious temper'. Her idea of hectoring and driving the girls was, he wrote, 'the most ignorant and the most fatal that could be possibly entertained;' she left soon after, and there was more turnover of staff to come.[23] But the girls were a more constant source of anxiety, if only because there were more of them, and because the Home possessed the disadvantages, as well as the advantages, of a voluntary institution. Its inmates could be selected, but only moral pressure could be exerted on them once they were in the Home. Dickens did not make his task too easy; he stuck out against Chesterton for accepting drunkards. 'As to there being no hope for drunkards,' he insisted, 'we mustn't start from that point. If we can't find hope ready-made (but I believe we can) we must try to make it. . . . The Saviour laid down no rules that kept the wretched at a distance from Him; and a noble effort like this should be, in that respect I think, as accessible and free.'[24] In the event, however, seemingly impossible cases were rejected, and girls who proved recalcitrant were expelled; Dickens learned the value of a decidedly firm policy in this matter, though he sometimes tried to transfer these girls who were too tough for Urania Cottage to some other institution 'where they take all sorts and conditions of impracticable girls in, if they will work'. Of course, all candidates were interviewed (usually by Dickens alone) before acceptance; he described the technique thus:

It has been observed, in taking the histories — especially of the more artful cases — that nothing is so likely to elicit the truth as a perfectly imperturbable face, and an avoidance of any leading question or expression of opinion. Give the narrator the least idea what tone will make her an object of interest, and she will take it directly. Give her none, and she will be driven on the truth, and in most cases will tell it. For similar reasons it is found desirable always to repress stock religious professions and religious phrases; to discourage shows of sentiment, and to make their lives practical and active. 'Don't talk about it — do it!' is the motto of the place.[25]

Dickens's perennial suspicion of mealy-mouthed 'model prisoners' was confirmed (to his manifest satisfaction) by several cases at the Home: the girl, for instance, who 'impressed me as being something too grateful, and too voluble in her earnestness', but who rapidly disappeared: or the case of 'that very bad and false subject, Jemima Hiscock'.

Jemima was the perpetrator of one of the disturbances at Urania Cottage, Dickens's spirited descriptions of which give to his correspondence with Miss Coutts an interest missing in the case-histories recorded by most social workers. For instance, one night when the Superintendents were out, Jemima

forced open the door of the little beer cellar with knives, and drank until she was dead drunk; when she used the most horrible language and made a very repulsive exhibition of herself. She induced *Mary Joynes*(!) to drink the beer with her; and that young lady was also drunk, but stupidly and drowsily . . . I have no doubt myself, that they had spirits from outside. I am perfectly sure that no woman of that Jemina Hiscock's habits could get so madly intoxicated with that weak beer. . . . This same woman made the most pious pretences of any in the place, and wrote the most hypocritical letters.[26]

Or there was the unsolved mystery, whether or not Julia Morley was carrying on with that young man seen hanging around the garden (the gardener was set to watch, for if she proved to be guilty of this association, 'that would be sufficient reason for immediately dismissing her') — or the similar case, about which there was no such lucky uncertainty, of Sarah Hyam, who was discovered in the parlour at four o'clock in the morning with the local policeman. A few other examples: there was the Irish girl, 'shewing a very national incapability of getting on with anybody on any subject — accompanied with expressions of a violent desire to "do for" the establishment in general;' or this dialogue with

Little Willis from the Ragged School, whose good-conduct marks had been stopped —

> I wish you could have seen her come in diplomatically to make terms with the establishment, 'O! Without her marks, she found she couldn't do her work agreeable to herself' — 'If you do it agreeable to us,' said I, 'that'll do.' — 'O! But' she said 'I could wish not to have my marks took away'. — 'Exactly so,' said I. 'That's quite right; and the only way to get them back again, is to do as well as you can.' — 'Ho! But if she didn't have 'em giv' up at once, she could wish fur to go.' — 'Very well,' said I. 'You shall go tomorrow morning.'

Lastly, Sesina, who soon struck Dickens as 'the pertest, vainest . . . and most deceitful little minx in this town — I never saw such a draggled piece of fringe upon the skirts of all that is bad'. She was involved in a cabal against the Superintendents, which Dickens and his colleagues on the Committee had firmly to suppress. 'I gave this young lady to understand, in the plainest and most emphatic words, that she appeared to us to misunderstand the place — and its object. That she must thoroughly change her whole feelings and demeanour,' and so on. Early next morning, however, Dickens was summoned to Urania Cottage; Sesina had been very insolent and was now staging a lie-down strike in her bedroom. She was duly expelled, and Dickens passed her on the road, 'walking in a jaunty way up Notting Hill, and refreshing herself with an occasional contemplation of the shop windows. . . . I think she would corrupt a Nunnery in a fortnight.'[27]

Enough has been said to show the strength and continuity of Dickens's interest in Urania Cottage, and the energy both of his activities on its behalf and his descriptions of its inmates. The good sense and understanding he brought to the task are equally notable. One scholar, noting Dickens's respect for the personal dignity of the recipients of charity (a sensitiveness not always common at that time), instances 'the imaginative sympathy and the incredible humanity and decency' with which he conducted this Home.[28] He could, as examples have shown, be firm and even ruthless, and he insisted that the girls should acknowledge to themselves the error of their past ways; but, thereafter, there were to be no reproaches about the past. The girls were forbidden to discuss it, and even the Superintendents were generally kept in ignorance of their charges' histories; the neighbours, too, were not to be told the nature of the Home and its occupants. Even the name 'Urania Cottage', which sounds quaintly mid-Victorian in our ears, was a kindly gesture at a time when other institutions founded for a similar purpose bore such forbiddingly explicit names as The British Penitent Female Refuge, The Home for Penitent Females, The London Female Penitentiary, and so on. (And who, one wonders, happily subscribed to the periodical entitled *The Magdalen's Friend and Female Homes' Intelligencer?*) In the *Appeal to Fallen Women* which he wrote for distribution, Dickens had made the point, in his more *vox humana* style: 'And do not think that I write you as if I felt myself very much above you, or wished to hurt your feelings by reminding you of the situation in which you are placed. God forbid! I mean nothing but kindness to you, and I write as if you were my sister.' His sympathy appears, more practically, in the letters. Some of these girls, he told Miss Coutts, must inevitably fall back into their old ways, 'unless we take them. . . . It is dreadful to think how some of these doomed women have no chance or choice. It is impossible to disguise from one's self the horrible truth that it would have been a social marvel and miracle if some of them had been anything else than what they are.' Accordingly, a girl was to be told, on arriving at the Home, that

> She has come there for *useful* repentance and reform, and because her past life has been dreadful in its nature and consequences, and full of affliction, misery, and despair *to herself*. Never mind society while she is at that pass. Society has used her ill and turned away from her, and she cannot be expected to take much heed of its rights and wrongs. It is destructive to *herself*, and there is no hope in it, or in her, as long as she pursues it.

This realistic and uncensorious passage comes from Dickens's first letter on the scheme, and he goes on to propose a method whereby the new girl may be induced to regain her self-respect.[29]

The emotional atmosphere of the Home seemed very important to him. Affectionate kindness and trustfulness were to be the basis of its appeal. Just before it opened he remarked, 'On the cheerfulness and kindness all our hopes rest'; and a year later he commented, 'The great thing to avoid, and the danger towards which I certainly think we rather tend at present, is the being too grim and gloomy.' He did what he could to prevent this, and to avoid the errors he found in the refuges already in existence. One recalls those forbidding names borne by most Institutions, and the comment of a prostitute interviewed by Henry Mayhew: 'She knew all about the Refuges. She had been in one once, but she didn't like the system; there wasn't enough liberty, and too much preaching, and that sort of thing.' It was such penitential grimness that Dickens wanted to avoid; after referring to the 'extraordinary monotony' of these places, he explains why he will not let the Home's Chaplain address the girls individually. They would already, he said, have developed an 'exaggerated dread' of religious forms and words, which were used excessively in such institutions, and they would therefore conclude that 'It's the old story after all' at Urania Cottage — 'and so we should lose them.'[30] As Chesterton's comments show, however, the young *filles de joie* were reluctant to believe that Dickens's Home was any less irksome than the rest, though he had done his best to reduce the institutional atmosphere there. Thus he rejected a uniform for the girls, and chose dresses for them, 'as cheerful in appearance as they reasonably could be — at the same time very neat and modest.' Some years later he wrote the much quoted letter, returning to Miss Coutts her sample of a dull cotton material called derry, which she had proposed for the girls' overalls and other garments:

> I return Derry. I have no doubt it's a capital article, but it's a mortal dull color. Color these people always want, and color (as allied to fancy), I would always give them. In these cast-iron and mechanical days, I think even such a garnish to the dish of their monotonous and hard lives, of unspeakable importance. One color, and that of the earth earthy, is too much with them early and late. Derry might just as well break out into a stripe, or put forth a bud, or even burst into a full blown flower. Who is Derry that he is to make quakers of us all, whether we will or no![31]

Similarly, the books read aloud to them while they sat at needlework were 'carefully chosen but always interesting' (the 'but' is instructive). Selections from Wordsworth and Crabbe (not overexciting, one would have thought) were suggested by one Superintendent, and Dickens approved, commenting that 'All people who have led hazardous and forbidden lives are, in a certain sense, imaginative; and if their imaginations are not filled with good things, they will choke them, for themselves, with bad ones'. Other outlets were the cultivation of little flower-beds (Dickens hoped to open the Home 'before it is winter weather, and while the garden is green and sunny'), and the singing of part-songs. Much of this seemed unncessarily genteel and luxurious to some of the charitable people of the time. Mrs Chisholm, for instance, asked Dickens 'if it were true that the girls at Shepherd's Bush "had *Pianos*". I shall always regret [he commented] that I didn't answer yes — each girl a grand, downstairs — and a cottage in her bedroom — besides a small guitar in the wash-house'.[32]

The girls did not spend much of their time, however, in merry songs and other recreation. They were constantly employed, and always overlooked, Dickens said, but he tried to 'make as great a variety in their daily lives as their daily lives will admit of'. For two hours every weekday morning they had lessons ('book education of a very plain kind'), but most of the time was spent in domestic training — 'Order, punctuality, cleanliness, the whole routine of household duties — as washing, mending, cooking. . . .' The girls were made to understand, however, that 'they were not going through a monotonous round of occupation and self-denial which began and ended there, but which began, or was resumed, under that roof, and would end, by God's blessing, in happy homes of their own'. Such girls as these needed to be *'tempted to* virtue. They cannot be dragged, driven or frightened' — and the best incentive was the hope of marriage. Dickens insisted on this, despite the doubts of Miss Coutts and of a Miss Cunliffe who was briefly on the staff; ungallantly hinting at the latter's maiden status, he remarked, 'You will not think me claiming much, if I claim to know much better than she does, or by any possibility can, what the force of that suggestion secretly is.'[33] The girls were not sent off as emigrants until they were deemed satisfactory, both as moral beings and as potential housewives or domestic servants; they were then despatched, but only in ships where their new-found honour could be guaranteed reasonably safe from temptation.[34] Dickens was indignant about similar institutions which neglected the after-care of their girls. It was, then, a sound practical course that his girls received — 'grounded in religion, most unquestionably,' he had said; 'It must be the basis of the whole system'[35] — but though the girls had their daily prayers, hymn-singing, and Bible-readings, he was watchful against any preachifying.

Dickens's dislike of exhortation appeared, very reasonably, in the way he reacted to Kay-Shuttleworth's suggestion that 'some greater *moral* stimulant' be introduced into the system. Would not practical 'incentives to good conduct' be more successful, he asked, both in the short and the long run? He had in mind an appropriate system of incentives, which was eventually adopted, after some opposition from Miss Coutts: it was a Marks System, such as was quite common in the 'progressive' schools of the period and which later became a central feature in English prisons. The

Urania Cottage scheme was based on the pamphlets and the personal advice of the great penal reformer Captain Maconochie, whose acquaintance with Dickens was mentioned in the last chapter, and whose ideas will be discussed more fully in Chapter VII. Dickens, as we shall see there, had some reserves about Maconochie and his system, but he was sure that under its influence a girl '*must* (I believe it to be in the eternal nature of things) rise somewhat in her own self-respect'. The scheme he devised is explained in several long letters and Memoranda to Miss Coutts, and in the *Household Words* article. Every girl was given marks daily for her attainments in several virtues; she could also lose marks for decidedly bad behaviour, but 'A bad mark is very infrequent, and occasions great distress in the recipient and great excitement in the community'. The girls all valued the marks highly (we have seen Little Willis's refusal to work without them), for they not only represented a recognition of achievement and conferred little privileges on their owners, but were also convertible into cash when a girl left the Home. The sums earned were about the average wages of an ordinary domestic servant.[36]

'I think I know them pretty well,' he had said of the first batch of girls he had interviewed and accepted. '. . . A most extraordinary and mysterious study it is, but interesting and touching in the extreme.' He brought to his task the memory of his observations of London's seamier side over many years, and he often proved very perceptive in his comments and diagnoses. 'Recollect that we address a peculiar and strangely-made character,' he was continually warning Miss Coutts, and he had from the beginning made some good guesses about it. In that first long letter on the subject he had, for example, foreseen that

> There is no doubt that many of them would go on well for some time, and would then be seized with a violent fit of the most extraordinary passion, apparently quite motiveless, and insist on going away. There seems to be something inherent in their course of life, which engenders and awakens a sudden restlessness and recklessness which may be long suppressed, but breaks out like madness. . . . This sudden dashing down of all the building up of months upon months, is, to my thinking, so distinctly a Disease with the persons under consideration that I would pay particular attention to it, and treat it with particular gentleness and anxiety.

Seven years later, experience had confirmed this: the restlessness tended to break out about six or eight months after admission. This violent instability is only one of the phenomena which he noted and tried to provide for (they are familiar enough to us now, in textbooks of psychology and social investigation). He commented, for instance, on the girls' fantasy-lives; even the most wretched of them pretended that their friends were well-off, though this psychological curiosity, he remarked, was considered inexplicable.[37]

His approach to Urania Cottage has been described as 'a characteristic blend of dramatic pathos and common sense'. The dramatic pathos is exemplified by his *Appeal to Fallen Women*, which certainly embarrasses us, though Dickens was assured by Chesterton, who had given it to suitable girls, that 'it affects them very heartily indeed'. In this respect, as over the pathos in the novels, we must make allowance for changes in public taste: indeed the peroration of this *Appeal* recalls the rhetoric of the novels.

> Whether you accept it or reject it, think of it. If you awake in the silence and solitude of the night, think of it then. If any remembrance ever comes into your mind of any time when you were innocent and very different, think of it then —

and so forth: this is very similar to a speech in *A Tale of Two Cities*, written a dozen years later, Lucie's appeal to her father.

> 'If you hear in my voice . . . any resemblance to a voice that once was sweet music in your ears, weep for it, weep for it! If you touch, in touching my hair, anything that recalls a beloved head that lay in your breast when you were young and free, weep for it, weep for it!'

— and, again, so forth.[38] Dickens's common sense is, however, much more conspicuous, in the actual running of the Home; once he has got down to work, he spends few words on the dramatic or sentimental aspects of the 'noble effort'. Rather, a healthy realism characterised his activities, as many of the passages quoted above have shown. One vital point of management was, he noted, 'never to treat the inmates as children.' One recalls his delightful satire, some years later, in the Ragged School episode in *Our Mutual Friend*, on people who forgot this:

> All the place was pervaded by a grimly ludicrous pretence that every pupil was childish and innocent. This pretence, much-favoured by the lady-visitors, led to the ghastliest absurdities. Young women old

in the vices of the commonest and worst life, were expected to profess themselves enthralled by the good child's book, the Adventures of Little Margery, who resided in the village cottage by the mill; severely reproved and morally squashed the miller when she was five and he was fifty; divided her porridge with singing birds; denied herself a new nankeen bonnet, on the ground that turnips did not wear nankeen bonnets, neither did the sheep who ate them; who plaited straw and delivered the dreariest orations to all comers, at all sorts of unseasonable times.[39]

The whole regime, both in its moral and psychological aspects, seems to have been shrewd, humane and practical. 'The projectors of this establishment,' he had explained (it will be remembered) in the *Household Words* article, 'were prepared . . . to consider their enterprise rewarded, if they in time succeeded with one third or one half of the cases they received.' The only statistics of its success are those given in the same article, written in 1853. Of the fifty-seven girls who had been through the Home by then, thirty had done well in Australia or elsewhere, seven of them having also found husbands. Of the rest, 'seven went away by their own desire during their probation; ten were sent away for misconduct in the Home; seven ran away; three emigrated and relapsed on the passage out.' Dickens's guess that about half should be reclaimable was about right; and it seems, in the circumstances, a creditable achievement. Another witness is Chesterton, who thought Miss Coutts 'had good cause to be satisfied with her charitable labours, for ample was the confirmation, from various colonies, of the credit-able conduct of, I think I may safely aver, all her protégées'. Some of the girls showed a proper gratitude, writing warm letters of thanks to Miss Coutts (a delightful specimen is printed in the *Household Words* article) and even returning in a glow of respectability to the dear old Home. Of one prize-pupil, on holiday from the Cape of Good Hope, Dickens writes:

> It was very pleasant to see Louisa Cooper, nicely dressed and looking very well to do. . . . She brought me for a present, the most hideous Ostrich's Egg ever laid — wrought all over with frightful devices, the most tasteful of which represents Queen Victoria (with her crown on) standing on the top of a Church receiving professions of affection from a British Seaman.[40]

Such is the reward of the successful social worker.

The later history of the Home is uncertain. If the published selection of the correspondence with Miss Coutts is more or less

representative of Dickens's activities in the matter, it would seem
that he spent less time on it from about 1854 onwards. His last
reference to it (that I have noted) is in the letter referring to the
affair of Sarah Hyam and the policeman, dated 14 April 1858.
This was just a month or so before the event which virtually ended
his friendship with Miss Coutts, and thus his association with
Urania Cottage — his separation from his wife.[41] This rupture in
his marriage was, almost certainly, precipitated by his passion for
the young actress Ellen Ternan. It is one of the ironies of Dickens's
life that his connection with Urania Cottage ceased through his
involvement in an affair which might have qualified yet another
girl for entrance into a Home for Fallen Women. Many years later,
Miss Coutts's secretary wrote that 'The Home at Shepherd's Bush
was carried on for some years with varying degrees of success.
There were gratifying cases of redemption with new starts in life,
and some successful efforts at emigration. But, on the whole, the
work proved even more difficult than Dickens had foreseen: and
after many discouragements and failures the scheme was given
up'.[24] This, however, must have been after Dickens's time.

His connection with the Home was not made common knowledge during his lifetime. His *Household Words* article was not only
anonymous, and never reprinted by himself; it contained no hint
that he or anyone else working for the journal was the author, or
was connected with the Home there described. (Its location, and
Miss Coutts's name, were also of course suppressed.) Dame Una
Pope-Hennessy suggests that some 'native instinct' warned him not
to 'invalidate the magic in his books' by disclosing his practical
philanthropy; but this was not, I think, his motive.[43] A comparison with the novels is appropriate again.

Dickens's contempt for people who advertised their philanthropic virtue appears in many passages; for instance, in Mr
Jarndyce's reflections upon those circles

> where benevolence took spasmodic forms; where charity was assumed,
> as a regular uniform, by loud professors and speculators in cheap
> notoriety, vehement in profession, restless and vain in action, servile
> in the last degree of meanness to the great, adulatory of one another,
> and intolerable to those who were anxious quietly to help the weak
> from falling, rather than with a great deal of bluster and self-
> laudation to raise them up a little way when they were down.

The novel from which this comes, *Bleak House*, contains a fine example in Mrs Pardiggle, whose infallible course was 'pouncing upon the poor, and applying benevolence to them like a strait-waistcoat': witness her visit to the brickmakers' home, which began ominously —

> 'Well, my friends,' said Mrs Pardiggle; but her voice had not a friendly sound, I thought; it was much too business-like and systematic. 'How do you do, all of you? I am here again. I told you, you couldn't tire me, you know. I am fond of hard work, and am true to my word.'

— a visit which ended, equally uncomfortably, when she

> pulled out a good book, as if it were a constable's staff, and took the whole family into custody. I mean into religious custody, of course; but she really did it, as if she were an inexorable moral Policeman carrying them all off to a station-house.

There are of course other such lively accounts of charitable busy-bodies in the novels, down to Mr Honeythunder in his final book, one of those Philanthropists who 'are always denouncing somebody . . . and are so given to seizing their fellow-creatures by the scruff of the neck, and . . . bumping them into the paths of peace'.[44] Dickens's own philanthropy, not only over Urania Cottage but also in scores of other instances, notably avoided these vices of insensitivity and self-congratulation.

The relation between the novels and Urania Cottage is illuminating in further respects. Mr Jarndyce was no doubt speaking for Dickens, in his reflections on heavy-handed and self-important philanthropy; but Jarndyce was no Dickens, though clearly Dickens delighted in his kindly generosity. There is an interesting comment by Esther Summerson when once again Jarndyce has forgiven Skimpole on the grounds that he is a child: 'It was so delicious to see the clouds about his bright face clearing, and to see him so heartily pleased, and to know, as it was impossible not to know, that the source of his pleasure was the goodness which was tortured by condemning, or mistrusting, or secretly accusing anyone.' Professor Houghton quotes this passage, in his excellent chapter on 'Sympathy and Benevolence' in *The Victorian Frame of Mind*, and he rightly notes 'the unabashed release of the sentimentality latent in benevolence'.[45] How unsentimental Dickens was, over actual fallen women, appears strikingly not only in his Urania Cottage activities, but also in his *Uncommercial Traveller* essay, 'The Ruffian,' where he recalls an occasion when he insisted that one such girl should be prosecuted for using foul language in the streets; the police and the magistrate were surprised and distressed by his persistence and his willingness that she should go to prison for her offence. The episode has often been misunderstood, and misdated; but it was, in the circumstances of the time, a sensible and public-spirited action by Dickens — sensible because the streets certainly needed to be saved from this notorious scandal of open profligacy, and public-spirited because few men would spare the time or risk the obloquy of initiating a prosecution.[46] None of his benevolent characters, however, unite his tough sensibleness and his generous impulses. What has been said of Jarndyce applies also to such figures as Mr Brownlow and the Cheerybles; Dickens presents them for our admiration and he himself is obviously moved and convinced by them, but the 'bad' philanthropists — like the 'bad' schools in the novels — are far better done (thus, Mr Jarndyce has much less vitality than Mrs Jellyby and Mrs Pardiggle, in the same novel). Moreover, Dickens was, in his own charitable activities, much less credulous, sentimental, and soft-headed than his Jarndyce, Brownlow and Cheerybles. He was much better at being a good man, than at describing and dramatising one.

The same disjunction between his life and his art is apparent in his handling of the girls who were the object of this philanthropy. As has been noted above, Martha Endell's behaviour was as conventionally melodramatic as that of any lost girl in his earlier stories or in the verses or plays or novels of contemporaries of his who lacked his strong interest in such girls and his skill in coping with them (and no important novelist of the age, except Mrs Gaskell, could rival his experience in such matters). Yet the Martha passages were written after he had been running Urania Cottage for three years with a realism quite absent in the novel. Certainly some reticences were obligatory for a novelist in that period, though Mrs Gaskell, for example, employed without scandal a vocabulary much blunter than Dickens's; even so, the falsity of Martha's appearances was gratuitous. The passages quoted from the letters, about Louisa Cooper and Little Willis and Jemima Hiscock and Sesina, are certainly altogether more lively and convincing than Martha's histrionics.

At one point in *David Copperfield*, however, he did draw upon the Urania Cottage idea, though again with a significant disparity.

Mr Peggotty, it will be remembered, had a plan similar to Dickens's: 'Theer's mighty countries, fur from heer. Our future life lays over the sea. . . . No one can't reproach my darling in Australia. We will begin a new life over theer!' And so they do, taking Martha with them; and Peggotty later reports on their success. Martha marries a decent young farm-labourer ('Wives is very scarce theer,' is Peggotty's ungallant but realistic comment), but Emily, though 'she might have married well a mort of times', chooses a life of repentant spinsterhood and good works.[47] Clearly one is intended to admire Emily's resolution (and her loyalty to Ham) more than Martha's earthier pursuit of happiness. Thus Dickens capitulates in his fiction to the view which he consistently rejected when Miss Coutts urged it as the policy for Urania Cottage. In most cases, he argued, it is almost impossible to produce a penitence which shall stand the wear and tear of this rough world without Hope — worldly hope' — and for girls of this age and disposition, marriage was the obvious bait. 'I am not quite sure that perfect penitence in these women — the best of them I mean — would lead them in all cases not to marry; for I can certainly (I think) descry a kind of active repentance in their being faithful wives and the mothers of virtuous children.'[48]

These contrasts between Dickens the novelist and Dickens the amateur social worker form an extreme example of the phenomenon I discussed at the end of my last chapter — his unwillingness or inability to express the whole truth (as he knew it) in his fiction. I there quoted Dr K. J. Fielding, who has written often and well on this matter. To my surprise, Dr Fielding finds the letters about Urania Cottage 'extremely unrevealing'; the interesting thing about Dickens's connection with the Home is, he says, that 'it tells us nothing about him, except that he had tremendous practical ability and a passionate love for administration'. The letters, surely, also show that he brought considerable insight, compassion, good sense and patience, to this decade of work at Shepherd's Bush? Some of these qualities belong, of course, to his equipment as a novelist — and the novelist is evident, too, in the brilliance of many of the descriptions and dialogues and characterisations which I have quoted. But if the novelist is often apparent in the social worker, the reverse is not true. As Dr Fielding has written elsewhere, 'Without recognising it himself, he had two sets of standards: one for fiction, and one for everyday use. . . . The general significance of Dickens's correspondence with Miss

Coutts . . . is largely that in the later novels his life and fiction remained disconcertingly mutually unassimilable.'[49] No-one would have guessed, from reading *David Copperfield* or any of the other novels which contain 'fallen' or delinquent girls, that their author really knew what he was talking about. We shall see further cases where the novels give an inadequate, even a very misleading, impression of what he knew and believed. Sometimes, as here, when he is writing about situations and types which are the subject of a strong literary convention, there is a total disparity between his observation and his writing; sometimes, there is a very partial selection, of the less agreeable or praiseworthy aspects of what he has observed. For the latter type of disparity, part of the explanation is of course that, as every journalist knows, disaster and folly and vice and violence are more newsworthy and easier to 'write up' than virtue, peace, and honest dealing. Good news is no news (to reverse the old adage). This discovery is not unique to journalists; novelists and poets, too, are generally less adept at dramatising virtue and sense than vice and folly; and this appears in Dickens's letters and articles, as well as his novels, though to a less extent.[50] The letters about Urania Cottage, as we have seen, are happier in their presentation of Dickens's sensible programme of education and training, than are the novels with their Brownlows and Cheerybles, sweet Ruth Pinches and Esther Summersons. But even in the letters, the memorable passages are those describing not the daily routine of practical education, but the rows and disasters; not the neat and modest appearance of the girls at their best, but such sights as poor Campbell, low-spirited because her hair had all been shaved off, 'looking something between the knob on the top of a pair of tongs — a chinese — and a scraped dutch cheese.'[51] Similarly, the *Household Words* article on Urania Cottage, though it gives in many ways a more coherent and intelligent account of his ideas about the Home, is less lively and quotable than the letters, where he allows his powers of imaginative expression a freer rein.

It must be admitted, moreover, that Dickens himself thought highly of the implausible paragons in his novels, as he did, also, of his pathetic waifs and his melodramatic fallen women. What may seem to us a conscious, perhaps even a cynical, capitulation to the literary clichés of his age (those juvenile death-beds, for instance, or Martha's invocation to the river) was for him as real, as affecting, and as finely-achieved, as anything else in his work. The vulgarities and the limitations of his writing cannot be accounted for by insincerity — though a more self-conscious and self-critical writer would no doubt have noticed and reduced the gap between the two standards, each held with a kind of sincerity, which govern his life and his art.

V

THE SEPARATE SYSTEM—
PHILADELPHIA AND THE BASTILLE

ON 8 March 1842, Dickens visited the most famous prison in the world — Cherry Hill, the Eastern Penitentiary in Phila-delphia. Opened only a dozen years before, it had become the international showplace for the Separate System, which the more advanced and articulate penologists of most countries tended to prefer: so when, seven months after that visit, Dickens published a long and uncompromising attack on it, he offended most leaders of professional opinion of this period. Nor could the friends of the system ignore this indictment by a writer of such international popularity. As the recent historians of Cherry Hill put it, they 'rallied to its defence heroically, calling in experts whose opinions were far more authoritative than those of the British author'.[1] The volume and persistency of the attempts to rebut Dickens's judg-ment was a gratifying tribute to his prestige — and not only in the Anglo-Saxon world: for when a German professor undertook an international tour in 1846, to report to the King of Prussia on current penal experiments, he too felt impelled to quote and dis-cuss Dickens's *American Notes* chapter on Philadelphia, since the views there expressed would, he said, influence German public opinion about prison discipline. He honoured no other layman, of any country, with such an attention. 'It is an unquestionable fact,' wrote another of his critics, in 1845, 'that the fictions of Mr Dickens have had, and are now having, a most prejudicial influence, not only on the public mind at home, but also on that of the Continent of Europe. In some of the French Reviews . . . even the hallucina-tions of Mr Dickens are referred to as weighty evidence!'[2] As was mentioned earlier, his criticism of Philadelphia was still being professionally disputed half a century later. Most well-informed writers of the period, indeed, entirely disagreed with his judg-ment on this prison.

It is this chapter of *American Notes*, however, that constitutes Dickens's main claim to a respectable place in penological history. Sidney and Beatrice Webb, for instance, applaud his 'burning indignation' over the cruelties of this system; Dr Max Grünhut praises his 'immortal prison stories' and his dissent from the general enthusiasm for the Philadelphia experiment — 'With the imagination of a poet he developed a psychology of solitary confinement.'[3] If these and other writers on penology had consulted some of his less-publicised statements on the subject, such as those quoted in the Coldbath Fields chapter, they would have realised that he was an unreliable ally in the campaign for greater humanity in prison-discipline. But they were certainly justified in honouring him for this *American Notes* chapter, which, despite some weaknesses, showed both good sense and a good heart. The most ambitious and the most famous, this was also his first substantial contribution to penology. It was preceded only by the descriptions of Newgate in *Sketches by Boz*, *Oliver Twist* and *Barnaby Rudge*, where his interest in prisons had been dramatic rather than analytical.

His contemporary opponents not only questioned his understanding and judgment of the Philadelphia system, and his assessment of the individual prisoners he described. They also impugned his sincerity, and questioned his right to comment at all after so short a visit. These are minor issues, but they should be mentioned and disposed of, particularly as the recent learned historians of the prison, Professors Teeters and Shearer, seem to have accepted without question these imputations, in their valuable chapter on 'Charles Dickens and his Cherry Hill Prisoners'. The charges are stated, in the intemperate language too common in the prison-pamphleteering of that period, by one of Dickens's earliest and most thorough critics — 'the immortal Adshead' whom Mr Rotch of Middlesex so much admired. Adshead's chapter 'The Fictions of Dickens upon Solitary Confinement', published in 1845, provided the basis for most of the subsequent attacks on *American Notes* during Dickens's lifetime. It was based on newspaper cuttings, and on information collected by several American observers — the Cherry Hill medical officer, a Philadelphian friend of Adshead's who was active in prison-reform, and the great authority Professor Lieber (who had invented the word 'penology'). For Adshead was an Englishman, who had not visited Philadelphia himself since Dickens had launched his attack.

Adshead's personal strictures on Dickens are as follows. Dickens, he says, admits that his stay in the city was 'very short', and a Philadelphia newspaper reported that he had spent only two hours in the prison — yet 'this fugacious prison inspector . . . with an effrontery unwarranted by his age or experience, questions the judgment and practice of veterans . . . in the cause of humanity and philanthropy'. Adshead then contrasts Dickens's onslaught on the Pennsylvania system with

> . . . the laudatory language which he employed when a guest at the dinner table with those officially connected with the Penitentiary. . . . Had he the ingenuous manliness, the moral courage . . . to tell them, face to face, they 'did not know what they were doing'? . . . When 'our distinguished guest' was proposed, his speech in return was characterised by a style the most complimentary, unequivocally conveying the *gratification he had at the Eastern Penitentiary*. . . . For the preceding facts we have the personal testimony of those importantly connected with the Eastern Penitentiary, and who were of the party where Mr Dickens sat an honoured guest. . . . A reflection is scarcely needed as to what will be the feelings of every well regulated mind upon the conduct evinced by Mr Dickens, on that occasion.

Other evidence might be given, Adshead continued, of the favourable verdict Dickens then expressed on the prison (indeed, an eyewitness recalled elsewhere that Dickens expressed 'not a word of criticism or of objection' to the prison or its system, but that he said on leaving it, 'Never before have I seen a public institution in which the relations of father and family were so well exemplified as this'). Adshead challenged Dickens to print a verbatim report of his post-prandial speech in the prison, so full of apparently-sincere praise — 'But a book had to be written; . . . the mere dry detail of fact was not contemplated, by him, as sufficiently exciting; the regions of fiction, therefore, had to be explored, to supply what truth could not furnish.' It was, indeed, wrote Adshead sarcastically, a fertile imagination, that could thus spin thirty pages of description out of a two-hour visit.[4]

Dickens was annoyed by these imputations, which were repeated in several books by defenders of the separate system, such as the Reverend Field's *Prison Discipline* (1846). Field, a cleric who combined lavender-water sanctimoniousness towards his flock with a holy combativeness towards his enemies, began his attack on *American Notes* peremptorily by referring to 'the shameful advantage which has been taken of the general want of information on this subject, by a writer whose works have obtained a wider circulation than his veracity deserved. The subject was of by far too serious a nature for discussion in a mere work of amusement'. Dickens was nettled by this last phrase, but he mildly suggested that perhaps Mr Field might like to hear the facts, which he had verified from his Diary, made up at the end of that day. (The quotation comes from an unsigned article, in which Dickens refers to himself in the third person.)

He left his hotel for the Prison at twelve o'clock, being waited on, by appointment, by the gentlemen who showed it to him; and he returned between seven and eight at night; dining in the Prison in the course of that time; which, according to his calculation, in despite of the *Philadelphia* Newspaper, rather exceeds two hours. He found the Prison admirably conducted, extremely clean, and the system administered in a most intelligent, kind, orderly, tender, and careful manner. He did not consider (nor should he, if he were to visit Pentonville to-morrow) that the book in which visitors were expected to record their observation of the place, was intended for the insertion of criticisms on the system, but for honest testimony to the manner of its administration; and to that, he bore, as an impartial visitor, the highest testimony in his power. In returning thanks for his health being drunk, at the dinner within the walls, he said that what he had seen that day was running in his mind; that he could not help reflecting on it; and that it was an awful punishment. If the American officer who rode back with him afterwards should ever see these words, he will perhaps recall his conversation with Mr Dickens on the road, as to Mr Dickens having said so very plainly and strongly.[5]

All this accords with what Dickens had written to Forster, five days after the event, and this letter, together with the quotation from the reply to Mr Field, seems to dispose of the merely personal charges made against him by Adshead and his followers:

I went last Tuesday to the Eastern Penitentiary near Philadelphia, which is the only prison in the States, or I believe, in the world, on the principle of hopeless, strict, and unrelaxed solitary confinement, during the whole term of the sentence. It is wonderfully kept, but a most dreadful, fearful place. The inspectors, immediately on my arrival in Philadelphia, invited me to pass the day in the gaol, and to dine with them when I had finished my inspection, that they might hear my opinion of the system. Accordingly I passed the whole day in going from cell to cell, and conversing with the prisoners. Every facility was given me, and no constraint whatever imposed upon any man's free speech. . . . I never shall be able to dismiss from my mind the impressions of that day. Making notes of them, as I have done, is an absurdity, for they are written, beyond all power of erasure, in my brain. I saw men who had been there, five years, six years, eleven years, two years, two months, two days; some whose term was nearly over, and some whose term had only just begun. Women too, under the same variety of circumstances. Every prisoner who comes into the gaol, comes at night; is put into a bath, and dressed in the prison garb; and then a black hood is drawn over his face and head, and he is led to the cell from which he never stirs again until his whole period of confinement has expired. I looked at some of them with the same awe as I should have looked at men who had been buried alive, and dug up again.

We dined in the gaol: and I told them after dinner how much the sight had affected me, and what an awful punishment it was. I dwelt upon this; for, although the inspectors are extremely kind and benevolent men, I question whether they are sufficiently acquainted with the human mind to know what it is they are doing. Indeed, I am sure they do not know. I bore testimony, as every one who sees it must, to the admirable government of the institution; and added that nothing could justify such a punishment, but its working a reformation in the prisoners. That for short terms — say two years for the maximum — I conceived, especially after what they had told me of its good effects in certain cases, it might perhaps be highly beneficial; but that, carried to so great an extent, I thought it cruel and unjustifiable; and further, that their sentences for small offences were very rigorous, not to say savage. All this, they took like men who were really anxious to have one's free opinion, and to do right. And we were very much pleased with each other, and parted in the friendliest way.

Like many of the long and brilliant letters to Forster from America, this contains the germ of the corresponding passage in *American Notes*, though he also kept a diary, which he consulted when writing the book a few months later.[6]

One other quotation, from another letter written soon after visiting the Penitentiary, is relevant: for it shows — what, indeed, he admitted in *American Notes* — that he had 'hesitated once, debating with myself, whether, if I had the power of saying "Yes" or "No", I would allow [this penal system] to be tried in certain cases, where the terms of imprisonment were short'. Two days after seeing the prison he wrote to an American friend:

I passed a whole day in the Penitentiary. . . . It is inexpressibly painful to see so many of the prisoners as I did, and to converse with them; but I fear that to a certain extent the system is a good one. I use the expression 'I fear', because it is dreadful to believe that it is ever necessary to impose such a torture of the mind upon our fellow creatures. But it seems, from all one can learn, to do good.[7]

There seems no excuse, then, for the allegation that Dickens spent only two hours in the prison, but one can guess how it was that the prison officials — sincere and veracious men, no doubt, like Dickens — failed to realise how deeply he distrusted the system: and one can understand their surprise and resentment when they read *American Notes*, three thousand copies of which were sold in Philadelphia inside half an hour — some sign of the furore it created.[8] Out of a polite sense of his obligations as a guest, Dickens had probably under-stated the objections he already felt. But also, while he was still digesting the experience, he was less sure than he soon afterwards became, that the system was entirely cruel and mistaken. There was nothing disgraceful in his having, for once, hesitated before arriving at a conclusion, nor in his changing his mind. Very rarely indeed, I think, can Dickens be convicted of insincerity or prevarication. He was an upright man, even in his follies.

As one would expect, he offers no closely-reasoned argument against the system he was condemning. He denounces it as intolerably cruel, and expresses his conviction that the suffering it inflicts on its victims produces no better results than the alternative Silent System, which is less unnatural and harmful and which 'has worked well, and is, in its whole design and practice, excellent'.[9] He is studiously respectful towards the advocates of the system he thinks so misguided, and towards the officials at Philadelphia. He displays, indeed, a restraint regrettably absent in his opponents. Not that he always refrained from making personal imputations against people whose ideas he disliked — but on this occasion he is not being wantonly provocative. He goes out of his way to speak well of his antagonists' sincerity and good intentions (as in the letter to Forster), not even suggesting by an ironical or comic phrase that they were soft-headed, or their system scatter-brained. By Dickensian standards, this is remarkably objective. He writes:

> In its intention, I am well convinced that it is kind, humane, and meant for reformation; but I am persuaded that those who devised this system of Prison Discipline, and those benevolent gentlemen who carry it into execution, do not know what it is that they are doing. I believe that very few men are capable of estimating the immense amount of torture and agony which this dreadful punishment, prolonged for years, inflicts upon the sufferers; and in guessing at it myself, and in reasoning from what I have seen written upon their

faces, and what to my certain knowledge they feel within, I am only the more convinced that there is a depth of terrible endurance in it which none but the sufferers themselves can fathom, and which no man has a right to inflict upon his fellow creature.

There is little more generalisation than this. The bulk of the chapter is an attempt to estimate the 'torture and agony which this dreadful punishment . . . inflicts', by 'guessing at it myself, and . . . reasoning from what I have seen written' on the faces of its victims. Like 'A Visit to Newgate', it is essentially the work of a journalist and creative writer, not of a professional observer concerned with systems and statistics and rational explanations. Posterity has agreed — even if Dickens's contemporaries on the whole did not — that here 'the imagination of a poet' got nearer to the truth than the arguments of the earnest professionals.

As in the letter to Forster, he describes dramatically the prison routine   how a new arrival is hooded as he enters 'this melancholy house' and is conducted to his cell, where he remains permanently unaware of the identity of his neighbours, or indeed whether he has any neighbours. 'He never hears of wife and children; home or friends; the life or death of any single creature. He sees the prison-officers, but with that exception he never looks upon a human countenance, or hears a human voice.' This was an exaggeration. After all, a number of the convicts spoke with Dickens, and he was not an uniquely-privileged stranger. They were also seen regularly (though not often) by officially-approved local Prison Visitors, and they did in fact discover quite a lot about their neighbours. The water-pipes were the great uncontrollable means of communication between cells; they have remained the traditional prison-telephone, as appears in scores of memoirs not only by former criminals, but also by political prisoners held in the severest possible custody in modern dictatorships. Moreover, though this was 'the most elaborate prison ever built', a change of plans during its construction frustrated the system, at least in some cell-blocks. To increase the prison's capacity, a second storey was added to these blocks, thus enabling men to talk quite easily to those housed above them, particularly during exercise in the individual yards attached to the cells.[10] (By 'men', incidentally, one should understand 'men and women', for this was a mixed prison, though the sexes were of course kept scrupulously apart.)

Still, the intention if not the effect was much as Dickens describes it, and the effect, if imperfect, was formidable enough. Thus, we are told, the prisoners remained entirely ignorant that the cholera had raged in their city, in the 1830s.[11] Moreover, Dickens is right in noting the prisoners' utter loss of personal identity, under this system. Only the Governor and the 'Moral Instructor' knew their names, let alone their offences. The prisoner, almost bereft of human contacts, was left idle in his cell, until he clamoured for work, and for something to read. Tools, and a Bible, were given to him, though liable to be withdrawn at any time as a punishment. Then he settled down to the unchanging routine of the prison. 'His loom, or bench, or wheel is there [in his cell]; and there he labours, sleeps and wakes, and counts the seasons as they change, and grows old.' Prisoners could, in fact, serve a dozen or more years under these conditions, though many served only a small proportion of their original sentence, as in the United States at that period there was a regular system whereby prisoners' friends exerted political pressure on the prison-authorities to obtain their early release.

Dickens then describes a dozen of the prisoners he visited. Some of them he judges to be desperate villains, others to be terrible humbugs in their professions of virtue and of gratitude for the day which brought them to this prison. But the emphasis is upon the pathos and horror of their situation — 'his lip trembled. . . . He gazed about him — Heaven knows how wearily! . . .' — '. . . a helpless, crushed, and broken man' — 'She was very penitent and quiet; had come to be resigned, she said (and I believe her); and had a peace at mind . . . but . . . she burst into tears, and . . . sobbed, poor thing!' — these phrases are typical of the tone. One longer quotation may be useful, for the prisoner it describes became the most famous in Dickens's prison portrait-gallery.

In another cell, there was a German, sentenced to five years' imprisonment for larceny, two of which had just expired . . . he had painted every inch of the walls and ceiling quite beautifully. He had laid out the few feet of ground, behind, with exquisite neatness, and had made a little bed in the centre, that looked by the bye like a grave. The taste and ingenuity he had displayed in everything were most extraordinary; and yet a more dejected, heart-broken, wretched creature, it would be difficult to imagine. I never saw such a picture of forlorn affliction and distress of mind. My heart bled for him; and when the tears ran down his cheeks, and he took one of the visitors aside, to ask, with his trembling hands nervously clutching at his coat to detain him, whether there was no hope of his dismal sentence being commuted, the spectacle was really too painful to witness. I never saw or heard of any kind of misery that impressed me more than the wretchedness of this man.

It is characteristic of the thoroughness with which Dickens's Philadelphia chapter was disputed, that we know the name, prison-number, previous record, prison history, and subsequent career of this man and of all the other prisoners whom Dickens describes. Adshead, using facts provided by his several informants, attempted a case-by-case rebuttal of his judgments, and recently Professors Teeters and Shearer have gone over the same ground more elaborately, basing their accounts mainly on the official prison-records, and on the investigation made at the time by William Peter, the British Consul-General in the city, at the request of the Philadelphia Prison Society.[12] Thus, we may discover that the German was a thirty-eight-year-old professional thief named Charles Longhamer or Langenheimer, serving a five year sentence for larceny. Under various aliases, he served thirteen further sentences in this Penitentiary and elsewhere. His crimes were petty ones, inefficiently carried out; he spent forty-three of his eighty years in gaol. William Peter could see no sign of distress or dejection in him — 'He was in excellent health and spirits. . . . He is an ingenious and clever fellow but a great hypocrite, and evidently saw Mr Dickens' weak side. . . . I have heard Mr Dickens accused of wilful misrepresentation. Of that I most fully absolve him. . . . His prison scenes are much akin to Sterne's. Still I believe that he never deceived another without having first deceived himself.' This is a more acceptable criticism, I think, than the Professors' rather odd rebuttal: Langenheimer, they say, 'was a troublemaker from the time he entered the prison. Four days after he arrived he attempted suicide.' He was certainly a difficult and obdurate prisoner, incurring various punishments for offences against discipline. The Moral Instructor noted: 'He seemed oppressed with the length of his sentence. . . . Seemed to have no sense of religion. . . . Made a second attempt to commit suicide and makes great promises of reform. *Not much hope.*'

I cannot see that this or the other evidence brought forward is a vindication of the prison's humanity or effectiveness, against Dickens's imputations. No doubt Dickens here allowed his pity to exclude other considerations, and the German, who indeed had a dismal record, probably played hard for his sympathy. But

Langenheimer scarcely represents a triumph for the Separate
System. Attempted suicides are doubtless a nuisance to prison
officials ('trouble-makers'!), and generally the attempts are not
pressed very hard, but they should excite some concern and compassion. Even wretched old lags like this German may be unhappy,
and claim our sympathy. I would not criticise Dickens for feeling
and expressing distress at this particular spectacle, so much as for
conspicuously failing to do so on other occasions, such as we have
noted, where vindictiveness inhibited the tears of human kindness.
If he wept too easily here, it was a fault in the right direction. And
even if one can believe the professions of gratitude which some of
the other prisoners whom Dickens interviewed are reported to have
made later, it remains doubtful whether the rigours of the system
could be justified because, in these cases, its subjects did go straight.

The record of success at Philadelphia was, in fact, by no means
remarkable; several of the 'rebuttals' of Dickens take the form of
criticising him for feeling pity towards prisoners whose later
careers proved them to be more or less incorrigible. As the subsequent history of the prison showed, he was justified in suspecting
that this system did not effect more, or more lasting, reformation
than its rivals. Moreover, the later modifications of the system,
both in Philadelphia and at other prisons which adopted it, were
the result of the accumulating evidence that this solitude was very
harmful to the prisoners' mental and physical health. Nor would
many people now reject Dickens's judgment that this regime,
however benevolent in its aim, was a terribly cruel imposition on
its subjects, whatever its permanent effects for good or ill upon
them.

One curious side-effect of *American Notes* may be mentioned.
The description of the German, though not notably different from
the others, caught the public imagination, and Langenheimer
became famous. Already the Penitentiary was, as its historians say,
a tourist attraction rivalling Niagara, the Capitol, and Sing-Sing
(the showplace of the Silent System), with as many as a hundred
visitors, official and otherwise, arriving every day from all parts
of the world. Now they all wanted to see Langenheimer. Thereafter he was never happy out of gaol — 'He pined for the curious
attention bestowed upon him by visitors, and boasted that he
would die in prison.' — Which he did, in 1884, having begged to
be admitted, though on this occasion he was guilty of no crime.[13]
The prison-authorities were, no doubt, anxious to demonstrate

that he was not as woebegone as Dickens had alleged, but they seem to have been foolish in allowing him to become a celebrity in this way.

Dickens's account of the Penitentiary was severe, though he tried to be fair and accurate. It does not, I think, warrant the Professors' recent dismissal of it as the product of 'fertile imagination . . . terms of vituperation . . .' and so on.[14] He made a few slips, and his judgment on some of the individual cases was doubtless insecurely founded on fact. Elsewhere in *American Notes*, to the joy of his opponents, he made some other minor bloomers — describing Auburn Prison as Mount Auburn, and putting a New York prison in the wrong place, and describing a difference (which did not exist) between the operation of the Separate System at Philadelphia and at Pittsburgh. A more serious limitation in his penological wisdom appeared in his uncritical eulogy, here as in later articles, of the Silent System and of the London prisons which had adopted it. Adshead had little difficulty in showing how unwise Dickens was in asserting that 'perfect order' prevailed at Coldbath Fields and Tothill Fields.[15]

The bitterly hostile reception which *American Notes* received in the United States was caused by many other features of the book than its penology, of course, and the vigour of the counter-attacks in defence of Philadelphia doubtless owed something to the general indignation which his sympathy for negroes excited. This sympathy appeared in the Penitentiary chapter, as well as elsewhere: he failed to make the appropriate automatic response to some coloured women prisoners. 'In the silence and solitude of their lives they had grown to be quite beautiful,' he wrote. 'Their looks were very sad, and might have moved the sternest visitor to tears.' Adshead produces a nasty knock-me-down argument in reply — 'They were of the inferior class of low women to whom the appelative, "beautiful," was inappropriate and unworthy; two of them were Mulattoes, and one of them a Negress!' What a pity, he continued, that Phiz had not been there to illustrate these three ladies! Even William Peter's more temperate protest, that they were confessedly 'very bad girls', who used to be drunk from morning to night in the brothels where they had led their unsavoury lives, seems no reason for rejecting Dickens's account.[16] For even thieving little hussies may be beautiful, and, like brutal housebreakers, may be reckoned to have some feelings which were unnecessarily violated by this extraordinary discipline. Cruelty done to instead of by criminals, and done legally and with the best intentions, still remains cruelty.

At one point in the chapter, however, the 'fertile imagination' of the novelist is at work, though not to bad effect either in literary or in social terms. 'As I walked among these solitary cells, and looked at the faces of the men within them, I tried to picture to myself the thoughts and feelings natural to their condition. I imagined the hood just taken off, and the scene of their captivity disclosed to them in all its dismal monotony. At first the man is stunned' — and for three or four pages Dickens pictures the mind of a prisoner at the various stages of his sentence. It is of course a repetition of the technique adopted in the 'Visit to Newgate' passage about the condemned cell — 'Conceive the situation of a man spending his last night on earth in this cell . . .' — and of the Fagin chapter in *Oliver Twist*. Most of his readers were duly moved by this passage. For instance, Lord Jeffrey, the old giant-killer of the *Edinburgh Review* a generation earlier, usually disliked the social-reformist Dickens, and told him that *American Notes* contained 'rather too much of . . . penitentiaries, &c., in general'. But this account of the silent or solitary system was 'as pathetic and powerful a piece of writing as I have ever seen'. This and other such passages in the book, he said, 'remind us that we have still among us the creator of Nelly, and Smike, and the schoolmaster, and his dying pupil, &c.' Jeffrey, it may be remembered, had declared that there had been 'nothing so good as Nell since Cordelia'; the Philadelphia chapter, it is clear, made an intense appeal to that element in the public taste which had responded so warmly to the pathos of *The Old Curiosity Shop*.[17]

On the several occasions when Dickens imagined the feelings of a man in a prison cell, he obviously enjoyed the dramatic and pathetic opportunities of the subject, and rose to the occasion with a strong piece of imaginative prose. Similarly, in a letter to Forster, he allowed his imagination to play on another aspect of the prisoner's lot, though he did not introduce this speculation into *American Notes*:

> At Pittsburgh I saw another solitary confinement prison: Pittsburgh being also in Pennsylvania. A horrible thought occurred to me when I was recalling all I had seen, that night. *What if ghosts be one of the terrors of the gaols?* I have pondered on it often, since then. The utter solitude by day and night; the many hours of darkness; the silence of death; the mind for ever brooding on melancholy

themes, and having no relief; sometimes an evil conscience very busy: imagine a prisoner covering up his head in the bedclothes and looking out from time to time, with a ghastly dread of some inexplicable silent figure that always sits upon his bed, or stands (if a thing can be said to stand, that never walks as men do) in the same corner of his cell. The more I think of it, the more certain I feel that not a few of these men (during a portion of their imprisonment at least) are nightly visited by spectres. I did ask one man in this last gaol, if he dreamed much. He gave me a most extraordinary look, and said — under his breath — in a whisper — 'No.'[18]

He should not, I think, be criticised for emotional self-indulgence in the *American Notes* passage. He had criticised the Philadelphia authorities, not as being wicked, or even foolish, men, but for a failure in imagination. They 'do not know what it is that they are doing', he had said; and he continued, 'I believe that very few men are capable of estimating the immense amount of torture and agony which this dreadful punishment, prolonged for years, inflicts upon the sufferers.' In claiming to be able to guess at and express it, he was asserting his right and duty as a novelist, a man of insight and of conscience. The chapter he wrote under this determination was both effective and salutary.

'For many years, every book of travels in America had been a party pamphlet, or had at least fallen among partisans, and been pressed into the service of one party or of the other,' wrote John Stuart Mill in his famous review of de Tocqueville's *Democracy in America*.[19] This was true in penology, as well as the larger issues of politics and institutions. There was a good market, among the general public as well as among specialists, for facts and impressions from America: witness Mr Weller's advice to Mr Pickwick to go there, instead of to the Fleet Prison — and 'then let him come back and write a book about the 'Merrikins as'll pay all his expenses and more, if he blows 'em up enough'.[20] Many European writers, men of letters and journalists as well as official delegations, inspected Philadelphia and Auburn or Sing-Sing, and recorded their votes in the prison-discipline debate: for it was generally agreed that (as Harriet Martineau put it) 'In the treatment of the guilty, America is beyond the rest of the world'. She decided that the Philadelphia system was the best yet tried; every one of the prisoners she interviewed there told her that 'he was under obligations to those who had charge of him for treating him "with respect" ', and she seems to have believed everything she heard about this 'work of mercy'. Another female visitor, Frederika Bremer, was so struck by the gentle Quaker atmosphere that, she said, 'I left the prison more edified than I had often been on leaving a church.' Not only the women were impressed. The popular novelists Captain Thomas Hamilton and Captain Marryat found the prisoners cheerful, and thought they suffered no harm, mental or physical.[21]

Most lay visitors, indeed, preferred Philadelphia to Auburn and Sing-Sing; and certainly, if the choice had to lie between these two systems, both carried to extremes in America, Philadelphia was the better. At least it was generous and hopeful in intention, whereas the rival prisons were conducted with a brutal repressiveness painful to read about. At Auburn, the officers carried whips, and enjoyed a large discretion to administer an exemplary flogging on the spot to anyone caught talking or otherwise contravening discipline. Early in his tour, Dickens told Forster of his great disappointment with the New York prisons he had seen, which despite their great reputation seemed to him much inferior to the London ones he knew: but, he added, 'It is very possible that I have not come to the best, not having yet seen Mount Auburn. I will tell you when I have.'[22] Unfortunately he did not manage to see Auburn or any of the other leading Silent System prisons. Had he done so, his complacency with that system might have been shaken.

Though professional opinion, and the verdicts of travellers who had seen both systems in operation in America, tended strongly towards the Philadelphia plan, lay opinion around 1840 was much less enthusiastic. Dickens found an ally in *The Times*, which shared with him the pillory set up by the immortal Adshead. 'An accursed system', *The Times* had called it, 'a cruel system,' 'a maniac-making system.' The last of these phrases occurs in a leading article in which the writer goes on to refer to Dickens:

> Those who wish to peruse a powerful and masterly sketch of the painfully-depressed and despondent feelings by which the imprisoned convict is in all probability racked, when he awakes to a full sense of the dismal monotony of his disastrous doom, have only to refer to Mr C. Dickens's *American Notes*, and they will see it drawn with no less force of language than semblance of truth.... Can human ingenuity devise a mode of punishment more cruel and insupportable?

Two prisoners had gone mad at Pentonville, within its first year of operation, it was reported in the same article.[23] As was mentioned earlier, *American Notes* was published only two months before Pentonville opened, and was naturally taken as an attack in advance on the Government's much-publicised experiment with the Separate System there. As we shall see, Pentonville attracted much criticism during its earlier years, on the grounds of its being cruel — and criticism from an opposite direction a few years later. Prisons were very much in the news, though much of what was written about them was ill-informed, unfair, and unbalanced.

Dickens's further investigations into the Separate System, in its European forms, seem to have been meagre, but he remained entirely hostile to it. In Lausanne in 1846 he became friendly with the prison-doctor, Monsieur Verdeil, from whom he learned that the Philadelphia system, adopted there some years back, had resulted in so many 'terrible fits, new phases of mental affliction, and horrible madness, among the prisoners', that Verdeil obtained its abolition except for sentences not exceeding ten months.

> It is remarkable [Dickens wrote] that in his notes of the different cases, there is *every effect* I mentioned as having observed myself at Philadelphia; even down to those contained in the description of the man who had been there thirteen years, and who *picked his hands* so much as he talked. He has only recently, he says, read the *American Notes*; but he is so much struck by the perfect coincidence that he intends to republish some extracts from his own notes, side by side with these passages of mine translated into French. I went with him over the prison the other day. It is wonderfully well arranged for a continental gaol, and in perfect order. The sentences however, or some of them, are very terrible. I saw one man sent there for murder under circumstances of mitigation — for 30 years. Upon the silent social system all the time! They weave, and plait straw, and make shoes, small articles of turnery and carpentry, and little common wooden clocks. But the sentences are too long for that monotonous and hopeless life; and, though they are well-fed and cared for, they generally break down utterly after two or three years. One delusion seems to become common to three-fourths of them after a certain time of imprisonment. Under the impression that there is something destructive put into their food 'pour les guérir de crime' (says M. Verdeil), they refuse to eat!

(These conversations with Verdeil, presumably, inspired the idea for a Christmas story, mentioned in the same letter, about 'a man imprisoned for ten or fifteen years: his imprisonment being the gap between the people and circumstances of the first part and the altered people and circumstances of the second, and his own changed mind'. But this story was never written.) Next year Dickens was briefly in Glasgow, where he visited the lunatic asylum and the prison — 'a truly damnable gaol,' he told Forster, 'exhibiting the separate system in a most absurd and hideous form. Governor practical and intelligent; very anxious for the associated silence system; and much comforted by my fault-finding.'²⁴ But, strangely enough, he seems not to have visited the much more famous Separate System prison on his own doorstep, for, a few months after that, he was writing to Joshua Jebb, the Surveyor General of Prisons, who had designed Pentonville Prison and was one of its Commissioners. Dickens hoped to interview a candidate for Urania Cottage, who was in custody there, and he would be extremely glad, he told Jebb, 'to make my long-deferred visit to Pentonville in your company.'²⁵ His apparently not having visited this great Model Prison, which had been open for over five years, shows how spasmodic and unsystematic was his interest in penology. I know of no evidence, indeed, that he ever did visit it, with Jebb or without him.

He did, however, write about Pentonville, both in his journalism and his fiction, in 1850. In my next chapter, I shall discuss these presentations of the English version of the Separate System, which differed a good deal from the American version. Before doing so, however, I want to notice a fictional re-creation of the Philadelphia visit. 'I never shall be able to dismiss from my mind the impressions of that day,' Dickens had told Forster just after leaving Philadelphia; '. . . they are written, beyond all power of erasure, in my brain.'²⁶ Nearly twenty years later, he wrote a novel, the plot of which provided an excellent opportunity for using these memories.

Of the prisoners he had seen at Philadelphia he wrote in the same letter to Forster: 'I looked at some of them with the same awe as I should have looked at men who have been buried alive, and dug up again.' The idea recurred in *American Notes* — 'every prisoner who comes into this melancholy house . . . is a man buried alive; to be dug out in the slow round of years; and in the meantime dead to everything but torturing anxieties and horrible despair.' Sitting in his solitary cell, 'every now and then there comes upon him a burning sense of the years that must be wasted in that stone coffin.'[27] Here in Philadelphia, it is clear, is one of the roots of *A Tale of Two Cities* (1859). The original title of this novel was 'Recalled to Life': it remains as the title of Book One, and as the password used by Mr Lorry 'on his way to dig someone out of a grave', as he travels to Paris to rescue Dr Manette. 'Eighteen years!' he thinks. 'Gracious Creator of day! To be buried alive for eighteen years!'[28]

These phrases recur throughout the novel, and in several guises. As Dr Morton Zabel has pointed out, 'Recalled to Life' is a dominant theme not only in Manette's liberation from the Bastille, but also in 'the drama of the Revolution, . . . Darnay's repudiation of his family's curse, even Jerry Cruncher's sinister trade as a body-snatcher ("resurrection man") . . . , down to the Scriptural phrases that come to Sydney Carton's mind as he mounts the guillotine: "I am the Resurrection and the Life, saith the Lord. . . ." It is the idea that gives the book its informing symbol: Resurrection'.[29] In the scene when Manette is 'restored to life' by his daughter Lucie (who is to be the one 'golden thread' tying him to the present and to reality), Dickens might well have used King Lear's words, 'You do me wrong to take me out of the grave.' He nearly does. At the end of that chapter, which is also the end of Book One, Mr Lorry asks Manette, 'I hope you care to be recalled to life?' And 'the old answer' comes: 'I can't say.'[30] The use of the reunion between father and daughter as a symbol of rebirth or resurrection, or of the relation between body and soul, is of course not peculiar to Shakespeare and Dickens: it reflects an universal emotional pattern. But it recurs particularly often in the later plays of Shakespeare, and throughout Dickens's work; one thinks of Little Nell and her grandfather, and of Florence Dombey, Louisa Gradgrind, and Little Dorrit, and their fathers.

Memories of Philadelphia and his attempt to 'picture to myself the thoughts and feelings' of its prisoners manifestly inform his presentation of Dr Manette. The 'prospect of release bewilders and confuses' the victims of the American system, Dickens had recorded:

> On the haggard face of every man among these prisoners, the same expression sat. I know not what to liken it to. It had something of that strained attention which we see upon the faces of the blind and deaf, mingled with a kind of horror, as though they had all been secretly terrified. In every little chamber that I entered, and at every grate through which I looked, I seemed to see the same appalling coun-

tenance. It lives in my memory, with the fascination of a remarkable picture. . . .

My firm conviction is that, independent of the mental anguish it occasions — an anguish so acute and so tremendous, that all imagination of it must fall far short of the reality — it wears the mind into a morbid state, which renders it unfit for the rough contact and busy action of the world. It is my fixed opinion that those who have undergone this punishment, MUST pass into society again morally unhealthy and diseased.[31]

'It lives in my memory, with the fascination of a remarkable picture' — and now, in *A Tale of Two Cities*, it was fused with other memories, of Carlyle's *French Revolution*, of Wilkie Collins's *The Frozen Deep*, and of several other plays and novels. Philadelphia certainly seems to me a more important 'source' than the one given prominence by Mr T. A. Jackson, and accepted by Mr Jack Lindsay in an otherwise perceptive account of the background of this novel. 'It is significant,' writes Mr Jackson, 'that the first novel Dickens wrote after the separation [from his wife] was constructed on the theme "Recalled to Life", and contains passionately moving descriptions of oppressors overthrown by a violent revolution.' This is, I must confess, one of my favourite owl-eyed comments in literary biography (it would have made even poor Catherine Dickens laugh); and Mr Lindsay's version also deserves high marks in the same category — 'The desire to break through obstructions and mate with Ellen [Ternan] turned into a desire to write about the French Revolution because some image or symbol made Dickens feel a basic coincidence between his own experience and the Revolution.'[32]

When Mr Lorry arrives at Monsieur Defarge's, he discusses Manette with him before visiting the garret where, as a 'free' man now, he is living.

'Is he alone?' [Mr Lorry] whispererd.
'Alone! God help him, who should be with him?' said the other, in the same low voice.
'Is he always alone, then?'
'Yes.' . . .
'He is greatly changed?'
'Changed!'
The keeper of the wine-shop stopped to strike the wall with his hand, and mutter a tremendous curse. No direct answer could have been half so forcible. . . .

'The door is locked then, my friend?' said Mr Lorry, surprised. . . . 'You think it necessary to keep the unfortunate man so retired?'

'I think it necessary to turn the key.' Monsieur Defarge whispered it closer in his ear, and frowned heavily. . . . 'Because he has lived so long, locked up, that he would be frightened — rave — tear himself to pieces — die — come to I know not what harm — if his door was left open.'[33]

They find Manette, working at the traditional prison-trade of shoe-making. It is with difficulty that they induce him to speak, or to make any real contact with them. His skin, like his clothes, have 'faded down to a dull uniformity of parchment yellow'; he has been so long secluded from light and air that it is only with the habitual submission of a helpless prisoner that he agrees to their letting a little more light into the room.

The faintness of the voice was pitiable and dreadful. It was not the faintness of physical weakness, though confinement and hard fare no doubt had their part in it. Its deplorable peculiarity was, that it was the faintness of solitude and disuse. It was like the last feeble echo of a sound made long and long ago. So entirely had it lost the life and resonance of the human voice, that it affected the senses like a once beautiful colour faded away into a poor weak stain. So sunken and suppressed it was, that it was like a voice underground.

Lucie appeals to him, and he responds to her warmth and kindness, but, as he is got ready for the journey to England,

No human intelligence could have read the mysteries of his mind, in the scared blank wonder of his face. Whether he knew what had happened, whether he recollected what they had said to him, whether he knew that he was free, were questions which no sagacity could have solved. They tried speaking to him; but, he was so confused, and so very slow to answer, that they took fright at his bewilderment, and agreed for the time to tamper with him no more. He had a wild, lost manner of occasionally clasping his head in his hands, that had not been seen in him before; yet, he had some pleasure in the mere sound of his daughter's voice, and invariably turned to it when she spoke.[34]

The only phrase which detracts from the moving reality of this description is the closing sentence, where Dickens relies on the literary convention that members of a family who have been long separated, or have never met before and do not yet realise that they are related, will nevertheless feel a mysterious, almost magical, bond of attraction.

After this scene, five years pass, and the Manette we now encounter has recovered his wits and re-established contact with reality. But he is a haunted man, subject to an 'abstraction that overclouded him fitfully, without any apparent reason'.[35] He has brought with him, not only his memories, but also the symbol, at once comforting and frightening, of his long imprisonment — the shoemaker's bench and tools, which stand in his bedroom in London, though he never mentions them or the period to which they belong. 'He is afraid of the whole subject,' Miss Pross guesses: and Mr Lorry wonders whether it is good for him 'to have that suppression always shut up within him.'[36] And then, when Lucie is marrying the heir of the man responsible for her father's imprisonment, the strain proves too much. Suddenly a low sound of knocking is heard. Manette has relapsed into his old solitary life, and cannot recognise Lorry and Miss Pross. His hand is 'a little out at first', but is 'growing dreadfully skilful' when, after nine days, he suddenly returns to the life around him, though uneasy in his half-knowledge of his relapse.[37]

There follows a delicately-managed conversation between him and Lorry, who hits on an indirect way of ending that suppression which has always been 'shut up within him'. Lorry puts to Dr Manette, as a physician, 'a very curious case' in which he is deeply interested — and thus enables Manette to become fully aware of what has happened, and to make some constructive suggestions about avoiding such breakdowns in the future, without being forced into the embarrassment of openly facing these painful experiences. Manette describes well the panic which lies behind the obsessional's behaviour.

'You see,' said Doctor Manette, turning to him after an uneasy pause, 'it is very hard to explain, consistently, the innermost workings of this poor man's mind. He once yearned so frightfully for that occupation, and it was so welcome when it came; no doubt it relieved his pain so much, by substituting the perplexity of the fingers for the perplexity of the brain, and by substituting, as he became more practised, the ingenuity of the hands, for the ingenuity of the mental torture; that he has never been able to bear the thought of putting it quite out of his reach. Even now, when I believe he is more hopeful of himself than he has ever been, and even speaks of himself with a kind of confidence, the idea that he might need that old employment, and not find it, gives him a sudden sense of terror, like that which one may fancy strikes to the heart of a lost child.'

(The final phrase about the 'lost child', while psychologically apt here, reminds one of another great Dickensian theme, which is obviously rooted in his painful memories of his own childhood; this is one of several pointers to a close relationship between Manette and his creator.) After a painful struggle, Manette agrees that it would be better if the bench and tools were removed, some time when he is out of the way, and at the first such opportunity Lorry hacks the bench to pieces, with Miss Pross standing by 'as if she were assisting at a murder'. The fragments of 'the body' are burned in the kitchen fire, and the tools and materials are buried in the garden. 'So wicked do destruction and secrecy appear to honest minds, that Mr Lorry and Miss Pross, while engaged in the commission of their deed and in the removal of its traces, almost felt, and almost looked, like accomplices in a horrible crime.'[38]

Manette relapses once more, during the anxieties of the imminent execution of his son-in-law. The passage about his tearing his hair and beating his feet upon the ground 'like a distracted child', when he cannot find his bench and tools now, was quoted in an earlier chapter.[39] When the family escape from Paris, he is still a 'helpless, inarticulately murmuring, wandering old man', and here the story ends — though Sydney Carton's vision of the future includes a picture of him 'aged and bent, but otherwise restored'. Whether this recovery is the result of another exercise in therapy by Mr Lorry, or merely of the passage of time, Dickens does not stop to say.[40]

'They do not know what it is that they are doing,' Dickens had said of the Philadelphia prison-authorities. On the basis of his observations and intuitions, he had tried to gauge the effects of a sentence under this system: a 'terrible endurance . . . which none but the sufferers themselves can fathom, and which no man has a right to inflict upon his fellow-creature'.[41] As we saw, his protest against the cruelty he alleged took the form of a dramatisation of the issue, by those pictures of the prisoners he saw, and by his imagining the feelings of a prisoner immured in the 'stone coffin' of a separate cell. In *A Tale of Two Cities* he again dramatises separate confinement, but retrospectively: Manette has been released from the Bastille before the novel begins. It is a powerful, and a plausible, rendering of the permanent damage to the personality which such an experience may inflict.

He had dealt with this topic also in the novel which preceded *A Tale of Two Cities* by two years, *Little Dorrit*. The Marshalsea had of course been a much less severe prison than the Bastille, and the 'prison taint' which Mr Dorrit and his children carry away with them is a subtler corruption than the brooding terror which afflicts Dr Manette, though the more dramatic effects of the *Tale* were anticipated in the wonderful scene when Mr Dorrit, sitting at the head of the High-Society dinner table in Rome, suddenly and disastrously relapses into his former position of honour as the Father of the Marshalsea. At that embarrassing moment, his daughter Amy — like Lucie, the 'golden thread' in her father's life, though little loved or regarded — remains unashamed of him. She had never been censorious of the selfishness, self-pity, snobbery, and greed which had long characterised his outlook and actions.[42] For, as she realises (using Dickens's metaphor for Philadelphia and the Bastille), he had spent twenty-three years in a 'living grave'. In 'a burst of sorrow and compassion' after the most humiliating of his self-exposures in the Marshalsea, she had said, with truth, 'No, no, I have never seen him in my life!' — for she had been born in the prison and had never known him before the 'gaol-rot' had 'worn into the grain of his soul'. In his maudlin self-pity, he had 'revealed his degenerate state to his affectionate child. No one else ever beheld him in the details of his humiliation'. They talk together:

'My love, you have had a life of hardship here. No companions, no recreations, many cares, I am afraid?'
'Don't think of that, dear. I never do.'
'You know my position, Amy. I have not been able to do much for you; but all I have been able to do, I have done.'
'Yes, my dear father,' she rejoined, kissing him. 'I know, I know.'
'I am in the twenty-third year of my life here,' he said, with a catch in his breath that was not so much a sob as an irrepressible sound of self approval, the momentary outburst of a noble consciousness. 'It is all I could do for my children — I have done it. Amy, my love, you are by far the best loved of the three; I have had you principally in my mind — whatever I have done for your sake, my dear child, I have done freely and without murmuring.'
Only the wisdom that holds the clue to all hearts and all mysteries, can surely know to what extent a man, especially a man brought down as this man had been, can impose upon himself. Enough, for the present place, that he lay down with wet eyelashes, serene, in a manner majestic, after bestowing his life of degradation as a sort of portion on the devoted child upon whom its miseries had fallen so heavily, and whose love alone had saved him to be even what he was.[43]

It is a blend of compassion and clear judgment which Dickens rarely achieves elsewhere. Mr Dorrit is one of his most remarkable achievements, and the more remarkable because Dickens himself is so obviously involved — for what he says of Little Dorrit is of course true of himself, haunted by memories of the King's Bench Prison: '. . . with a remembrance of her father's old life in prison hanging about her like the burden of a sorrowful tune.'[44]

These imaginative achievements embody a wiser and more tolerant penology than is often present in Dickens's journalistic writings on the subject. There, he might demand the perpetual imprisonment of felons, without stopping to consider the individual or the social effects of this simple policy. When his imaginative sympathy was engaged, he knew these well enough. But in *Little Dorrit* and *A Tale of Two Cities* he is of course dealing with victims of the law who do not strain his charity by being guilty of those major crimes against the person and against property which tend to arouse indignation, disgust, and the desire for revenge. Dorrit is imprisoned for debt, under laws which, as Dickens's contemporaries agreed, were unjust and impolitic (they were finally repealed in the 1860s). Manette is a good man, the innocent victim of an oppressive regime which has political reasons for wanting him out of the way. Very few prisoners serving long sentences are so little culpable, and so obviously deserving our pity. Pentonville, built to receive convicts with sentences of not less than fifteen years, raises the more normal problems of crime and punishment, and we must now see how Dickens's comments on this prison in 1850 — mid-way between *American Notes* and *A Tale of Two Cities* — are related to his repudiation of the modern American and the *ancien régime* French versions of solitary confinement.

VI

THE PENTONVILLE EXPERIMENT

JUST about a year after Pentonville opened, one of its prisoners died and an inquest was held. The Coroner, the redoubtable Thomas Wakley, remarked that 'Out of doors there is a strong feeling against this place, and some persons can hardly find terms vehement enough to use in speaking of it', so he insisted on a very full investigation. He called, among other witnesses, the Reverend Whitworth Russell (an Inspector of Prisons, and Commissioner of Pentonville), who 'explained the regulations of the prison, some of which were rather startling, and elicited a good deal of observation from the Coroner'. But he concluded his evidence: 'Whatever the public may now think of this prison, I am much more afraid that by and by they will say that the inmates are too well treated, rather than not well enough.'[1] It was a shrewd prophecy, and Dickens proved to be one of the spokesmen of changing public opinion on this issue — and not just a spokesman, for according to several well-informed contemporaries it was he more than anyone else who brought about this change in public opinion.

Dickens was always an opponent of the Separate System, but under this term were comprised several very different disciplinary schemes. American penologists of that period, like American literary critics today, tended to go to extremes, and to favour a system in its 'pure' state; the British, by comparison, displayed, and display, their traditional proclivity for compromise (or muddling through). Some American States had, indeed, experimented with a much 'purer' system of separation than Pennsylvania — cells that were not only separate, but unlit and even underground, and from which even the chaplains were excluded. How effective this system would have been as an encouragement to penitence and reformation was never discovered, since so many prisoners died, went mad, or collapsed before the allotted spell was served, that the experiments had to be called off. As an eighteenth-century English penal reformer had said, 'Criminals have always been judged a fair subject of hazardous experiments, to which it would be unjust to expose the more valuable members of the State.'[2]

In Great Britain, the severity and the daily routine of the Separate System varied a good deal from prison to prison; there were, as Walter Clay pointed out, at least five common patterns, the most important of which were those operating at Pentonville, Reading, and Preston. People who set up as opponents of the Separate System should, said Clay, make clear to themselves and to their readers just which version or versions they were attacking. Clay's father, the Chaplain at Preston, thought Dickens had not sufficiently noted the differences between these variants of the system. Dickens had, apparently, been in correspondence with him, and Clay replied, urging him to visit Preston, for it might cause him to modify his wholesale opposition to the Separate System —

> I am very anxious to induce you to think as favourably as you honestly can of the *Preston* system, which differs in many important points from the 'separate system' as it *did* exist at Pentonville, and *does* yet, I believe, at Reading. . . . It is rather singular that poor Mr Russell, the late inspector of Pentonville and chief originator of the separate system, used your expression in writing to me seven years ago, when he found that his views and mine on separate confinement 'differed', so as to exclude all hope of agreement. In his view I opposed the separate system, in yours I am thought its advocate. . . .[3]

A year after this letter, Dickens visited Preston to get 'local colour' for *Hard Times*, but I do not know whether he visited the prison. Probably not: Clay's biography does not mention any such visit (as surely it would have done, if the great novelist had gratified the old chaplain by accepting his invitation). There is only Clay's sad comment in a letter a few months later: 'I see that Mr Dickens, in *Hard Times*, has a laugh at my "tabular statements", and at my credulity. He is not the only man I have met with who prefers to rely on his own theories and fancies rather than on well-ascertained facts.' (Whether Dickens was indeed laughing at Clay is uncertain; the 'Coketown' of *Hard Times* was based upon Preston, but was by no means a representation of that town and its personalities; but Clay certainly was famous for his statistical tables, many of which were influential nationally as well as locally.)[4] Perhaps, after these warnings from Clay and his son, we should summarise the 'well-ascertained facts' about Pentonville, the English Separate-System prison which did attract Dickens's explicit interest, before we see what 'theories and fancies' of his own entered into his description of it.

Separate confinement had been tried out locally in a few English prisons around 1800, but their example had been less influential at home than in America, whence the idea returned in much greater strength in the mid-1830s. Impressed by the advocacy of its official delegate to America, and of the Prison Inspectors, the Government rejected a House of Lords Committee's recommendation of the Silent System, and took what the Webbs described as 'perhaps the most momentous official decision in English prison history' — the decision in favour of the Separate System.[5] Lord John Russell (Home Secretary 1835-9) wrote to local magistrates, drawing their attention to the Inspectors' condemnation of the Silent System ('the plan which has of late years been most generally adopted'), and urging them to adopt the Separate System in any prisons built in the future and, as far as was practicable, in all existing prisons.[6] In 1839, again on the Inspectors' advice, Russell got a Bill through Parliament, empowering the Government to build and administer a Model Prison on this plan, and later that year the construction of Pentonville began. By the time it opened, in December 1842, Russell was out of office, but his successors as Home Secretary, Sir James Graham and Sir George Grey, continued his policy. In Britain, as in most of Europe, the Separate System had triumphed.

Pentonville was a relatively small-scale experiment, on a system different in many respects from that obtaining at Philadelphia. The prison contained about five hundred separate cells (Coldbath Fields took nearly three times as many prisoners), though later many additions were made. Its strongly-built blocks and cells are, alas, still standing and in full use. The original inmates were picked men — convicts with sentences of not less than fifteen years, and aged between eighteen and thirty five, who were certified physically strong enough to endure the rigours of separate confinement and who seemed likely to respond to the prison's reformatory programme. Most of them were therefore first offenders. Pentonville was meant to be what Parkhurst was for juvenile offenders — a prison, not of oppressive punishment, but of instruction and probation. As Sir James Graham explained in his famous letter to the Pentonville Commissioners, just before the great experiment began, only convicts sentenced to transportation would be eligible for this prison; thus, they would realise that their future lives lay overseas, and that, from the day they entered Pentonville, they were beginning a new career. Their imprisonment would be 'a period of probation', lasting not more than eighteenth months. They would be taught trades which would earn them a good livelihood in Van Diemen's Land, and would also receive moral and religious instruction to guide their future lives. After eighteen months, the men would go to Australia, and those who had behaved well would be given an immediate ticket-of-leave (which was equivalent to freedom); those who had done badly would be transported to less eligible convict-stations, and under stricter terms. Eighteen months of the Pentonville discipline should be sufficient, said Graham: 'In that time the real character will be developed, instruction will be imparted, new habits will be formed, a better frame of mind will have been moulded, or else the heart will have hardened, and the case be desperate.'[7]

It was, in intention, a benevolent and optimistic scheme — not dissimilar in its aim, though using different means, from Dickens's own plan for Urania Cottage. Colonisation was, of course, one of the century's great panaceas for 'over-population', poverty and crime; it was Acton's great remedy for prostitution, too — 'For the sufferings of labour, for the immorality of the community, my nostrum is, marry and colonize — colonize — colonize.'[8] The relatively mild form of Transportation proposed for the more successful graduates from Pentonville was one example of this belief in the efficacy of a 'new start' in the virgin lands.

Pentonville differed from Philadelphia, then, in that prisoners did not serve the whole of their long sentences there — only eighteen months in 'a kind of penal purgatory' (as Mayhew put it) 'where men are submitted to the chastisement of separate confinement, so as to fit them for the after state'.[9] But the system was soon further modified. Almost all the colonies refused to take further convicts, whether or not they had been purified by Pentonville, so, after 1852, the men had to proceed to English Convict Prisons such as Portland and Dartmoor after their initial spell of separate confinement. Moreover in 1848–9 important changes had been made in the entrance-qualifications and length of sentence. The prison was no longer reserved for convicts selected for their high moral potentialities, and the basic eighteen months' period was reduced to fifteen and then to twelve. The actual period served in Pentonville was often, indeed, reduced by a further two or three months, because so many convicts were waiting to get in, and, even so, part of the period was spent in gardening or other working parties 'in association'. One of the reasons for these changes was the inevitable re-organisation of the English penal system, as Transportation ceased to exist; another was the sudden death in 1847 of the two most powerful and extreme of the Pentonville Commissioners, Whitworth Russell and Crawford. Their departure made it possible for Jebb, the prison's builder and one of its leading figures, and for Joseph Kingsmill, its chaplain, to mitigate the length and severity of the period served there, as they had long wanted to do. The most important reason, however, was the disquieting evidence that the original scheme was leading to a good deal of mental and physical illness. The depressing influence of such complete separation 'took all the starch out of the prisoners' characters, and rendered both their wits and their wills limp and flabby', as one contemporary said.[10] The Commissioners were reluctant to admit this, and were still claiming in 1847 that the moral training had been 'attended with *a success which we believe is without parallel in the history of prison discipline*'.[11] There was much argument, and obfuscation, about both the moral and the physical results of the system, and about the effects of the changes made from 1848 onwards.

The staff were not unanimous in their verdict. Kingsmill, the senior chaplain, agreed that the original sentences were too long for safety, but his assistant, the Reverend John Burt, looked back on the early days of Pentonville as its Golden Age, remarkable for its moral and spiritual achievements, and he defended everything in the early scheme, from its generous dietary and its bill of health to the 'conversation and demeanour' of its earliest inmates. During the last few years, Burt complained in 1852,

> The rigour of the system has been relaxed; the term of the imprisonment has been reduced; the prospects of the prisoners upon removal have greatly deteriorated; and these and other changes have incidentally, but inevitably, resulted in a decrease of moral instruction. Thus the integrity of the system has in reality been surrendered; a mixed system has superseded it. . . . Those indications by which the visitor was formerly convinced of powerful moral influence, as he passed from cell to cell, are no longer met with to the same extent. . . . Time will not soon efface from my memory the susceptibility to moral influence which characterised a very large proportion of [the original eighteen-monthers]. . . . It was always as the original term of imprisonment ran on, and with the more depraved, *chiefly towards its close*, that . . . they one by one yielded to the correction of the place.[12]

Soon after this, however, the maximum period of separate confinement, at Pentonville or elsewhere, was still further reduced, from twelve to nine months, the figure which remained constant till the end of the century. This reduction was the result, not of further pressure on accommodation, but of further medical evidence that nine months was the limit of safety. Experience, not only at Pentonville but at similar prisons all over the world, showed that the incidence of mental illness was up to ten times as great under the Separate, as under any other penal system. The earlier batches of prisoners leaving Pentonville for Australia had been (said the ship's surgeon) 'slow in comprehending orders, and equally slow in obeying them, though evidently tractable and willing; in fact, they had lost their gregarious habits, and did not again acquire them until after some weeks'; those who had been longest in separation seemed 'less robust', or 'positively delicate', and they articulated their speech less correctly.[13] As an immediate measure, brisker and longer exercise-periods were introduced, but it is clear that the Pentonville regime in the mid-forties was lowering to the constitution and cruel in its effects, and that even after the reforms of 1848–9 it was terribly severe — though, as at Philadelphia, the authorities were idealists, men of the highest integrity, earnestly seeking a humane and effective way of reclaiming their charges to virtue. Their blindness to the consequences of their system-ridden policy is sad to contemplate: 'the brutality of good intentions,' as Henry James has it.

The daily routine did not alter much, during these changes of policy. The men did not spend all their time in their cells, as at Philadelphia. Every day they attended Divine Service, and on two full days a week they returned to Chapel for lessons. In the corridors and on other occasions when they could see one another, they had to pull down the peaks of their caps, which formed a mask over their faces; they walked at ten-yard intervals, and were thus, in theory, never able either to communicate with or to recognise one another. (The masks were abolished in 1853, for the good reason that the men did see one another both before and after their spell in Pentonville, and that the masks had never prevented their recognising one another, anyhow. And, of course, prisoners did communicate with their neighbours, through the invaluable water-pipes and ventilation-shafts.) In Chapel the men doffed their masks, for they could not then see one another; they sat in little individual boxes, like pigeon-holes, ranged in tiers in a way oddly combining 'the chief architectural features of a theatre and a menagerie'.[14] Back in their cells, the men worked mainly at the traditional prison-trades of cobbling and tailoring; they had individual tuition from the school-masters and trade-instructors, and regular visits from the devoted chaplains. There they worked, ate and slept. Every cell contained a water-closet, wash-basin, hammock, and a bell with which to summon a warder in emergency. The food, it was generally agreed, was ample and good, and a special heating system kept the prison pleasantly warm. On the whole, the prisoners were docile, and committed few offences; Adshead was able to point out that punishments there ran at a yearly average of 11·48 per cent per prisoner, compared with 161·92 per cent at Coldbath Fields.

On this point, the opponents of Pentonville had an obvious reply, and Dickens made it in his first published remark on the prison: 'You are spending I am afraid to say how much every year out of the rates, to keep men in solitude, where they *can't* do any harm (that you know of) and then you sing all sort of choruses about their being good.'[15] This was published in the second issue of *Household Words*, on 6 April 1850. Three weeks later, Dickens published his full scale attack on Pentonville and its influence on other British prisons — the article from which I have quoted in earlier chapters, 'Pet Prisoners.' As in the *American Notes* attack on Philadelphia, Dickens tries hard to be less pugnacious than his antagonists on this blood-heating question. 'A little calm considera-tion and reflection' was necessary, he said, and he would state his objections 'temperately, and without considering it necessary to regard everyone with whom we differ, as a scoundrel, actuated by base motives.'[16] He does, however, manage to make one of them look a fool: but a great fool that man already was, as we shall see.

Dickens still objects to the 'extreme severity' of the Philadelphia version of the system, but he accepts the official assurances that the Pentonville version, though admittedly dangerous if protracted for eighteen months, no longer produces any ill effects, now that twelve months is the maximum. 'We are content to regard the system as dissociated in England from the American objection of too great severity,' he concludes after no further discussion, thus begging one of the major questions involved. He proceeds to enlarge on one of his favourite themes in prison-affairs — the disparity between the Pentonville prisoners' conditions and those of the poor man in the work-house or in his wretched cottage; the dangers of this type of argument have already been discussed. Here Dickens adopts a further tactic, which is journalistically effective though weak in its argument. The annual cost per head in Pentonville in 1848 was thirty-six pounds: compare this, he says, not only with the twelve shillings a week on which many rural labourers have to keep their families, but with the board-residence offered in the *Times* advertisements for middle-class lodgers. The argument ignores the obvious fact that middle-class lodgers do not require the intensive supervision, the lockers-up, the high walls, and the many other expensive and artificial arrangements necessary to ensure discipline and security in a prison. His last financial argument is the contrast between the huge costs of building and maintaining Pentonville, and the insignificant sums spent on education, emigration, and other such worthy social needs. Certainly Governments had been spending generously on this penal experiment, from which they hoped so much, and were niggardly in their grants towards these other important activities, but Dickens should have known that no Government, urged or forced to decrease expenditure in one department, devotes the money saved to some other and better purpose. The remedy was, not to cut the meals or the educational facilities at Pentonville, but to improve the other social institutions by increasing taxation.

It was not only or mainly on these financial grounds, however, that Dickens criticised the Pentonville idea. The money was spent, he thought, not only unjustly but also ineffectively. He rightly noted that all the precautions of masks and strict cellular custody did not prevent prisoners from talking with and identifying one another: but his more important allegation against the system is 'the condition of mind produced by the seclusion'. He has dismissed, from the start, the contention that a mere twelve months' seclusion could be cruel or harmful; his objection is, instead, that

The state of mind into which a man is brought who is the lonely inhabitant of his own small world, and who is only visited by certain regular visitors, all addressing themselves to him individually and personally, as the object of their particular solicitude — we believe in most cases to have very little promise in it, and very little of solid foundation. A strange absorbing selfishness — a spiritual egotism and vanity, real or assumed — is the first result. It is most remarkable to observe, in the cases of murderers who become this kind of object of interest, when they are at last consigned to the condemned cell, how the rule is (of course there are exceptions), that the murdered person disappears from the stage of their thoughts, except as a part of their own important story; and how they occupy the whole scene. *I* did this, *I* feel that, *I* confide in the mercy of Heaven being extended to *me*; this is the autograph of *me*, the unfortunate and unhappy; in my childhood I was so and so; in my youth I did such a thing, to which I attribute my downfall — not this thing of basely and barbarously defacing the image of my Creator, and sending an immortal soul into eternity without a moment's warning, but something else of a venial kind that many unpunished people do.

Here, no doubt, Dickens makes a shrewd point, though his argument relies too heavily on the very special case of a murderer awaiting execution. In cases where the dread of death is not present, he continues, there is instead 'every possible inducement, either to feign contrition, or to set up an unreliable semblance of it'.

Here again Dickens was on strong ground. He quotes, not unfairly, from a book entitled *Prison Discipline: the Advantages of the Separate System of Imprisonment, as established in the New County Gaol of Reading*. Its author was the prison's Chaplain, the Reverend John Field — evidently an enthusiastic but credulous man. For instance Field had reprinted this letter (which Dickens quotes as a sample of 'pattern penitence'), saying that it was inserted as 'a specimen of many rather than because superior to most'. A twenty-year-old felon writes home:

'Don't fret, my dear sister, about my being here. I cannot help fretting when I think about my usage to my father and mother: when I think about it, it makes me quite ill. I hope God will forgive me; I pray for it night and day from my heart. Instead of fretting about imprisonment, I ought to thank God for it, for before I came here, I was living quite a careless life; neither was God in all my thoughts; all I thought about was ways that led me towards destruction. Give my respects to my wretched companions, and I hope they will alter their wicked course, for they don't know for a day nor an hour but what they may be cut off. I have seen my folly, and I hope they may see their folly; but I shouldn't if I had not been in trouble. It is good for me that I have been in trouble. Go to church, my sister, every Sunday, and don't give your mind to going to playhouses and theatres, for that is no good to you. There are a great many temptations.'[17]

It is not only Dickens who would feel inclined to dismiss this as nauseous humbug, unless a good deal more objective evidence was forthcoming than Field provides. Field's book is pervaded by what some might call *sancta simplicitas* and others sanctimonious idiocy. This is how Field describes the lasting benefits of separate imprisonment with a Bible at hand:

> Seclusion, under such circumstances, renders society more inviting, whilst its corrective tendency prepares the subject of it for the increased pleasure which more virtuous companionship shall afford. . . . The advantages of his seclusion will be thankfully borne in mind [after his release], and occasional secrecy therefore chosen; but converse will have increased charms; the deprivation will have made it a privilege; company therefore, but that of a better character than before, will be sought, and will prove a source of more profitable enjoyment.

Solitude, far from leading to evil thoughts, will provide 'opportunities, which few can possess' for the reception of Grace, since the Bible is about the only resource available in the cell: 'Hours which would have been otherwise wearisome are spent in its perusal, and whilst it prevents despondency it proves attractive. The truth being thus received in the love thereof regulates the life, and the sinner becomes wise unto salvation.' Similarly, Divine Service relieves the monotony of the cell, and thus acquires pleasurable associations.[18] Field, one should add, did not command universal respect, even among adherents to the Separate System, but he was not simply ignored, as he deserved to be, as a dangerously naïve eccentric; his book had gone into a second edition within two years.

Dickens had, then, some justification for his complaint that the Separate System embodied some hopes and practices of very dubious wisdom. His other quotations from Field are equally ludicrous, and quite fairly chosen. Another prisoner writes about his past 'follies' and his desire to reform his mother, and Dickens reasonably asks:

> Does this overweening readiness to lecture other people, suggest the suspicion of any parrot-like imitation of Mr Field, who lectures him, and any presumptuous confounding of their relative positions? We venture altogether to protest against the citation, in support of this system, of assumed repentance which has stood no test or trial in the working world. We consider that it proves nothing, and is worth nothing, except as a discouraging sign of that spiritual egotism and presumption of which we have already spoken. It is not peculiar to the separate system at Reading. . . .

— and he cites further evidence from Harriet Martineau about Philadelphia, and from 'the calm and intelligent report' by Kingsmill, the Pentonville chaplain.

Kingsmill was a much more sensible man than Field, though he seems to have indulged unwisely in an emotional brand of religiosity. He describes the effects of his address to a new intake of convicts: 'As is usually the case, the tear stood in many an eye. . . . I did not touch, however, on domestic ties. Enough feeling had been excited.' And his diary presents a touching mixture of naïvety and honest puzzlement: he tours the prison one evening, for instance, and finds most of the men (as usual) reading the Bible. Among those who ask him questions about it is a prisoner, once 'the greatest of blackguards', but now a communicant — 'His full acknowledgement of sin is one of the hopeful signs of conversion. It is singular, however, that criminals professing repentance towards God are less moved and less humbled than those whom one sees among less guilty persons.'[19] Kingsmill was surely right to be troubled and doubtful; but his assistant, Burt, was untouched by any such scepticism about the religious or the organisational principles of the system. Burt praises the Pentonville classes, as 'pre-eminently calculated to reform, being occupied both with lessons of worldly prudence, and with the saving doctrines of revelation', and he asserts that they cultivate 'a habit of reflection', which (he charmingly adds) 'is, of course, powerfully stimulated by the return of the prisoner to his cell.'[20]

The role of prison chaplain was, as I briefly remarked in the last chapter, a very controversial item in the prison-discipline debate, partly, though not wholly, because many of the books and pamphlets on prison questions were written by the Chaplains, who were no doubt handier with a pen than the Governors or other interested parties. The activities of some of these Chaplains would have excited controversy, to say the least, at any period. Especially in Separate System prisons, they enjoyed great power: there had even been a remarkable experiment at Millbank in the 1830s, when the Reverend Daniel Nihil united the offices of Governor and Chaplain — an application of the Platonic idea of uniting the King and the Philosopher, which had foreseeably disastrous results. The prison discipline broke down; Nihil was credulous about the pious professions of the more astute convicts (many, he said, 'evinced a softened and subdued tone of feeling, and thanked God they had been brought to the Penitentiary'); when it appeared that the prisoners' health was deteriorating under the strict separation which he considered essential for their moral and spiritual reform, he refused to alter his rules. 'Health is certainly a great consideration,' he agreed, 'but are morals less? Ought health to be sought by the rash demolition of an important moral fence?' The number of deaths under this regime, in a prison which was already notoriously unhealthy because of its site and construction, made the Millbank of this period 'a capital substitute for capital punishments', as *Punch* put it.[21]

Dickens never wavered in his suspicions against prison-chaplains, and often returned to the attack. Ten years after 'Pet Prisoners', he wrote to an *All the Year Round* contributor, enclosing a pamphlet for review. In the main, he said, it 'expresses the views I have often urged respecting Prison Discipline, . . . sensibly shews what evil is done by injudicious Gaol-Chaplains, and points out in what glaring respects their set ways of carrying on are wrong'.[22] The hostility was reciprocated. Dickens was attacked in several books by prison-chaplains, and Mayhew found *Household Words* conspicuously absent from the reading-matter provided for the convicts in the Woolwich Hulks. 'The chaplain objects to it being in the library,' he was told.[23]

Prison-chaplains, of course, varied, and it was not always they who were responsible for the religious excesses in prisons. It was, for instance, the magistrates in one prison who had the brainwave of locking prisoners in their cells with nothing but a Bible — and it was the chaplain who remonstrated, urging that at least the Bibles should have marginalia: whereupon the magistrates replied, superbly, 'No, let them puzzle out the meaning for themselves.'[24] Among the more famous chaplains, whom we have mentioned, Field was much the most foolish, with Burt a good second. Kingsmill's humanity was combined with some good sense, while Clay of Preston — described by the recent historian of *Religion in Prison* as 'almost . . . the patron saint of prison chaplains' — possessed all the virtues: piety, zeal, diligence, acuteness, flexibility, a sound but not cynical worldly wisdom, and a respect for facts whether statistically presented or not.[25] Dickens was by no means alone, nor was he unjustified, in his doubts about most prison-chaplains. 'A felonious hypocrite with his tongue in his cheek, gulling a rose-water chaplain, was long accepted by the British public as the symbol of religion in Gaols,' writes Clay's son; '. . . grave judges, able editors, popular novelists, and even "our philosopher Mr Punch", had endorsed the opinion.' (As Clay keeps referring to *Punch*, perhaps one example of its prison wit at this period should be quoted. A few months after Dickens's 'Pet Prisoners' it had the following joke about a recent escape. 'The Model Prison at Pentonville is so comfortable a place that some people may wonder what induced Hackett to run away from it. It has been surmised that he did so because he was disgusted by the humbug.')[26] Opposing *Punch* and its allies, Clay continued, 'there were only a few simple-minded chaplains, some enthusiastic Christians, and the Bible.' The chaplains had, he said, in comparison with their colleagues in prison-administration, received 'almost a monopoly of abuse and ridicule', but they had in fact been 'by far the most open-eyed and common-sensible'.[27]

The chaplains' position was indeed a difficult one, and Dickens was too much given to seeing issues in simplified black-and-white terms to be able to appreciate the complexities of their situation and the mixture of good and bad in their activities. He sees only the case against them. He was certainly right in thinking that the Separate System, in Pentonville and many other prisons, almost incited its subjects to religious humbug, and that few chaplains entirely resisted the temptation to exaggerate the efficacy of their devoted work. Their Annual Reports, one critic said with justice, 'in too many cases are full of descriptions of prisoners "deeply affected", . . . with accounts of their own indefatigable efforts, disclosing, through a thin veil, a placid self-satisfaction.'[28] In the prison-hierarchy, the chaplain stood only second to the governor; a good deal, therefore, depended on his reports on a prisoner — his privileges, the length and severity of his separate confinement, the 'Class' in which he was discharged to the colonies or to the 'associated' convict-prisons. As Dickens and others complained, the Separate System offered few temptations to prisoners. There were not many misdeeds they could commit in their separate cells, so one of the few ways in which they could make good a claim to be 'reformed characters' was by making pious professions to the chaplain. Naturally many prisoners tried this on. Moreover, the chaplains' marked preference for the Separate System was sometimes based on a very questionable view of their religious duties and opportunities. They enjoyed a very captive congregation; as Kingsmill put it, separation was 'of no small value . . . as an auxiliary to the great remedial means appointed by God'. One of his opponents — the writer of the pamphlet which Dickens commended to his colleague — retorted: 'Might not the rack and thumb-screws equally be found useful "auxiliaries" of "conversion"?' What Kingsmill called the 'subdued and softened state of mind' of his charges was merely, wrote this critic, what the Medical Superintendent at Millbank had diagnosed as the mental condition 'approaching to decided imbecility' which was the inevitable result of this unnatural life.[29] There was a good deal of pious self-deception in chaplains, and much deliberate deception was attempted upon them by their charges. The warders at Pentonville assured Mayhew 'that the prisoners know the very footsteps of the chaplain, and that many of them fall down on their knees as they hear him coming, so that he may find them engaged in prayer on visiting their cells; whereas, immediately he has left, they put their tongue in their cheek, and laugh at his gullibility'.[30] Even the most modest and alert chaplains must have found it difficult to distinguish between the false and the true, and their *amour-propre* as well as their faith in the efficacy of Grace would naturally incline them to believe rather than otherwise. God knows (literally speaking) how often they were mistaken.

That they were often unwise and naïve was Dickens's judgment, and I suspect that he was right. The tone of many of their writings inspires little confidence in their knowledge of human nature; and the task they were set, or had set themselves, was a difficult if not an impossible one. In Philadelphia, the chaplains had believed that crime 'could be cured through religious conversion, and all their activities were centred on personal salvation'.[31] Many chaplains of prisons on this plan believed that *only* through religious conversion could this end be accomplished; it was a perilous all-or-nothing policy, with very intractable material, and it led to such fantastic nonsense as Field's work at Reading. Field clearly believed he was advancing the cause of religion and virtue when he judged his prisoners' advance towards salvation by the number of Bible-texts they could repeat, and he presents for the reader's admiration such exercises as this — a 'good' prisoner's written answer to the question, 'Give reasons why we should speak the truth?': '1. Because it is the express command of God. Ex. xx. 16, xxiii. 1; Lev. xix. 11; Numb. xxx. 2; Deut. v. 20; Matt. xix. 18; Rom. xiii. 19; Eph. iv. 25.' and so on, with four more 'reasons' supported by a similar number of Biblical references.[32] It was small wonder that the chaplains aroused widespread derision and hostility.

The most sensible and dignified reply to the sneers against them all for trying to plough this hard furrow came, as one would expect, from Clay of Preston. He wrote to Dickens: '. . . our, and especially my, efforts are directed to the humanizing, civilizing, Christianizing of the wretched or misguided persons that come under our care. . . . As a minister of religion, I cannot be expected to support any other view.'³³ Clay was often saddened by the reactions of educated church-going people when religion for criminals was mentioned: they would 'retail vapid jests and put their whole trust in *Punch* instead of the Bible'. Their lack of faith showed, he said, the flimsiness of English Christianity. He often found himself ridiculed for being over-sanguine and credulous, but he would reply that he had no business to be a chaplain unless he was sanguine. How, he asked, would his critics behave, if they were chaplains? — 'It would be barren work, I think, going from cell to cell to let the prisoners know how 'cute and wide awake you were yourself, and what hypocritical scoundrels you thought them. It is hard enough, I can tell you, working in such a place, hoping against hope; and our gratitude, therefore, is not very profound to the kind monitors who think us a pack of fools for our pains.'³⁴ Clay was more aware than some of his brethren, too, that religious exhortation and witness could not accomplish everything; he also investigated the social roots of crime, and laboured to obtain honest jobs for his men on their discharge.

The chaplains, indeed, with all their faults, provided much of the moral leaven to the prisons. Most of them at least represented some sort of hopefulness for the sinner, as a corrective to the policy of deterrence and repressiveness. Prison governors were mostly, like Chesterton and Tracey, former officers of the armed services — upright, efficient, good organisers and disciplinarians, but not often imbued with Christian charity, or psychological understanding, or a readiness or ability to examine and try out new ideas. The chaplains were, by comparison, men of education; by profession, they stood for moral instead of physical influences, so they could exert their considerable powers in favour of the new penological ideas which, despite their huge errors, were an improvement on what had gone before. Chaplains still retain much more power in prisons than clergymen do in the world outside, though they have now been joined by a host of specialists, psychological and technical and medical, who have greatly reduced their importance and responsibilities. This development is one

instance of the evolution which Dr Grünhut sees in prison-reform
and prison-discipline — from the religious and humanitarian
approach to the scientific — and what he says of the Separate
System may, perhaps, be applied also to the excessive prestige and
very mixed performance of the prison chaplains. 'From an historical point of view,' he writes, 'solitary confinement was a necessary
step on the way to progress. Under the exciting influence of a
forceful idea the chaotic state of the old gaols was definitely
removed. After the disastrous wavering between collusive negli-
gence and brutal arbitrariness, the new order introduced a
wholesome atmosphere of earnestness and dignity into prisons.'[35]

The attitudes expressed in 'Pet Prisoners' recurred in many other
articles in *Household Words* and its successor. A few weeks later,
Dickens's right-hand man, W. H. Wills, was duly echoing his
master's voice in an article on 'The Great Penal Experiments',
which contrasted the feather-bed conditions at Pentonville,
against which Dickens had already protested, with the terrible
rigours of Millbank, the squalor of the Hulks, and the shocking
chaos of such London prisons as Giltspur Street Compter. Wills
ended his article on a typical *Household Words* note — the great
experiment *never* tried, though 'immeasurably safer, more humane,
and incalculably cheaper . . . is NATIONAL EDUCATION'.[36] What
happened to contributors who did not toe the line which Dickens
had drawn, appeared in his handling of Morley's article on
Frederic Hill's book, described in a previous chapter. It was
therefore presumably with Dickens's concurrence that Wills had
praised Carlyle's 'Model Prisons', which had appeared on 1
March 1850 — that is, about three or four weeks before Dickens
wrote 'Pet Prisoners'. Dickens never, to my knowledge, mentions
Carlyle's essay, but contemporary readers did not doubt that it
had influenced him.

'Pet Prisoners', appearing anonymously, seems not to have
caused much stir, but seven months later Dickens returned to the
attack, dramatising the issues in the final number of *David
Copperfield*, which was (of course) published under his own name.
This certainly caught the public eye, and reviewers assumed that
Carlyle lay behind Chapter LXI, 'I am shown Two Interesting
Penitents.' The reviewer in *Fraser's Magazine* reprinted two
passages, from Carlyle and Dickens respectively, side by side. The
collocation showed, he said, that Dickens 'follows as junior on

the same side', and that both arrive at 'an entire condemnation of the whole system'. He adds: 'When from points of view so widely different two independent observers have come to the same conclusion, we have the strongest presumption that the said conclusion is right.'[37] One could wish that Dickens's point of view had been as widely different from Carlyle's as this reviewer asserted; in fact, Dickens had long admired Carlyle more than any other contemporary 'thinker', and did not part company with him over *Latter Day Pamphlets*, as did so many of his thoughtful and decent contemporaries.[38]

The relation between Dickens, Carlyle, and the movement of penal reaction is admirably plotted by the invaluable Walter Clay.

> The controversy about prison-discipline, which revived in 1847, increased the next year, grew vigorous in 1849, and culminated in 1850. By degrees, almost the whole press, which had been generally favourable to the plan of separation in 1847, veered round into brisk hostility. Early in 1849 the *Times* began to fulminate; presently the *Daily News*, with other newspapers, took part (though with mitigated vehemence) in the attack. And of course their 'facetious contemporary', follow-my-leader *Punch*, immediately flung his squibs at the unpopular system. But the journalists had no monopoly of the wrangle. The din stirred up a multitudinous flock of pamphlets. . . . In the spring [of 1850] Carlyle flung 'Model Prisons' at the belaboured system; and in autumn Dickens, in the final number of *David Copperfield*, gave it the unkindest cut of all. . . . The rattling fun of the caricature told powerfully on the British public, which always believes without any question in the ridiculous absurdity of everything that is cleverly quizzed. The able editors and the literary magnates failed to upset the separate system, but their efforts produced some effect. A partial reaction against reformatory discipline set in. . . .[39]

The *David Copperfield* chapter had, of course, the practical advantage of being part of a genial comic novel: it was, perhaps, all the more insidiously effective for that. 'Model Prisons' is only too plainly the work of a man who has lost his temper and his ability to think: it was perilous, for instance, to ask the rhetorical question, 'Does the Christian or any religion prescribe love of scoundrels, then?' — for the obvious if unwelcome answer is 'Yes'. To leave *David Copperfield* aside for a moment, and to compare like with like, Dickens's article 'Pet Prisoners' was much more reasonable and temperate than Carlyle's pamphlet. Dickens does not follow Carlyle, in invoking the Gods and 'the universe and its laws': as usual, his arguments are entirely secular. He had begun by comparing the prisoners' happy lot with the rural labourer's, and even the middle class lodger's: Carlyle completely enters the world of fantasy, by comparing it to a Duke's — 'No Duke in England is, for all rational purposes which a human being can or ought to aim at, lodged, fed, tended, taken care of, with such perfection. . . . Which Duke . . . has cocoa, soup, meat, and food in general, made ready, so fit for keeping him in health . . .? Which Duke has a House so thoroughly clean, pure and airy . . .? No Duke that I have ever known.'[40] Carlyle must have known some very indigent Dukes, afflicted with an uncommon lust for cocoa. Dickens, happily, never becomes quite as foolish as the 'thinker' he admired, nor does he here show Carlyle's nasty relish for killing prisoners (grandly described to the felon as 'sending thee back into the whole Universe, solemnly expelling thee from our community') or for managing lesser offenders by 'a collar round the neck, and a cartwhip flourished over the back'.[41]

The *David Copperfield* chapter is very funny, if confused in its penology. Dickens's anxiety to have another crack at the Pentonville system is apparent from the fact that this is the only contemporary matter in the novel, and that it is introduced quite unnecessarily.[42] Dickens has to revive a character who had left the novel over fifty chapters earlier, as a pretext — Mr Creakle, David's former schoolmaster, who now writes to him out of the blue to announce that he has become a Middlesex Magistrate and wishes to show him 'the only true system of prison discipline; the only unchallengeable way of making sincere and lasting converts and penitents — which, you know, is by solitary confinement'.[43] The tender-hearted Creakle of this chapter, absurdly solicitous about the quality of the prisoners' cocoa, milk and meat, and guilelessly confident of their reformation, has in fact only the most nominal connection with the brutal schoolmaster of earlier in the story. David Copperfield duly visits the prison, and notices what his creator had noticed in 'Pet Prisoners' — the huge and costly building, the concern for the 'supreme comfort of prisoners, at any expense', the high feeding, the superstitious reliance on 'the system', its ineffectiveness in preventing the men's talking to one another, and above all the 'pattern penitence' of the wily prisoners, who so easily hoodwink the authorities (though not the down-to-earth warders — 'who, I suspected, from certain latent indications . . . , knew pretty well what all this stir was worth'). The only comfort

David can get from this visit is that 'Perhaps it's a good thing . . . to have an unsound Hobby ridden hard; for it's the sooner ridden to death'.

The episode has at least one usefulness in the story — it enables the malefactors Uriah Heep and Mr Littimer to make a final appearance, suitably enough in gaol awaiting transportation (Uriah, at least, for Life). They get in some fine and characteristic parting shots at their old enemy, David. They are, of course, 'Model Prisoners' (as Dickens calls them, with a punning allusion to Carlyle's pamphlet); indeed, they are the pride of the magistrates. 'I heard so much of Twenty Seven,' says David of the prisoner who turns out to be Uriah, 'of his pious admonitions to everybody around him, and of the beautiful letters he constantly wrote to his mother (whom he seemed to consider in a very bad way), that I became quite impatient to see him.' Uriah is, inevitably, discovered reading a Hymn Book, and gladly accepts this chance to deliver a homily to his visitors. He is 'far more comfortable here, than ever I was outside', he explains, because now he can see his 'follies'.

'Now, Twenty Seven,' said Mr Creakle, . . . 'is there anything that any one can do for you? If so, mention it.'

'I would umbly ask, sir,' returned Uriah, with a jerk of his malevolent head, 'for leave to write again to mother. . . . I am anxious about mother. I am afraid she ain't safe. . . . Immortally safe, sir. . . . I should wish mother to be got into my state. I never should have been got into my present state if I hadn't come here. I wish mother had come here. It would be better for everybody, if they got took up, and was brought here.'

This sentiment gave unbounded satisfaction — greater satisfaction, I think, than anything that had passed yet.

'Before I come here,' said Uriah, stealing a look at us, as if he would have blighted the outer world to which we belonged, if he could, 'I was given to follies; but now I am sensible of my follies. There's a deal of sin outside. There's a deal of sin in mother. There's nothing but sin everywhere — except here.' . . .

[Mr Creakle is delighted by Uriah's assurance that he is now 'quite changed', and he invites him to address David Copperfield.]

'You knew me a long time before I came here and was changed, Mr Copperfield,' said Uriah, looking at me; and a more villainous look I never saw, even on his visage. 'You knew me when, in spite of my follies, I was umble among them that was proud, and meek among them that was violent — you was violent to me yourself, Mr Copperfield. Once, you struck me a blow in the face, you know.'

General commiseration. Several indignant glances directed at me.

'But I forgive you, Mr Copperfield,' said Uriah, making his forgiving nature the subject of a most impious and awful parallel, which I shall not record. 'I forgive everybody. It would ill become me to bear malice. I freely forgive you, and I hope you'll curb your passions in future. I hope Mr W. will repent, and Miss W., and all the sinful lot. You've been visited with affliction, and I hope it may do you good; but you'd better have come here, and Miss W. too. The best wish I could give you, Mr Copperfield, and give all of you gentlemen, is, that you could be took up and brought here. When I think of my past follies, and my present state, I am sure it would be best for you. I pity all who ain't brought here!'

He sneaked back into his cell, amidst a little chorus of approbation; and both Traddles and I experienced a great relief when he was locked in.

Mr Littimer gives a similar lecture to David and Traddles on the sinfulness of young men, blames David for the 'follies' which have brought him to prison, and expresses the hope that David and Traddles and the magistrates, and their families, 'will also see your wickedness, and amend!'

The 'rattling fun' (as Clay acknowledged it) of these speeches is, very clearly, a heightened version of the letters quoted in 'Pet Prisoners', written by the Reverend Field's prize-parishioners. Dickens was not as completely in the realm of fantasy as one might have supposed. It is instructive, however, to compare his fictional-propagandist technique with that of his contemporary, Charles Reade, in his prison-novel of 1856, *It is Never too Late to Mend*. Reade was also protesting against the Separate System, but not on the grounds of the softness or the credulity of its adherents. Inspired by the Birmingham Prison scandal, his novel was more akin to *Oliver Twist* or *American Notes* in its indictment of the insolent cruelty of office. But it differs from *David Copperfield* not only in its penological idea; its mode of operation, too, is quite un-Dickensian. Dickens of course, unlike Reade, was a comic novelist, but there are other reasons for their different approaches to contemporary fact. Reade was trying to write 'A Matter-of-Fact Romance' (this is the sub-title of the novel), and he took much more trouble than Dickens ever did to master the documentary evidence about his subject and to base his story upon it. His main source was the *Report of the Commissioners appointed to enquire into the Condition and Treatment of Prisoners confined in Birmingham Borough Prison ... together with the Minutes of Evidence* (1854). The —— Gaol of

his novel is, transparently, Birmingham, and many of the characters
and episodes are immediately recognisable to anyone acquainted
with the evidence. The relation between Reade's fact and fiction
has recently been examined by Miss Sheila M. Smith, of Notting-
ham University. Reade's system, she shows, can be summed up as
'the use of a great deal of fact and of a little imagination', though
the facts were, in effect, continually 'distorted by the violence of
the author's feelings'. Miss Smith proves the justice of the allegation in the *Edinburgh Review* that the novel 'hardly contains a single
statement of a matter of fact which can be entirely depended upon,
though every statement . . . which it contains, is founded upon
something mentioned in the Report'. As she concludes: 'The
cumulative effect of Reade's slight but persistent exaggeration of
the cruelties inflicted by [the Governor] Hawes and his officers,
the suppression of any taint in [the prisoner] Josephs's character or
behaviour, and the creation of [the chaplain] Mr Eden, are not a
convincing and impressive protest against cruelty, but a sensational
picture of a melodramatic struggle between devilish brutality and
angelic mercy. . . . Reade's novel is not one of patient exploration,
but of dogmatic statement.'[44]

Dickens makes no pretence at a 'matter-of-fact' texture, nor
does he suggest even such qualifications to his thesis as Reade,
albeit inartistically, introduces. In *David Copperfield*, for once, it is
the magistrates instead of the prison-chaplains who appear as the
representatives of a futile religious policy, but there is no suggestion here or elsewhere that there might be some element of good
in this approach, or that not all chaplains are fools. Reade has his
'Model Prisoners', probably a reminiscence of Uriah and Littimer
— the most hardened old lags told the magistrates that 'the best
thing that ever happened to them was coming to —— Gaol. They
thanked Heaven they had been pulled up short in an evil career
that must have ended in their ruin, body and soul. As for their
present situation, they were never happier in their lives . . .' and
so on.[45] Reade also has his credulous prison-chaplain, a zealot for
strict separation and for learning biblical texts — the Reverend
Lepel from 'a gaol in the North of England' (probably an amalgam
of Clay of Preston, and Field of Reading).[46] But 'It is never too late
to mend' — Reade is more optimistic, and tries harder to be fair,
than Dickens. The canting hypocrites are balanced by the prisoner
Robinson, who after some backsliding becomes a respectable
citizen; and Mr Lepel is contrasted both with a feeble and

neglectful old-style chaplain, Mr Jones, and with the hero of the story, the indefatigable reforming chaplain Mr Eden, an improbable paragon who unites energy and good sense with earnest and inspiring piety. In a fever, Eden has a vision. 'His eye was flashing, and he spoke in bursts, and then stopped awhile and seemed to be listening in irritation to some arguments with which he did not agree. The enthusiast was building a prison in the air . . .', and at the end of the novel he is shown beginning to put these ideas into practice. They are quite sensible ideas, too, derived (without acknowledgment) from the Irish System.[47] Dickens neither had a coherent vision of the future of penology, nor was he given to expressing any positive policy on this or on other public issues through the thoughts or actions of his fictional characters. He would certainly have rejected Mr Eden's programme of useful industrial work, a form of group-counselling, individual encouragement, charity without sloppiness, and sound Christianity.

Dickens's lively satire in *David Copperfield*, though not altogether unjustified, was impressionistic and irresponsible. He did not indicate an alternative policy to Mr Creakle's; as Clay pointed out, he played into the hands — to put it no more strongly — of the vicious reactionaries whose excesses at Birmingham were to inspire Reade's novel a few years later. It was not the first, nor the last, time that his satire on the excesses of a reformist movement, or on the foibles of its advocates, had a reactionary implication, or at least seemed to his readers at the time to have one. His digs at Training Colleges in *Hard Times* and *Our Mutual Friend*, for instance, hardly sounded an encouragement to the idea of training teachers: the satire is negative enough to have convinced a recent writer on *Dickens on Education* that 'he attacked intervention by the state in respect of its efforts to train teachers'. This seems to me a misunderstanding of Dickens's ideas and techniques — excusable enough, except in someone who is writing a scholarly book about him. For what is really an attack on existing Training College methods (as Dickens understood them) can easily be taken, or rather mistaken, for an attack on Training Colleges as such, or on the Government's busying itself with them: and doubtless it was taken in this sense by many of his readers. Similarly, Dickens's former friend Lord Denman was no doubt right in thinking that his picture of Mrs Jellyby in *Bleak House* was a discouragement to efforts to put down Slavery and the Slave Trade, though wrong in charging him with having deliberately 'done his best to replunge the world into barbarism' in this respect.[48] Dickens did not always stop to think about the likely consequences of his satire — which were not always by any means what he would have wished. His lack of seriousness allowed him, moreover, to introduce a curious inconsistency into the satire in *David Copperfield*, which has not (I think) been noticed before.

Mr Creakle, it will be remembered, was a Middlesex Magistrate — but as *The Times* remarked a few years earlier, and in another connection, 'Have the magistrates of Middlesex the right of inspecting the prison at Pentonville, which is situate within their county? No such thing.'[49] But it is manifestly Pentonville that Dickens is attacking here, as in 'Pet Prisoners', though that prison is specified only in the article and not in the novel. Pentonville was, in fact, controlled not by any magistrates but by a special Government Board of Commissioners. Moreover, as appeared in the chapter on Coldbath Fields, the Middlesex Magistrates were conspicuous for their adherence to the Silent System, for a decade after *David Copperfield* and long after most other prison-authorities had accepted the Government's and the Inspectors' insistence that the Separate System was preferable. Why, then, did Dickens in the novel, and in his manuscript Number-plan for it, carefully specify the Middlesex Magistrates as his butts?[50]

Dickens was, I suspect, engaging in a private joke here, against his old enemy Benjamin Rotch, the magistrate who had resented his activities at Coldbath Fields and who had so bitterly quarrelled with its Governor, Chesterton. Rotch, unlike the majority of his fellows on the Middlesex Bench, was, it will be remembered, a strong believer in the Separate System. The 'contamination of Gaol Association' was, he said, 'almost electrical, . . . so rapidly does it take effect.' He had accordingly invoked Adshead — one of Dickens's fiercest enemies — and had been warmly praised by another, the Reverend Mr Field of Reading.[51] As we have seen, there was little tolerance between the rival cliques in the penological debate, and neither Rotch nor Dickens was notable for moderation and forbearance. Their disagreement was not only doctrinal but personal. Rotch is named in several of Dickens's letters. Just before Urania Cottage opened, he mentions his suspicions about a candidate from Coldbath Fields: '. . . she was produced to me by Mr Chesterton . . . as a model. She was the matron's model, and the head female turnkey's model, and the peculiar pet and protégée of Mr Rotch the magistrate who is a very good man, and takes infinite pains in the prisons — though I doubt his understanding of the company he finds there.' Six months later, relations between Dickens and Rotch have clearly deteriorated. He writes to Miss Coutts about another Coldbath Fields candidate for the Cottage, who was later to disappoint them: 'In case you should, by any evil chance, in visiting Stonnell, encounter a magistrate of the name of Rotch, let me advise you to say nothing to him, either about her, or the Home. For whatever is said to him, he is as certain to pervert, if it should suit his purpose, as the Sun is to rise tomorrow morning.'[52] As the phraseology of these letters suggests, Rotch had, in Dickens's opinion, the gullibility of a Mr Creakle, JP; as my earlier account of his quarrel with Chesterton showed, he was, like most advocates of the Separate System, more fanatical, and more optimistic about reforming prisoners, than Dickens or Chesterton. It was demonstrably inaccurate of Dickens to identify the Middlesex Magistrates with the Separate System: and their tough policy at Coldbath Fields, despite its occasional modifications, could never be charged with the faults which Dickens detects in Mr Creakle's gaol. A prison run by Mr Rotch, however, might well have been something like this. But why did Dickens depart from the facts which were widely known about London prisons? Why did he compromise the success of his lampoon of Pentonville methods, by attributing them to an authority conspicuously associated with a different policy?

If I am right in seeing Rotch as an underlying, though unrecognised, subject of the Creakle episode, this is a further example of a trick of Dickens's mind which was first pointed out, I believe, by Dr K. J. Fielding. Every reader of Dickens is aware of his satire on identifiable social institutions: here in *David Copperfield*, 'soft' methods of prison discipline, and specifically the Pentonville experiment in separate confinement. What had not been noticed is that Dickens sometimes also indulges in private jokes, even at the expense of the consistency of his satire; he introduces personal references which, though topical, were neither spotted nor meant to be spotted. Their purpose, says Dr Fielding, 'was not so much satire for the amusement of the readers, but because they delighted Dickens himself and stimulated his zest in writing.'[53] From Chesterton's account of Rotch, and from Dickens's letters, it is clear that there were some old scores to be paid off; presenting him as Mr Creakle may have seemed an agreeable, if esoteric, way of doing so.

VII

THE MARKS SYSTEM

THE implication of the *David Copperfield* chapter on the 'Interesting Penitents' was of course negative. 'Pet Prisoners' had ended with a salute to the tread-wheel and to the idea of felons' being given work of a suitably unique and degrading kind, but its conclusions were not solely repressive and retaliatory (as Carlyle's *Latter Day Pamphlet* had been). 'Let anything with a ray of hope in it be tried,' Dickens urged, but, he added, 'only as a part of some general system for raising up the prostrate portion of the people of this country, and not as an exhibition of such astonishing consideration for crime, in comparison with want and work.' As a gesture at least of fair-mindedness, he had even suggested that the Separate System might be tried out 'on a limited scale, if you will, with fair representatives of all classes of prisoners'. With more conviction, he had said: 'Let Captain Maconochie's system be tried.' Earlier in the article, when arguing that the Silent System, though 'not in the abstract a good secondary punishment', was superior to the Separate System, he had remarked:

> We are not acquainted with any system of secondary punishment that we think reformatory, except the mark system of Captain Macconnochie, formerly governor of Norfolk Island, which proceeds upon the principle of obliging the convict to some exercise of self-denial and resolution in every act of his prison life, and which would condemn him to a sentence of so much labour and good conduct instead of so much time. There are details in Captain Macconnochie's scheme on which we have our doubts (rigid silence we consider indispensable); but, in the main, we regard it as embodying sound and wise principles.[1]

Maconochie, as this quotation suggests, was not an admirer of the Silent System — nor of the Separate System, with which his ideas were even more incompatible. He had originally called his plan 'the Social System' (until he found that people then confused it with Owenite Socialism), for one of its fundamentals was that convicts should work together in groups which would share a common responsibility for rewards and punishments. He held that

164

'The proper object of prison discipline is to prepare men for discharge', and he saw that the artificiality of separate confinement provided no training for that life outside prison to which almost all prisoners must sooner or later return.[2] Moreover, he realised (as Field of Reading did not) that 'It is vain to talk of ignorant, inert and corrupt minds profiting by their unassisted reflections'. Nor did he want mere docility, whether obtained by a chaplain or by a flogger: 'A good prisoner,' he said, 'is usually a bad man.' Practical training, in a communal setting, with real incentives for good work, seemed to him a much more promising policy. His attitude was 'parental, not vindictive', 'prospective rather than retrospective' in regard to the prisoner. He considered no man incorrigible: 'Vice is a disease,' he wrote, 'and penal science just moral surgery' — and he thought that he had discovered the right surgical devices.[3] The 'Marks' for which his system became known represented only the means, not the end; every prisoner was to be awarded marks for good conduct and behaviour, or docked them as a punishment, and he could earn further marks by denying himself some of the little extra comforts or privileges of prison life. His promotion to a better 'class' in a progressive-stages system — and, if only the law could be changed, even his discharge from prison at all — would depend wholly upon his having amassed the specified number of marks.

Maconochie returned to England in 1846, and began a prolonged pamphlet-campaign to publicise his theories, but he was too far ahead of his time to carry officialdom with him. His Reports, said the influential civil servant Sir James Stephen, were 'the production of a man much less fitted for active than for contemplative life, who had very much to learn before he could be of very much use even in that way'.[4] Maconochie was, however, much better qualified than Stephen to pronounce on these matters, having commanded with striking success the great penal station of Norfolk Island (a terrible 'Devil's Island' in the Pacific, for the most recalcitrant convicts transported to Australia). But his reputation was unluckily clouded by two misfortunes: both at Norfolk Island, and later at Birmingham Gaol, his successors abandoned his policy and thus provoked notable riots — scandals for which he and his 'soft' methods were quite unfairly blamed. It was to Dickens's credit that he supported Maconochie back in 1846–7, when many officials shared Stephen's view of him.

Just how and when they met is not recorded by the biographers or the extant letters of either. Maconochie's recent and excellent biographer, Mr Justice Barry, to whose book I am much indebted, suggests to me that possibly they met about 1836, just before Maconochie left England, since there is a similarity that may be more than coincidental between the proceedings of the Pickwick Club (described in that year) and the affairs of the Royal Geographical Society in which Maconochie (as its first secretary) was involved. This speculation may perhaps be confirmed by the discovery of further correspondence; certainly Dickens was in contact with him early in 1846.[5] In May of that year he sent to Miss Coutts the splendid letter outlining for the first time his idea of Urania Cottage, and there Maconochie's plan appears as the basis of the Home's discipline. 'I do not know of any plan, so well conceived, or so firmly grounded in a knowledge of human nature, or so judiciously addressed to it, for observance in this place, as what is called Captain Maconnochie's Mark System' (which he then summarises).[6] Shortly before the Home opened, eighteen months later, Dickens tells Miss Coutts: 'I have avoided Macconochie's ideas, as they hardly seemed (or I fancied so) to meet with your full approval, and as they were perhaps unsuited to so small an establishment.' He had, presumably, met with opposition some time before, when he stressed that it was '*some modification* of [Maconochie's plan], I am so strongly inclined to recommend for adoption'.[7] He was still in contact with Maconochie; on the question, how much temptation to allow the girls to undergo in the Home, he could 'easily take the opinion of Macconnochie', he said — adding how pleased he was to hear that the Government was giving him the chance to try his system on some convicts at Weymouth.[8]

Not that Dickens was an uncritical admirer. He writes in May 1848 — 'Maconnochie has sent me a kind of protocol concerning such Institutions, which seems to me to be wrong from beginning to end. I will make my notes upon it, and shew it you. His head seems to be so full of the Mark System, that he has not room to turn another idea in it.'[9] It was not an unjust criticism: Maconochie himself had told a friend he would 'go the whole hog' on penal reform, even if he came to seem 'extravagant' instead of the 'quiet judicial person enough' he had so far appeared to be, and his biographer, Mr Justice Barry, admits that his zeal in the good cause led him into a fanaticism unrelieved by any detachment or sense of humour.[10] Dickens had little patience with 'Whole Hogs' (he wrote an article under this title in *Household Words*, satirising such single-minded fanatics). A moderate prison-governor like Chesterton, not over-optimistic about any penal system, was more to his taste. But he was attracted to Maconochie's scheme, as being both hopeful and practical, so he modified it, and eventually got it introduced at Urania Cottage. He much preferred a down-to-earth calculable device like this, to any idea of exhorting or shaming or converting the girls to virtue. This preference appeared, as was mentioned in the Urania Cottage chapter, in his disagreement with his illustrious colleague on the Committee of Management.

> I have considered Mr Kay Shuttleworth's desire to introduce some greater *moral* stimulant into this system, and do not descry any means by which it can hopefully be done. But I submit this consideration for his reflection — whether incentives to good conduct, successfully addressed to the reason and prudence of people and obviously tending to their welfare, be not likely to become, imperceptibly, the awakeners of a real moral sentiment — suggesting, in the first instance, the wisdom of virtue and the folly of vice: and, afterwards, the inherent beauty of the former, and deformity of the latter? In this, my hope of the system as a moral influence, mainly lies.[11]

This note of cautious realism recurs throughout Dickens's correspondence about Urania Cottage, where, as we noted, he displayed a serviceable mixture of charity, firm discipline, and reasonable hope.

His suggestions to Kay-Shuttleworth come at the end of a long Memorandum, in which he explains to Miss Coutts the workings of the 'Mark Table' at the Home. He had limited it to 'as few heads as possible, in order that it may be rendered the plainer to the comprehension of the young women themselves' — and he considered their state of education, too, when proposing that every girl should herself keep a duplicate copy of the daily Mark-paper, since 'Besides the probability of its producing some moral effect upon her, it would be a lesson in arithmetic, in which she could not fail to have a personal interest'. Up to four marks a day could be earned under nine separate headings — Truthfulness, Industry, Temper, Propriety of Conduct and Conversation, Order, Punctuality, Economy, Cleanliness, and Temperance (in the larger meaning of 'moderation, patience, calmness'). Originally Dickens had suggested a further heading — clearly inspired by Maconochie — 'Voluntary self-denial.' He explained to Miss Coutts that a reward under this heading would be obtainable for 'abstinence from beer, on the part of those employed in the laundry', or from tea and sugar by those otherwise employed — but, he foresaw, 'It is not unlikely that some young woman may now and then deny herself beer or tea, because she is sulky.' Perhaps for this reason, this heading was eventually dispensed with. Some other headings were changed or dropped also, but this example, though using the earlier nomenclature, illustrates well enough how the scheme worked:

> Supposing such a case as once occurred with Emma Lea, when she called another girl by opprobrious names, and threatened her, and was otherwise violent and defiant. Such an extreme case would involve, under this table, a bad mark for 'temper', a bad mark for 'propriety of deportment', a bad mark for 'propriety of language', and a bad mark for 'improvement' — every one of which, I would certainly have entered.

Conduct of a 'particularly objectionable' kind not merely meant that no marks were earned. The culprit could also be awarded a bad mark, in red ink, which lost her forty good ones. The girls seem to have enjoyed the competitive, and monetary, aspects of this elaborate game, though, the cash value of the marks being only six shillings and sixpence per thousand, one could swear quite a lot for threepence.[12]

The more mechanical 'marks' element in Maconochie's system was adopted in English prisons in the 1860s, though its essential spirit was ignored. In the previous decade, however, the Irish prisons under Sir Walter Crofton's reorganisation had been greatly influenced by Maconochie. Irish convicts, like English, began their sentence with nine-months' separate confinement, to cool them off, but then they went through a more carefully defined and intelligently devised sequence of Progressive Stages, ending with a distinctive Intermediate Stage (a 'filter between prison and community') when convicts worked without supervision and lived in an ordinary hut — a sort of 'open prison'. At this stage, 'Individualisation' was the ruling principle, and men worked in small groups. This was followed by their conditional discharge, under an effective after-care system. (Here, as so often in Victorian penal history, one finds in full operation practices which, a century later, are being hailed as exciting new developments.) Neither the

Irish system, nor Maconochie's own plans and performance, were soft. Maconochie maintained that society had no right to inflict pain or punishment on prisoners except in so far as it reformed them — but, he added, reform could only be effected 'through the medium of a *well-arranged adversity*', disinterestedly devised to promote moral effort by the prisoner.[13] To many rival penologists, however, he seemed insufficiently severe, and too hopeful, and many prison-officials were equally opposed to the Irish system — claiming that its more successful elements were copied from England, and that its overall claim to success was ill-founded. They were patently jealous of its growing prestige.

Dickens, as we have seen, had some reserves about Maconochie's scheme, but he supported it much more strongly than one might have expected in view of his more bloodthirsty and vindictive pronouncements on penology. Similarly, contributors to *All the Year Round* were allowed to praise the Irish system, as superior to the English. An article on 'The Irish Convict's Progress' accepts reformation as the basic principle of all civilised penology, and gives an enthusiastic account of the Irish system.[14] Three years later a contributor reviews Mary Carpenter's book *Our Convicts*, and agrees with her criticism of the English system as 'a costly and a grievous failure'; he describes the ineffective English procedure, and contrasts it with the Irish system, the results of which, for over eleven years now, 'have been in every way satisfactory.'[15] Both contributors rightly name and praise Maconochie as the inspirer of Sir Walter Crofton's successful plan; both note that a 'great battle of the systems' is beginning, the debate now having moved from Separate *versus* Silent to English *versus* Irish. The new debate was often as acrimonious as the old. Most of the more forward-looking reformers, such as Mary Carpenter of the Reformatory School movement and Matthew Davenport Hill the great Recorder of Birmingham, regarded the Irish System as much sounder and more hopeful, and it was indeed through the influence of the Irish System on American prisons, and later of the American prisons on the English, that Maconochie ultimately brought some hope and light into the penal system of his own country. Maconochie's short period as Governor of Norfolk Island was, historically, the beginning of the reformatory movement in prison-discipline, as a recent history of criminology states.[16] It is pleasant to find Dickens, in his support of Maconochie and through his journals' praise of the Irish System, coinciding for once with the more intelligent and

generous-minded of his contemporaries and with the penologists
of posterity.

Unfortunately, there seems to be no direct evidence of Dickens's
attitude to the explicitly reformative Irish System. The *All the Year
Round* articles would certainly not have been printed, had he deeply
disapproved of them; he may, for all I know, even have instructed
or encouraged their authors to write them. Who their authors are,
I do not know — nor, indeed, whether the articles were written by
two contributors, or by the same man. Certainly Dickens's praise
for Maconochie, a decade or so earlier, shows that even when he
was advocating the tread-wheel his penological attitude was not
entirely deterrent. He never repudiated the merely penal and
vindictive ideas he had expressed; but he never quite lost faith in
the possibility of reforming some criminals.

It is impossible, I think, to discover a consistent attitude, or a clear
development, in Dickens's various pronouncements on penal
discipline. The most that one can say is that, throughout his
career, he approved of severe penal measures, and inclined more
towards a deterrent than a curative policy, and that the inclination
became stronger, and was more vehemently expressed, the older he
grew. Back in 1842, he had written from Baltimore to his friend
Macready, confessing his disappointment and disillusion with
American society and political institutions. 'You know that I am
truly a Liberal,' he said, but 'the man who comes to this country a
Radical and goes home again with his opinions unchanged, must
be a Radical on reason, sympathy, and reflection, and one who has
so well considered the subject that he has no chance of wavering.'[17]
The man who never wavers in a liberal attitude towards penology
must have based his ideas on a particularly strong foundation of
'reason, sympathy, and reflection' (to borrow Dickens's words),
for the temptation to abandon charity and patience is both strong
and recurrent. Our first thought, especially when some notably
disgusting crime has been committed or when some crime-wave
occurs, is to hit back as hard as possible: and it is always easy to
rationalise this impulse, which springs both from self-defence and
from vindictiveness, as honest indignation, firmness, a virtuous
exercise of public duty. To remain constant to wiser second thoughts
requires an emotional and intellectual self-control that was
beyond Dickens.

'Mr Dickens is a great observer and a great humorist,' wrote

Henry James in a review of *Our Mutual Friend*, 'but he is nothing of a philosopher. Some people may hereupon say, so much the better; we say, so much the worse. For a novelist very soon has need of a little philosophy.'[18] About the same time, the *Westminster Review* was complaining that 'his views, both on life and morals, are imperfect and of the first impression; being, in fact, just what would occur to an ordinary warm-hearted person who had not reflected on the subject'.[19] Sometimes, it is fair to say, Dickens's ideas were less obvious than the *Westminster Review* alleges; sometimes, too, 'the first impression . . . of an ordinary warm-hearted person' was juster, as well as more generous, than the better-informed and more fully argued policy of the *Westminster Review*. In his recoil from the well-meant barbarity of the Philadelphia Penitentiary, Dickens was wiser as well as more humane than the experts. A warm heart and common sense are invaluable in penology, as in other social activities, but they are not enough. A more searching enquiry into the roots of crime, and a firm attachment to reasonable principle, are necessary if one is not to be at the mercy of every momentary crisis or reaction. Dickens lacked the requisite patience, and the intellectual habits and capacity. A commentator more sympathetic towards him than Henry James and the *Westminster Review*, makes a judgment akin to theirs, but subtler in its understanding of the man. One of the many shrewd assessments that John Forster offers is this:

> . . . apart from that wonderful world of his books, the range of his thoughts was not always proportioned to the width and largeness of his nature. His ordinary circle of activity, whether in likings or thinkings, was full of such surprising animation, that one was apt to believe it more comprehensive that it really was; and again and again, when a wide horizon might seem to be ahead of him he would pull up suddenly and stop short, as though nothing lay beyond. For the time, though each had its term and change, he was very much a man of one idea, each having its turn of absolute predominance. . . .

— and, as Forster remarks later in his biography, 'His literary work was so intensely one with his nature that he is not separable from it, and the man and the method throw a singular light on each other.'[20]

On penology, as on other matters, he was indeed 'very much a man of one idea, each having its turn of absolute predominance'; rarely does he offer a careful balance of considerations, nor recognise how difficult are the problems under discussion and how tentative must be the solutions offered. The ideas predominating in his mind at any particular moment were, in general, those most current in public opinion. When it changed, he changed, whether slightly before or slightly after. If, however, his being unphilosophical, not having considered the subject so well that he had no chance of wavering, makes him chancy and untrustworthy as a penologist, at least it makes him the more valuable as an indicator of the climate of opinion. As Dicey said of him, in another connection, 'Just because he was no systematiser, he reflected with the greater rapidity and truth the varying sentiment of the age in which he lived.'[21] Of course, public opinion was not always wrong, and even when it took a really undesirable turn there was substance in some of the arguments most commonly adduced. Thus, the dietary at Pentonville in 1850 was indeed unfairly superior to that in many other prisons and in workhouses, and, I have argued, the zealous activities of the Chaplains were often ill-advised: but this does not, of course, mean that a tough policy of tread-wheel and terror was preferable, let alone perfect.

In 1842, Dickens had expressed the predominant lay opinion that the American Separate System was cruel, and he was right. In 1850, he was again reflecting public opinion when he criticised the English Separate System for the opposite reason — but on this occasion, as so often in the history of penal developments, what was needed, and what the newspapers and journals failed to provide, was a balanced assessment, restraining the public from an excessive reaction though not ignoring the remediable defects in the system. The same was true, a dozen years later, when London was stricken by an epidemic of garotting in the winter of 1862-3. Matthew Davenport Hill, a wise and experienced jurist, wrote to Lord John Russell at the time, arguing that the present dangers to life and property were less formidable than the possibility that the Government would be panicked into 'a resort to expedients of which history has demonstrated the worthlessness'.[22] Such temperate views did not prevail. Dickens's colleagues in *All the Year Round* joined *The Times*, the House of Lords, and other popular spokesmen, in demanding severe measures: the Government was indeed panicked into passing the 'Garotters' Act', which revived the perennial panacea of flogging, and into appointing the Carnarvon Committee, whose fierce Report of 1863 led to the disastrously reactionary Prisons Act of 1865.[23] Similarly, throughout the '50s and '60s, Dickens and his colleagues kept repeating the popular —

and not entirely unjustified — distrust of the Ticket-of-Leave system. To give one other example of Dickens's general coincidence with public opinion: I have mentioned elsewhere the fierce *Uncommercial Traveller* article entitled 'The Ruffian', which appeared in *All the Year Round* in October 1868. It called for more drastic police measures towards released convicts whose reformation was dubious, and for stronger legal sanctions against professional thugs and thieves. Dickens's peremptory tone here, and his lack of charity towards criminals, has surprised and distressed some of his biographers, who have been driven to an explanation in terms of his sexual frustration in his later years.[24] As I pointed out, this article is not surprising, if one has noted his many similar remarks in earlier years; I may now add that he was again, on this occasion, expressing a widespread topical concern. Mr Douglas C. Browne, in his book on *The Rise of Scotland Yard*, quotes leading articles from the *Daily News*, the *Penny Illustrated Paper*, and the *Daily Telegraph*, written within a month of 'The Ruffian', making the same points and in much the same tone of voice. 'Obviously,' Mr Browne comments, 'there was some truth in this flood of fault-finding, flouts, and jeers.'[25] A few months later, Parliament passed without much ado the Habitual Criminals Act, which met many of the criticisms rightly or wrongly made by the 'able editors'. So, once again, Dickens had been expressing a majority view.[26]

VIII

THE BENCH

'Hɪs notions of the law ... are precisely those of an attorney's clerk,' wrote the lawyer Sir James Fitzjames Stephen in his famous onslaught on Dickens in the *Edinburgh Review*.[1] Dickens had, indeed, begun his working life in a solicitor's office ('I didn't much like it,' he later wrote — it was 'a very little world, and a very dull one'). He had then become a reporter in the Consistory Court of Doctors' Commons — 'a little out-of-the-way place,' as he makes Steerforth explain to David Copperfield, 'where they administer what is called ecclesiastical law, and play all kinds of tricks with obsolete old monsters of acts of Parliament.' He also did a little Police Court Reporting, on the side. Thence he graduated to the Press Gallery in Parliament: on this experience, David Copperfield speaks for him — 'I am sufficiently behind the scenes to know the worth of political life. I am quite an Infidel about it, and shall never be converted.'[2] His memories of 'monkish attorneys', the expensive 'private theatricals' of the courts, and the archaic inefficiency of the law, had a similar effect upon him. Mr Bumble was slow in arriving at his famous discovery that 'the law is a ass — a idiot'; Dickens had known it from his youth upwards, and he never lost this conviction. 'Wiglomeration,' he called it in *Bleak House*: and a month before his death he was writing, 'I have that high opinion of the law of England generally, which one is likely to derive from the impression that it puts all the honest men under the diabolical hoofs of all the scoundrels.'[3]

Neither Parliament nor the law was quite as bad as Dickens intemperately thought, but again he expresses the common man's view. Lawyers, as a profession, neither warm the heart nor excite the admiration of the great British public; the prejudice Dickens imbibed from his brief experience of the legal world was reinforced by a long tradition of popular and literary hostility towards lawyers, who generally appear — in, say, Jacobean and Restoration drama, and in eighteenth-century fiction — either as musty crabbed half-wits or, more often, as unscrupulous rogues. His friend Douglas Jerrold was writing well within this popular tradition, when he said that 'Turkey has her eunuchs, Russia her Cossacks, and England her attorneys'.[4] In his last novel, *Edwin Drood*, indeed, Dickens portrays the other legal archetype, which for some reason or other has tended in modern literature to replace earlier ones — the trusty and devoted family solicitor. But more often he remains true to the folk-mind: Dodson and Fogg, Sampson Brass, Uriah Heep and Mr Vholes are creations more typical of his outlook than Mr Grewgious. No wonder Mr Jaggers is so constantly washing his hands with scented soap. The most offensive thing Dickens can think of saying about some Americans is that their advocacy of certain principles 'would disgrace . . . Old Bailey lawyers'.[5] Intellectuals, of course, do not bother much about solicitors and barristers: they save their bitterest comments for Judges, enough of whom, to be sure, maintain a standard of complacent stupidity and ignorance well calculated to keep that prejudice happily alive. Dickens was, perhaps, showing his non-intellectual bias when he spoke so often with respect about Her Majesty's Judges: but he made up for it by feeling a special venom towards magistrates.

Fitzjames Stephen was right: Dickens's knowledge of the law was never at all professional. He was stronger on civil law than on the criminal law which is our concern. But even an attorney's clerk can 'get the hang of it', and a lad so observant as Dickens could pick up a good deal not only of the detail but also of the atmosphere of the law and its personnel. Sir William Holdsworth, whose monumental *History of English Law* (1923–38) is no less authoritative in its field than Stephen's *History of the Criminal Law of England* (1883), had a greater respect than his predecessor for this aspect of Dickens's achievement. In his lectures on *Charles Dickens as a Legal Historian* he asserts that his pictures of the law and lawyers are 'a very valuable addition to our authorities', since they give us information which we can get nowhere else and 'were painted by a man with extraordinary powers of observation, who had first-hand knowledge'. Dickens's novels provide, indeed, 'a source of information which, in its range and lifelike character, is superior to that possessed by the historian of any other period.' Holdsworth notes that Dickens is best acquainted with the lower reaches of the legal world: 'his knowledge of the higher ranks of the legal profession is less extensive. Neither barristers nor king's counsel play any great part,' and the novels contain only one judge.[6] Dickens makes a few slips in his law of court-procedure; as he confessed to the United Law Clerks Society, in the case *Bardell* v *Pickwick* 'the pleading, the evidence, the summing up, and the verdict were all equally wrong'.[7] But generally he is accurate in his detail, and — given his heightening mode — is very informative about the atmosphere of the legal world of his earlier years. Scarcely one of his novels, from *Pickwick Papers* to *Edwin Drood*, is without lawyers and law-clerks and magistrates. Dickens made his brief experience of the law stretch a long way. He often needed to use these memories, and his later glimpses of the legal world, since the plots of 'sensation novels' so constantly turn upon legacies, birthrights, thefts and deeds of violence.

What we have seen of prison developments in Dickens's period applies also, of course, to other aspects of the law and its administration: this was pre-eminently 'The Age of Reform', even if some of the reforms were slow in coming, and incomplete or ill-advised when at last they came. Basically, the institutions of a rural and semi-feudal England were being re-shaped for an increasingly urban, industrial and democratic society. The reforms in local and national government, the Factory Acts, the Repeal of the Corn Law, the development of popular education — all belonged together, in this respect: and changes in the law and its administration are part of the same process. Many features of the Courts and their procedure, and of the law both civil and criminal, were radically amended. In my opening chapter, I briefly mentioned some examples — the virtual restriction of capital punishment to cases of murder, the more decent mode of inflicting both capital and corporal punishment, the ending of Transportation, the establishment of an efficient police force. Many 'obsolete old monsters of acts of Parliament', which engaged the attention of Doctors' Commons during Dickens's time there, were repealed or drastically overhauled during his lifetime; that Court itself was abolished in 1857. After 1873, Serjeants — such as the great Serjeant Buzfuz — were no more; after 1869, there was no imprisonment for debt; the Chancery Procedure Acts of 1852 ended many of the scandals against which Dickens was protesting in *Bleak House* and elsewhere. There are dozens of other examples, even if one confines one's attention to those aspects of the law which attracted Dickens's lasting, or passing, attention. He had opinions — varying in merit — on many of these developments, and in the present chapter I shall discuss some of his attitudes towards the criminal law and its administration. I shall leave aside two important topics, which interested him particularly and which therefore deserve fuller treatment in separate chapters — the police, and capital punishment. As before, I shall try to mix, and relate together, passages from his novels and from his non-fictional writings. Then, in two final chapters, I shall confine myself to the novels and shall trace his artistic development, as shown in his treatment of the theme of murder.

Dickens, like David Copperfield, felt considerable contempt both for the Courts and for Parliament. He declined several invitations to stand for various constituencies: but he did, in his earlier years, think of becoming a lawyer and, indeed, a magistrate.

Back in 1834, while he was still a journalist, he told the Steward of New Inn that he intended 'entering at the Bar as soon as circumstances will enable me to do so.'[8] Nothing seems to have come of this: but late in 1839 he did enter his name at the Middle Temple. Serjeant Talfourd and Edward Chapman were his sponsors, and Forster seems to have ensured that he filled in the right forms ('It's the right Temple, I take for granted', Dickens trustfully wrote to him). It was several years, however, before he began eating his dinners there (apparently about 1849).[9] In 1854, he was still paying his dues of ten guineas, and enquiring how many more Terms he had to keep before qualifying to be called. 'I have no belief whatever that I shall ever keep them now,' he admitted; 'but I should like — for the gratification of an innocent curiosity — to know how many I *have* kept, after all the boredom I have suffered in that noble Institution of my country.' Presumably the answer was discouraging, for six months later he finally withdrew his name from the Temple, and petitioned, with success, for the return of his Deposit money, one hundred pounds.[10] At one period, at least, he had more specific intentions in regard to the law. Forster records that, in 1846, he heard 'with some surprise' that Dickens had opened communication with a leading member of the Government 'to ascertain what chances there might be for his appointment, upon due qualification, to the paid magistracy of London'. The reply did not encourage him to pursue the matter, however.[11] About the same time Dickens was telling another friend: 'I am (nominally, God knows!) a Law student, and have a certain number of "terms to keep" before I can be called to the Bar; and it would be well for me to be called, as there are many little pickings to be got, — pretty easily within my reach, — which *can* only be bestowed on Barristers.'[12] What Forster fails to mention — probably he never knew of it — is the fact that this desire to be a magistrate was more than a mere 'outbreak of momentary discontent' in 1846, but represented a long-held ambition. For in 1843 Dickens had written to Lord Brougham:

> Since I had the pleasure of seeing you, I have gone very much about the Jails and bye-places of London, and although they are old sights to me, am more than ever amazed at the Ignorance and Misery that prevail. . . . I would that I were a Police Magistrate, and could take and hold this question from such a 'vantage ground at its lowest and most wretched end. I think I should be a pretty good one, with my knowledge of the kind of people that come most commonly within their Jurisdiction; and I would never rest from practically shewing all classes how important it has become to educate, on bold and comprehensive principles, the Dangerous Members of Society. I have often had this desire in my mind, but never so strongly as now.[13]

What was the meaning of these inconclusive episodes? In 1834 he may have intended to make a career of the law, but it is doubtful whether in 1839 he had any expectation of ever practising in the Courts; probably he would have been like Forster, who declined all connection with the law excepting the name of barrister. The title of barrister was, among other things, a certificate of gentility (as Sampson Brass reminded Mr Witherden); it also qualified its holder for certain lucrative 'pickings', particularly if his acquaintance lay among the bestowers of patronage. Dickens's wish to be called to the Bar must partly have been an insurance-policy of this kind, and probably it was the relative failure, financially, of *Martin Chuzzlewit* (1843-4), followed by the *Daily News* fiasco early in 1846, that prompted him to renew enquiries a few months later about the possibility of becoming a stipendiary magistrate. One should not, however, attribute merely financial and prudential motives for his desire for such a post. He was certainly sincere in telling Brougham of his passionate concern over 'the Ignorance and Misery that prevail', and doubtless also in feeling some confidence that he would do the work well. 'What a court his would have been!' as the reviewer of my book in *The Magistrate* longingly exclaimed.

Lawyers have of course a traditional connection with the stage and light literature (witness the membership of the Garrick Club). Several of Dickens's friends, such as Talfourd and Jeffery, showed how possible it was to combine letters and the law; another friend, Gilbert à Beckett, the popular comic and political journalist and founder-member of *Punch*, was a lawyer who later achieved Dickens's ambition by becoming a Metropolitan police magistrate. (*Punch* has always had this contact with the Bar and the Bench.) But probably the most powerful influence was Henry Fielding, whose novels Dickens deeply admired, and whose work as a Westminster magistrate had resulted in some notable reforms. Dickens must have hoped to emulate him, in this respect as in others, and to gather fresh materials for his novels from this daily experience of the seamier side of London life. Dickens was not alone in feeling this two-fold kinship with Fielding. Thackeray, another warm admirer of his novels, also hankered after his magisterial bench; in 1849, his friend Monckton Milnes tried to obtain for him a vacant Metropolitan magistrateship. He was not eligible, having only been called to the Bar a year before, but in order to qualify for a future vacancy he kept his name-plate displayed on the doors of chambers.[14] In 1849, when Dickens was eating his dinners at the Middle Temple, a sixth son was born to him, and he broke his habit of naming his boys after contemporary writers with whom he was friendly, by christening this one Henry Fielding Dickens. The augury and honour were not lost upon the child. He alone of the seven Dickens boys was called to the Bar, at which he achieved some distinction; like his father, he was a Middle Temple man.

Dickens's suspicions about the law and lawyers were not, then, so extreme as to prevent his contemplating a career in the Courts, if all else failed. He knew and admired a number of the Metropolitan stipendiary magistrates. In the course of his charitable work for Miss Coutts, he often writes of his reliance on the help and judgment of à Beckett, of Broderip of the Thames and later the Westminster Police Court ('a very good magistrate. I know him intimately'), and of John Hardwick of Marlborough Street.[15] Similarly he was acquainted with the 'nobly patient and humane' Coroner for West Middlesex, Thomas Wakley, whom he several times praised in public.[16] Of course, he also knew of full-time magistrates who were less admirable, and one of them has become famous through his fiction.

In 1837 Dickens wrote to a Mr Haines, who had charge of the

Press reporters for the City Courts: 'In my next number of Oliver Twist, I must have a magistrate; and, casting about for a magistrate whose harshness and insolence would render him a fit subject to be "shewn up" I have, as a necessary consequence, stumbled upon Mr Laing of Hatton Garden celebrity. I know the man's character perfectly well; but as it would be necessary to describe his personal appearance also, I ought to have seen him, which (fortunately or unfortunately as the case may be) I have never done.'[17] He asked Haines therefore to smuggle him in to Laing's court for a few moments. This subterfuge was necessary because, as he complained in *Oliver Twist* (where Laing appears, barely disguised, as Fang), 'Although the presiding genii in such an office as this, exercise a summary and arbitrary power over the liberties, the good name, the character, almost the lives, of Her Majesty's subjects, especially of the poorer class; and although, within such walls, enough fantastic tricks are daily played to make the angels blind with weeping; they are closed to the public, save through the medium of the daily press.' — 'Or were virtually, then,' he later adds in a footnote.[18] He always, said Forster, showed some satisfaction in admitting the identity of Laing and Fang, and, according to Forster, the *Oliver Twist* chapter had some effect — '. . . shortly after, on some fresh outbreak of intolerable temper, the home-secretary found it an easy and popular step to remove Mr Laing from the bench.' It is difficult to know how much Dickens's intervention counted in the campaign against Laing, which had long been mounting and which finally succeeded in January 1838, six months after the *Oliver Twist* chapter was published. The comic magazine *Figaro in London* claimed the credit; its readers would recollect, it remarked at the time, that 'we have frequently promised to be unwearied in our exertions to procure for society the boon of the dismissal of Laing', and it was notorious that 'to this publication, and to this alone, is the public indebted for the ferocities of Laing being exposed'. This penny satirical journal had been started, as Henry Vizetelly later pointed out, during the Reform agitation, and 'originated those periodical comments on magisterial decisions which subsequently became general in the newspapers, under the title of "Justices' Justice" '.[19] By 1837, then, Laing was being widely attacked; in *Oliver Twist*, 'the renowned Mr Fang,' is discovered 'perusing a leading article in a newspaper of the morning, adverting to some recent decision of his, and commending him, for the three hundred and fiftieth

time, to the special and particular notice of the Secretary of State
for the Home Department'.[20] At this distance of time, it is impossible to apportion the credit for Laing's removal, without a
detailed study of the newspapers, and of the Home Office papers,
which I have not made. Forster's claim, like most assertions about
Dickens's 'influence' by his biographers, must be regarded with
caution. But it was, at least, sustained by Serjeant Ballantine, who
recalled that the Home Secretary received a complaint against
Laing from a clergyman (who was 'shortly afterwards convicted of
stealing a silver spoon at a charity dinner at which he presided').
Laing had, once again, displayed some irritability in court —
'and the authorities were not sorry to follow the lead of a popular
author, and dismissed him.' He was, said Ballantine, 'notwithstanding an unfortunate temper, a thoroughly honourable man, a
good lawyer, and accomplished scholar,' though 'I never saw him
without thinking of a shrivelled crab apple'.[21]

It was not mainly the paid magistrates that Dickens attacked,
however. As we have seen, he knew and esteemed several of them
— as he did also many of the leading Judges. At one of his dramatic
performances, indeed, he observed in the front row a notable bevy
of his legal friends: the Lord Chief Justice (Campbell), the Lord
Chief Baron (Pollock), Mr Baron Bramwell, and Mr Justice
Willes; as he commented, Cockburn, the new Chief Justice of the
Common Pleas, rather spoiled the effect by coming on another
night.[22] He was on friendly terms with the three men who served
as Lord Chief Justice between 1832 and 1880, and praised their
qualities — Denman, Campbell, and Cockburn. He was particularly fond of Denman, and of Pollock, but the strength of his
friendships with the Bench seems to have borne little relation to
the juridical or penological reputation of these various men of law.
Denman was, by the modest standards of the Bench, a humane and
open-minded man; Campbell and Cockburn and Pollock were
decidedly not.[23] 'Denman delights me,' Dickens had said — and his
affection was reciprocated, at least until Denman's fierce objection
to *Bleak House*; when he retired from the Bench, a highly laudatory
sonnet on him, by Talfourd, appeared in *Household Words* ('. . .
justice kept from rigour's flaw By beautiful regards . . .')[24] With
the other Judges, Dickens's contacts were cordial, but less intimate.
Edmund Yates has an amusing account of Cockburn at one of
the Public Readings: he had revelled in the *Carol*, but during
'The Trial from Pickwick' he 'pish'd and psha'd throughout,'

particularly at Dickens's impersonation of Mr Justice Stareleigh, and at the end he stigmatised the performance as 'perfectly ridiculous, a mere broad farce or exaggerated pantomime'.[25] As, no doubt, it was: nevertheless Dickens was generally thought to have caught exactly, in *Pickwick Papers*, the tones and mannerisms of Mr Justice Gazelee, who was indeed very deaf, very short, and comically pompous and eccentric. These traits — already (according to Denman's biographer) 'an endless source of amusement to the Bar' — Dickens 'immortalised, and scarcely caricatured, . . . under the punning sobriquet of Mr Justice Stareleigh'.[26]

Mr Justice Stareleigh was the only Judge shown in action in the novels. When Charles Darnay is tried at the Old Bailey, the judge is hardly mentioned; in *Bleak House*, the Lord Chancellor makes only a brief appearance ('his manner was both courtly and kind . . . so affable and polite; by which he certainly lost no dignity, but seemed to us to have gained some').[27] Dickens thought well enough of the Judges not to depict them in his novels; they are let off lightly, with an occasional injunction to 'expose themselves to feel what wretches feel' — such Carlylean apostrophes as 'Oh ermined Judge, whose duty to society is, now, to doom the ragged criminal to punishment and death, hadst thou never, Man, a duty to discharge in barring up the hundred open gates that wooed him to the felon's dock . . . !'[28] But generally they receive fulsome praise; there were 'no authorities in England so deserving of general respect and confidence, or so possessed of it', he wrote — though he wished that the Courts would dispense with the 'false and ridiculous' flummery of wigs, black caps, and other such theatrical paraphernalia.[29] Magistrates — the ordinary unpaid sort — were a very different matter. When he was planning a weekly magazine in 1839, he said that one feature would be 'a series of satirical papers purporting . . . to describe the administration of justice in some country that never existed, and record the proceedings of its wise men. The object of this series . . . would be to keep a special look-out upon the magistrates in town and country, and never to leave those worthies alone'.[30] He had not left them alone in his earlier novels and essays, and he kept up the attack during the remaining thirty years of his life: but the trend of his allegations against them changed in the course of time.

'Among the Shallows' was the title of one *Household Words* paper. Dickens and his colleagues were, again, drawing on a long literary tradition of magistrate-baiting, most famously exemplified in Shakespeare's Shallow and Silence. Mr Nupkins, Mayor of Ipswich, before whom Mr Pickwick is hailed, is an early example of this bumbling pomposity and pride of place. When Pickwick demands to know on what charge he has been brought there, Nupkins has to whisper to his Clerk, 'Must I tell him?' As Sam Weller remarks, 'This is a wery impartial country for justice. There ain't a magistrate goin' as don't commit himself, twice as often as he commits other people.'[31] The apotheosis of this 'solemn Jackass' appears at the other end of Dickens's career, in Mr Sapsea of *Edwin Drood*, who at one point 'wanders into a denser haze and maze of nonsense than even a mayor might be expected to disport himself in'.[32] Variants on this type had appeared in the *Barnaby Rudge* Lord Mayor, in the wooden-headed effigies of magistrates at the Mudfog Association meeting, and in Mr Tulrumble, Mayor of Mudfog, who makes a fool of himself by instituting a 'Show', and by acting on the Middlesex Magistrates' great discovery that music in pubs leads to crime and immorality.[33] Most of Dickens's earlier magistrates are asses, killjoys or bullies; the bully type appears most viciously in Fang, and in the rural landowner who insults and persecutes Barnaby Rudge and his mother ('a country gentleman of the true school. . . . He was in the commission of the peace, and could write his name almost legibly'). It is his 'evidence' against Barnaby that prevents his being acquitted on the capital charge, later in the story. These magistrates are seen from the point of view of the poor whom they oppress; and when the poor answer back, they are impervious. Recall the magistrate in *The Old Curiosity Shop*, arraigned by the convict's mother: ' "You are desperate," said the gentleman, taking out his snuff-box, "and I am sorry for you".'[34]

The most famous example of this type is, of course, Alderman Cute of *The Chimes*. Accompanied by Mr Filer and another friend, he comes upon poor Trotty Veck eating his humble tripe-dinner.

'Now, you know,' said the Alderman, addressing his two friends, with a self-complacent smile upon his face, which was habitual to him, 'I am a plain man, and a practical man; and I go to work in a plain practical way. That's my way. There is not the least mystery or difficulty in dealing with this sort of people if you only understand 'em, and can talk to 'em, in their own manner. Now, you Porter! Don't you ever tell me, or anybody else, my friend, that you haven't always enough to eat, and of the best, because I know better. I have tasted your tripe, you know, and you can't "chaff" me. You understand what "chaff" means, eh! That's the right word, isn't it? Ha, ha, ha! Lord bless you,' said the Alderman, turning to his friends again, 'it's the easiest thing on earth to deal with this sort of people, if you only understand 'em.'

Famous man for the common people, Alderman Cute! Never out of temper with them! Easy, affable, joking, knowing gentleman!

'You see, my friend,' pursued the Alderman, 'there's a great deal of nonsense talked about Want — "hard up," you know: that's the phrase, isn't it? ha! ha! ha! — and I intend to Put it Down. There's a certain amount of cant in vogue about Starvation, and I mean to Put it Down. That's all! Lord bless you,' said the Alderman, turning to his friends again, 'you may Put Down anything among this sort of people, if you only know the way to set about it!'

He continues in this vein, talking of other social mischiefs he intends to Put Down. When he hears that young Meg intends to get married, he warns her of various marital disasters which he will not allow, ending with the direst possibility —

'. . . And if you attempt, desperately, and ungratefully, and impiously, and fraudulently attempt, to drown yourself, or hang yourself, I'll have no pity on you, for I have made up my mind to Put all suicide Down. If there is one thing,' said the Alderman, with his self-satisfied smile, 'on which I can be said to have made up my mind more than on another, it is to Put suicide Down. So don't try it on. That's the phrase, isn't it! Ha, ha! now we understand each other.'[36]

Everyone recognised this as a lampoon of Sir Peter Laurie, Alderman and former Lord Mayor of the City of London, and Middlesex Magistrate. Sir Peter himself did so, and was astonished and hurt at what he considered 'ungracious treatment, after his civilities' — for he had met Dickens, entertained him at dinners, and obtained facilities for him to visit London gaols as a background for *Barnaby Rudge*. In his journal reviewing 1844, he wrote:

Dickens in his annual Xmas Tale this year introduced me as Alderman Cute resolved to '*put down*' everything connected with the Poor because I in 1841 'put down' suicide by sending two persons for trial. The fact was in two months there were *23* attempts at Blackfriars Bridge. Pathos and pity only seemed to increase the evil — The Grand Jury found a Bill, they were convicted and for the two following months Novr. and Dec: instead of *23* only *2*. . . . The newspapers gave my name but all abused the Tale as setting the poor against the rich and it was in all reviews condemned except the Edinburgh Review — It was dramatised and brought out at the Adelphi and Lyceum but was not successful and the Aldermans '*Put Down*' produced no effect. This was the more disgraceful for Dickens [because] I had taken his Wife to the Lord Mayor's dinner and was upon terms of civility with him — he is a dangerous man to meet — I was greatly hurt at the circumstance but I soon forgot it. . . . These are the penalties all public men pay — particularly those who have made their own fortune.[37]

The Chimes was not the last occasion on which Dickens attacked him: four years later, reviewing a Metropolitan Police Report, he noted that 'Old Sir Peter Laurie's sagacity does not appear by these returns to have quite "put down" suicide yet,'[38] and, two years after that, Laurie made a foolish attack on Dickens, which gave him an irresistible opportunity to strike back. At a meeting of the Marylebone Vestry, Sir Peter opposed spending the ratepayers' money on Industrial Training Schools for pauper children — a scheme as ephemeral, he said, as a recent proposal to improve the sanitation of Jacob's Island, which 'only existed in a work of fiction, written by Mr Charles Dickens ten years ago [*roars of laughter*].' In a new Preface to *Oliver Twist*, written a few weeks later, Dickens quoted this sally, and with heavy irony agreed that all places and persons ceased to exist when described by a novelist — in which case, 'Sir Peter Laurie having been himself described in a book (as I understand he was, one Christmas time, for his conduct on the seat of justice), it it is but too clear that there *can* be no such man!' Privately, at this time, Dickens described Laurie as 'that incarnation of a Vulgar Soul and a thoroughly mean and sordid spirit.'[39]

Laurie was not quite as bad as this: and there was some justice in the defence of his methods, expressed in his journal. He should have received some praise from Dickens, for having done so much to open the magistrates' courts to the Press and public and to make public executions more decent and merciful.[40] He was very active in supervising the City and Middlesex gaols, though his policies were of the tough 'commonsense' kind (his guffaws at Mr Rotch, and at prison-chaplains, have been mentioned earlier in this book). In 1835, he was impenitent when the terrible state of Newgate was exposed: 'I do not think you could improve it,' he said.[41] He was a violent opponent of the Separate System, though he thought that no system of prison-discipline offered any 'reasonable expectation of reformation of Prisoners generally.'[42] He also opposed spending money on rebuilding prisons, many of which were already made too comfortable 'by the humane excesses of some people', or on Industrial Schools to prevent boys from poor homes falling into a dishonest life, or on Houses of Occupation for the Refuge and Employment of Prisoners after their discharge. The last of these projects was started by a kinsman of his — to whom Dickens wrote an appreciative letter — but Sir Peter considered that this would put a premium on dishonesty. 'As to reforming a thief, he considered it was quite out of the question. He would go twenty miles to see a reformed convict.'[43] Laurie made this much-remembered statement to his fellow Middlesex Magistrates; he was a typical member of that unadventurous fraternity.

His most famous 'saying' was, of course, the one that Dickens repeats: that he would 'put down' suicide. Whether he ever actually used this unfortunate expression is, however, doubtful; Mr Michael Slater, who is making a special study of *The Chimes*, tells me that he has not been able to trace any record of his doing so, and a member of the Laurie family explicitly denied that he had done so. Certainly there was a general impression current in the early 1840s that he had used these words (Mr Slater guesses that it was *Punch* that had put them into his mouth); and certainly they represent fairly enough both the tone of his pronouncements and the policy towards suicide he had been operating. In 1841, a starving man had attempted to commit suicide — very inefficiently, said the police, who regarded it as merely a device for attracting sympathy. Sir Peter blamed the 'morbid sympathy' that encouraged such deeds, and sentenced the man to a month on the tread-mill, adding that he would 'look very narrowly' into any similar cases brought before him. Two days later, he sent forward for trial a girl rescued from Blackfriars Bridge (a place notorious for suicides), with the warning that 'when any crime became prevalent . . . it was the duty of the Magistrates to suppress it, if necessary, with severity.' It was six weeks before he had another such case before him, and he noted that his prompt action had greatly reduced the incidence of this offence, which had previously been occurring at the rate of three or four a week; many impostors had been making money by 'tumbling into the Thames', as sympathetic newspaper readers sent cash to these 'desperate' people. The *Illustrated London News* praised him for ending this 'drowning-mania' by 'boldly encountering the risk of being rated for want of feeling.'[44] And when, after several years of this campaign, he had before him a seduced girl, charged with trying to poison herself, he sent her for trial at the Old Bailey. He had no doubt, he said, that she would be transported. 'He had put an end to persons attempting to drown themselves; he would now try the same cure for attempted poisoning.' Douglas Jerrold, in *Punch*, commented that 'His conquest of suicide by water and poison is, perhaps, among the greatest triumphs of the public mind.'[45] This episode occurred just when Dickens was beginning on *The Chimes*.

Dickens was by no means the only person who found Laurie ludicrous and insensitive. Sir Peter probably surpasses even Colonel Sibthorpe, M.P., as the favourite butt of *Punch* throughout the 1840s. *Punch*'s first joke about him — not one of its best — appears in its second week of publication: '*Fashionable Arrivals . . .* Sir Peter Laurie has arrived at the conclusion — that Solon was a greater man than himself.'[46] There are thirty more in the first half-yearly volume, and I have counted over one hundred attacks on him during *Punch*'s first decade. 'The Pig-Skin Solomon' was one of its favourite names for him: others included 'Peter the Great', 'the eminent anti-suicide', and 'Peter the Putter-down'. Many items hound him for his 'putting-down' policy, but other aspects of his public life excited similar derision. 'Rally round your Cesspools: a Song for Sir Peter' appeared when he opposed the 'pernicious interference' of Dr Southwood Smith and his sanitary colleagues; 'Laurie and Lunacy' recorded a case of the blind leading the blind — his having become a Governor of Bedlam; 'Signs of a Hard Winter', another item was headed — 'A pamphlet was recently seen in Albemarle Street, written by Sir Peter Laurie.'[47] The tone of these attacks is very similar to Dickens's in *The Chimes*: and most of them were written by his friend Jerrold.

Laurie was certainly right in thinking that many 'attempted suicides' were a spectacular form of begging, but much too peremptory in regarding all cases as amenable to a tough policy of tread-mill or transportation. An energetic and well-meaning magistrate, he was sometimes bluffly generous towards cases before him, but his generosity and wisdom moved within narrow bounds. A self-made man, he enjoyed being a 'character' — a canny, no-nonsense, John-Bullish wiseacre. Even when Lord Mayor, he cracked his homespun jokes, which some people thought incompatible with the civic dignity. 'He devotedly loves his joke: it is a thing he could not be without — it is essential to his being.'

Dickens nicely hits off this hearty jocularity, in *The Chimes*; indeed, quite apart from identifying him with Cute through the (possibly apocryphal) 'putting-down' slogan, he catches many of Laurie's mannerisms very recognisably. 'Quaint and conceited, but with plenty of good sound sense and an honourable character,' Serjeant Ballantine thought him. 'His zeal may sometimes take an eccentric direction,' admitted an admirer in the *Illustrated London News*, though 'On the whole he has the fullest right to be the first in our series of "City Magistrates".'[48] This would not strike Dickens as a high distinction; he had little time for City aldermen and magistrates. Just after the *Illustrated London News* praised Laurie in these terms, Dickens was writing (to Douglas Jerrold, appropriately enough) about 'the City aristocracy' he had heard speechifying at a dinner and expressing 'such sentiments as any moderately intelligent dustman would have blushed through his cindery bloom to have thought of. Sleek, slobbering, bow-paunched, over-fed, apoplectic, snorting cattle, and the auditory leaping up in their delight!'[49]

It was not, then, only the apparent harshness of Sir Peter's 'putting down' policy that aroused the animosity of Dickens and Jerrold, but its emanating from this prosperous and complacent background of City dinners. *Punch* and *The Chimes* do not, of course, offer a balanced estimate of his achievement, but their comment on his shortcomings was not grossly unfair. Maybe he never actually used that 'putting-down' phrase; certainly he meant well, in that as in other of his public activities. But, along with some innocently silly idiocyncrasies, he had an aggravatingly cocksure manner and was on the whole a dangerously stupid reactionary. When challenged about his contention that Jacob's Island was a figment of Dickens's imagination, he indignantly defended his original remarks;[50] he must bear some responsibility for the deaths from cholera there. 'And when he joked the little children died in the streets.' One can hardly spare much sympathy for his 'hurt feelings' when he was pilloried as Alderman Cute. Here was a case where Dickens was justified in discerning the insolence of office.

Often, however, he was not so justified. He generally assumed that magistrates were guilty unless proved innocent. His suspicion was common: *Punch* shared it ('The Pig-Skin Solomon' was only the most conspicuous of its magisterial butts), so did *Figaro in London*, so did Fonblanque of *The Examiner*, and many other

Radical journalists. Probably Dickens, as a young man on the staff of the *Morning Chronicle*, had been a good deal influenced in this direction by its editor, John Black, whom he revered and who was (wrote John Stuart Mill) 'the first journalist who carried criticism and the spirit of reform into the details of English institutions . . . the writer who introduced Bentham's opinions on legal and judicial reform into newspaper discussion.' His almost daily leading articles against an Unpaid Magistracy — mainly written by Fonblanque — hammered the point home *ad nauseam*.[51] There were some objective grounds for this (Sir Peter, after all, was considered one of the *best* of the City magistrates), but much more important, I would guess, was social and political prejudice. The rural magistracy was, on the whole, the squirearchy — a class obnoxious to Dickens and his fellows on several grounds. The town magistrates were successful merchants, of the kind Dickens heard at the City dinner, or lesser men rewarded for political services such as Dickens could not respect. ('Vestry' was a swearword for him.) 'How do you suppose he comes to be a Middlesex Magistrate?' David Copperfield asks, when he hears of Mr Creakle's elevation. 'Oh, dear me!' replied Traddles, 'it would be very difficult to answer that question. Perhaps he voted for somebody, or lent money to somebody, or bought something of somebody, or otherwise obliged somebody, or jobbed for somebody, who knew somebody who got the lieutenant of the county to nominate him for the commission.'[52] Dickens could, perhaps, feel more tolerance for Judges than for magistrates, because they mostly came from or moved into a social class several times removed from the one in which he himself was born and to which he always instinctively belonged. The class one most hates is the one just above one's own. Dickens was warmer towards the aristocracy, than towards the self-made commercial bourgeoisie.

Moreover, magistrates mattered more than Judges, because there were more of them and because they impinged more obviously on the poor. 'The Nupkinses and Fangs,' as Humphry House points out, 'are the instruments of Government which touch the people most closely, and it is in them that the conception of government held by the ruling class can be most clearly seen. It is an almost entirely negative conception; its end is Public Order, and the only means to the end is "putting-down".' Dickens could see the inadequacy and the harshness, often involuntary, of this outlook, but his own powers of thought and imagination were inadequate to devise anything more positive, except in the vaguest terms. As so often, I find myself anticipated, and my ideas clarified, by Humphry House, who writes, just after the sentences I have just quoted:

> . . . it is significant that . . . he never once attempted to give one of his benevolent characters any public office; there is no portrait in any of his fiction of a good judge, a good bishop, or a good magistrate. . . . His problem all through his writing life was to find a kind of political and social power, a government, which he could approve; and in the end he failed. He was not a man of great political understanding and vision, not a prophet; his imagination worked on the data society gave him. . . .[53]

Dickens had, of course, some positive ideas about the state of the law. He shared the common layman's opinion that legal language was a mumbo-jumbo devised by lawyers to render themselves necessary and valuable. He asked ironically, in one of the opening numbers of *Household Words*: 'Supposing, we were materially to simplify the laws, and to abrogate the absurd fiction that everybody is supposed to be acquainted with them, when we know very well that such acquaintance is the study of a life in which some fifty men may have been proficient perhaps in five times fifty years, I wonder whether laws would be respected less?' It was a theme to which his journals often reverted.[54] The loopholes of the law, and the high costs of litigation, were other obvious grievances which he and his colleagues explored; Grand Juries were one of their particular hatreds.[55] Dickens was increasingly impatient with English court procedure — for being, as he thought, much too favourable to the criminal ('learned judges taking uncommon pains to prevent the prisoner from letting out the truth'). The accused should have no option about being questioned in court, he thought.[56] In 'Five New Points of Criminal Law' he ironically suggests some amendments which should ensure still further protection for poisoners; he reiterates his favourite gibe that 'the real offender is the Murdered Person'.[57]

'A due respect for the Law is the basis of social existence,' Dickens agreed, but he was sickened by laudation of the existing English law, and of our proverbial respect for it.

> We avow for our own part, that whensoever, at public meeting, dinner, testimonial-presentation, charity-election, or other spoutation ceremony, we find (which we always do), an orator approaching an Englishman's respect for the Law, our heart dries up within us, and terror paralyses our frame. As the dreadful old clap-trap begins to

jingle, we become the prey of a deep-seated melancholy and a miserable despair. We know the thing to have passed into a fulsome form, out of which the life has gone, and into which putrefaction has come. On common lips we perceive it to be a thing of no meaning, and on lips of authority we perceive it to have gradually passed into a thing of most pernicious meaning.

Citizens were leaving too much to the police; they should take a hand themselves.[58] Similarly, Judges should have regard to the spirit of the law, if to follow its letter would result in the injustice of malefactors' escaping altogether or getting off too lightly. As often when at his least sensible, Dickens very appropriately adopts the style and tone of Carlyle. Here he imagines the outraged Law speaking to such a culprit:

> 'Attend to me yet, knave. Hold your peace! You are one of those landmarks whose eyes have twinkled to see the driving of coaches and six through Acts of Parliament, and who come up with their dirty little dog's meat carts to follow through the same crooked ways. But you shall know, that I am something more than a maze of tortuous ins and outs, and that I have at least, one plain road — to wit, the road by which, for the general protection, and in the exercise of my first function, I mean to send you into safe keeping; fifty thousand Acts, and a hundred thousand Caps, and five hundred thousand Secs, notwithstanding.
>
> 'For, Beast of Prey, above the perplexed letter of all Law that has any might in it, goes the spirit. If I be, as I claim to be, the child of Justice, and not the offspring of the Artful Dodger, that spirit shall, before I gabble through one legal argument more, provide for you and all the like of you, as you deserve. If it cannot do that of itself, I will have letter to help it. . . .'[59]

In the article in which this unwise suggestion occurs, Dickens had been describing, without mentioning names, a case in which he himself had been long involved — against an unsavoury blackmailer and impostor who for years past had been persecuting the heiress Miss Coutts. Dickens had taken a hand in earlier attempts to bring him to justice, none of which had been satisfactorily conclusive. 'I should very much like . . . to state this Dunn's case, as from a public knowledge of it, in Household Words,' he wrote when the case came up again in 1853. 'I think I could cast a little more reproach and disgrace about the gentleman than the Judges do.' In the article, in fact, it is the lower courts that he most attacks — 'incapable country justices, and dim little farthing rushlights of the law', through whose technical errors ('because the Law is a Law of the peddling letter and not of the comprehensive spirit') Dunn escapes 'any punishment worthy of the name, for his real offence.'[60] One can understand Dickens's impatience, especially as he had other experiences of the law's delays and imperfections. He had found the law very inefficient in protecting his copyright, and on other occasions, when he insisted that petty wrong-doers be charged in the police courts, he received little encouragement or gratitude for this public service. He recounts several instances of this — for instance, the time when he insisted on having a girl charged for using foul language in the streets. The police were surprised, but courteous, the magistrate by no means so courteous: 'I was evidently regarded as a much more objectionable person than the prisoner.' Asked whether he really wanted the girl sent to prison, 'I grimly answered, stating: "If I didn't, why should I take the trouble to come here?" ' but she got off with a ten shillings fine.[61] Another such experience was his prosecution of a fraudulent begging-letter writer — a class from whom he suffered a good deal —

> I presented myself at a London Police-Office with my testimony against him. The Magistrate was wonderfully struck by his educational acquirements, deeply impressed by the excellence of his letters, exceedingly sorry to see a man of his attainments there, complimented him highly on his powers of composition, and was quite charmed to have the agreeable duty of discharging him. A collection was made for the 'poor fellow', as he was called in the reports, and I left the court with a comfortable sense of being universally regarded as a sort of monster. Next day comes to me a friend of mine, the governor of a large prison. 'Why did you ever go to the Police-Office against that man,' says he, 'without coming to me first? I know all about him and his frauds. . . .'[62]

The prison-governor was, presumably, Chesterton. Dickens's acquaintance with Chesterton and his prison had a more amusing result, in another police-court case in which Dickens was involved. He and his friend Mark Lemon, the editor of *Punch*, had chased and caught a lad who was picking Lemon's pocket. At the police station, Dickens said that he thought that he recognised the lad, having seen him at Coldbath Fields prison. The boy agreed: he, too, recognised Dickens — as a 'swell-mob man' who trafficked in stolen goods, and had been 'inside' for six months as against his own sentence of only two.[63] Dickens was indeed free from the vice of which he accused his fellow-citizens, failing to take a hand in bringing wrong-doers to justice. Other cases have been reported, of his taking the initiative and giving firm evidence in the courts.[64]

In most of these instances, where Dickens is plaintiff or victim, his complaint about the magistrates is, not that they are rough and oppressive, but that they are credulous and lenient. In his public pronouncements, this allegation becomes more common in the second half of his career. Mr Creakle, in *David Copperfield* (1849–1850), marks a turning-point. Most of the magistrates in the earlier stories had, as I have mentioned, been seen from the point of view of the bewildered, innocent and badly-used prisoner. We see Mr Nupkins through the eyes of Mr Pickwick: Mr Fang through Oliver's and Mr Brownlow's: the country magistrate through Mrs Rudge's: Alderman Cute through Trotty Veck's and Will Fern's. This character and viewpoint do not appear in the later novels. Soft-hearted and soft-headed Mr Creakle is seen through the eyes of the intelligent citizens, David Copperfield and Traddles, and in relation to two undoubted villains, Uriah Heep and Mr Littimer. He is 'coddling' his prisoners, and believes any sanctimonious lie they tell. Most of Dickens's later comments on the administration of justice are written from David Copperfield's point of view.

Of course, he could always find cases to criticise in these terms. A complaint he and his colleagues on the periodicals often made was that sentences for offences against the person were too lenient, especially when compared with sentences for offences against property. He refers ironically, for instance, to the penalties inflicted on ruffians who maim policemen for life — 'I constantly read in the newspapers of such an offender being committed to prison with hard labour, for one, two or even three months.' Dickens demanded much longer sentences, in nastier prisons, and without any option; fines, he said, were a 'barbarous device, quite as much out of date as wager by battle'. As for street-violence, the magistrates, with a few exceptions, 'know nothing about it but what the Police choose to tell them.'[65] Their sentences were erratic, if generally erring towards leniency. One *Household Words* article analysed the figures for a recent Quarter Sessions in six counties, purporting to show how much depended on the wisdom and temper of the magistrates presiding. One group of four dozen prisoners, who between them had stolen a total of £12.9.1, received sentences amounting to 376 years of transportation, while another four dozen got a total of sixteen and a half years for thefts totalling over four hundred pounds.[66] Such complaints were common in the Press, and often justified; there had been a particularly strong outcry about the disparity between sentences for larceny and for assault in the winter of 1851, but the topic had long been prominent in *Punch*, for instance.[67]

During this period when Dickens was condemning the magistracy more often for softness than for harshness, he continues to rise in defence of two classes of the oppressed — children and ordinary working men. During the first winter of *Household Words*, he wrote 'A December Vision', in which he saw the untaught children of London being 'hunted, flogged, imprisoned'; a few weeks later, the Old Year looked back on its grievous record of unjust punishments inflicted on children who could know no better.[68] Very often, in defending popular amusements, particularly on the Sabbath, he attacks the 'bigwigs' who try to close parks and stop music-licences, and who malign the ordinary man by stating or insinuating that he is by nature a drunken beast.[69] Mr Gradgrind is a typical magistrate in this respect: when he reads the circus folk's bill-poster, he mentally 'consigns them to the House of Correction'.[70] At the end of *Hard Times*, Mr Gradgrind, though a Justice of the Peace, contrives, at some expense, to get his thieving son Tom overseas so that he may evade prosecution; neither Dickens nor the judicial authorities take him to task for this, since he is by then a broken and chastened man. Outside fiction, however, Dickens had a keener eye for class-bias in the administration of justice — for the magistrate, for instance, who ensured special privileges for a 'gentleman' prisoner.[71]

I must not exaggerate the difference between Dickens's earlier and later attitudes to the Bench. Throughout his life he was eager to ensure that malefactors were hauled up and punished, and equally he was ready to denounce the oppressive treatment of minor offenders or of the innocent. But in his later years he was more likely to notice and write about cases where, in his opinion, the public was not being given the protection it deserved, because sentences were too light; earlier, it was cases of judicial bullying that more often attracted his attention and excited his indignation. No doubt, instances of both kinds of judicial error occurred every day, at all stages of his career — as, indeed, at any period, including our own. One notices the kind of error one wants to notice: a comparison between the newspapers of 1961 makes that obvious enough — some habitually report the apparent excesses, others the apparent soft-headedness, of the courts, though criticisms of either kind are much more restrained than in Dickens's day. The later Dickens most often comments on cases of murder and assault, for which any sentence short of death or life-imprisonment may easily seem too light. The earlier Dickens is drawn towards cases where decent people like Pickwick and Oliver and Mrs Rudge and Will Fern find themselves up for judgment; they deserve an acquittal, indeed an apology, but only through good luck do they get either. This shift in Dickens's choice of subject (and thus of attitude) does not, I think, reflect an objective change in the state of crime, or the administration of justice, nor a conscious development in his convictions on these issues. Rather, it falls in with that change in public feeling towards criminals and prisons, examples of which we have seen, and further examples of which we shall see in a later chapter. It is also related to changes in Dickens himself — but these are emotional changes, not intellectual or ideological.

THE POLICE

Dickens had, said one of his colleagues, 'a curious and almost morbid partiality for communing with and entertaining police officers. . . . He seemed always at his ease with these personages, and never tired of questioning them.' The affection was reciprocated, or so Dickens thought. 'Any of the Detective men will do anything for me,' he said.[1] He wrote a good deal about them; he is generally credited with introducing the detective into English fiction, while his journalistic articles on the subject were much admired and copied at the time, and have been lavishly quoted by almost every historian of British police development. If highly-coloured, these articles are, indeed, of great historical value, as among the earliest and most vivid accounts of the personalities and activities of this new branch of Scotland Yard. 'Charles Dickens may be said to have discovered the modern detective,' wrote a contemporary. 'His papers in *Household Words* were a revelation to the public, and the life portraits he drew of some of the most notable men employed in this comparatively new branch of criminal pursuit were the just rewards accorded to those excellent officers.'[2] Some of his readers, however, deplored the 'almost hyperbolical language' which he used on this subject, and several recent commentators have discussed this 'almost fanatical devotion' to the Metropolitan police (as Humphry House puts it, in a valuable couple of pages on the topic), and have noted the contrast between his admiration for the police and his contempt for, or indifference towards, other public functionaries — politicians, magistrates, officers in the armed services, civil servants and local government officials.[3] Gratefully taking some hints from these predecessors, I propose to examine, more fully than their purposes permitted, the nature and significance of Dickens's interest in the police.

They were of course a new phenomenon. Dickens's lifetime, as was mentioned in the opening chapter, saw the establishment and rapid development of the police as we know them. Peel had set up the Metropolitan force less than seven years before Dickens's first books appeared; certain provincial towns and cities were permitted to appoint a paid constabulary by the Municipal Corporations Act of 1835, and the system was extended to other towns and to county areas by further Police Acts of 1839 and 1856. Under the 1856 Act all local authorities were obliged to set up police forces, and the Government offered financial inducements towards efficiency. As all historians of the British police remark, the two Commissioners of Metropolitan Police appointed in 1829 — Colonel Charles Rowan, and Richard Mayne — showed remarkable prescience. Their scheme of police organisation and duties, and the relations which they established between police and public, not only became the model for the many Constabularies founded in the next few decades, but have also remained the guiding principle down to today. The primary duty of the police was to prevent crime, through co-operation with the local community. Perhaps the Commissioners hoped too much from this policy, in their early years; certainly the task of detecting the perpetrators of crimes which had not been prevented still remained to be done, and in 1842 the Commissioners gave official recognition to this by establishing a Detective Department. This was done unostentatiously; the first mention of 'the detective force' in a criminal case did not occur, apparently, until the famous trial of Hocker, the Hampstead murderer, in 1845.[4]

Before 1829, England was still being policed by the antique system of parish-constables and watchmen, which had not improved much since Shakespeare's time: nor had the jokes changed much, either, for Dogberry and Verges, and Elbow, reappear in Messrs Grummer and Dubbley of unreformed Ipswich, in *Pickwick Papers*.[5] Between 1750 and 1780, the Fielding brothers, Henry and John, had improved the safety of London by establishing the Bow Street Runners and Patroles, and these, later augmented, and joined by the Thames River Police, were much the most efficient English police-force before the Peelers.[6] But the gross inadequacies of London's defences were shown, not only by the huge amount of undetected crime, but also by such crises as the Gordon Riots of 1780. As we saw, Dickens in *Barnaby Rudge* attributes these disorders to 'bad criminal laws, bad prison regulations, and the worst conceivable police', and he describes the main guardians of the peace — the watchmen and constables — comically but not altogether unfairly. The watchmen, he says, 'being selected for the office on account of excessive age and extraordinary infirmity, had a custom of shutting themselves up tight in their boxes on the first symptoms of disturbance, and remaining there until they disappeared,' while the constables are represented by this reply of the Lord Mayor, beset by a gentleman who demands protection for his property — 'Would a javelin-man do? — Or, there's Philips the constable, — *he's* disengaged, — he's not very old for a man at his time of life, except in his legs, and if you put him up at a window he'd look quite young by candle-light, and might frighten 'em very much.'[7] It has often been said that Dickens was nostalgic for the past — for a pre-industrial stage-coach England — but this tendency in him has been much exaggerated. The new police seemed to him one of the unqualified advantages of modernity.

He was not even nostalgic for the Bow Street Runners, whose exploits had long been famous. The Runners were primarily a detective force, and were generally held to be much superior at such work, until they were disbanded ten years after the Metropolitan Police were established (though three years before they had a Detective Department of their own). Dickens's crusty old butt, Sir Peter Laurie, for instance, 'was positive that the Metropolitan Police could not supersede the Runners,' and he instanced the famous Forrester brother of the City Police, who had only to look at the scene of a crime and would then 'tell you directly, by inspection, whether it had been done by an old or by an inexperienced thief'. Serjeant Ballantine was another great admirer of the Runners, who he thought were more skilful and self-effacing than their Scotland Yard successors, though he acknowledged that the ordinary constables were a great improvement on the old 'Charlies'.[8] The inferiority of the Metropolitan Police was, of course, sedulously maintained by the Runners themselves, and by the Police Magistrates who were losing power, under the new system, to the Commissioners at Scotland Yard.[9] Dickens had no truck with this particular nostalgia. Introducing an article on the modern detectives, he briskly dismissed their predecessors:

> We are not by any means devout believers in the old Bow Street Police. To say the truth, we think there was a vast amount of humbug about these worthies. Apart from many of them being men of very indifferent character, and far too much in the habit of consorting with thieves and the like, they never lost a public occasion of jobbing and trading in mystery and making the most of themselves. Continually puffed besides by incompetent magistrates anxious to conceal their own deficiencies, and hand-in-glove with the penny-a-liners

of that time, they became a sort of superstition. Although as a
Preventive Police they were utterly ineffective, and as a Detective
Police were very loose and uncertain in their operations, they remain
with some people a superstition to the present day.[10]

Dickens's magisterial judgment is one of the *loci classici* in police
history. It recurs, inevitably, in most books on the subject, nearly
always being quoted with approval.[11] Recently, however, it has
been challenged by Mr Patrick Pringle, in his excellent Introduction to *Memoirs of a Bow Street Runner*, the case-book of one of the
most famous of the fraternity, Henry Goddard. Mr Pringle also
quotes and criticises a well-known letter Dickens wrote in 1862, to
a young colleague who wanted information on this subject:

> The Bow Street runners ceased out of the land soon after the intro-
> duction of the new police. I remember them very well as standing
> about the door of the office in Bow Street. They had no other uniform
> than a blue dress-coat, brass buttons (I am not even now sure that
> that was necessary), and a bright red cloth waistcoat. The waistcoat
> was indispensable, and the slang name for them was 'red-breasts',
> in consequence.
>   They kept company with thieves and the like, much more than
> the detective police do. I don't know what their pay was, but I have
> no doubt their principal complements were got under the rose. It was
> a very slack institution, and its head-quarters were The Brown Bear,
> in Bow Street, a public-house of more than doubtful reputation,
> opposite the police-office; and either the house which is now the
> theatrical costume maker's, or the next door to it.
>   Field, who advertises the Secret Enquiry Office, was a Bow Street
> runner, and can tell you all about it; Goddard, who also advertises
> an enquiry office, was another of the fraternity. They are the only
> two I know of as yet existing in a 'questionable shape'.[12]

As Mr Pringle points out, Dickens's memory was certainly at
fault about the Runners' dress, for they wore no uniform; the
costume and nickname he describes belonged, not to them, but to
the Bow Street Patroles. More important are Dickens's allegations
about their honesty and efficiency. Certainly the Runners depended upon rewards and private fees for most of their income,
and their activities had sometimes included the arrangement of
compromises whereby stolen cash or goods were restored to their
owners without prosecutions being entered — but this occurred, as
a Parliamentary Committee of 1823 found, with the Magistrates'
sanction and generally at the owners' request. 'Not one of the Bow

Street Runners,' writes Mr Pringle, 'was ever charged with a criminal offence or, as far as I know, dismissed on suspicion of being corrupt.' They certainly frequented the Brown Bear, a 'flash-house' or thieves' rendezvous, and even used it as a lock-up, but there is no evidence (he continues) that their motives or behaviour were any more improper than those of later detectives who have, in the course of duty, familiarised themselves with the haunts of their clients.[13] Dickens seems to Mr Pringle as unfair towards the Runners as he was uncritical towards their successors: his 'naive belief that the detectives of Scotland Yard were incorruptible' was, he asserts, 'soon proved wrong.' Here Mr Pringle must be referring to the scandals of the late 1870s — but these happened a decade after his death, and a quarter-century after his main writings on the subject.[14] The Metropolitan police had received much criticism and calumny during Dickens's lifetime, but there had been a striking absence of important allegations of corruption.[15]

Mr Pringle, in challenging Dickens's assessment of the Runners, is rejecting also the judgment of most later historians of the police.[16] Certainly the fortunes left by some of the Runners seem to a later age too large to have been earned by legitimate fees and rewards alone. But I cannot claim to have done such sustained original work on police documents from this period as might entitle me to say whether Dickens or his critic is nearer the truth. Very likely Dickens saw the matter too much in terms of black and white (such was his habit of mind), but there is no doubt that the Metropolitan Police, including the Detective Department, were soon much more effective than the Bow Street officers. How much this was due to the superior organisation of police work, and how much to the relative incorruptibility of the New Police, I cannot say; nor do I know how far the notable decrease in crime was due to their activities, and how far to other social improvements. A decrease certainly occurred — though in the early years of Scotland Yard it was confined to London, for many professional criminals transferred their operations from the metropolis to the ill-policed provinces.[17] This was, indeed, a tribute, for, as Gibbon Wakefield pointed out, the best authority on police efficiency were the experienced thieves. He was in Newgate when the Scotland Yard regime began. The old lags, he reported, never mentioned the old police except with contempt and derision — 'until, indeed, the establishment of the new Police, whereupon the regular thieves, who entered Newgate about that time, spoke with affection of the old system.' Inevitably, comparisons between the old and new regimes were the great topic of Newgate conversation: 'the former was universally praised, and the latter mentioned in terms of strong dislike.' As Wakefield concluded, 'The hatred which the thieves bear to the new Police proves that the new is superior to the old system, but not that it is perfect,' and he went on to urge that a special detective branch be established (though this did not come about for some years).[18]

The Bow Street Runners appear in two of Dickens's novels, in both cases investigating crimes committed outside the metropolitan area — as, like their Scotland Yard successors, they were often called upon to do. In *Oliver Twist* (1837–9) they are called to Chertsey after Bill Sikes and his gang have been house-breaking, and in *Great Expectations* (1860–1) to Kent after the assault upon Mrs Joe Gargery. In the latter book, Dickens makes his customary sneer at the much-lauded Runners. 'It was characteristic of the police people,' he comments, 'that they all more or less suspected poor Joe.' They

> were about the house for a week or two, and did pretty much what I have heard and read of like authorities doing in other such cases. They took up several obviously wrong people, and they ran their heads very hard against wrong ideas, and persisted in trying to fit the circumstances to the ideas, instead of trying to extract ideas from the circumstances. Also, they stood about the door of the Jolly Bargemen, with knowing and reserved looks that filled the whole neighbourhood with admiration: and they had a mysterious manner of taking their drink, that was almost as good as taking the culprit. But not quite, for they never did it.[19]

In the earlier book, written before Dickens began his love-affair with the Metropolitan Police, he was less critical. Blathers and Duff were, certainly, vulgar fellows, and the latter had 'a rather ill-favoured countenance, and a turned-up sinister-looking nose' (as well as an unpromising surname). They fail to solve the crime, largely because Mr Losberne and his household are withholding the relevant evidence, though they spend a lot of time consulting together in great 'secrecy and solemnity'. But, though mildly satirical, Dickens is impressed by their professional pride, expertise and patter ('We had better inspect the premises first, and examine the servants arterwards. That's the usual way of doing business').

They decide that this was not 'a put-up thing' — that is, they explain, not a robbery by the servants.

> 'We find it was a town hand,' said Blathers, continuing his report; 'for the style of work is first-rate.'
>
> 'Wery pretty indeed it is,' remarked Duff, in an undertone . . .
>
> 'Ah!' said Mr Blathers, not holding his wineglass by the stem, but grasping the bottom between the thumb and forefinger of his left hand, and placing it in front of his chest; 'I have seen a good many pieces of business like this, in my time, ladies.'
>
> 'That crack down in the back lane at Edmonton, Blathers,' said Mr Duff, assisting his colleague's memory.
>
> 'That was something in this way, warn't it?' rejoined Mr Blathers; 'that was done by Conkey Chickweed, that was.'
>
> 'You always gave that to him,' replied Duff. 'It was the Family Pet, I tell you. Conkey hadn't any more to do with it than I had.'
>
> 'Get out!' retorted Mr Blathers; 'I know better. Do you mind that time when Conkey was robbed of his money, though? What a start that was! Better than any novel-book I ever see! . . . It was a robbery, miss, that hardly anybody would have been down upon. This here Conkey Chickweed . . . kept a public-house over Battlebridge way. . . .'

— and Dickens then holds up the action for two pages, while Blathers describes how Conkey was detected in a fraud by Jem Spyers, 'an active officer' (as plain-clothes detectives were then called).[20] The tones and the relish of this account, and its uneducated idiom, anticipate Dickens's more famous and more adulatory presentation of the Scotland Yard detectives a dozen years later.

One of the less savoury aspects of the pre-Metropolitan police was its heavy reliance on paid informers. This, like the Runners' collaboration with thieves and fences, was probably inevitable if stolen property was ever to be restored, or malefactors prosecuted, under a police system so haphazard and ill-manned, but the use of spies naturally aroused widespread resentment and it was the policy of the New Police to do without them as far as possible. In several novels dealing with the old days, Dickens reflects the popular detestation of the informer. One recalls Mr Pickwick's embarrassment when he is suspected of being one, and the reptilian group of characters who do actually make a living from this disgraceful trade — Noah Claypole, Barsad and Cly, and Mr Gashford.[21]

For the ordinary Peeler on his beat, Dickens expresses great respect, though not the awe he reserves for the detective branch.

In his early *Sketches by Boz* (1836) he notes with satisfaction that the London apprentices, who used to enjoy terrifying the citizens 'whenever it pleased them to take offense in their heads and staves in their hands', are now restrained by a 'wholesome dread of the New Police'. He also refers to the perils of Walworth in 1800 — 'the police of London were a very different body in that day.'[22] In another early work, *The Old Curiosity Shop* (1840–1), appears a police characteristic which often recurs later: the constable whom Sampson Brass summons to arrest Kit Nubbles is *imperturbable*.

> This functionary being, of course, well used to such scenes; looking upon all kinds of robbery, from petty larceny up to housebreaking or ventures on the highway, as matters in the regular course of business; and regarding the perpetrators in the light of so many customers coming to be served at the wholesale and retail shop of criminal law, where he stood behind the counter; received Mr Brass's statement of facts with about as much interest and surprise as an undertaker might evince if required to listen to a circumstantial account of the last illness of a person whom he was called in to wait upon professionally; and took Kit into custody with a decent indifference.

The imperturbability of the British policeman was soon, indeed, a part of the national mythology. *Punch*, for instance, pointed out how every country's police reflected the national temperament. 'The Englishman is as laconic as an electric telegraph's message. The Frenchman is as lengthy and as pompous as an American President's message. . . . The English Policeman says briefly and sharply, "Move on there." '[23] It was another sign of the times, perhaps, that in *Dombey and Son* (1846–8) Mrs MacStinger uses the local policeman to knock her up early on spring-cleaning days; relations between the police and their community had not been so happy and familiar a few years before.[24]

The apotheosis of the Bobbie occurs, however, in *Bleak House* (1852–3). Thus, soon after Nemo's dead body has been found, a policeman is on the scene.

> A policeman has already walked up to the room, and walked down again to the door, where he stands like a tower, only condescending to see the boys at his base occasionally; but whenever he does see them, they quail and fall back. . . . The beadle, though generally understood in the neighbourhood to be a ridiculous institution, is not without a certain popularity for the moment, if it were only as a man who is going to see the body. The policeman considers him an imbecile civilian, a remnant of the barbarous watchmen-times; but gives him

admission, as something that must be borne with until Government shall abolish him. . . .

. . . Policeman seen to smile at potboy. Public loses interest, and undergoes reaction. Taunts the beadle, in shrill youthful voices, with having boiled a boy; choruses fragments of a popular song to that effect, and importing that the boy was made into soup for the workhouse. Policeman at last finds it necessary to support the law, and seize a vocalist; who is released upon the flight of the rest, on condition of his getting out of this then, come! and cutting it — a condition he immediately observes. So the sensation dies off for the time; and the unmoved policeman . . . with his shining hat, stiff stock, inflexible great-coat, stout belt and bracelet, and all things fitting, pursues his lounging way with a heavy tread: beating the palms of his white gloves one against the other, and stopping now and then, at a street-corner, to look casually about for anything between a lost child and a murder.

A yet more impressive tribute, in the same novel, is Dickens's treatment of the constable who 'moves on' Jo, the crossing-sweeper boy whom we are intended to love. Though this 'one grand recipe' for Jo is presented as a symbol of society's wicked neglect of such waifs, the policeman is exonerated. He is fulfilling his instructions, impersonally. He speaks, 'calmly, with a slight professional hitch of his neck involving its better settlement in his stiff stock'; he gives Jo only 'a passionless shake'.[25]

One of the greatest compliments a novelist can pay to his characters is to let them harm the 'good' characters with impunity. In *Bleak House*, Inspector Bucket also proceeds against Jo, and against Gridley and George Rouncewell as well, without ever being meant to forfeit our approval. Bucket's claim to be the first police-detective in English fiction has been sustained in the most recent scholarly study of the development of the detective novel, by Mrs A. E. Murch.[26] He is the father of a long line (and it is surprising to see how many of his characteristics are inherited by his literary successors), but he himself inherits much from the detectives Dickens had described in a series of articles two years before. A few months after *Household Words* began, its assistant-editor W. H. Wills contributed an article on 'The Modern Science of Thief-Taking', extolling the Detective Department and the local divisional Detectives, and contrasting their experienced skill with the clumsiness of the ordinary constable. During the following month, two similar articles by Dickens himself appeared, under the title 'A Detective Police Party', and a month later he contributed 'Three "Detective" Anecdotes'. This series of articles formed a prominent feature in the new magazine, and attracted a good deal of attention. Next year, Dickens wrote 'On Duty with Inspector Field' and collaborated with Wills on an article describing a night at Bow Street Station, 'The Metropolitan Protectives.' A further article by Dickens, on the Thames River Police, appeared in 1853 — 'Down with the Tide.'[27]

All these papers are laudatory, indeed awestruck. The tone is represented well enough by these passages from the beginning and the end of 'A Detective Police Party'.

> ... the Detective Force organised since the establishment of the existing Police, is so well chosen and trained, proceeds so systematically and quietly, does its business in such a workmanlike manner, and is always so calmly and steadily engaged in the service of the public, that the public really do not know enough of it, to know a tithe of its usefulness.
>
> .   .   .   .
>
> Such ... is the peculiar ability, always sharpening and being improved by practice, ... for which this important social branch of the public service is remarkable! For ever on the watch, with their wits stretched to the utmost, these officers have, from day to day and year to year, to set themselves against every novelty of trickery and dexterity that the combined imaginations of all the lawless rascals in England can devise, and to keep pace with every such invention that comes out. ...
>
> These games of chess, played with live pieces, are played before small audiences, and are chronicled nowhere. The interest of the game supports the player. Its results are enough for Justice.[28]

Several of these articles were based on nights out with the police — in the slums and common lodging-houses and thieves' dens of the St Giles area, or down the river, or in the busy Station-houses. Dickens relished these slumming expeditions under police guidance, whether in London or New York or Liverpool. About the latter, he wrote another adulatory article, in 1860, while his visit to 'an infamous receptacle of rogues' in New York was commemorated in another and more surprising way — the area, formerly called Five Points, was renamed Dickens Place in his honour.[29] Such forays were quite a novelty at that time: but so was the journalistic 'interview', on which the other articles were based. Dickens invited the whole Detective Department to some evening parties at the *Household Words* offices; as its full strength was only two Inspectors and six Sergeants, this was not impossible, and Dickens recorded that they were all present except one.[30] In 'A Detective Police Party' he describes all his visitors from the Yard one by one, under the flimsiest of pseudonyms — 'Stalker' for Walker, 'Dornton' for Thornton, and so on — and sums up their general appearance thus:

> They are, one and all, respectable-looking men; of perfectly good deportment and unusual intelligence; with nothing lounging or slinking in their manners; with an air of keen observation and quick perception when addressed; and generally presenting in their faces, traces more or less marked of habitually leading lives of strong mental excitement. They have all good eyes; and they all can, and they all do, look full at whomsoever they speak to.[31]

Nowhere else in his work does Dickens indulge this vein of boyish hero-worship.

According to his friend Sala, who was present at some of these detective parties, Dickens greatly over-estimated his guests' skill — and one can well believe this, for no men could be quite the paragons of virtue and sagacity he here describes. Another young colleague, Fitzgerald, agrees with Sala, and cites this hyperbolical respect for detectives as an example of an amiable weakness in Dickens — his proclivity for exaggerating the merits of the people he loved.[32] His closest colleague, Wills, shared the enchantment, however: these detectives, he wrote, could often tell what a rogue had been up to, simply by looking into his eyes.[33] Later policemen seem to have lost this convenient knack of divination.

What Sala says about one of the policemen who was a frequent guest at *Household Words* dinners is of particular interest: 'There was something, but not much, of Dickens's Inspector Bucket about Inspector Field; and I venture to think that he was a much acuter and astuter detective in *Bleak House* than he was in real life.' Field reminded him rather of the old Bow Street Runners, like Blathers and Duff.[34] Inspector Charles Frederick Field has been regarded as the 'original' of Inspector Bucket ever since the novel appeared, and Dickens even took the unusual step of writing to *The Times* to comment on this rumour. Some statements in that newspaper, he wrote, 'represent me as having availed myself of the experiences of that excellent police-officer, Mr Inspector Field, in *Bleak House*, and so as having undertaken to write the said excellent officer's biography. Allow me to assure you that, amid all the news in *The Times*, I found nothing more entirely and completely new to me than these two pieces of intelligence.'[35] Though not an explicit denial, this has the air of being one; but it is disingenuous. For some prominent features of Bucket were very clearly derived from Field (or from what Dickens took Field to be) — which is not to say, of course, that Bucket *is* Field.

His appearance and mannerisms certainly reappear in Bucket. Inspector 'Wield' is described appreciatively in one of the *Household Words* articles as 'a middle-aged man of a portly presence, with a large, moist, knowing eye, a husky voice, and a habit of emphasising his conversation by the aid of a corpulent forefinger, which is constantly in juxtaposition with his eyes or nose'. Appearing in another article under his own name, Field is said to be 'of a burly figure', 'sagacious, vigilant,' 'polite and soothing', and to possess an almost supernatural facility for knowing every place inside-out, for being everywhere, and for knowing everyone.

> Inspector Field's eye is the roving eye that searches every corner of the cellar as he talks . . . [He] stands in this den, the Sultan of the place. Every thief here cowers before him, like a schoolboy before his schoolmaster. . . . Come across the street here, and, entering by a little shop, and yard, examine these intricate passages and doors, contrived for escape, flapping and counter-flapping, like the lids of the conjurer's boxes. But what avail they? Who gets in by a nod, and shows their secret working to us? Inspector Field . . . I should like to know where Inspector Field was born. In Ratcliffe Highway, I would have answered with confidence, but for his being equally at home wherever we go.

Dickens's account sounds hyperbolical, indeed, but a remarkably similar description of a tour of thieves' dens, with Field as guide, is given by a young Guards officer.[36] Field does seem to have been a remarkably omniscient, and quietly formidable, policeman. In letters written about this time, Dickens further describes his 'horrible sharpness, . . . knowledge and sagacity', and remarks on his discretion (he 'is used in all sorts of delicate matters and is quite devoted to me').[37]

Inspector Bucket's appearance, habits, qualities, personality and speech-idiom are all very close to these descriptions of Field. For Bucket, too, is 'a stoutly built, steady-looking, sharp-eyed man in black, of about the middle-age'; he seems to possess 'an unlimited number of eyes', and to be omni-present. He 'takes in everybody's look at him, all at once, individually and collectively, in a manner that stamps him a remarkable man'. The 'velocity and certainty' of his interpretations are 'little short of miraculous'. He is firm but kindly towards his victims, solicitous (for instance) about whether the handcuffs he is putting on to a suspected murderer are comfortable — 'like a most respectable tradesman, anxious to execute an order neatly, and to the perfect satisfaction of his customer.'[38] Towards his prospective prisoners, or towards anyone who might unwittingly give him useful information, he is dexterously easy, affable and reassuring. And, like Inspector 'Wield', he makes play with his fat forefinger:

> Mr Bucket and his fat forefinger are much in consultation together under existing circumstances. When Mr Bucket has a matter of this pressing interest under his consideration, the fat forefinger seems to rise to the dignity of a familiar demon. He puts it to his ears and it whispers information; he puts it to his lips, and it enjoins him to secrecy; he rubs it over his nose, and it sharpens his scent; he shakes it before a guilty man, and it charms him to destruction. The Augurs of the Detective Temple invariably predict, that when Mr Bucket and that finger are in much conference, a terrible avenger will be heard of before long.
>
> Otherwise mildly studious in his observation of human nature, on the whole a benignant philosopher not disposed to be severe upon the follies of mankind, Mr Bucket pervades a vast number of houses, and strolls about an infinity of streets: to outward appearance rather languishing for want of an object. He is in the friendliest condition towards his species, and will drink with most of them. He is free with his money, affable in his manners, innocent in his conversation — but, through the placid stream of his life, there glides an under-current of forefinger.
>
> Time and place cannot bind Mr Bucket. Like man in the abstract, he is here today and gone tomorrow — but, very unlike man indeed, he is here again the next day.
>
> .   .   .   .
>
> Thoughtful Mr Bucket is; as a man may be, with weighty work to do; but composed, sure, confident. From the expression of his face, he might be a famous whist-player for a large stake — say a hundred guineas certain — with the game in his hand, but with a high reputation involved in his playing his hand out to the last card, in a masterly way. Not in the least anxious or disturbed is Mr Bucket. . . .

And this is how Esther describes him, during the pursuit of Lady Dedlock:

All this time, kept fresh by a certain enjoyment of the work in which he was engaged, he was up and down at every house we came to; addressing people whom he had never beheld before, as old acquaintances; running in to warm himself at every fire he saw; talking and drinking and shaking hands at every bar and tap; friendly with every waggoner, wheel-wright, blacksmith, and toll-taker; yet never seeming to lose time, and always mounting to the box again with his watchful, steady face, and his business-like 'Get on, my lad!'[39]

There are further similarities between Bucket and the Field or 'Wield' of the articles, but these quotations will suffice to show how close they are akin — and how dramatic, indeed romantic, is Dickens's view of the detective's life.

Field himself, however, seems to have seen it very much in the same way. Dickens had complained about the old Runners' habit of 'making the most of themselves' and of being 'hand-in-glove with the penny-a-liners': but Field — a former Runner himself, according to Dickens — was afflicted by the same temptation, and 'had a reputation for boasting and playing to the gallery'.[40] This is very apparent in an account of one of his cases, printed in *The Times*. How accurate the account is, I do not know, but what matters is that this is how Field put himself across to the Press, for the story must have been based on his own narration. He was employed by the solicitors of a family named Smyth, to trace an impostor who was claiming to be Sir Richard Smyth but whose real name was Tom Provis. (Field, it should be mentioned, had retired from the Metropolitan Police a few months earlier, and had set up a Private Enquiry Office.)[41] He received his instructions: 'Scratching his ear . . ., he said, "Well, we'll see what can be done," and immediately set to work in his peculiar way.' Having discovered, through enquiries made 'in a quiet, incidental way', that an old woman of the Provis family lived in Warminster, he realised that she would remain silent if she knew that he was a detective.

Mr Field, therefore, assumed a character which might win him the old woman's heart. He appeared at her gate one day, an invalid, broken down by bodily sickness, brought on by family trouble, who had come down to Warminster for the benefit of the Wiltshire air. The old lady . . . was highly pleased with the sick visitor — he was such a nice, civi l well-behaved gentleman; while he, in turn, was delighted, for the old lady reminded him so much of his mother! Indeed, he was (so he said) so much struck by the resemblance, that

he should like to lodge in the old lady's house during his stay —
it would remind him so much of old times. . . . Mr Field soon installed
himself in the cottage, and those who know him will not wonder that
he was also soon installed in his landlady's good graces. He chatted
with her about the news of the place, not forgetting the famous
Warminster onions; told her many funny things, and quite won
her heart, when, on going to bed at night, he said that he had not felt
so comfortable for many years.

He then told her how much he had suffered from bad relatives,
which provoked her to exclaim, 'Why, one of our family, Tom
Provis, is the greatest rascal living!' Spying 'land ahead', Field
gave her a packet of best tea, and took a cup with her; then he
complained of stomach-ache, and produced his 'medicine', a
bottle of gin, which she also shared. Thus lubricated, the woman
gave him a very full account of Tom Provis's villainies, whereupon
Field invented an excuse for leaving, and took up the chase
elsewhere.

As the newspaper reporter commented, the incident showed that
Field was 'a man of great shrewdness, coolness, patience, and
perseverance'. In a briefer account of another case he remarked on
another of Field's specialities, which recurs in Inspector Bucket —
his arresting a man kindly, 'as his rule was to treat everybody who
became his prisoner.'[42] Field's cunning in making unobtrusive
arrests appears in another journalistic article based on an interview.
Ordered to arrest a Birmingham Chartist leader 'in a quiet
manner', he pretended to be drunk, and jostled the wanted man.
A watchman duly 'arrested' Field, and the Chartist accompanied
him to the lock-up, to charge him with assault — only to find himself arrested instead, and charged with sedition.[43]

The elaborate game with the old woman in the Provis case
reminds one of Inspector Bucket's deceptive affability with the
Bagnet household, when he arrives to arrest George for murder,
and of his use of disguise to obtain access to Gridley's hideout.
Having discovered where Gridley is, by some adroit observation
through a skylight, he presents himself at the door as 'a very
respectable old gentleman, with grey hair, wearing spectacles, and
dressed in a black spencer and gaiters and a broad-rimmed hat'.[44]
Inspector 'Wield' and several of his colleagues are also said to be
skilful at impersonation, and they all delight in it as much as
Dickens delights in them. Not the least attractive feature of their
work, no doubt, to a man so fond as Dickens was of dressing-up

and acting, was their having a professional excuse to indulge in this pleasant hobby. Field's tales probably lost nothing in the telling, but he seems to have enjoyed acting up to a romantic *persona* of the plain-clothes detective. His disguises and trickeries, like Inspector Bucket's, seem more a self-indulgence than a professional necessity. Bucket's behaviour has often been criticised as improbably circuitous, but it is clear that Field — who was perhaps the most famous detective of his time — sometimes behaved in a fashion not much less extraordinary. He had indeed been very keen on amateur theatricals, and only the poor financial prospects prevented his becoming a professional actor instead of a policeman.[45] One is not surprised to discover this actor *manqué* in Field — nor, after reading some of these antics, to hear that he was once rebuked from the Bench 'for presuming to speak of his "honour" '.[46]

The *Times* article shows, too, that Field was very much a 'character' — another feature which he shares with Bucket, who passes it on to later fictional detectives. A famous example is the great Sergeant Cuff of the Detective Police in Wilkie Collins's *The Moonstone* (1868) with his passion for growing roses and his unconstabular appearance — 'a grizzled, elderly man, . . . he might have been a parson, or an undertaker — or anything else you like, except what he really was.'[47] Another example, famous in its day, is Hawkshaw, 'the cutest detective in the force,' in Tom Taylor's popular play *The Ticket-of-Leave Man* (1863), who has an enjoyable time disguised as a drunken navvy in wig and whiskers and speaking in a rough country dialect. Fictional detectives of this period seem, indeed, to divide their time between looking almost ostentatiously ordinary — like the 'stranger of gentlemanly address and clerical appearance' who arrests Charles Reade's prison-hero — and donning the most exotic of disguises. The hint taken from *Bleak House* was, no doubt, amplified by the bogus *Recollections of a Detective Police-Officer*, by 'Waters', produced in 1856 — a book which was so hugely popular that it led to an immediate vogue for yellow-back detective stories. 'Transformed by the aid of a flaxen wig, broad-rimmed hat, green spectacles, and a multiplicity of waistcoats and shawls, into a heavy and elderly, well-to-do personage, I set forth . . .' — so begins a typical adventure.[48] The juvenile amateur-theatrical ambitions of Charles Frederick Field have, perhaps, a lot to answer for.

It was not, however, only the imputed individual skill and resource of Field and Bucket that excite Dickens's admiration, but also their belonging to a superbly efficient organisation. In his article 'On Duty with Inspector Field', he puts himself in the shoes of the miscreant: 'And to know that I *must* be stopped, come what will. To know that I am no match for this individual energy and keenness, or this organised and steady system!'[49] The articles of 1850–3, the account of the Liverpool police in 1860, and *Bleak House* and *Our Mutual Friend* (1864–5) all contain many references to the smooth working of the system, and the mysterious rapport existing between the constables and their superiors. To quote from the Liverpool essay:

> In Mr Superintendent I saw, as anybody might, a tall, well-looking, well set-up man of a soldiery bearing, with a cavalry air, a good chest, and a resolute but not by any means ungentle face. He carried in his hand a plain black walking-stick of hard wood; and whenever and wherever, at any after-time of the night, he struck it on the pavement with a ringing sound, it instantly produced a whistle out of the darkness, and a policeman. To this remarkable stick, I refer an air of mystery and magic which pervaded the whole of my [expedition].[50]

In the article about a night at Bow Street, written with Wills, and even more in the novels, he describes police-stations as places of wonderful calm efficiency. Mr Bucket, for instance, takes Esther Summerson to one, where he hands in a description of her lost mother ('It was very accurate indeed,' she notes). It was copied and sent out. 'All this was done with the greatest dispatch, and without the waste of a moment; yet nobody was at all hurried.'[51] A dozen years later, Dickens remains equally impressed; in *Our Mutual Friend*, Gaffer Hexam and Mortimer Lightwood go to a Police Station to enquire about the Harmon murder.

> ... they found the Night-Inspector, with a pen and ink, and ruler, posting up his books in a whitewashed office, as studiously as if he were in a monastery on the top of a mountain, and no howling fury of a drunken woman were banging herself against a cell-door in the back-yard at his elbow. With the same air of a recluse much given to study, he desisted from his books to bestow a distrustful nod of recognition upon Gaffer, plainly importing, 'Ah! we know all about you, and you'll overdo it some day;' and to inform Mr Mortimer Lightwood and friends, that he would attend to them immediately. Then, he finished ruling the work he had in hand (it might have been illuminating a missal, he was so calm), in a very neat and methodical manner, showing not the slightest consciousness of the woman who

was banging herself with increased violence, and shrieking most
terrifically for some other woman's liver.

'A bull's-eye,' said the Night-Inspector, taking up his keys. Which
a deferential satellite produced. 'Now, gentlemen.'[52]

This Mr Inspector, though a less important character than Bucket,
maintains his tradition of being imperturbable, omnicompetent,
firm but genial, and an accomplished actor. Thus, when he reads
an affidavit naming the murderer he is seeking, he 'mounted to
that (for him) extraordinary pitch of emotion that he said, "Does
either of you two gentlemen happen to have a pinch of snuff about
him?" Finding that neither had, he did quite as well without it
and read on'.[53]

Dickens's fascination with the police can be accounted for, in part,
simply by reference to his common-man *News of the World* interest
in crime, or to the ordinary detective-story-addict's delight in the
solution of mysteries. The possibilities of self-identification for the
reader — and of course the writer — of detective fiction were
nicely discussed by a reviewer in *The Times Literary Supplement*
recently: 'The peculiar attraction of the detective story can be
explained in many ways, flattering or unflattering, according to
taste. One plausible reason is that a detective is the ideal adven-
turer for an intellectual to identify himself with. His triumphs are
cerebral and even sedentary. Bishops and dons and schoolmasters
have to stretch their imagination outrageously to see themselves as
pirate chiefs or intrepid explorers: but they have no difficulty in
being Sherlock Holmes or Nero Wolfe, shrewdly observing what
others have missed, expounding the proper deductions from facts
that their colleagues have doltishly misunderstood.'[54] Moreover,
the criminal areas in which the police operated had always been
very much Dickens's country, as far back as his boyhood years
when he developed that 'profound attraction of repulsion to St
Giles's'.[55] He remained, in adult life, a frequent visitor to this and
other notorious districts of London, right up to the end of his life:
a tour, under police protection, of the opium-dens of Shadwell
inspired some notable characters of *Edwin Drood*.[56] Many of these
criminal areas had appeared in earlier novels and essays. Moreover,
of course, most of the novels had contained murders or thefts or
mysteries and pursuits of a non-criminal kind.

Thus, in almost every novel somebody is shadowing or pursuing
someone else, for reasons virtuous or sinister. Monks follow Oliver

Twist, Little Nell flees from Quilp, Stagg tracks down Mrs Rudge, Mr Dombey chases Carker, Guppy tries to solve the Dedlock mystery, and so on. Dickens has many such amateur detectives, sometimes investigating serious crimes. The disguised stranger calling himself Datchery was, it is clear, collecting the vital clues in *The Mystery of Edwin Drood*; for this reason, Dickens had been vague about how, at an earlier stage, the search for the missing Edwin had been 'pressed on every hand', and he had prevented anything important being discovered then. (The police are never specified, as having tried and failed, though the action of the novel took place at a period when policemen were on their beats.) [57] Dickens had introduced the professional police detective into English fiction nearly twenty years earlier, but he never outgrew his fondness for the amateur, who can, of course enjoy the fictional advantage of being emotionally involved with the victim or the villain. Datchery was certainly a detective of this type; another late example is Beckwith, in the short-story 'Hunted Down' (1859), who adopts various ruses and disguises to track down and convict his sweetheart's murderer.

Much the most elaborate example, however, had occurred before the 'detective' articles and novels, in *Martin Chuzzlewit* (1843–4). The shady financier Tigg Montague employs a confidential agent, Nadgett, to discover any discreditable facts about his clients.

> ... he was born to be a secret. He was a short, dried-up, withered old man, who seemed to have secreted his very blood, for nobody would have given him credit for the possession of six ounces of it in his whole body. How he lived was a secret; where he lived was a secret; and even what he was, was a secret. In his musty old pocket-book he carried contradictory cards, in some of which he called himself a coal-merchant, in others a wine-merchant, in others a commission-agent, in others a collector, in others an accountant, as if he really didn't know the secret himself. He was always keeping appointments in the City, and the other man never seemed to come. ... He was mildewed, threadbare, shabby; always had flue upon his legs and back; and kept his linen so secret by buttoning up and wrapping over, that he might have had none — perhaps he hadn't. He carried one stained beaver glove, which he dangled before him by the forefinger as he walked or sat; but even its fellow was a secret.
>
> .   .   .   .
>
> Jonas had no more idea that Mr Nadgett's eyes were fixed on him than he had that he was living under the daily inspection and report of a whole order of Jesuits. Indeed, Mr Nadgett's eyes were seldom

fixed on any other objects than the ground, the clock, or the fire; but every button on his coat might have been an eye, he saw so much.

The secret manner of the man disarmed suspicion in this wise; suggesting, not that he was watching any one, but that he thought some other man was watching him. He went about so stealthily, and kept himself so wrapped up in himself, that the whole object of his life appeared to be to avoid notice and preserve his own mystery. . . . He rang the bell in a covert underhanded way, as though it were a treasonable act; and passed in at the door, the moment it was opened wide enough to receive his body. That done, he shut it immediately with his own hands.[58]

Through Nadgett, Montague discovers that Jonas Chuzzlewit has (as he thinks) murdered his father. It is Nadgett who intercepts Jonas at the docks, when he tries to escape abroad out of the range of Montague's blackmail; and later it is Nadgett again who arrives with the police, having shadowed Jonas and proved that he has killed his tormentor. As my quotations suggest, Nadgett is like Bucket, a 'character'. He moves in the melodramatic atmosphere of mystery, diligence, patience, and uncanny perceptiveness which Dickens later transfers to the more respectable police detectives.

The Nadgett passages, like those about Blathers and Duff a few years earlier, display a delight in a professional mystery (in the old as well as the modern sense of the word), which is amplified when Dickens describes the Scotland Yard men, of whom he can approve more completely. He was always fascinated by the intricacies, private language, and trade secrets of occupational groups: recall how lovingly he presents his undertakers, clerks, lawyers, actors, and medical students — to name only a few examples. He never shows great inwardness with their professional problems or techniques, partly because he was ignorant of them, but also because he preferred the outside, layman's view: intrigued but mystified by glimpses of these special little worlds. With the police, he can pursue this interest, and with particular satisfaction. As we have seen, the police were concerned with situations and persons that made a strong imaginative appeal to him; their techniques were such as he could both understand and relish; and he could regard their work — unlike that, say, of lawyers — as socially beneficial. Their duties involved them, moreover, in danger; they needed to be courageous as well as clever, but unlike soldiers they did not operate in areas which were outside Dickens's experience or where his moral judgment was uncertain. A thief or a murderer must be captured, there was no doubt about that, and Dickens could freely admire the men who boldly did the catching.

A further reason for this admiration may be seen in Forster's comment on one of the tensions in his character: '. . . underneath his exterior of a singular precision, method, and strictly orderly arrangement in all things, . . . [he had] something in common with those eager, impetuous, somewhat overbearing natures, that rush at existence without heeding the cost of it.'[59] These two sides of his nature correspond to his adoration of the police and his imaginative understanding of criminals. For, as we have seen, it was not only the glamour, excitement, and usefulness of the detective police that attracted him, but also their belonging — as he saw it — to a superbly efficient organisation. Readers are often surprised to discover how strictly Dickens organised his own professional, domestic and social life. He had a mania for tidiness, punctuality, routine and efficiency — to the amusement, and sometimes exasperation, of his family and friends. 'As to his system of work,' wrote his eldest son, 'it was the same wherever he was. No city clerk was ever more methodical or orderly than he; no humdrum, monotonous, mechanical task could ever have been discharged with more punctuality or with more business-like regularity, than he gave to the work of his imagination and fancy.'[60] He expected those around him to conform to his standards; he was, indeed, somewhat of a martinet in the home. Correspondingly, many of his social policies contain, as Humphry House remarked, a strong authoritarian strain which has often been overlooked. This, said House, helps to explain his uncritical devotion to the police.[61] Even without this instinctive reaction against disorder, whether in the home or the nation, and this relish for efficiency, Dickens had of course good objective reasons for admiring the new police, if not for being quite so starry-eyed about them. Britain badly needed such a civilising agency, and the new policemen, faced with many initial difficulties and much opposition, came through these testing early decades triumphantly. Dickens, one should remember, was not their only admirer, though he was prompter and more vocal than most.

He had, then, several reasons for admiring the police: but perhaps almost as important was the fact that he had nothing against them. The widespread early prejudice against them, and indeed the reason why their establishment had been so long postponed, arose from the suspicion that an efficient police force must inevitably become the instrument of political repression.[62] The very word 'police' was suspect, being French; and though we can now see that these fears were unjustified, there seemed at the time good reason to associate police with tyranny. There is no hint of this fear in Dickens. To be sure, by the time he began writing, the Metropolitan Police had been in existence for several years, and had proved almost ostentatiously untyrannical in political matters. By the end of the 1830s, of course, they were sometimes being used against the Chartists, but in this they would excite Dickens's sympathy, not his indignation. He knew little about Chartism, which was much stronger in the Midlands and North and West than in London (his spiritual as well as physical home). His middleclass fear of Chartist violence may be gauged, however, from his presentation of the terrifying bands of unemployed labourers whom Little Nell meets on her journey through the Midlands, and from *Barnaby Rudge*, where the Gordon Riots are seen as a parable for the 1840s. Sympathetic though Dickens was to the unemployed and untaught and misled, his final instinct was to side with the forces of law and order. Of the nicer problems of free speech and association in a policed community, he seems unaware. His mind was not theoretical enough for that, and his interest in politics was fitful and immediate. He had strong views on particular social issues that presented themselves at the moment, but only the sketchiest general ideas about political principles. If it had come to the point, he would probably have been prepared to sacrifice some political freedoms for better drains, schools and workhouses, and a more efficient governmental machine.

About other public officials than the police, he was rarely less than scathing, as we have seen. It is noteworthy that, on the few occasions when he criticises the conduct of the police, he manages to blame not them but their masters. Thus, his remarks on the Ministerial responsibility for the Hyde Park Riots of 1855 (in which the police injured many citizens) were expressed so trenchantly at Lord John Russell's dinner-table as to provoke the famous exclamation of his fellow-guest, Meyerbeer — 'Ah, mon ami illustre! que c'est noble de vous entendre parler d'haute voix morale, à la table d'un ministre!'[63] Or, in that late essay 'The Ruffian', he deplores the fact that the police stand around merely 'contemplating' the notorious criminals who are obviously planning further crimes (as we saw, this was written when there was much popular feeling of this kind). Dickens continues to speak well here of the police, however, though not of the magistracy who try the men whom they arrest. The Inspectors 'are all intelligent men', he writes. '. . . The Police, all things considered, are an excellent force, and I have borne my small testimony to their merits. Constabular contemplation is the result of a bad system; a system which is administered, not invented, by the man in uniform, employed at twenty shillings a week. He has his orders, and would be marked for discouragement if he overstepped them.'[64] Dickens concludes by urging the public to take the law into its own hands — a recommendation which shows how little he had reflected on these large social issues.

It is characteristic that nowhere does he praise the officials, Rowan and Mayne, who had devised and administered the police system he so ardently admired. He does not think in such large-scale terms. He can understand the workings of the small Detective Department, but cannot identify himself with the remote officials who run the whole Force. When he thinks of such high bureaucrats, it is for purposes of ridicule — the Circumlocution Office with its clan of do-nothing Barnacles. The failure of his imagination here is partly due to the limitations of his experience, but more (I think) to his social prejudices. Though he became an important and affluent man, welcome in the highest Society circles, he remained at heart the *petit-bourgeois* of his birth. He never enters into the mind of men responsible for major legislative or executive activities — Ministers of the Crown, high-ranking officers of the armed services, bishops, judges or civil servants. When such men appear in his novels — which is not often — they are figures of fun. As we have seen, he made some surprisingly cordial remarks about judges: but no wise and good judge appears in the novels. Magistrates he viewed with more hostility, and though, again, he knew and praised some good magistrates, his imagination does not warm to them as fictional subjects. Doubtless all these classes of functionary had their faults, which he was quite entitled to satirise, but the underlying emotional attitude is a lower-middle-class suspicion of 'them' — social superiors who enjoy power and honour and office without sweating for it. Nor do any of his 'good' lower or middle-class characters feel any inclination to sweat for it.[65]

The police were almost the only group of officials who would not arouse these prejudices in Dickens. They came, almost exclusively, from the lower social groups. To prevent the New Police becoming a prey to jobbery, Peel had laid down that all posts except those of Commissioner should be filled by promotion from the ranks, and the original Superintendents and Inspectors recruited in 1829 had almost all been former Warrant Officers and NCOs from the army.[66] From the start, there was no separate 'officer class' in the police, nor were the pay, conditions and status such as would normally attract 'gentleman' recruits. Some gentlemen did join, of course, out of enthusiasm, or because they were desperate for employment, or for some more arcane reason — but they were few and untypical.[67] Dickens notes this in *Martin Chuzzlewit*, where one of the less reputable of the Chuzzlewit family, Chevy Slyme, becomes a policeman only, as he tells them, 'on purpose to shame you. . . . Perhaps even you may feel it some disgrace to your own blood to be employed in this way. I'm to be bought off.'[68] All the policemen in his novels and articles, except Mr Inspector in *Our Mutual Friend*, talk and act in a way which emphasises their humble origins. Inspector Bucket is always addressing his client as 'Sir Leicester Dedlock, Baronet', and committing other such solecisms. But all the police are, of course, deferential to the middle-class public, including Dickens. 'Sir,' they call him — as magistrates and mayors and their superiors would not. As Percy Fitzgerald said, the detectives invited to the *Household Words* evening parties must have responded gratefully, not to say obsequiously, to the great novelist's flattering interest in them. Always, along with his admiration for the police, there is a sure reminder that they are not his social equals. Important among his reasons for praising them so heartily was his being able also to patronise them.

THE PUNISHMENT OF DEATH

The good old laws were garnished well with gibbets, whips, and
    chains,
With fine old English penalties, and fine old English pains,
With rebel heads and seas of blood once hot in rebel veins:
For all these things were requisite to guard the rich old gains
      Of the fine old English Tory times;
      Soon may they come again!

— So ran Dickens's revised version of 'The Fine Old English
Gentleman, to be said or sung at all Conservative dinners', composed in 1841. 'By Jove, how radical I am getting!' he wrote to
Forster about that time. 'I wax stronger and stronger in the true
principles every day.'[1] There was, then as at most times, a rough
correlation between political radicalism and penal reformism,
though there were many exceptions of course, as there still are —
members of 'the stupid party' who oppose capital punishment, and
Labour MPs who defend flogging as passionately as the proverbial
ladies at Conservative Party Conferences. Dickens's criticisms of
the law and its administration were part of his generally Radical
outlook at this period: and this, I have suggested, was closely
bound up with his social prejudices against the class which represented privilege and tradition. But, if he 'waxed stronger and
stronger in the true principles every day', he never — in my view
— progressed very far in political Radicalism. He never wanted,
or even envisaged, a society much different from his own in its
social and political and economic organisation. Likewise, in penal
reform, he regarded himself as a moderate.

He had made this clear in *American Notes*, when casting doubt
on the 'humanity' of reforming prisons so much that they no longer
seemed places of 'ignominious punishment and endurance'. He
hoped that he would

> . . . not be misunderstood on this subject, for it is one in which
> I take a strong and deep interest. I incline as little to the sickly feeling
> which makes every canting lie or maudlin speech of a notorious criminal

a subject of newspaper report and general sympathy, as I do to those good old customs of the good old times which made England, even so recently as in the reign of the Third King George, in respect of her criminal code and her prison regulations, one of the most bloody-minded and barbarous countries on the earth. If I thought it would do any good to the rising generation, I would cheerfully give my consent to the disinterment of the bones of any genteel highwayman (the more genteel, the more cheerfully), and to their exposure, piece-meal, on any sign-post, gate, or gibbet, that might be deemed a good elevation for the purpose. My reason is as well convinced that these gentry were utterly worthless and debauched villains, as it is that the laws and gaols hardened them in their evil courses.[2]

The happy medium between maudlin sentimentality and hard-heartedness is not easy to achieve and maintain, and Dickens rarely thought his contemporaries had found it. When, in Italy a few years later, he learned that two ladies of quality were keeping up a constant prayer for the souls of some men just hanged, he took this as evidence that 'a morbid sympathy for criminals is not wholly peculiar to England, though it affects more people in that country perhaps than in any other'.[3] He was equally convinced, however, that the Bloody Code of the 'good old times' had been cruel and inefficient, and was well out of the way.

Barnaby Rudge had been full of his disgust for the practice of hanging many people for slight offences. He mentions both in the text and in the Preface the notorious case of Mary Jones, hanged in 1771 for shoplifting (her husband had been press-ganged, and her children were starving). 'And in times to come,' says the hang-man Dennis, recounting the story and emphasising Dickens's point still further, 'if our grandsons should think of their grandfathers' times, and find these things altered, they'll say "Those were days indeed, and we've been going down hill ever since".'[4] Hugh the Bastard's mother, abandoned by her aristocratic seducer, and hanged at Tyburn, with her six-year-old son looking on, for passing forged notes, is a fictional variant on Mary Jones, and Hugh's participation in the Riots is, in part, his revenge against a society which could commit such an outrage. He too ends on the gallows, and Dickens gives him a Dying Speech, of such wild implausibility that one cannot regret that none of the other condemned men in the novels are accorded this privilege. Hugh, brutalised by his upbringing, cannot make much of the 'faith and strong belief' urged on him by the Chaplain, especially after he has been disappointed in the belief that did mean something to him — that the idiot Barnaby would be spared execution.

'If this was not faith and strong belief!' cried Hugh, raising his right arm aloft, and looking upward like a savage prophet whom the near approach of Death had filled with inspiration, 'where are they? What else should teach me — me, born as I was born, and reared as I have been reared — to hope for any mercy in this hardened, cruel, unrelenting place? Upon these human shambles, I, who never raised his hand in prayer till now, call down the wrath of God! On that black tree, of which I am the ripened fruit, I do invoke the curse of all its victims, past and present, and to come. On the head of that man who, in his conscience, owns me for his son, I leave the wish that he may never sicken on his bed of down, but die a violent death as I do now, and have the night wind for his only mourner. To this I say, Amen, amen!'[5]

This legal system has its defender, of course, in Dennis, since it brings him such constant employment in a job so near his heart. He is confident that, despite his enthusiastic participation in the Riots, he will escape punishment.

When he remembered the great estimation in which his office was held, and the constant demand for his services; when he bethought himself how the Statute Book regarded him as a kind of Universal Medicine, applicable to men, women, and children of every age and variety of criminal constitution; and how high he stood, in his official capacity, in the favour of the Crown and both Houses of Parliament, the Mint, the Bank of England, and the Judges of the land; when he recollected that whatever Ministry was in or out, he remained their peculiar pet and panacea; and that for his sake England stood single and conspicuous among the civilized nations of the earth, — when he called these things to mind and dwelt upon them, he felt certain that the national gratitude *must* relieve him from the consequences of his late proceedings, and would certainly restore him to his old place in the happy social system.[6]

Dickens had, of course, taken this character from history, and the actual Dennis did in fact obtain pardon for exactly this reason.[7] Dickens rejected this finely ironical episode, to gain other advantages. His Dennis takes a much fuller part in the Riots than his historical forbear had done, and thus exhibits on a grand scale the nihilism and brutality of his trade; and when he himself approaches the gallows (ruefully aware that 'Some other man has got my old opinions at this minute. . . . Somebody's longing to work me off') he verifies the old adage that a bully is always a coward. His demeanour when facing execution is compared with Hugh's.

> Although one of these men displayed, in his speech and bearing, the most reckless hardihood, and the other, in his every word and action, testified such an extreme of abject cowardice that it was humiliating to see him, it would be difficult to say which of them would most have repelled and shocked an observer. Hugh's was the dogged desperation of a savage at the stake; the hangman was reduced to a condition little better, if any, than that of a hound with the halter round his neck. Yet, as Mr Dennis knew, and could have told them, these were the two commonest states of mind in persons brought to their pass. Such was the wholesale growth of the seed sown by the law, that this kind of harvest was usually looked for as a matter of course.
>
> In one respect they all agreed. The wandering and uncontrollable train of thought, suggesting sudden recollections of things distant and long-forgotten and remote from each other — the vague restless craving for something undefined, which nothing could satisfy — the swift flight of the minutes, fusing themselves into hours, as if by enchantment — the rapid coming of the solemn night — the shadow of death always upon them, and yet so dim and faint that objects the meanest and most trivial started from the gloom beyond, and forced themselves upon the view — the impossibility of holding the mind, even if they had been so disposed, to penitence and preparation, or of keeping it to any point while that hideous fascination tempted it away, — these things were common to them all, and varied only in their outward tokens.[8]

This is of course a reminiscence of 'A Visit to Newgate' and 'Fagin's Last Night alive' — but now Dickens is not only creating a dramatic effect. He is expressing some of the arguments against capital punishment.

By 1841, when *Barnaby Rudge* was written, there can have been only a very few Tory backwoodsmen who regretted the abolition of the Bloody Code. Dickens was on very safe ground, in belabouring the 'good old times' and lampooning the more far-gone guests at Conservative dinners who still sang the praises of 'the gibbet, whip, and chain'. He was more adventurous when he claimed, in this novel, that 'this last dreadful and repulsive penalty' of hanging 'never turned a man inclined to evil, and has hardened thousands who were half inclined to good'.[9] How and when he came to oppose capital punishment is uncertain. He was sympathetic to the cause, at least, in May 1840, when he wrote to the prominent abolitionist Henry Gilpin: 'I should be most happy to promote your object, but I fear it is not in my power to do so. The worthiness of your work, no one, I imagine, can question for a moment.'[10] But perhaps the crucial experience was his seeing an execution about five weeks after this letter was written.

Many years later he was asked for his views on capital punishment, and replied: '. . . the descriptions in Oliver Twist and Barnaby Rudge are ideal, but are founded on close observation and reflection.'[11] No execution is, in fact, described in *Oliver Twist* — only the vast crowd, 'pushing, quarrelling, joking,' assembled around 'the black stage, the cross-beam, the rope, and all the hideous apparatus of death'. Fagin, like Dennis, is terrified though, like him, he had thought capital punishment 'a fine thing' until he became its victim. 'Dead men tell no tales,' was his earlier attitude; 'dead men never bring awkward stories to light. Ah, it's a fine thing for the trade! Five of 'em strung up in a row, and none left to play booty, or turn white-livered!' — for, like Jonathan Wild, he had often used the hangman, or the threat of him, to remove or silence unreliable allies.[12]

In *Barnaby Rudge*, the description of the 'hideous apparatus of death' is more prolonged. The atmospheric clock-striking device used in the two 'condemned cell at Newgate' pieces now registers the mounting excitement of the crowd instead of the sleepless panic of the victim. The gallows, 'its nooses dangling in the light like loathsome garlands,' is an 'obscene presence' which should never have been thrust upon the sight of the spectators. 'Even little children were held up above the people's heads to see what kind of toy a gallows was, and learn how men were hanged.' Every inch of space 'swarmed with human life. . . . It was terrible to see . . . the world of eager eyes, all strained upon the scaffold and the beam'.[13]

This was published in November 1841, and written not long before. In July 1840, Dickens had witnessed the execution of Courvoisier, and memories of that experience certainly shaped this chapter and indeed influenced him throughout the novel. The Courvoisier case was one of the most famous murders of the century, not because it was particularly daring or ingenious, but because the murderer was a foreigner and his victim was the aged Lord William Russell, uncle of the Cabinet Minister. The trial had caused great excitement, and forty thousand people watched the execution. Dickens had been disgusted to learn that his brother Fred planned to join some journalists who were covering the event, but on the eve of the hanging he suddenly decided to walk down to Newgate and 'see what was being done by way of preparation'.[14] His brother-in-law Henry Burnett, and the painter Maclise, happened to be spending the evening with the Dickenses, so the three men went off together, leaving the ladies at home. They found huge crowds already awaiting the execution. Burnett recalled Dickens as 'somewhat painfully interested and taking mental notes', and as saying, about one o'clock in the morning: 'Just once I should like to watch a scene like this, and see the end of the Drama.' So they hired a room with a view, where they spent 'a ghastly night in Hades with demons', watching the terrible behaviour of the crowd, rifled by pickpockets. 'In the midst of all this devilment, Dickens . . . suddenly cried out, "Why there stands Thackeray!" ' but they could not catch his attention.

Thackeray had come with Monckton Milnes, who had recently voted in favour of Ewart's parliamentary motion to abolish capital punishment. A fortnight later, Thackeray was still haunted by Courvoisier's face: 'I can see Mr Ketch at this moment, with an easy air, taking the rope from his pocket; . . . I feel myself ashamed and degraded at the brutal curiosity which took me to that brutal sight; and . . . I pray to Almighty God to cause this disgraceful sin to pass from among us, and to cleanse our land of blood.' This comes from his famous essay 'Going to see a man hanged', which appeared in *Fraser's Magazine* in August 1840. 'It seems to me,' he wrote, 'that I have been abetting an act of frightful wickedness and violence, performed by a set of men against one of their fellows. . . . I fully confess that I came away . . . that morning with a disgust for murder, but it was for *the murder I saw done*.'[15]

Dickens felt a similar disgust — though not, I think, Thackeray's self-reproaches for having gone at all — but on this occasion he did not rush into print about it. Memories of it affect *Barnaby Rudge*, I have suggested, but it was not until 1846 that he wrote explicitly about the Courvoisier hanging, in a letter to the *Daily News*:

I was, purposely, on the spot, from midnight of the night before; and was a near witness of the whole process of the building of the scaffold, the gathering of the crowd, the gradual swelling of the concourse with the coming-on of day, the hanging of the man, the cutting of the body down, and the removal of it into the prison. From the moment of my arrival, when there were but a few score boys in the street, and those all young thieves, and all clustered together behind the barrier nearest to the drop — down to the time when I saw the body with its dangling head, being carried on a wooden bier into the gaol — I did not see one token in all the immense crowd; at the windows, in the streets, on the house-tops, anywhere; of any one emotion suitable to the occasion. No sorrow, no salutary terror, no abhorrence, no seriousness; nothing but ribaldry, debauchery, levity, drunkenness, and flaunting vice in fifty other shapes. I should have deemed it impossible that I could have ever felt any large assemblage of my fellow-creatures to be so odious. I hoped, for an instant, that there was some sense of Death and Eternity in the cry of 'Hats off!' when the miserable wretch appeared; but I found, next moment, that they only raised it as they would at a Play — to see the Stage the better, in the final scene.

Of the effect upon a perfectly different class, I can speak with no less confidence. There were, with me, some gentlemen of education and distinction in imaginative pursuits, who had, as I had, a particular detestation of that murderer; not only for the cruel deed he had done, but for his slow and subtle treachery, and for his wicked defence. And yet, if any one among us could have saved the man (we said so, afterwards, with one accord), he would have done it. It was so loathsome, pitiful, and vile a sight, that the law appeared to be as bad as he, or worse; being very much the stronger, and shedding around it a far more dismal contagion.[16]

This passage occurs in the first of a series of four long letters to the *Daily News*, which conclude, more unequivocally than *Barnaby Rudge*, by advocating 'the total abolition of the Punishment of Death, as a general principle, for the advantage of society, for the prevention of crime, and without the least reference to, or tenderness for any individual malefactor whatever'. Indeed, he continues, dissociating himself from that 'mawkish sentimentality' he so often detected in other penal reformers, 'in most cases of murder, my feeling towards the culprit is very strongly and violently the reverse.' On this issue, he for once found himself and his cause attacked in terms he had so often used against others. Macaulay had described the abolitionists as being victims of 'a kind of effeminate feeling'. Dickens quotes him, and asks 'what there may be especially manly and heroic in the advocacy of the gallows?' He 'hints a doubt, in all good humour, whether this be the true Macaulay way of meeting a great question?'[17] It was a temperate and pointed riposte. One of Dickens's friends had described his conversation, a couple of years before: 'He hates argument; in fact, he is unable to argue — a common case with impulsive characters who see the whole truth, and feel it crowding and struggling at once for immediate utterance.'[18] This is generally as true of his writings as of his conversation, but these *Daily News* letters are exceptional. He presents his case against capital punishment lucidly, marshalling very ably the several kinds of objection to hanging. He uses psychological insight, emotional appeal, statistics, and pertinent references to the literature on the subject. He argues at unusual length, too (some twelve thousand words); I cannot, indeed, recall his *arguing* at such length about any other social question.

Clearly he felt much concerned about this issue at this period. His contributions to the *Daily News*, during his brief connection with it, were few — just this series, a letter on 'Crime and Education' (chiefly about Ragged Schools), the 'Hymn of the Wiltshire Labourers', and his travel-sketches *Pictures from Italy*. Crime, therefore, was the dominating social issue, and capital punishment was the subject of four of the five items devoted to it. Dickens was, in fact, using up ideas he had mooted a year or so before, when trying to fulfil an engagement to contribute to the *Edinburgh Review*.[19] A project for an article on Infant Labour had been discussed in 1841, but came to nothing; two further projects, discussed in 1843–4 and 1845, were concerned with Ragged Schools and capital punishment. These too were never published — never, in fact, written. Biographers have assumed that Dickens proved too outspoken for the *Review*; actually, he was always finding excuses for not writing the articles he had promised. He obviously felt no enthusiasm for publishing in a journal so alien to his intellectual habits.[20] Far from wanting to outrage the susceptibilities of its readers, however, he had been studiously conciliatory in his correspondence with its editor. Thus, when Napier had (apparently) urged that rape should remain a capital offence, Dickens stuck to his guns — declining to accept that '*any* crime affects the broad philosophy of the question: still less a crime so very difficult of proof', but adding: 'I espy a way, I think, of not compromising you on this head. And you may rely on my being gentle and discreet.'[21]

His first letter to Napier on the proposed capital punishment article provides a convenient summary of most of the points developed more fully in the *Daily News* letters, so a lengthy quotation will, I hope, be excused.

> Society having arrived at that state, in which it spares bodily torture to the worst criminals: and having agreed, if criminals be put to Death at all, to kill them in the speediest way: I consider the

question with reference to society, and not at all with reference to the criminal. Holding that in a case of cruel and deliberate murder, he is already mercifully and sparingly treated.

But, as a question for the deliberate consideration of all reflective persons, I put this view of the case. — With such very repulsive and odious details before us, may it not be well to inquire whether the Punishment of Death be beneficial to society. I believe it to have a horrible fascination for many of those persons who render themselves liable to it, impelling them onward to the acquisition of a frightful notoriety; and (setting aside the strong confirmation of this idea afforded in individual instances) I presume this to be the case in very badly regulated minds, when I observe the strange fascination which everything connected with this punishment or the object of it, possesses for tens of thousands of decent, virtuous, well-conducted people, who are quite unable to resist the published portraits, letters, anecdotes, smilings, snuff-takings, &c &c &c of the bloodiest and most unnatural scoundrel with the gallows before him. I observe that this strange interest does not prevail to anything like the same degree, where Death is not the penalty. Therefore I connect it with the Dread and Mystery surrounding Death in any shape, but especially in this avenging form; and am disposed to come to the conclusion that it produces crime in the criminally disposed, and engenders a diseased sympathy — morbid and bad, but natural and often irresistible — among the well-conducted and gentle.

Regarding it as doing harm to both these classes, it may even then be right to enquire, whether it has any salutary influence on those small knots and specks of people, mere bubbles in the living ocean, who actually behold its infliction with their proper eyes. On this head, it is scarcely possible to entertain a doubt; for we know that robbery and obscenity and callous indifference are of no commoner occurrence anywhere than at the foot of the scaffold. Furthermore, we know that all exhibitions of agony and Death have a tendency to brutalise and harden the feelings of men, and have always been the most rife, among the fiercest people. Again, it is a great question whether ignorant and dissolute persons (ever the great body of spectators, as few others will attend) seeing *that* murder done, and not having seen the other, will not, almost of necessity sympathise with the man who dies before them; especially as he is shown, a martyr to their fancy — tied and bound — alone among scores — with every kind of odds against him.

I should take all these threads up at the end by a vivid little sketch of the origin and progress of such a crime as Hocker's — stating a somewhat parallel case, but an imaginary one, pursuing its hero to his death, and showing what enormous harm he does, *after* the crime for which he suffers. I should state none of these positions in a posi-

tive sledge-hammer way, but tempt and lure the reader into the discussion of them in his own mind; and so we come to this at last —
whether it be for the benefit of society to elevate even this crime to the
awful dignity and notoriety of death; and whether it would not be
much more to its advantage to substitute a mean and shameful punishment, degrading the deed and the committer of the deed, and leaving
the general compassion to expend itself upon the only theme at present
quite forgotten in the history, that is to say, the murdered person.[22]

The *Daily News* series follows much this pattern, with a few
additions and alterations. Instead of offering a 'vivid little sketch'
of an imaginary case based on young Hocker's, he describes at
some length Hocker himself (he was a vicious little popinjay, not
unlike Simon Tappertit), and gives a further instance of murder
for notoriety — the pot-boy named Oxford who had shot at Queen
Victoria in 1840.[23] He adds a good deal of statistical evidence:
referring to foreign experience, to show that abolition does not
cause an increase in capital crimes, and using the much-quoted
figures of the prison-chaplain Roberts, of Bristol, who had attended
167 prisoners under sentence of death, and found only three who
had not been spectators at other men's executions. Another argument he adds is the familiar and important one, that judicial
mistakes occur, and are irreparable if their victim has been hanged;
he adduces several examples, and quotes at length from the Report
of a New York State Select Committee, which had used this and
other arguments in coming to the conclusion that execution should
be abolished.[24] He discusses the publicity given to murderers:

The smallest circumstance in the behaviour of these . . . wretches is
noted down and published as a precious fact. And read, too —
extensively and generally read — even by hundreds and thousands
of people who object to the publication of such details, and are disgusted by them. The horrible fascination surrounding the punishment, and everything concerned with it, is too strong for resistance.
. . . But it is neither just nor reasonable to charge their publication on
the newspapers, or the gleaners for the newspapers. They are published because they are read and sought for. They are read and sought
for: not because society has causelessly entered into a monstrous and
unnatural league on this theme (which it would be absurd to suppose), but because it is in the secret nature of those of whom society is
made up, to have a dark and dreadful interest in the punishment at
issue.

The only effective way of stopping this morbid trade, he argues, is
to abolish the death-penalty upon which it battens. (He under-

estimates, indeed, the fascination of murder as such.) Forgers and other minor criminals ceased to excite this unhealthy interest, he says, when their offences were no longer capital. 'Coining, when the coiner was dragged (as I have seen one) on a hurdle to the place of execution; or Burglary, or Highway Robbery — did these crimes ever wear an aspect of adventure and mystery, and did the perpetrators of them ever become the town talk, when their offences were visited with death? Now, they are mean, degraded, miserable criminals; and nothing more.'[25]

Dickens handles the factual and statistical part of his argument competently, but what are more interesting (and more akin to his work as a novelist) are his speculations about the effect of capital punishment on the various people involved — the spectators and newspaper readers, the judge and jury, the hangman, and of course the murderer himself. Enough has been quoted to illustrate his contention that its 'horrible fascination' was as harmful as it was irresistible to ordinary well-conducted people. The figures quoted to show its inefficiency as a deterrent are of a kind familiar in all such arguments, but Dickens also attempts to show why, far from being a deterrent, it may sometimes be an incentive. He surveys the commonest motives for murder, and argues the irrelevance of hanging to most of them and its fatal attraction for some types of murderer, of whom the most obvious and least interesting are the exhibitionist Hockers and Oxfords. He exercises his imaginative insight further, and plausibly, on cases of greater psychological complication: for instance, murders committed in deliberate revenge. Here, he says, the murderer often makes no secret of his guilt — 'I killed him. I'm glad of it. I meant to do it. I am ready to die.' Dickens asks:

> Now, what is this but a false arguing of the question, announcing a foregone conclusion, expressly leading to the crime, and inseparably arising out of the Punishment of Death? 'I took his life. I give up mine to pay for it. Life for life; blood for blood. I have done the crime. I am ready with the atonement. I know all about it; it's a fair bargain between me and the law. Here am I to execute my part of it; and what more is to be said or done?' It is the very essence of the maintenance of this punishment for murder, that it *does* set life against life. It is in the essence of a stupid, weak, or otherwise ill regulated mind (of such a murderer's mind, in short), to recognise in this set off, a something that diminishes the base and coward character of murder. . . .

A mind incapable, or confounded in its perceptions — and you must argue with reference to such a mind, or you could not have such a murder — may not only establish on these grounds an idea of strict justice and fair reparation, but a stubborn and dogged fortitude and foresight that satisfy it hugely.[26]

Another type of murderer who feels more justified, simply because he may be executed, is (Dickens argues) the man, say, who feels 'a slow, corroding, growing hate' of his woman. Violent quarrels, full of reproaches and recrimination, end in his exclaiming that 'he wouldn't mind killing her, though he should be hanged for it'. This phrase, so frequent in such cases, possessed for Dickens 'a deeper meaning than is usually attached to it'. The idea of murder is generally not new to such a man; after a quarrel, or in mounting irritation, he broods over his 'unformed desire' to rid himself of this bane of his life —

'Though he should be hanged for it.' With the entrance of the Punishment into his thoughts, the shadow of the fatal beam begins to attend — not on himself, but on the object of his hate. At every new temptation, it is there, stronger and blacker yet, trying to terrify him. When she defies or threatens him, the scaffold seems to be her strength and 'vantage ground'. Let her not be too sure of that; 'though he should be hanged for it.'

Thus, he begins to raise up, in the contemplation of this death by hanging, a new and violent enemy to brave. The prospect of a slow and solitary expiation would have no congeniality with his wicked thoughts, but this throttling and strangling has. There is always before him, an ugly, bloody, scarecrow phantom, that champions her, as it were, and yet shows him, in a ghastly way, the example of murder. Is she very weak, or very trustful in him, or infirm, or old? It gives a hideous courage to what would be mere slaughter otherwise; for there it is, a presence always about her, darkly menacing him with that penalty whose murky secret has a fascination for all secret and unwholesome thoughts. And when he struggles with his victim at the last, 'though he should be hanged for it,' it is a merciless wrestle, not with one weak life only, but with that ever-haunting, ever-beckoning shadow of the gallows, too; and with a fierce defiance to it, after their long survey of each other, to come on and do its worst.

Present this black idea of violence to a bad mind contemplating violence; hold up before a man remotely compassing the death of another person, the spectacle of his own ghastly and untimely death by man's hands; and out of the depths of his own nature you shall assuredly raise up that which lures and tempts him on.[27]

Here, as in the chapter on the Philadelphia prisoners, Dickens the novelist is trying to get beyond the statistics and the overt facts of crime and punishment, to the intricate 'secret history' of the individual case, which he presents dramatically. The theme stimulates him, indeed, to a more sustained exploration of unconscious motives than is common in his novels at this period.

He offers some interesting insights, too, when referring to the Judges, then as ever overwhelmingly opposed to a diminution of capital punishment. He writes of them very temperately: a fine exercise of forbearance, when one recalls the Bench's disgraceful record on issues of penal reform. (The depressing but instructive tale has been re-told recently, with ample documentation, by two learned counsel in *The Law Quarterly Review*.)[28] Dickens gives two main reasons for this judicial conservatism. First, the obvious one, that men 'contract a general liking for those things which they have studied at great cost of time and intellect, and their proficiency in which has led to their becoming distinguished and successful'. Lawyers thus become inclined not merely to a passive blindness to the law's defects, but to 'an active disposition to advocate and defend them'. He cites examples of the many ludicrous judicial defences of laws, the abolition of which did not result in the disasters foretold — though he fairly acknowledges, and names, some of the exceptions to this rule that Judges are disastrous penologists. He adds — and it sounds a fair guess —

> There is another and stronger reason still, why a criminal judge is a bad witness in favour of the Punishment of Death. He is a chief actor in the terrible drama of a trial, where the life or death of a fellow creature is at issue. No one who has seen such a trial can fail to know, or can ever forget, its intense interest. I care not how painful this interest is to the good, wise judge upon the bench. I admit its painful nature, and the judge's goodness and wisdom to the fullest extent. . . . I know the solemn pause before the verdict, the hush and stilling of the fever in the court. . . . I know the thrill that goes round when the black cap is put on, and how there will be shrieks among the women, and a taking out of some one in a swoon. . . . I know all this, I can imagine what the office of the judge costs in this execution of it; but I say that in these strong sensations he is lost, and is unable to abstract the penalty as a preventive or example, from an experience of it, and from associations surrounding it, which are and can be, only his, and his alone.[29]

The general public, he has argued, have an unhealthy interest in the gallows, though a very ambivalent attitude towards it. This is shown not only by their natural tendency to pity the man who dies before them 'tied and bound — alone among scores — with every kind of odds against him', but also, he suggests, in their attitude to the hangman who carries out the law on their behalf.

> I learn from the newspaper accounts of every execution, how Mr So-and-so, and Mr Somebody else, and Mr So-forth shook hands with the culprit, but I never find them shaking hands with the hangman. All kinds of attention and consideration are lavished on the one; but the other is universally avoided, like a pestilence. I want to know why so much sympathy is expended on the man who kills another in the vehemence of his own bad passions, and why the man who kills him in the name of the law is shunned and fled from? Is it because the murderer is going to die? Then by no means put him to death. Is it because the hangman executes a law, which, when they once come near it face to face, all men instinctively revolt from? Then by all means change it.[30]

This revulsion against the law and its operation was increasing, he asserted. Juries were registering their protest, if not by acquittals, then by questionable verdicts of 'insanity'. Probably, he says, they reconcile their consciences to such verdicts by reflecting that 'grave doctors have said all men are more or less mad'. He is troubled by this double-think, but adds his suffrage to the device. We should blame rather the existing law, he says, and should abolish the punishment which juries flinch from inflicting.

> And the question will always suggest itself in jurors' minds — however earnestly the learned judge presiding, may discharge his duty — 'which is the greater wrong to society? To give this man the benefit of the possibility of his being mad, or to have another public execution, with all its depraving and hardening influences?' Imagining myself a juror, in a case of life or death: and supposing that the evidence had forced me from every other ground of opposition to this punishment in the particular case, as a possibility of irremediable mistake, or otherwise: I would go over it again on this ground; and if I could, by any reasonable special pleading with myself, find him mad rather than hang him — I think I would.[31]

'His face used to *blaze* with indignation at any injustice or cruelty, and be awful, almost, over horrors,' recalled a close friend, after his death. 'I remember well the intense feeling of horror over the only execution he ever saw — *Never again* would he go to one.'

She was misinformed, or remembering incorrectly, but still she was closer to the truth than, say, Dame Una Pope-Hennessy, who asserts that 'he had considerable experience of executions', or than Mr Julian Symons, who states that he was 'always eager to attend' them.[32] I have heard many well-informed people say much the same (such is the new orthodoxy that has replaced, in smart circles, the old-hat belief in Dickens the Reformer), so it is worth enquiring what evidence these biographers might have adduced but did not. He was not, in fact, a masculine Madame Defarge. To my knowledge he certainly attended three, and probably attended four, executions.

Burnett's account infers that Courvoisier's in 1840 was the first, and I see no reason to doubt this. Then, in 1845, he went to see a beheading in Rome, which he found no more edifying than a hanging in London. As he pointed out in the *Daily News*, pickpockets were equally active at both ceremonies: so much for the salutary terrors of the scaffold! The severed head was set up on a pole — 'a little patch of black and white, for the long street to stare at, and the flies to settle on. . . . There was a great deal of blood.' He gives a horrified description of the scene, and of the cadaver.

> Nobody cared, or was at all affected. There was no manifestation of disgust, or pity, or indignation, or sorrow. . . . It was an ugly, filthy, careless, sickening spectacle; meaning nothing but butchery beyond the momentary interest, to the one wretched actor. Yes! Such a sight has one meaning and one warning. Let me not forget it. The speculators in the lottery, station themselves at favourable points for counting the gouts of blood that spirt out, here or there; and buy that number. It is pretty sure to have a run upon it.[33]

Two months later he declined to witness a further example of Italian justice — a double hanging in Genoa. 'I was afraid to go,' he wrote, 'for I know how they manage things here: and knew I should be horrified. It was very dreadful, I understand. . . . Roche went, and could eat nothing for a long time afterwards.'[34]

He may have witnessed another execution during his Continental travels. This is not mentioned in any letters or biographies, that I know of, but in an essay he contributed to *Household Words* in 1855. It is a partly-fictional partly-autobiographical piece, recalling adventures he had experienced at various inns where he had lodged. Most of these adventures certainly occurred to Dickens (we have other accounts of them), but one that is otherwise undocumented is the 'story which worked itself out at a little Inn in

Switzerland, while I was staying there' one winter. The corpse of a young man was discovered under a huge stack of firewood outside the inn. The culprit was easily discovered and arrested.

> I saw the murderer that day . . . and I see him now, lying shackled with cords on the stable litter, among the mild eyes and the smoking breath of the cows, waiting to be taken away by the police. . . . I saw him once again, on the day of my departure from the Inn. In that Canton the headsman still does his office with a sword; and I came upon this murderer sitting bound to a chair, with his eyes bandaged, on a scaffold in a little market-place. In that instant, a great sword (loaded with quick-silver in the thick part of the blade), swept round him like a gust of wind or fire, and there was no such creature in the world. My wonder was, not that he was so suddenly dispatched, but that any head was left unreaped, within a radius of fifty yards of that tremendous sickle.

Parts of this essay are certainly fictional, but this episode has the ring of truth in it, and there are several possible occasions when Dickens was in Switzerland during the winter months and could thus have 'come upon this murderer sitting . . . on a scaffold'.[35]

The other execution which he certainly saw was perhaps the most notorious of the century. On 13 November 1849, Mr and Mrs George Manning were hanged together on top of Horsemonger Lane Gaol — the first husband-and-wife execution, it was said, since 1700. It had been a sordid little murder, chiefly for gain; they had killed their lodger, Patrick O'Connor, and buried him in quicklime beneath their kitchen floor in Bermondsey. But Maria Manning had captured the public imagination. She was a Belgian, of intrepid and passionate temperament. During the trial, she kept interrupting the Judge with cries of 'There is no law nor justice to be got here! Base and degraded England!' In prison, she behaved furiously and violently, cursing all the officers, and making a remarkably bold attempt to commit suicide. (It is generally accepted that Dickens used her as the model for Hortense, the murderous Frenchwoman in *Bleak House* three years later.) Her husband was less impressive, except for his memorably laconic confession about how he treated O'Connor, whom his wife had shot: 'He moaned; I never liked him well, and I battered his head with a ripping chisel.'[36] The lack of co-operation and cordiality between the two defendants had added a spice of interest to their trial. Some thirty thousand witnessed their execution, which had a famous effect on Victorian costume — for Mrs Manning

wore black satin for the ceremony, and it was decades before that
material came back into fashion. Interest in the case was maintained
long after the execution; a publisher found it worth his while to
issue *The Authentic Memoirs of Maria Manning*, a bulky compilation of
over eight-hundred pages, in penny-numbers of sixteen pages each.[37]

On this occasion, Dickens did plan in advance to witness the
execution, though he was in two minds about it. A week before the
event he wrote to his friend Leech, the artist, that he had decided
not to go: 'I give in, about the Mannings. The doleful weather, the
beastly nature of the scene, the having no excuse for going (after
seeing Courvoisier) and the constantly recurring desire to avoid
another such horrible and odious impression, decide me to cry off.'
Leech presumably had 'an excuse for going' — he was the leading
cartoonist of *Punch*, where his famous cut 'The Great Moral Lesson
at Horsemonger Lane' appeared the following week.[38] As we shall
see, it was an issue upon which *Punch* had strong feelings. Leech
met Dickens a few days before the execution, and perhaps it was
he that persuaded him to go, after all. Anyway, on the eve of the
execution Dickens wrote to him again, saying 'We have taken the
whole of the roof (and the back kitchen) for the extremely moderate sum of Ten Guineas, or two guineas each'.[39] Their expedition
resulted, not only in Leech's cut, but also in Dickens's most
famous pronouncement on capital punishment — his letters to *The
Times*, the first written on the day of the execution, and the second
a few days later. These attracted far more attention than the longer
and more searching *Daily News* series of three years earlier, mainly,
no doubt, because the circulation and influence of *The Times* were
much greater than the *Daily News* could command in its opening
months. Moreover, Dickens was now arguing for a more limited
change in the law — one which, he thought, was more likely to be
obtained, as indeed proved to be the case.

The *Times* letters deliberately do not raise the issue, whether or
not capital punishment should be abolished. They are confined to
arguing the harmfulness of public executions, and to suggesting
how hangings could be carried out inside prison walls, justly and
more decorously. The scene in Horsemonger Lane is described
with great passion and eloquence.

> I believe that a sight so inconceivably awful as the wickedness and
> levity of the immense crowd collected at that execution this morning
> could be imagined by no man, and could be presented in no heathen
> land under the sun. The horrors of the gibbet and of the crime which

brought the wretched murderers to it faded in my mind before the atrocious bearing, looks, and language of the assembled spectators. When I came upon the scene at midnight, the *shrillness* of the cries and howls that were raised from time to time, denoting that they came from a concourse of boys and girls already assembled in the best places, made my blood run cold. . . . When the two miserable creatures who attracted all this ghastly sight about them were turned quivering into the air, there was no more emotion, no more pity, no more thought that two immortal souls had gone to judgment, no more restraint in any of the previous obscenities, than if the name of Christ had never been heard in this world, and there were no belief among men but that they perished like the beasts.

I have seen, habitually, some of the worst sources of general contamination and corruption in this country, and I think there are not many phases of London life that could surprise me. I am solemnly convinced that nothing that ingenuity could devise to be done in this city, in the same compass of time, could work such ruin as one public execution, and I stand astounded and appalled by the wickedness it exhibits. I do not believe that any community can prosper where such a scene of horror and demoralisation as was enacted this morning outside Horsemonger Lane Gaol is presented at the very doors of good citizens, and is passed by unknown or forgotten.[40]

Many other reports confirm this condemnation of the crowd. For days past, the neighbourhood had been like a great Fair, with huge crowds collecting round the prison, wrote the *Times* reporter; those present at the execution itself were 'the dregs and offscourings of the population', and when the final moment came they 'exhibited no feeling except one of heartless indifference and levity'. The *Times* leading-article, however, while praising Dickens's 'knowledge of the human heart and its workings under the infinite varieties and accidents of modern life', was 'not prepared . . . to follow' him to his conclusion. The 'mystery' of private executions would be intolerable; the populace must be able to see that rich murderers as well as poor ones were hanged. 'Nor do we think it altogether fair to infer the real feelings, much less the abiding impression, of the spectators from the horrid, hysterical mirth produced by a night's exposure, an immense crowd, and a long suspended expectation.'[41] Several more letters appeared during the next few days, both for and against Dickens's proposal. A nice argument started, whether the more 'respectable' spectators were being logical and proper, or disgusting, when they used operaglasses to gain a closer view.

At his home, Dickens was soon, he wrote, 'in the midst of such a roaring sea of correspondence, brought upon me by those two letters in The Times, that I seem to have no hope of land.'[42] To some of these letters, and to the *Times* correspondence and leader, he replied in a further and longer letter printed in *The Times* on 19 November. He had little difficulty in disposing of the suggestion that the crowd's 'real feelings' were more wholesome than might appear. 'The mirth was not hysterical,' he replied, 'the shoutings and fightings were not the efforts of a strained excitement seeking to vent itself in any relief. The whole was unmistakably callous and bad.' Invoking the authority of Henry Fielding, who had urged a century earlier that executions should be 'in some degree private', he goes on to suggest in more detail how this should be so accomplished that, despite the 'mystery', justice could be seen to be done.

> From the moment of a murderer's being sentenced to death, I would dismiss him to ... obscurity. ... I would allow no curious visitors to hold any communication with him; I would place every obstacle in the way of his sayings and doings being served up in print on Sunday mornings for the perusal of families. His execution within the walls of the prison should be conducted with every terrible solemnity that careful consideration could devise. Mr Calcraft, the hangman (of whom I have some information in reference to this last occasion), should be restrained in his unseemly briskness, in his jokes, his oaths, and his brandy. To attend the execution I would summon a jury of twenty-four, to be called the witness jury, eight to be summoned on a low qualification, eight on a higher, eight on a higher still! so that it might fairly represent all classes of society.[43]

Other prison and judicial officers should be present, and should sign a death-certificate, to be publicly displayed. Less wisely, Dickens suggests that, during the hour of the body's hanging, all the city's shops should be shut, and its church bells tolled.

A more rancorous note enters the letter when he refers to another class of objectors to his proposal — those who, 'desiring the total abolition of capital punishment, will have nothing less, and who, not doubting the fearful influence of public executions, would have it protracted for an indefinite term, rather than spare the demoralisation they do not dispute, at the risk of losing sight for a while of their final end. But of these I say nothing, considering them, however good and pure in intention, unreasonable, and not to be argued with.'[44] He had suffered, and was to suffer more, from the attacks of the total abolitionists, many of whom deplored his advocating the more limited reform. He referred jocularly to the reputation they were giving him, as a bloodthirsty pro-hangman, at a dinner a day or so later; and, in a letter, he expressed more bitterly his annoyance with their attitude. Because they would accept nothing but total abolition, nothing would get done at all, he thought; they were 'utterly reckless and dishonest (generally speaking), and would play the deuce with any such proposition in Parliament, unless it were strongly supported by the Government, which it would certainly not be, the Whig motto (in office) being "*laissez aller*" '.[45] Many of the abolitionists, however, were equally angry with him, and equally sure that his policy was disastrous. If this half-measure were accepted, they thought, the idea of total abolition would be shelved and forgotten; hanging, once out of sight, would be out of mind. The leaders of the movement were, indeed, divided on this issue. Thus, Charles Gilpin, founder of the Society for Promoting the Abolition of Capital Punishment, had formerly been willing to compromise, by accepting private executions, while William Ewart, who had in 1840 introduced the first Parliamentary motion and long remained the chief spokesman in the House for total abolition, was always devastating in his criticism of proposals to end public executions, holding that this would merely prolong the fundamental evil of capital punishment itself.[46] A good case could be made out for either policy, though later history suggests that the purist one would have been more effective in the long run, for, in other European countries where public executions continued as late as 1890, capital punishment soon afterwards was abolished or fell into disuse.[47]

Dickens soon heard from both parties. Henry Christy, a rich philanthropist, obtained his permission to reprint the *Times* letters as a pamphlet, copies of which he hoped to enclose in magazines sympathetic to the cause and in the next Number of *David Copperfield* (then being serialised).[48] Gilpin, however, was not satisfied by Dickens's going on record as a supporter of private execution. He wanted him to attend an abolitionist meeting, but Dickens declined, on the ground that 'the general mind is not in that state in which the total abolition of capital punishment can be advantageously advocated by Public meetings . . . for a long time to come', though many good people who could not 'conscientiously abrogate capital punishment in extreme cases' would strongly support the lesser, and necessary, reform.[49] (Three years ealier, Dickens had been willing to attend one of Gilpin's abolitionist meetings — 'I cannot positively *promise* to attend . . . but I hope to do so, and if I can I certainly will.')[50] More personally distressing was an exchange of letters with his friend Douglas Jerrold. Dickens remonstrated with him for using the catch-phrase about the 'mystery' of private executions — 'I wish I could induce you to feel justified in leaving that word to the platform people.' Jerrold was equally nettled, and lamented Dickens's public statement: 'The sturdy anti-abolitionist may count it as upon his side. I am grieved that the weight of your name, and the influence of your reputation, should be claimed by such a party. . . . Sorry am I, my dear Dickens, to differ from any opinion of yours — most sorry upon an opinion so grave; but both of us are only the instruments of our convictions.' The disagreement led to a temporary estrangement between them.[51]

Dickens did not soon forget the horror of this day at Horsemonger Lane, though he was haunted as much by the bestiality of the crowd as by the obsenity of hanging this man and woman. To a foreign friend he wrote about this time: 'You have no idea what that hanging of the Mannings really was. The conduct of the people was so indescribably frightful, that I felt for some time afterwards almost as if I were living in a city of devils. I feel at this hour, as if I never could go near the place again.'[52] Three years later, in a paper about 'Lying Awake' at night, he recalled the Mannings, hanging together on the top of the prison.

> In connexion with which dismal spectacle, I recall this curious fantasy of the mind. That, having beheld that execution, and having left those two forms dangling on the top of the entrance gateway — the man's, a limp, loose suit of clothes as if the man had gone out of them; the woman's, a fine shape, so elaborately corseted and artfully dressed, that it was quite unchanged in its trim appearance as it slowly swung from side to side — I never could, by my uttermost efforts, for some weeks, present the outside of that prison to myself (which the terrible impression I had received continually obliged me to do) without presenting it with the two figures still hanging in the morning air. Until, strolling past the gloomy place one night, when the street was deserted and quiet, and actually seeing that the bodies were not there, my fancy was persuaded, as it were, to take them down and bury them within the precincts of the gaol, where they have lain ever since.[53]

'My letters have made a great to-do, and led to a great agitation of the subject,' he wrote a few weeks after the event. With these *Times* letters, indeed, 'there began an active agitation against public executions which never ceased until the salutary change was effected which has worked so well:' so John Forster claimed in his *Life of Dickens*, and the claim is repeated in many later biographies and in many surveys of nineteenth-century penology.[54]

The claim cannot, however, be sustained. Public executions were not abolished until 1868, though a Select Committee of the House of Commons had unanimously recommended it in 1856. (As usual, the House of Lords stopped this reform.) The eventual change in the law was a direct result of the Report of the Royal Commission of 1864–6, led by the Duke of Richmond. Nearly twenty years had by then elapsed since Dickens's letters, however, and it seems unwise to assert that they did more than contribute remotely to the Parliamentary decision of 1868. A more immediate, and doubtless a greater, influence was *The Times*, which had been tardily converted to the idea of private executions by the terrible scenes at Franz Müller's hanging in 1864. Moreover, Dickens, important though he was — 'the greatest instructor of the Nineteenth Century', *The Times* called him when he died — had been by no means the only, nor the first, advocate of this reform. Thackeray's 'Going to see a man hanged' had been published in 1840 — and Thackeray was never in the forefront of reform, either. As was mentioned, Thackeray's companion at the Courvoisier execution was a Member of Parliament who had recently voted for Ewart's motion to abolish capital punishment altogether; this was the first of many such motions, and the support it had received was not negligible (it was lost by 90 votes to 161). Another Member introduced a motion, the following year, for private executions.[55]

The 1840s, which saw Dickens's letters to the *Daily News* and to *The Times*, was indeed a decade notably favourable to further reforms in capital punishment. During the previous two or three decades, the number of capital offences had been drastically reduced; after 1841, only seven remained, and in effect only murderers were hanged. It seemed quite likely that these few survivors of the two-hundred-odd capital crimes of a few years ago would soon go the way of the rest, and there were many writers and public men eager that they should. Even Carlyle was an abolitionist in 1842; so — to mention a few other writers — were

Thackeray, Fonblanque of the *Examiner*, William and Mary Howitt, Bulwer Lytton, and of course Douglas Jerrold.[56] The first number of *Punch*, published in July 1841, had contained Mark Lemon's manifesto, 'The Moral of *Punch*.' Referring to the magazine, as so often, through allusions to the Punch and Judy show, he pointed out that a gallows always appeared in the old story, and he added: 'How clearly PUNCH exposes the fallacy of that dreadful law which authorises the destruction of life! PUNCH sometimes destroys the hangman, and why not? Where is the divine injunction against the shedder of man's blood to rest? None *can* answer!'[57]

Jerrold was abroad when *Punch* began, but soon he returned, and became its most prolific and influential contributor during the 1840s. It was mainly he who conducted its campaign against capital punishment and public executions throughout that period. In 1842, for instance, he was describing with savage irony the 'Old Bailey Holidays' — 'and it is with great delight we quote these words from *The Times* — "and this is the moral influence of capital punishments!"'[58] Jerrold had a knack of noting his opponents' least happy remarks, and repeating them *ad nauseam*: this one often recurs — in, for example, an item published a few weeks before Dickens's *Daily News* letters, 'The "Moral Lesson" of the Gallows,' which ends with the confident statement that 'the gallows is doomed, is crumbling, and must down — overthrown by no greater instruments than a few goose-quills'.[59] Two years later, Mr Jack Ketch was 'advertising' in *Punch*, urging his patrons to avail themselves of their few remaining opportunities of witnessing his 'Scientific and Moral Exhibitions', as 'in consequence of what is called Public Opinion, J. K. seriously apprehends that they must Shortly Terminate'.[60] *Punch*, still opposed to capital punishment '*under any circumstances*', was indeed 'a mortal enemy to Jack Ketch', often in a quite personal way — gleefully pointing out how ineffective its 'moral influence' had been, when the great Calcraft was summoned for refusing to help his pauper mother, and when the wife of another hangman was found guilty of stealing potatoes, even though she had enjoyed 'the elevating benefits of a close companionship with such a national moralist'. As was mentioned above, Leech illustrated 'The Great Moral Lesson at Horsemonger Lane Gaol' with a cartoon of the brutalised crowd; it was one of half-a-dozen items about the Mannings' execution. This is a sample of scores of items on this topic in *Punch* during that decade. Many of them appeared in Jerrold's famous 'Q' papers, which were acknowledged to be 'a power in the land' and to have gained for *Punch* an influence 'second only to that enjoyed by *The Times*'.[61]

Dickens's *Daily News* letters were published in 1846, the year which perhaps registered the highest point of the campaign. Like the prison-reform campaign, which it paralleled, it was international. Several countries had recently abolished capital punishment, or public executions, and various great literary men, such as Victor Hugo, had taken a hand in the campaign. Dickens had been pleased to find in New York, in 1842, that executions took place decently and solemnly inside prisons, and in 1849 he was 'waiting to explode . . . on the first man of mark who gives me the opportunity' the fact that the British Government itself permitted private executions in New South Wales, 'with decidedly improved results.'[62] In 1846, it seemed a good moment for Gilpin to launch the Society for Promoting the Abolition of Capital Punishment — an organisation with a more uncompromising title than the Society for Diffusing Information on the Subject of Capital Punishment, founded in 1828. A *Magazine of Popular Instruction on Capital and Secondary Punishments* had begun in 1845. The years 1845-7, too, if my impression is correct, see the culmination of the pamphlet-controversy on this issue. Dickens refers to some of these items — the New York Report, the papers published by Lord Nugent's Aylesbury committee of 1845, and the Reverend Henry Christmas's *Capital Punishments unsanctioned by the Gospel* (1845).[63]

Much controversy hinged on whether the text 'Whoso sheddeth man's blood, by man shall his blood be shed' was textually valid, and if so whether it was contradicted by 'Thou shalt not kill' or superseded by the New Testament message. Dickens had a short way through the theological difficulties: 'If any text appeared to justify the claim, I would reject that limited appeal, and rest upon the character of the Redeemer, and the great scheme of His Religion, where, in its broad spirit, made so plain — and not this or that disputed letter — we all put our trust. But, happily, such doubts do not exist' — for he was quite convinced by Mr Christmas's textual arguments that the Authorised Version misrepresented *Genesis* here.[64] Not all clerics and theologians took this view. A Prebendary of St Paul's classed 'the advocate of the murderer's life' with 'the desecrator of the Lord's-day, the enemy of Church

Establishments, and the Romanizing allegorist', while from across the Atlantic came the even more formidable insinuation, from a clerical McCarthy, that abolitionism was most associated with 'all who are known as most radical, most revolutionary, most afloat on all that has long been regarded as first principles in politics and religion'.[65] Certainly, as Jerrold pointed out, the Bench of Bishops was not conspicuous in the abolitionist campaign, though many other Christians — notably, of course, the Quakers — were among its leaders. The issue was thoroughly thrashed out, on the religious as well as the secular level, in many treatises, sermons and pamphlets in the mid-forties.[66] Nor of course were *Punch* and the *Daily News* the only journals which devoted a good deal of space to this very topical debate.[67]

To oppose capital punishment in 1846, and public executions in 1849, was therefore by no means a bold or original gesture. Rather, it was the expected thing, in literary and journalistic circles. It is, however, a great tribute to Dickens's standing with his public that he has so frequently been given the credit for 'starting' the campaign against public executions. (His early demand for total abolition has been less often remembered.) This claim has been made, moreover, not only by such partial witnesses as his biographers, and by later historians who have, perhaps, been better up in their Dickens than in their Thackeray or Jerrold or in the files of *Punch* and other periodicals. A more convincing contemporary tribute comes from Frederic Hill, who, as a former Prison Inspector, was presumably well aware of the state of public opinion, within which he and his fellow Inspectors had to manoeuvre. In his book on *Crime* in 1853, he discusses the evil effects of a public execution — 'a performance notorious for its accompaniment of drunkenness, tumult, and vice, but never pictured to the public mind in all its deformity till portrayed by the masterly hand of Charles Dickens.'[68]

When Dickens compromised on the hanging issue in 1849, he was at pains to point out privately that he remained, 'on principle, opposed to capital punishment,' hopeless though he was of its being abolished in the foreseeable future.[69] Not unreasonably, he was accepting the notion of politics as the art of the possible. In 1846 the total abolition of capital punishment had been politically conceivable, though not highly likely, but Dickens was probably right in thinking that, by 1849, this possibility had receded. (As we have noted, there was a general reaction against penal reformism in the late 1840s.) But within a few years, he himself had abandoned his opposition to hanging. Previous commentators seem to have overlooked this fact.[70]

Just when and why he changed his mind is uncertain. As I have said in other connections, he was rarely self-conscious or explicit about the sources or developments of his thought. The only passage I know where he justifies his later attitude on this issue occurs in a short letter written in 1864 to a Quaker who wanted to use his name in an argument against hanging. 'Distinguish if you please in quoting me between Public Executions and Capital Punishment,' he replied. 'I should be glad to abolish both, if I knew what to do with the Savages of civilisation. As I do not, I would rid Society of them, when they shed blood, in a very solemn manner but would bar out the present audience.'[71] As this letter suggests, he never abandoned his hatred of public executions. In 1851 he contributed to *Household Words* a striking article entitled 'The Finishing Schoolmaster', about the hangman, 'the only State Education the State can adjust to the perfect satisfaction of its conscience,' and his periodicals contained a number of other items in similar vein.[72] Several years after this, he ran into the crowds coming away from a very popular execution — 'such a tide of ruffians as never could have flowed from any point but the Gallows. Without any figure of speech, it turned one white and sick to behold them.'[73] And in *A Tale of Two Cities*, when Charles Darnay is on trial for his life, he reverts to the point he had made so often —

> The sort of interest with which this man was stared and breathed at, was not a sort that elevated humanity. Had he stood in peril of a less horrible sentence — had there been a chance of any one of its savage details being spared — by just so much would he have lost in his fascination. The form that was to be doomed to be so shamefully mangled, was the sight; the immortal creature that was to be so butchered and torn asunder, yielded the sensation. Whatever gloss the various spectators put upon the interest, according to their several arts and powers of self-deceit, the interest was, at the root of it, Ogreish.[74]

But when public executions ceased in 1868, he made — as far as I can see — no comment: he uttered no sigh of relief and gratitude. As over several other issues and activities, a spell of keen enthusiasm was followed by indifference or boredom. By 1868 he no longer cared passionately about the ethics of execution.

Long before this, and long before the letter to his Quaker correspondent, he had withdrawn his opposition to hanging as such. The earliest unambiguous indication I have noticed comes in a letter dated 25 August 1859, which Forster printed in a footnote as 'too characteristic of the writer to be lost'. It concerned the celebrated trial of a surgeon, Thomas Smethurst, found guilty of poisoning his bigamous 'wife'. The Judge — 'our brave and excellent friend' (as Dickens called him) Sir Frederick Pollock — had strongly expressed his concurrence in this verdict, but there was much public debate about its correctness, and the Home Secretary was being urged to quash or commute the sentence. Dickens applauded Pollock's stand on this issue.

> I followed the case with so much interest, and have followed the miserable knaves and asses who have perverted it since, with so much indignation, that I have often had more than half a mind to write and thank the upright judge who tried him. I declare to God that I believe such a service one of the greatest that a man of intellect and courage can render to society. Of course I saw the beast of a prisoner (with my mind's eye) delivering his cut-and-dried speech, and read in every word of it that no one but the murderer could have delivered or conceived it. Of course I have been driving the girls out of their wits here, by incessantly proclaiming that there needed no medical evidence either way, and that the case was plain without it. Lastly, of course (though a merciful man — because a merciful man I mean), I would hang any Home Secretary (Whig, Tory, Radical, or otherwise) who should step in between that black scoundrel and the gallows. I cannot believe — and my belief in all wrong as to public matters is enormous — that such a thing will be done.[75]

An unpleasantly emotional note intrudes here, which is absent in the more impersonal letter to the Quaker stranger: and it recurs in a letter about another notorious murder case a few years later, that of Franz Müller. 'I hope that gentleman will be hanged,' he wrote, 'and have hardly a doubt of it, though croakers contrariwise are not wanting.'[76] The expression 'croakers' is ungenerous, to describe the party to which Dickens himself had belonged not so long before.

Finally, in the last year of his life, he introduced an abolitionist for the first time in one of his novels. It was the egregious 'philanthropist' Mr Honeythunder, who also represents other 'good causes' which Dickens now abominates: one notices in this passage the hits at the Peace Society and at the Jamaica Committee which had sought to prosecute Governor Eyre for his colonial excesses.

Though it was not literally true, as was facetiously charged against him by public unbelievers, that he called aloud to his fellow-creatures: 'Curse your souls and bodies, come here and be blessed!' still his philanthropy was of that gunpowderous sort that the difference between it and animosity was hard to determine. You were to abolish military force, but you were first to bring all commanding officers who had done their duty, to trial by court-martial for that offence, and shoot them. You were to abolish war, but were to make converts by making war upon them, and charging them with loving war as the apple of their eye. You were to have no capital punishment, but were first to sweep off the face of the earth all legislators, jurists, and judges, who were of the contrary opinion. You were to have universal concord, and were to get it by eliminating all the people who wouldn't, or conscientiously couldn't, be concordant. You were to love your brother as yourself, but after an indefinite interval of maligning him (very much as if you hated him), and calling him all manner of names.[77]

It is a lively passage — and the Honeythunders do, indeed, exist. A splendid example comes to hand as I write this chapter. Sir Thomas Moore, a Conservative MP, urging on Parliament the appropriateness of flogging for certain offences, quoted from one of the few letters he had received from opponents of his motion. 'Don't you dare bring that birch back,' it ran, 'and don't you ever open your big mouth about it again.' It was signed 'World Youth Organiser', which gave Sir Thomas an obvious opening for the retort, 'God help world youth.' Still, the Honeythunders are not the most favourable, and probably not the most typical, representatives of the abolitionist cause — and even if they are, this does not, of course, affect the validity or otherwise of the cause which they discredit. Characteristically, Mr Honeythunder later becomes irrationally violent in his denunciation of Neville Landless, who is wrongly suspected of having murdered Edwin Drood, and he has to be put in his place by a long speech from Canon Crisparkle about his 'destestable platform manners'.[78]

In 1846 and 1849, Dickens had spoken, if not for the majority, at least for a very substantial minority, and in moving, some time in the 1850s, to an acceptance of capital punishment he was also reflecting a widespread change of opinion. Carlyle, abolitionist in 1842, was no longer content, eight years later, to 'protect' scoundrels — 'The scoundrel that *will* hasten to the gallows, why not rather clear the way for him!' — and he bade his readers reflect on the fact that 'The Ancient Germans . . . had no scruple about public executions'.[79] So different a man as John Stuart Mill, who had been so appalled by *Latter Day Pamphlets* that he broke off relations with Carlyle, moved in the same direction; an abolitionist in the 1840s, he opposed an abolitionist Bill in the House twenty years later.[80] *Punch* also had stopped opposing Mr Ketch, and as for its former contributor, Thackeray, this is how his editor George Saintsbury commented on his 'Going to see a man hanged' — 'The anti-capital-punishment fad was one of the special crotchets of mid-century Liberalism, and he kept to it for some time: but in his later and wiser days admitted that he was wrong.'[81] By the 1860s, indeed, the abolitionist movement was virtually dead. In 1862 the Society for the Abolition of Capital Punishment was 'a very small Society, which previously had temporarily suspended its operations several times, owing to a lack of support and to other causes'. When the Richmond Report was published in 1866, recommending private executions, the Society, now hopeless of achieving its object, decided to disband; it was, however, persuaded to reconstitute itself on broader lines, and thus the Howard Association was born. Since 1865, wrote the Society's last Secretary, forty years later, 'some half-a-dozen Societies for the Abolition of Capital Punishment have, in succession, been formed, or at least announced. But for the most part, they have met with very little public support, or attention.' The Howard Association found newspapers willing to accept discussion on any penological topic except capital punishment.[82] No further significant change in the law took place until 1957.

In the first of his *Daily News* letters, Dickens had discussed the 'horrible fascination' which hanging exerted even on 'good and virtuous and well-conducted people'. It was, he asserted, 'generally speaking, irresistible' though 'odious and painful, even to many of those who eagerly gratify it by every means they can compass.... The attraction of repulsion being as much a law of our moral nature, as gravitation is in the structure of the visible world, operates in no case (I believe) so powerfully, as in this case of the punishment of death; though it may occasionally diminish in its force, through strong re-action'. This 'attraction of repulsion', of which Dickens was always very conscious, seemed to him 'a metaphysical truth, which, however wild and appalling in its aspect, was a truth still'.[83] Later generations are too familiar with the idea to share Dickens's awed surprise at this discovery, through introspection or observation, of psychological ambivalence. Dickens himself was not so extreme an example in this respect as Monckton Milnes, for instance, who, despite his abolitionism, gathered a large collection of murderers' and hangmen's autographs, and scrap-books containing letters, relics, and newspaper accounts of the most odious criminals. 'On Sunday mornings . . . he would sometimes amuse himself by watching his guests recoil before a piece of the dried skin of a notorious murderer, which he kept pressed between the pages of some appropriate book.'[84]

Dickens did not stimulate his sensations in this fashion, but he did let his imagination play on the process of hanging. Dennis in *Barnaby Rudge* is always sizing up his companions with a professional eye. Briefly, in *Nicholas Nickleby*, the Newgate scaffold is seen from the victim's point of view — 'in the mass of white and upturned faces, the dying wretch, in his all-comprehensive look of agony, has met not one — not one — that bore the impress of pity or compassion.'[85] More startlingly, in 'The Lazy Tour' of 1857, Mr Goodchild (the *persona* for Dickens) has a conversation with an old man who unexpectedly enters his room at a Lancaster inn:

'. . . They hang condemned criminals at the Castle, I believe?'
'*I* believe so,' said the old man.
'Are their faces turned towards that noble prospect?'
'Your face is turned,' replied the old man, 'to the Castle wall. When you are tied up, you see its stones expanding and contracting violently, and a similar expansion and contraction seem to take place in your own head and breast. Then, there is a rush of fire and an earthquake, and the Castle springs into the air, and you tumble down a precipice.'
. . . 'A strong description, Sir,' [Mr Goodchild] observed.
'A strong sensation,' the old man rejoined.

The old man turns out, of course, to be the ghost of a murderer, haunting the scene of his death.[68]

In the novels, however, Dickens rarely gave himself a chance to describe hangings, though he depicted plenty of hangable criminals. There were of course the political executions in *Barnaby Rudge* and *A Tale of Two Cities*, but Dickens was raising different issues there: the victims were more or less innocent, and he was too intent on pointing the political moral to engage in exploiting the more sensational possibilities. Some of the murderers are, of course, caught and executed — but the actual process is never described. Fagin is last seen in the condemned cell; Hortense, proved guilty of killing Mr Tulkinghorn, fades out of sight in Inspector Bucket's custody; Rudge had been seen by Gabriel Varden riding to the gallows, and Gabriel later hears 'that to the last he had been an unyielding obdurate man; that in the savage terror of his condition he had hardened, rather than relented, to his wife and child; and that the last words which had passed his white lips were curses on them as his foes'.[87] One wonders how far beyond the condemned cell Dickens would have carried John Jasper, had he lived to complete *Edwin Drood*.

His literary instinct was right here, of course. Not only is the description of a hanging likely to be distasteful, but also, as he had insisted in his letters against public executions, the solitary victim before our eyes tends to attract an excessive sympathy, however heinous his crime. But the readers' demands for justice must be satisfied, so Dickens generally contrives to punish his malefactors adequately and tidily, without the delay and tedium of a trial, and without risking the emotional conflict that a judicial hanging may excite. He uses time-honoured expedients. Recall, for instance, the end of Shakespearean tragedies — Othello committing suicide, Iago taken off under arrest: Edmund killed in combat, Regan poisoned, and Goneril dead by her own hand. The reviewer of crime-fiction in 1875 who complained that 'Our modern novelists have abolished the gallows, and suicide is almost invariably the penalty', was allowing his moral preoccupations to obscure his sense of literary precedent.[88]

Some of Dickens's murderers, too, manage to commit suicide. Jonas Chuzzlewit takes poison, and so does Slinckton in 'Hunted Down'. Of his lesser villains, Ralph Nickleby hangs himself, and Mr Merdle cuts his veins in a bath. More often, accidents or natural disasters, so opportune as to seem indeed an Act of God, cut short the lives of the wicked. Rigaud is crushed to death when the house collapses; Rogue Riderhood and Bradley Headstone drown, grappling together in the weir; Obenreizer is carried away by an avalanche ('I am racking my brains for a good death to that respectable gentleman,' Dickens had told his collaborator Wilkie Collins).[89] Again, it is not only murderers, or would-be murderers, who end like this. Quilp, Steerforth, Compeyson, and Gaffer Hexam all drown; Carker, more original, is struck by a railway train.

Most fitting of all is the death of Bill Sikes, who hangs himself when trying to escape from his pursuers. Ever since he has murdered Nancy, he has been haunted by her eyes. Now he has climbed on to the roof of the house on Jacob's Island where he has been cornered, and he hopes to drop down to the ditch and escape in the darkness and confusion. His faithful dog is still with him. He ties a rope round a chimney-stack, and prepares to lower himself to within a safe distance from the ground, when he will cut the rope with a knife, and drop.

> At the very instant when he brought the loop over his head previous to slipping it beneath his arm-pits, . . . the murderer, looking behind him on the roof, threw his arms above his head, and uttered a yell of terror.
>
> 'The eyes again!' he cried, in an unearthly screech.
>
> Staggering as if struck by lightning, he lost his balance and tumbled over the parapet. The noose was on his neck. It ran up with his weight, tight as a bowstring, and swift as the arrow it speeds. He fell for five-and-thirty feet. There was a sudden jerk, a terrific convulsion of the limbs; and there he hung, with the open knife clenched in his stiffening hand.
>
> The old chimney quivered with the shock, but stood it bravely. The murderer swung lifeless against the wall. . . .
>
> A dog, which had lain concealed till now, ran backwards and forwards on the parapet with a dismal howl, and, collecting himself for a spring, jumped for the dead man's shoulders. Missing his aim, he fell into the ditch, turning completely over as he went; and striking his head against a stone, dashed out his brains.[90]

This episode provided a splendid melodramatic ending to Dickens's *Sikes and Nancy* Reading. Sikes's attempt to cheat the gallows has, by poetic justice, been thwarted by his vision of Nancy's accusing eyes, and he becomes his own hangman. The dog's death, however, is quite another matter. Equally unnecessary to the plot and to the moral theme, it is a gratuitous touch of sadism, such as often occurs elsewhere at similar moments in the novels. Part of Dickens's 'attraction of repulsion' towards murder, execution, and other forms of violent death, is manifested in the unnecessary violence with which he punishes some of his villains, and in the superfluous detail with which he recounts their deaths. (This can also occur, however, when the victim is sympathetic, and the means of his death abhorrent to Dickens: I am thinking of his detailed descriptions of the burning of heretics, in *A Child's History of England*.) In fiction, Dickens can let himself go in this way, only with his villains. The obvious examples are the deaths of Carker and Quilp.

Carker is not a violent criminal, though a mean and villainous creature. He has tried to seduce Edith Dombey, and is pursued by her husband, who catches up with him at a railway station. Carker is so taken by surprise, that he staggers back on to the railway track.

> He heard a shout — another — saw the face [of Mr Dombey] change from its vindictive passion to a faint sickness and terror — felt the earth tremble — knew in a moment that the rush was come — uttered a shriek — looked round — saw the red eyes, bleared and dim, in the daylight, close upon him — was beaten down, caught up, and whirled away upon a jagged mill, that spun him round and round, and struck him limb from limb, and licked his stream of life up with its fiery heat, and cast his mutilated fragments in the air.[91]

Quilp, too, dies when trying to escape from the prosecution that is at last threatening him. He runs off into the pitch-dark night, as his accusers are knocking at the gate of his 'summer-house' by the river, and he falls into the water. The process of his drowning is lovingly described, and 'The End of Quilp' was illustrated by an engraving, as were the penultimate moments of Sikes and Fagin, presumably on Dickens's instructions.

> For all its bubbling up and rushing in his ears, he could hear the knocking at the gate again — could hear a shout that followed it — could recognise the voice. For all his struggling and plashing, he could understand that they . . . were all but looking on, while he was drowning; that they were close at hand, but could not make an effort to save him; that he himself had shut and barred them out. He answered the shout — with a yell, which seemed to make the hundred fires that danced before his eyes tremble and flicker, as if a gust of wind had stirred them. It was of no avail. The strong tide filled his throat, and bore him on upon its rapid current.
>
> Another mortal struggle, and he was up again, beating the water with his hands, and looking out, with wild and glaring eyes that showed him some black object he was drifting close upon. The hull of a ship! He could touch its smooth and slippery surface with his hand. One loud cry now — but the resistless water bore him down before he could give it utterance, and, driving him under it, carried away a corpse.
>
> It toyed and sported with its ghastly freight, now bruising it against the slimy piles, now hiding in mud or long, rank grass, now dragging it heavily over rough stones and gravel, now feigning to yield it to its own element, and in the same action luring it away, until, tired of the ugly plaything, it flung it on a swamp . . . and left it there to bleach.[92]

The death-penalties that Dickens awards these characters do not show much moral superiority to the legal form of capital punishment which he was, at this period, rejecting. *Naturam expellas furca, tamen usque recurret.*

Such passages in his fiction may, no doubt, be partly accounted for by the fact that Dickens was a 'Sensation Novelist', working inside a tradition of violent and bloodthirsty incident. But the same quest for gruesome sensation appears also in some of his non-fictional activities — in the necrophilia, for instance, which took him to the Paris Morgue. 'He went at first rather frequently to the Morgue,' records Forster, 'until shocked by something so repulsive that he had not courage for a long time to go back.'[93] If he rarely attended the executions of criminals, he followed their trials avidly, and was not above visiting the scene of the crime. Thus, late in 1849, when he was wondering where to go for a bachelor jaunt with some friends, it was a notorious recent murder, as well as the bad weather, that decided him against Salisbury Plain or the Isle of Wight. It would be better, he told Forster, 'to make an outburst to some old cathedral city we don't know, and what do you say to Norwich and Stanfield-hall?' Norwich seems to have been chosen, then, instead of Ely or Durham or whatnot, because, only a month before, the Recorder of Norwich, who lived at the near-by Stanfield Hall, had been shot dead, and three members of his household wounded. Dickens went there, and described the place as having 'a murderous look that seemed to invite such a crime'. Norwich disappointed him, 'all save its place of execution, which we found fit for a gigantic scoundrel's exit,' so he and his party moved on to Yarmouth and Lowestoft — and that is the reason, I think, why *David Copperfield*, begun a few days later, has its opening chapters set in that coast.[94] Nearer home, his daily walks from Gad's Hill often took him past the place where a lunatic named Dadd — an acquaintance of several of Dickens's friends — had murdered his father. Dickens would re-enact the whole scene, with great dramatic force.[95]

Most famous was Dickens's expedition to Harvard University, to see the laboratories where Webster, its Professor of Chemistry, had tried to dispose of his victim's body. Dickens had met him socially, a few years before the murder. Now he wrote to Wilkie Collins:

Being in Boston last Sunday, I took it into my head to go over the medical school, and survey the holes and corners in which that extraordinary murder was done by Webster. There was the furnace

— stinking horribly, as if the dismembered pieces were still inside it — and there are all the grim spouts, and sinks, and chemical appliances, and what not. At dinner, afterwards, Longfellow told me a terrific story. He dined with Webster within a year of the murder, one of a party of ten or twelve. As they sat at their wine, Webster suddenly ordered the lights to be turned out, and a bowl of some burning mineral to be placed on the table, that the guests might see how ghostly it made them look. As each man stared at all the rest in the weird light, all were horrified to see Webster *with a rope round his neck*, holding it up, over the bowl, with his head jerked on one side, and his tongue lolled out representing a man being hanged! Poking into his life and character, I find (what I would have staked my head upon) that he was always a cruel man.

Whenever he thought of this story, he wrote later, he felt like the lady in *Nicholas Nickleby* who had 'a sensation of alternate cold, and biling water running down her back ever since' — and no wonder.[96]

'He was always a cruel man:' Dickens was gratified to confirm his guess about Professor Webster, for he had always shared the common assumption that murderers are, by temperament, monsters of vice. He never seems to have realised that many murderers are, instead, weak and stupid or temporarily over-wrought. Even in his abolitionist days, he had never accepted this item in the usual case against capital punishment. For him, murderers were always wholly vile, never pitiful; one of his main objections to capital punishment, and later to public executions, was indeed that hanging a man made him too much an object for sympathy, and that a reform in the law would 'leave the general compassion to expend itself on the only theme at present quite forgotten in the history, that is to say, the murdered person'. It is a phrase, and a point, to which he often reverts, with increasing asperity.[97] Abolitionists are still, of course, often accused of devoting so much pity to the murderer that they have little or none to spare for his victim — doubtless sometimes with some justice. But that Dickens could so often make this allegation, even during his own abolitionist phase, shows how little he partook of what one might loosely call the abolitionist temperament.

He resembled those opponents of blood-sports who think foxes a pest and do not mind how they die, but regard hunting as bad for the souls of its devotees. It was on similar grounds that he had objected to flogging in 1852 —

The late brutal assaults. I strongly question the expediency of advocating the revival of whipping for those crimes. It is a natural and generous impulse to be indignant at the perpetration of inconceivable brutality, but I doubt the whipping panacea gravely. Not in the least regard or pity for the criminal, whom I hold in far lower estimation than a mad wolf, but in consideration for the general tone and feeling, which is very much improved since the whipping times. It is bad for a people to be familiarised with such punishments. When the whip went out of Bridewell, and ceased to be flourished at the cart's tail and at the whipping-post, it began to fade out of madhouses, and workhouses, and schools and families, and to give place to a better system everywhere, than cruel driving. It would be hasty, because a few brutes may be inadequately punished, to revive, in any aspect, what, in so many aspects, society is hardly yet happily rid of. The whip is a very contagious kind of thing, and difficult to confine within one set of bounds. Utterly abolish punishment by fine — a barbarous device, quite as much out of date as wager by battle, but particularly connected in the vulgar mind with this class of offence — at least quadruple the term of imprisonment for aggravated assaults — and above all let us, in such cases, have no Pet Prisoning, vain glorifying, strong soup, and roasted meats, but hard work, and one unchanging and uncompromising dietary of bread and water, well or ill; and we shall do much better than by going down into the dark to grope for the whip among the rusty fragments of the rack, and the branding iron, and the chains and gibbet from the public roads, and the weights that pressed men to death in the cells of Newgate.[98]

The sociological argument is reasonable, though the dietary proposals are harsh and ludicrous. But one sees how anxious Dickens is here, as elsewhere, to dissociate himself from those penal reformers who might be suspected of being 'soft' towards ruffians and murderers. On flogging, he had surprisingly little to say: the campaign against it was a parallel to the campaign against capital punishment, and attracted much the same lot of supporters.[99] Both campaigns had once been able to claim Dickens as an illustrious ally, but he was an independent and an unreliable one. For, as was noted in a previous chapter, he later turned against the anti-flogging campaign, and came to display an emotional relish for this form of punishment, the more extreme, perhaps, in reaction against the uncongenial restraint of his former attitude. Of the ruffian, it will be remembered, he then wrote: 'I would have his back scarified often and deep.'[100] *Naturam expellas* . . . indeed.

MURDER: FROM BILL SIKES
TO BRADLEY HEADSTONE

'I USED, when I was at school,' wrote Dickens, 'to take in the *Terrific Register*, making myself unspeakably miserable, and frightening my very wits out of my head, for the small charge of a penny weekly; which considering that there was an illustration to every number, in which there was always a pool of blood, and at least one body, was cheap.' As a young man, he still had a 'passion for sensational novels', which he would 'carry away by the pile' from his circulating library.[1] Boys and men of all periods have shared these tastes, for which popular literature and drama has catered in various fashions. Often the sensational stories have been set in the past, or in a foreign country where evil notoriously flourishes, or in both. Italy was a favourite for Elizabethan dramatists, as for Gothic romancers: the 'Westerns' of today, and Mr Graham Greene's sultry settings, are variants on the old methods of escape into violence and vice. Early in his career, Dickens began exploiting this, along with his other strong suits — humour, pathos, and social reformism. *Sketches by Boz* contained two short stories of melodramatic type, 'The Black Veil' and 'The Drunkard's Death'; he was proud of these, and Edgar Allan Poe highly praised the former, but they are wretched efforts — as are the stories of violence interpolated into *Pickwick Papers*, the significance of which has been discussed in a famous passage by Mr Edmund Wilson.[2] But before *Pickwick* was begun, Dickens had already formed the idea for two novels which were to present evil and violence more fully and successfully — *Barnaby Rudge* and (as Professor Kathleen Tillotson has recently argued) *Oliver Twist*.[3]

As everyone has noted, *Barnaby Rudge* might have been given the sub-title of *Waverley* — '*Tis Sixty Years Since* — and Scott is certainly an important impulse behind this novel.[4] Scott was much the most popular novelist of any repute before Dickens; his influence was omnipresent, and had been felt in the sensation-novel as well as elsewhere. Ainsworth's Preface to *Rookwood* (1834) does not mention Scott, but Scott provides half the formula: 'I resolved to attempt a story in the bygone style of Mrs Radcliffe (which had always inexpressible charms for me), substituting an old English squire, an old English manorial residence, and an old English highwayman, for the Italian marchese, the castle, and the brigand of the great mistress of Romance.' Romance, he thought, was 'destined shortly to undergo an important change', as the structure inherited from Horace Walpole, Monk Lewis, Mrs Radcliffe and Maturin was modified by the influence of the recent German and French writers, Hoffman, Tieck, Hugo, Dumas, Balzac and Lacroix. *Rookwood*, set in the mid-eighteenth century, and centred on Dick Turpin, was vastly popular, and a few years later Ainsworth repeated the formula, with even greater success, in *Jack Sheppard* (1839), the hero of which is a housebreaker instead of highwayman, the period being now Jonathan Wild's London. With this novel, Ainsworth became 'the literary lion of the day', a contemporary recalled. 'For a time Dickens's star paled.'[5] Ainsworth was not alone in this field, of course. Lytton's *Paul Clifford* (1830) had a highwayman-hero, and his *Pelham* (1828), *Eugene Aram* (1832), *Ernest Maltravers* (1837) and *Alice* (1838) also had crime-themes, while in 1834 Charles Whitehead published his *Autobiography of Jack Ketch* and *Lives of the Highwaymen*.

Reviewers began talking of a 'Newgate School of Novelists', and they included *Oliver Twist* among its products. At the end of the 1830s, Thackeray serialised in *Fraser's Magazine* (1839–40) his anti-Newgate School novel *Catherine*, and there Dickens stands accused beside Bulwer Lytton and Ainsworth. A couple of years later, an early number of *Punch* contained among its 'Literary Recipes' some advice about how to cook up 'A Startling Romance' —

Take a small boy, charity, factory, carpenter's apprentice, or otherwise, as occasion may serve — stew him well down in vice — garnish largely with oaths and flash songs — boil him in a cauldron of crime and improbabilities. Season equally with good and bad qualities — infuse petty larceny, affection, benevolence, and burglary, honour and housebreaking, amiability and arson — boil all gently. Stew down a mad mother — a gang of robbers — several pistols — a bloody knife. Serve up with a couple of murders — and season with a hanging-match.

N.B. Alter the ingredients to a beadle and a work-house — the scenes may be the same, but the whole flavour of vice will be lost, and the boy will turn out a perfect pattern. — Strongly recommended for weak stomachs.[6]

Again, Dickens — though more suitable for 'weak stomachs' — finds himself indicted with Ainsworth, Lytton, Mrs Trollope and others here glanced at: and much the same being said by other reviewers, preachers, and social workers. A Police Commissioner reported several young delinquents as testifying to the popularity of *Oliver Twist*. 'On Sundays,' said one of them, describing his fellow youngsters at Common Lodging Houses, 'they play cards, dominoes, and pitch-halfpenny, read *Jack Sheppard*, *Oliver Twist*, *Martha Willis*, and publications of the kind, and plan robberies.'[7]

Dickens was very annoyed to be put in this category. He admired *Pelham* and *Paul Clifford* ('admirable and most powerful'), and he was personally friendly with Lytton and Whitehead. In 1838 he and Ainsworth and Forster formed a 'Trio Club' — they were inseparable companions at this period.[8] He had inserted a footnote in *Sketches by Boz* praising *Rookwood*, but in the 1839 edition he deleted it, having changed his mind on the subject, doubtless because, having been attacked in the reviews along with Ainsworth, he realised how little, in fact, their fictional aims coincided, and wanted to dissociate himself from Ainsworth as far as was decent. It was difficult to do so explicitly, not only because Ainsworth was a close friend, but also because *Jack Sheppard* had begun appearing in *Bentley's Miscellany* shortly before Dickens handed over to him the editorship of this journal. The further fact, that Cruikshank illustrated both *Oliver Twist* and *Jack Sheppard*, doubtless encouraged the public and the reviewers to exaggerate the resemblance between the two novels. Dickens wrote privately to a friend in 1839: 'I am by some jolter-headed enemies most unjustly and untruly charged with having written a book after Mr Ainsworth's fashion. Unto these jolter-heads and their intensely concentrated humbug I shall take an early opportunity of temperately replying.' He wanted to 'disavow any sympathy with that school', and he had no sympathy at all for 'the late lamented John Sheppard', but he had to wait for a suitable opportunity to do so and to shield himself without seeming 'ungenerous and unmanly'.[9]

The preface to the 1841 edition of *Oliver Twist* provided an occasion for 'saying a few words in explanation of my aim and object'. Fortified by an epigraph from *Tom Jones*, and invoking 'examples and precedents . . . in the noblest range of English literature' (Fielding, Defoe, Goldsmith, Smollett, Richardson, and

Mackenzie), he defends his choice of characters 'from the most criminal and degraded of London's population' and his method of presenting them.

> I had read of thieves by scores — seductive fellows (amiable for the most part), faultless in dress, plump in pocket, choice in horseflesh, bold in bearing, fortunate in gallantry, great at a song, a bottle, pack of cards or dice-box, and fit companions for the bravest. But I had never met (except in Hogarth) with the miserable reality. It appeared to me that to draw a knot of such associates in crime as really do exist; to paint them in all their deformity, in all their wretchedness, in all the squalid poverty of their lives; to show them as they really are, for ever skulking uneasily through the dirtiest paths of life, with the great, black, ghastly gallows closing up their prospect, turn them where they may; it appeared to me that to do this, would be to attempt a something which was greatly needed, and which would be a service to society.

He excludes *Paul Clifford* from his imputations (though in fact its moral casuistry is decidedly vulnerable, rather in the way of Mr Graham Greene, the Bulwer Lytton *de nos jours*), and it is clearly *Rookwood* and *Jack Sheppard* that he has most in mind, though he mentions no names. He also attacks the Italianised Gothic romances and dramas — or, at least, those people who are enchanted by 'a Massaroni in green velvet' but find 'a Sikes in fustian . . . insupportable'.[10] 'I will not, for these readers, abate one hole in the Dodger's coat, or one scrap of curl-paper in the girl's dishevelled hair,' he proclaims, though he assures the reader that, while telling 'the stern and plain truth, . . . unattractive and repulsive', he will 'banish from the lips of the lowest character . . . any expression that could by possibility offend; and rather lead to the unavoidable inference that its existence was of the most debased and vicious kind, than to prove it elaborately by words and deeds'.[11] In later editions, indeed, as Professor Tillotson has shown, he progressively bowdlerised the mild vocabulary that resulted from this policy, though in its original edition even the nineteen-year-old maiden Queen Victoria was able to read it without scandal. She found it 'excessively interesting'.[12]

Dickens certainly was justified in distinguishing his purposes from Ainsworth's. 'Turpin was the hero of my boyhood,' Ainsworth had acknowledged in the Preface to *Rookwood*; and, referring to the famous 'ride to York' passage, he wrote, 'So thoroughly did I identify myself with the flying highwayman that, once started, I found it impossible to halt.' (He wrote the whole hundred pages, indeed, at one sitting of twenty-four hours.) He made no pretence of a moral purpose: 'I fear I have but imperfectly fulfilled the office imposed upon me; having, as I will freely confess, had, throughout, an eye rather on the reader's amusement than his edification.' And at the end of the novel he offered a final salute to his hero: 'Turpin (why disguise it?) was hanged at York in 1739. His firmness deserted him not at the last. ... Oh rare Dick Turpin! ... Perhaps, we may have placed him in too favourable a point of view; and yet we know not. ...'[13] Jack Sheppard's exploits were recounted with a similar frank sensationalism, uncontrolled by any moral curiosity.

Dickens never indulges his criminals like this: nor does he attempt the more ambitious 'metaphysical speculation and analysis' that Bulwer Lytton had claimed as his sanction for presenting his criminals so sympathetically. Eugene Aram, according to Lytton, was 'a person who, till the detection of the crime for which he was sentenced [murder], had appeared of the mildest character and the most unexceptionable morals ... so benevolent that he would rob his own to administer to the necessities of another, so humane that he would turn aside from the worm in his path. ...' Dickens had no interest in such alleged complexities of character (for him, as we have seen, murderers were always men of vicious temperament), nor did he in *Oliver Twist* or elsewhere, make a central issue of what Lytton claimed as his two-fold object in *Paul Clifford*:

> First, to draw attention to two errors in our penal institutions — viz., a vicious Prison-discipline, and a sanguinary Criminal Code — the habit of corrupting the boy by the very punishment that ought to redeem him, and then hanging the man, at the first occasion, as the easiest way of getting rid of our own blunders. ... A second and lighter object ... was to show that there is nothing essentially different between vulgar vice and fashionable vice — and that the slang of the one circle is but an easy paraphrase of the cant of the other.[14]

Dickens was willing to use such arguments on behalf of minor offenders, such as Nancy, or of characters whose crimes (generally unspecified) were committed long ago, like Magwitch: but he never condones or invites a sympathetic understanding for his major and active criminals.

Nevertheless, despite his differences from the 'Newgate School', he belonged to it. *Oliver Twist*, it should be remembered, was the first novel he had written off his own bat. The idea of *Pickwick* had not been his, but its huge popularity was an invitation to him to repeat its success with a further comic novel. He surprised and to some extent disappointed his public by writing *Oliver Twist* instead. *Oliver* belongs very much to the late 1830s, and could not have been written at any other time. 'Un Roman au Gout du Jour', is Professor Monod's appropriate title for his useful chapter on this novel in *Dickens romancier*. Though protesting explicitly and implicitly against some of the moral obliquities of the 'Newgate Novel', Dickens was drawn to the subject of *Oliver Twist* — as to the earlier 'Visit to Newgate' — more by the desire to exploit this exciting material than by any high-minded cathartic intention.[15] Even Thackeray, whose *Catherine* was much more explicitly and insistently an anti-Newgate novel, found himself developing a moral wobble as he became involved in his subject. It was 'a mistake all through', he decided soon afterwards — 'it was not made disgusting enough that is the fact, and the triumph of it would have been to make readers so horribly horrified as to cause them to give up or rather throw up the book and all of it's kind, whereas you see the author had a sneaking kindness for his heroine, and did not like to make her utterly worthless.'[16] Thackeray was, rightly, less severe upon *Oliver Twist* than upon Lytton's 'juggling and thimblerigging with virtue and vice' and Ainsworth's amorality, and he chiefly attacked *Oliver Twist* at its weakest point (in this respect) — the virtues imputed to Nancy. Anyway, he argues, such novels 'familiarise the public with notions of crime. . . . In the name of common-sense, let us not expend our sympathies on cut-throats, and other such prodigies of evil!'[17]

Few would now wish to attack or defend Nancy on moral grounds, her unreality as a literary creation removing her from the area of discussion: it is an index of changing taste and outlook that she could, at that time, arouse such denunciations, or, indeed, high praise from many critics who had misgivings about the moral tendency, or the literary quality, of other aspects of the book.[18] It is not Nancy, but Bill Sikes, who still excites our interest, and raises critical and moral problems, and we of course have a further interest in this character, which was denied to the original readers and reviewers. I refer to the Public Reading, *Sikes and Nancy*, which Dickens delivered in the last years of his life — a performance greatly admired, and deplored, at the time, and said by some of his friends to have caused, or hastened, his death.

As he claimed in his Preface to *Oliver Twist*, Dickens had stripped
crime of the charms and allurements which it bore in many contemporary novels and plays. 'The cold, wet, shelterless midnight
streets of London; the foul and frowsy dens, where vice is closely
packed and lacks the room to turn; the haunts of hunger and
disease, the shabby rags that scarcely hold together: where are
the attractions of these things?' Nancy's behaviour, he said, was
based on what he had often seen and read of 'in actual life around
me', and he had, 'for years, tracked it through many profligate
and noisome ways.'[19] He did not merely rely on the common
repute of the Saffron Hill area where Fagin lives, its thieves' dens,
'flash-houses,' and stolen-handkerchief trade; he knew the area
well. Many independent reports of it provide striking parallels, and
several readers familiar with the facts acknowledge the accuracy
of *Oliver Twist* as a guide to Metropolitan criminal life of this
period. Fagin was, as everyone saw, based on the famous Jewish
fence, Ikey Solomon, and his methods of employing and training
boy pick-pockets were the standard practice, and remained so for
several decades.[20] Even Sikes, it has been said, was based on an
actual criminal. A friend of Cruikshank's recorded that a burglar
named Bill was among the visitors to Cruikshank's parlour, and
so were a girl and a boy on whom Nancy and Oliver were based.
' "Jaw away, Bill," Dickens would say, and Dickens took shorthand notes while Cruikshank did the sketching.' But this story is
clearly as apocryphal as Cruikshank's fantastic claim that it was
he, not Dickens, that devised *Oliver Twist*.[21]

Within his self-imposed limits of a decent reticence, Dickens
creates a convincing and accurate picture of the London underworld, rather over-emphasising the squalor and misery, and
suppressing its feckless jollity. Beyond its documentary value —
which is considerable — the novel remains of course a powerful
symbol of moral evil and darkness.[22] Fagin, Dickens told Forster
when writing the concluding chapters, 'is such an out and outer
that I don't know what to make of him;' Sikes, he wrote in the
Preface, was one of those 'insensible and callous natures that do
become, at last, utterly and irredeemably bad'.[23] Sikes had been bad
enough, at the beginning of the book. He is first introduced, shouting
oaths and kicking his already much-injured dog across the room:

> The man who growled out these words, was a stoutly-built fellow
> about five-and-thirty, in a black velveteen coat, very soiled drab
> breeches, lace-up half-boots, and gray cotton stockings, which in-

closed a bulky pair of legs, with large, swelling calves — the kind of legs, which, in such costume, always look in an unfinished and incomplete state without a set of fetters to garnish them. He had a brown hat on his head, and a dirty belcher handkerchief round his neck; with the long, frayed ends of which he smeared the beer from his face as he spoke. He disclosed, when he had done so, a broad, heavy countenance with a beard of three day's growth, and two scowling eyes; one of which displayed various parti-coloured symptoms of having been recently damaged by a blow.[24]

His coarse brutality is insisted upon at every subsequent entrance: so are the squalor and uncertainty of his criminal life. The hideout in Spitalfields to which he retreats after the Chertsey housebreaking is described as 'a mean and badly-furnished apartment, of very limited size; lighted only by one small window in the shelving roof, and abutting on a close and dirty lane. . . . A great scarcity of furniture, and total absence of comfort, together with the disappearance of all such small movables as spare clothes and linen, bespoke a state of extreme poverty'.[25] He bullies, indeed terrifies, the pathetic boy-hero Oliver; then he brutally murders his mistress Nancy, when she, having been touched by Oliver's sufferings, has tried to help him to escape from the clutches of the gang. It is, however, at this point that Sikes becomes, in a sense, a sympathetic character.

This has been much discussed by recent writers, but it was of course noticed at the time. Thus, R. H. Horne, while applauding Dickens for not 'making a morbid hero of him in any degree, or being guilty of the frequent error of late years, that of endeavouring to surround an atrocious villain with various romantic associations', thought that in the climax of the novel 'the author over-shoots his aim'. Dickens hunts Sikes down like a wild beast — indeed 'with ten-fold more ferocity than ever was fox, or boar, or midnight wolf — having scarce a chance of escape' — but with the result that

> . . . our sympathies go with the hunted victim in this his last extremity. It is not 'Sykes the murderer', of whom we think — it is no longer the 'criminal' in whose fate we are interested — it is for that one worn and haggard man with all the world against him. . . . In truth, we would fairly have had him escape. . . . We are with this hunted-down human being, brought home to our sympathies by the extremity of his distress; and we are *not* with the howling mass of demons outside. . . . It will then appear that Mr Dickens has defeated his own aim,

and made the criminal an object of sympathy, owing to the vindictive fury with which he is pursued to his destruction, because the author was so anxious to cut him off from *all* sympathy. The overstrained terror of the intended moral, has thus an immoral tendency.[26]

Certainly it is Sikes's mind, not his pursuers', that Dickens traces — and at considerable length: noticing even such details as what happens when he tries to burn the club with which he had killed Nancy. 'There was hair upon the end, which blazed and shrunk into a light cinder, and, caught by the air, whirled up the chimney. Even that frightened him, sturdy as he was. . . .' Taking flight from London, he finds himself pursued by rumours of the murder and, worse, by his memories of Nancy's eyes and corpse ('. . . but such flesh, and so much blood!')

> He went on doggedly; but as he left the town behind him, and plunged into the solitude and darkness of the road, he felt a dread and awe creeping upon him which shook him to the core. Every object before him, substance or shadow, still or moving, took the semblance of some fearful thing; but these fears were nothing compared to the sense that haunted him of that morning's ghastly figure following at his heels. He could trace its shadow in the gloom, supply the smallest item of the outline, and note how stiff and solemn it seemed to stalk along. He could hear its garments rustling in the leaves, and every breath of wind came laden with that last low cry. If he stopped it did the same. If he ran, it followed — not running too, that would have been a relief, but like a corpse endowed with the mere machinery of life, and borne on one slow melancholy wind that never rose or fell. . . .
>
> Let no man talk of murderers escaping justice, and hint that Providence must sleep. There were twenty score of violent deaths in one long minute of that agony of fear.

At length he suddenly decided to return to London: 'There's somebody to speak to there, at all events.'[27] But even his fellow-criminals are silent and horrified when he forces his presence upon them: and then he is cornered by his pursuers. 'Of all the terrific yells that ever fell on mortal ears, none could exceed the cry of the infuriated throng . . . one loud furious roar . . . a cry of triumphant execration. . . . The cries and shrieks of those who were pressed almost to suffocation, or trampled down and trodden under foot in the confusion, were dreadful. . . . The man had shrunk down, thoroughly quelled by the ferocity of the crowd, and the impossibility of escape. . . .'[28] It might be Dickens describing the terrible scenes at a public execution: and, a moment later, that is of course exactly what occurs, when Sikes slips and hangs himself.

That Dickens's effects and intentions were more complicated than R. H. Horne's analysis suggests, was made clear when, in 1869, Dickens gave the *Sikes and Nancy* Reading. None of the other Readings involved violence and horror; comedy had predominated in them, though often with a substratum of pathos. Back in 1863 he had told a friend: 'I have been trying, alone by myself, the Oliver Twist murder, but have got something so horrible out of it that I am afraid to try it in public.' But years before that, he had realised the dramatic force of his achievement. 'Nancy is no more,' he had written to Forster, while at work on *Oliver Twist*. 'I showed what I have done to Kate last night, who was in an unspeakable *"state"*: from which and my own impression I augur well.'[29] He had, at the time, wanted to dramatise the novel, and had offered to do so for two managers, Macready and Yates. Nothing came of these proposals, but soon he saw how the adaptations made by other hands excited audiences to such a frenzy of horror and of anger towards Sikes that for a long period the Lord Chamberlain banned all performances.[30]

It should, incidentally, be noted that contemporary reviewers and moralists, when deploring the social effects of the 'Newgate Novels' and other forms of popular fiction, were referring at least as much to the debased theatrical versions as to the novels themselves. In these dramatisations, over which the original author had no control whatever, *Oliver Twist* probably seemed much more like *Jack Sheppard* and *Paul Clifford* than it really was. As a somewhat hostile reviewer explained in 1845, 'In estimating the probable effects of these writings of Mr Dickens, we must remember that, in the shape of plays, they have been represented at most of the theatres in the country. In the process of transmutation the better and more sober parts necessarily disappear. . . .'[31] This, for instance, is how a theatrical manager described the audiences at the Victoria Theatre during E. F. Savile's performance as Bill Sikes: 'It was a heavy leaden mass when the play was dull and didactic, but with a fifty-ironclad store of reserved force, which, like a slumbering volcano, could be roused into violent action at any moment. . . . The "murder of Nancy" was the great scene. . . . No language ever dreamt of in Bedlam could equal the outburst. A thousand enraged voices, which sounded like ten thousand, . . .

filled the theatre, and . . . when the smiling ruffian came forward and bowed, . . . expressed a fierce determination to tear his sanguinary entrails from his sanguinary body.'[32]

The popularity and the dramatic tension of the *Oliver Twist* plays must have excited Dickens's envy and his wish to perform these juicy roles himself, though the disturbances among the audiences must at the same time have made him question the wisdom of doing so. Anyway, the idea haunted him, and when in 1868 he was preparing his Farewell Series he decided that a new attraction was necessary, and that this should be it, though he realised that on various grounds it was a bold and a questionable undertaking. To Forster he wrote:

> I have made a short reading of the murder in *Oliver Twist*. I cannot make up my mind, however, whether to do it or not. I have no doubt that I could perfectly petrify an audience by carrying out the notion I have of the way of rendering it. But whether the impression would not be so horrible as to keep them away another time, is what I cannot satisfy myself upon. What do you think? It is in three short parts: 1. Where Fagin sets Noah Claypole on to watch Nancy. 2. The scene on London Bridge. 3. Where Fagin rouses Claypole from his sleep to tell his perverted story to Sikes: and the Murder, and the Murderer's sense of being haunted. I have adapted and cut about the text with great care, and it is very powerful.

Forster, like most of his friends and family, advised against it — partly on grounds of taste, and partly because they feared its effect upon his health; 'a painful correspondence' passed between them on the subject.[33] Dickens decided on the unusual device of giving a Trial Reading in private, to his friends and advisers; meanwhile, he rehearsed at home with an abandon that startled his family. 'The finest thing I have ever heard,' said his eldest son, after coming upon one of these rehearsals by accident one day, 'but don't do it.'[34]

Originally the Reading had ended with Sikes leaving the place of the murder. Dickens's friends Wilkie Collins and Charles Kent urged him, however, after the Trial Reading, to extend the narrative to include the death of Sikes. 'My dear fellow,' Dickens replied to Kent, 'believe me, no audience on earth could be held for ten minutes after the girl's death. Give them time, and they would be revengeful for having had such a strain put upon them. Trust me to be right. I stand there, and I know.'[35] Even with the shorter version delivered at the Trial Reading, he had created a remarkable enough effect. He described it to a friend, with considerable relish:

> Now you must know that all this company were...unmistakably pale, and had horror-stricken faces. Next morning Harness (... did an edition of Shakespeare — old friend of the Kembles and Mrs Siddons), writing to me about it, and saying it was 'a most amazing and terrific thing', added, 'but I am bound to tell you that I had an almost irresistible impulse to *scream*, and that, if anyone had cried out, I am certain I should have followed.' He had no idea that, on the night, Priestley, the great ladies' doctor, had taken me aside and said: 'My dear Dickens, you may rely upon it that if only one woman cries out when you murder the girl, there will be a contagion of hysteria all over this place.' It is impossible to soften it without spoiling it, and you may suppose that I am rather anxious to discover how it goes on the Fifth of January!!! We are afraid to announce it elsewhere, without knowing, except that I have thought it pretty safe to put it up once in Dublin. I asked Mrs Keeley, the famous actress, who was at the experiment: 'What do *you* say? Do it or not?' 'Why, of course, do it,' she replied. 'Having got at such an affect as that, it must be done. But,' rolling her large black eyes very slowly, and speaking very distinctly, 'the public have been looking out for a sensation these last fifty years or so, and by Heaven they have got it!' With which words, and a long breath and a long stare, she became speechless. Again, you may suppose that I am a little anxious![36]

But by the time he wrote this, he was experimenting with the more violent ending that, a few weeks before, he had rejected as intolerable. 'I have got together in a very short space the conclusion of Oliver Twist that you suggested,' he wrote to Wilkie Collins, 'and am trying it daily with the object of rising from that blank state of horror into a fierce and passionate rush for the end. As yet I cannot make a certain effect of it; but when I shall have gone over it as many score of times as over the rest of that reading, perhaps I may strike one out.' Two days after the Trial Reading, and seven weeks before he gave the first public performance, he wrote to W. P. Frith inviting him to 'Come early in January, and see a certain friend of yours do the murder from Oliver Twist. It is horribly like, I am afraid! I have a vague sensation of being "wanted" as I walk about the streets'.[37]

This and other such remarks have been much discussed, as indicating a higher degree of identification than is usual between a performer and his role. Certainly Dickens generally referred to the Reading as if he were Sikes: 'I am ... murdering Nancy ...,' 'I do not commit the murder again ... until Tuesday ... ', 'my murderous instincts,' and so on.[38] The day after the first performance he apologised for his delay in replying to a letter, having been busy with his 'preparations for a certain murder. ... The crime being completely off my mind and the blood spilled, I am (like many of my fellow-criminals) in a highly edifying state today'. Other letters describe the effect of his performance upon his audiences. To an American friend he writes: 'I begin to doubt and fear on the subject of your having a horror of me after seeing the murder. I don't think a hand moved while I was doing it last night, or an eye looked away. And there was a fixed expression of horror of me, all over the theatre, which could not have been surpassed if I had been going to be hanged to that red velvet table. It is quite a new sensation to be execrated with that unanimity; and I hope it will remain so!' At one performance, he tells his daughter, 'we had a contagion of fainting. And yet the place was not hot. I should think we had from a dozen to twenty ladies borne out, stiff and rigid, at various times. It became quite ridiculous.' The audience's reactions had to be 'set apart from all our other efforts', he told his Manager, 'and judged by no other "Reading" standard.' The audiences 'were frozen while it went on, but came to life when it was over and rose to boiling-point'. His prophecy to Forster, that he could 'perfectly petrify an audience' by this Reading, proved accurate enough. He even stunned the professionals — both the ladies and gentlemen of the acting profession, to whom he gave a special run of day-time performances, and the great veteran Macready, who, to Dickens's obvious delight, gasped 'In my — er — best times — er — you remember them, my dear boy — er — gone, gone! — no — it comes to this — er — *two Macbeths*!'[39]

At this point, I may be forgiven, I hope, for intruding with some personal experience in this affair. I do not much resemble Dickens in character, let alone talent, but I share with him a devotion to amateur acting, with an immodest preference for lengthy roles which provide splendid, if hammy, histrionic opportunities. I have given public 'Readings from Dickens', including the *Sikes and Nancy* one; and I have also — unlike Dickens, but like Macready (only less effectively) — played Macbeth. Even in my paler and less practised version, which omits the first third of Dickens's reading-text, I certainly find *Sikes and Nancy* is 'two Macbeths' in terms of the physical and emotional strain on the performer.

Moreover, it is 'two Macbeths' in the satisfaction it gives — to my lower, more exhibitionist self. Its effects are crude, but powerful, and anyone who enjoys 'holding' an audience, and who has enough talent to perform this Reading at all competently, must find it exhilarating. The satisfaction must have been immensely stronger for Dickens than for me. He was incomparably more illustrious — his Readings were the Greatest One-man Show on Earth. He had the kudos of having written, as well as performing, the piece; and he had much less reserve than I feel about its literary quality. When dismissing Forster's objections to the *Sikes and Nancy* project, he explained that 'I wanted to leave behind me the recollection of something very passionate and dramatic, done with simple means, if the art would justify the theme'.[40] It gave him opportunities which none of the other Readings provided, for 'passionate' melodramatic acting such as was admired in the theatres of the period, and which he himself had enjoyed in some of the amateur theatricals such as *The Frozen Deep* and *The Lighthouse*. He was, by all accounts, very good at it, and no wonder he enjoyed it. As Mr Wilson puts it, 'Dickens had a strain of the ham in him, and, in the desperation of his later life, he gave in to the old ham and let him rip.'[41] On these purely histrionic grounds, then, we can to a large extent account for his devising this Reading, and delivering it with such zest and frequency. In a similar way, too, his phrases about 'I am murdering Nancy' should be understood, in the first place, as the normal mode of discourse and banter among actors. Biographers who have hastened to take these expressions seriously should spend five minutes at a rehearsal or in a dressing-room; and those over-anxious to identify Dickens with Sikes should remember, too, that his impersonation of Nancy was praised and remembered quite as much.

Though I think these considerations important, and too little regarded by recent commentators, I would however agree that his addiction to this Reading was excessive, and cannot be accounted for entirely in terms of a keen actor's enjoyment of creating a striking effect. It had been no accident that the paid Readings began in 1858, about a month before his separation from his wife. 'I must do *something*, or I shall wear my heart away,' he had told Forster at the time. 'I can see no better thing to do that is half so hopeful in itself, or half so well suited to my restless state.'[42] The Readings were an outlet and a compensation for the disappointments of his personal life, and for this reason his addiction to *Sikes and Nancy* is certainly significant. He had his favourites among the other items in the repertoire, but to none of them did he become so passionately attached. An addiction it certainly was. He gave it as many as ten times in a week, and when his manager, George Dolby, pointed out one day that three out of four of the items Dickens had put down in the draft programme for a forthcoming week were 'Murders', a scene occurred such as Dolby had never witnessed before.

> 'Have you finished?' he said, angrily.
> 'I have said all I feel on the matter,' was my reply.
> Bounding up from his chair, and throwing his knife and fork on his plate (which he smashed to atoms), he exclaimed —
> 'Dolby! your infernal caution will be your ruin one of these days!' ...
> I left the table, and proceeded to put my tour list in my writing-case. Turning round, I saw he was crying ... and, coming towards me, he embraced me affectionately, sobbing the while —
> 'Forgive me, Dolby! I really didn't mean it; and I know you are right. We will talk the matter over calmly in the morning.'
> In all my experiences with the Chief, this was the only time I ever heard him address angry words to any one. ...

Much later, he confessed to Dolby that it was 'worse than madness' to have given this Reading with such frequency.[43] He made the same confession to another close friend, Wills, adding that 'My ordinary pulse is 72, and it runs up under this effort to 112. Besides which it takes me ten or twelve minutes to get my wind back at all; I being in the meantime like the man who lost the fight...'.[44] He had to be supported to his dressing-room, and his doctor recorded pulse-rates of up to 124 while he lay prostrate on his sofa, unable to speak a rational or consecutive sentence. Moreover, says Dolby: 'These shocks to the nerves were not as easily repelled as for the moment they appeared to be, but invariably recurred later on in the evening, either in the form of great hilarity or a desire to be once more on the platform, or in a craving to do the work over again.'[45]

This 'invariable' consequence, like the episode when he shattered the plate, certainly shows a Dickens deeply, and morbidly, disturbed by the experience of giving this Reading. It is not surprising to find his specialist medical adviser, the distinguished physician Sir Thomas Watson, recording the 'first threatenings of brain mischief' in April 1869.[46] 'I shall tear myself to pieces,' he whispered to a friend, as he walked towards the platform for his final public performance of the 'Murder', and it is clear that this is what he had been doing, with dangerous regularity, for months past. Another friend records, on good authority, that a day or two before he died, he was found in the grounds of Gad's Hill acting the murder scene.[47] Wilkie Collins was not alone in thinking that it 'did more to kill Dickens than all his other work put together' — but, it should be added, this diagnosis, dramatically attractive and poetically just though it is, receives little support from Dr W. H. Bowen, a physician who has recently examined Dickens's medical history.[48]

When the idea of paid Readings was first mooted, Forster argued that these nightly exhibitions of himself were undignified — 'a substitution of lower for higher aims.' But they appealed to many elements in Dickens — his love of acting and of seeing and hearing from his audience, his nomadic tastes, his desire to lose himself in intense physical activity. 'It is much better to go on and fret, than to stop and fret,' he had told Forster, when 'the skeleton in his domestic closet' was becoming pretty big. 'As to repose — for some men there's no such thing in this life.'[49] He lacked internal resources against misery and disappointment, and in his later years he was writing much less and was therefore getting less satisfaction that way. It is a nice question, whether he wrote less because the Readings absorbed his energies and satisfied his creative urge, or whether he devoted more time to the Readings because he felt less impulse or ability to write.

He certainly proved a very talented performer; the Readings were immensely popular, the public showed its affection for him nightly, and he made considerably more money than he could earn by spending the same time at his desk. When Dolby asked him how he liked returning to fiction-writing, with *Edwin Drood*, he replied that he 'missed the pressure' of former days: by which Dolby understood him to mean that 'as his circumstances were comfortable now, the work was irksome'. It was probably not just through lack of practice that he wrote the first two instalments of *Edwin Drood* twelve pages short — far the largest miscalculation of his career.[50] *Sikes and Nancy* was 'a novelty', the first new item in his repertoire for some time, and strikingly different from the others. 'I must do *something*' — and this was his most spectacular 'doing'. More crudely than the other Readings, it was an emotional self-indulgence, and his wanting to perform it so much more often than any other item, despite its obviously damaging effect upon him, showed what a strong stimulant he now craved. But, of course, he had written *Oliver Twist* thirty years before and, as we shall see, his imagination had often followed this track in other novels since then. The 'Murder' Reading was the climax of a long process, not an unique episode in his imaginative life.

'It is two Macbeths:' the comparison may suggest two final comments on the Reading. First, that Dickens was not unusual among artists in being attracted to evil and murderous characters. Shakespeare wrote his play about Macbeth, not about Macduff or Duncan; and actors of any ambition and talent prefer playing the title-part to the more virtuous supporting characters. Second, that the comparison makes Dickens look very inferior. Dickens's comic characters can well stand beside Shakespeare's, dissimilar though their artistic methods are, but Macbeth belongs to a quite different order of achievement from Sikes. The 'Murder' chapters are indeed effective, whether read or performed, but like most of Dickens's horrifics they lack restraint, subtlety and depth. Critics who have recently discovered 'the macabre Dickens' have tended to over-praise this aspect of his work, because it had been too little noticed and regarded before, and because of its biographical interest to a generation of readers who prefer their artists to be, or seem, neurotic, complex, ambivalent. Certainly he surpasses his English contemporaries, of the 'Newgate School' and outside it, in this kind of sensation — as he did in the pathetic, also. But it would be foolish to pretend that these areas of his work constitute his claim to be a major novelist.

Nicholas Nickleby (1838–9), the novel which followed *Oliver Twist*, had no murders or violent crime. It contained various mysteries and rogueries, of course, such as the wicked machinations of Mulberry Hawk, Snawley, Squeers, Brooker, Gride and Peg Sliderskew. Dotheboys Hall was a variant on the prison and the workhouse of the two preceding novels, and Smike's death, though less dramatic than Nancy's, was firmly blamed on two of the villains, who were duly punished in accordance with poetic justice: Ralph Nickleby died by suicide, and Squeers got seven years' Transportation. The next two novels, *The Old Curiosity Shop* (1840–1) and *Barnaby Rudge* (1841), continued to use the hoary old mysteries of long-lost relatives and love-children. The former did without murder, but had some very lively rogues in Daniel Quilp and his creatures, Sampson and Sally Brass.

Quilp is a major creation. An exultant bourgeois Richard III, he continues and expands Fagin's and Squeers's robust delight in villainy. As he never commits a really dreadful crime, Dickens can indulge him in his enjoyable sadistic habits — forcing Sampson to smoke and to drink fierce doses of liquor, taunting his chained-up dog by performing 'a kind of demon-dance round the kennel', hammering a figure-head which he uses as a totem for Kit Nubbles, looking at his wife 'like a dismounted nightmare', even making sexual advances on Little Nell and leering at the chambermaid at an inn, and trying to kiss her, when she enquires whether he will want a bed.[51] A superb pantomime villain, he 'ate hard eggs, shell and all, devoured gigantic prawns with the heads and tails on, . . . drank boiling tea without winking, bit his fork and spoon till they bent . . .', at the breakfast table; in his own den, he drank half a pint of boiling rum straight out of the hot saucepan. When tired of business, 'he varied its monotonous routine with a little screeching, or howling, or some other innocent relaxation of that nature.' A hideous dwarf, he terrifies and dominates all who come into contact with him. 'I'll bite you,' he warns his wife. 'I hate your virtuous people!' he says on another occasion, throwing off a bumper of brandy, 'Ah! I hate 'em every one!'[52] He is a figure to compel the imagination — and Dickens adds the nice point that he is attractive despite, or through, his repulsiveness. Tom Scott adores him, and even the wretched Mrs Quilp has this to tell the ladies who have just been shocked by his tea-table behaviour:

'It's all very fine to talk,' said Mrs Quilp, with much simplicity, 'but I know that if I was to die to-morrow, Quilp could marry anybody he pleased — now that he could, I know!'

There was a scream of indignation at this idea. Marry whom he pleased! They would like to see him dare to think of marrying any of them; they would like to see the faintest approach to such a thing. One lady (a widow) was quite certain she should stab him if he hinted at it.

'Very well,' said Mrs Quilp, nodding her head, 'as I said just now, it's very easy to talk, but I say again that I know — that I'm sure — Quilp has such a way with him when he likes, that the best-looking woman here couldn't refuse him if I was dead, and she was free, and he chose to make love to her. Come!'

Everybody bridled up at this remark, as much as to say, 'I know you mean me. Let him try — that's all.' And yet for some hidden reason they were all angry with the widow, and each lady whispered in her neighbour's ear that it was very plain the said widow thought herself the person referred to, and what a puss she was![53]

It is in *Barnaby Rudge* that Dickens returns to murder, with many reminiscences from *Oliver Twist* and anticipations of the murder that was to occur in the next novel, *Martin Chuzzlewit* (1843–4). Years before the story of *Barnaby Rudge* opens, Reuben Haredale was murdered on a suitably ominous night, 'blowing a hurricane, raining heavily, and very dark.' As Dickens comments:

> There are times when, the elements being in unusual commotion, those who are bent on daring enterprises, or agitated by great thoughts, whether of good or evil, feel a mysterious sympathy with the tumult of nature, and are roused into corresponding violence. In the midst of thunder, lightning, and storm, many tremendous deeds have been committed; men, self-possessed before, have given a sudden loose to passions they could no longer control. . . .
> Whether the traveller was possessed by thoughts which the fury of the night had heated and stimulated into a quicker current, or was merely impelled by some strong motive to reach his journey's end, on he swept, more like a hunted phantom than a man, nor checked his pace. . . .[54]

It requires little percipience to guess that this unnamed stranger was the guilty man, that he is the supposedly-dead steward Rudge, and that therefore the story of the murder just told by Solomon Daisy must be incorrect. After a few instalments had appeared, Edgar Allan Poe published a forecast of the solution of the mystery, accurate enough to have evoked (so it is said) Dickens's exclamation that 'The man must be a devil!'[55] But Poe's forecast, though clever, was not uncanny: Dickens's puzzle was poor, as usual and as he never seems to have realised. Poe's notes on his failure in '*pure* narration', his excessive use of coincidence, and his inability to devise a mystery that was both 'fair' and difficult, can be applied to many later novels, for Dickens never mastered the techniques of Poe or Collins, and he had little natural talent in this direction.[56] 'What dark history is this?' ponders Gabriel Varden, having noticed the sinister stranger haunting Mrs Rudge's cottage.[57] Dickens does not tantalise the reader too long; a quarter of the way through the story, the mysterious wanderer's identity is disclosed, and later we learn exactly how the crime was committed. Later still, Geoffrey Haredale arrests Rudge and brings him to justice, after a long investigation and pursuit: he is Dickens's first amateur detective. Such interest as Rudge lends to the novel does not, however, lie in this mystery-and-detection plot, but in the presentation of a guilty mind.

Rudge's crime occurred long ago, and in the novel itself he is given little to do except skulk around in the darkness. He lacks Fagin's and Sikes's opportunities for action, but he is in effect a *reprise* of them. Like Sikes, he is cut off from society by his deed, even though his guilt is unknown. Members of the underworld 'as uncouth and fierce' as himself shrink from him 'with an involuntary dread'. No-one knows who he is, but his 'constant restlessness' gives rise to strange rumours. His appearance and demeanour certainly seem to invite comment — 'Besmeared with mire; his saturated clothes clinging with a damp embrace about his limbs; his beard unshaven, his face unwashed, his meagre cheeks worn into deep hollows, — a more miserable wretch could hardly be.'[58] This is obviously a good deal too close to Sikes, for Rudge is not on the run. Twenty years have passed since the murder, and he was never suspected. Forster called this 'as powerful a picture as any in his writings of the inevitable and unfathomable consequences of sin', but Dickens is in fact guilty of gross over-writing. Rudge is entirely unconvincing. Dickens's moral intentions had been insistent enough in *Oliver Twist* (his impersonation of Sikes's horror after killing Nancy, said Charles Kent, 'had about it something of the articulation of an avenging voice not against Sikes only, but against all who ever outraged, or ever dreamt of outraging, the sanctity of human life'), but in *Barnaby Rudge* these excellent intentions operate too mechanically. As Poe objected, 'That Rudge should so long and so deeply feel the sting of conscience is inconsistent with his brutality.'[59] Macbeth's is a more plausible murderer's progress, and no less salutary:

> Direness, familiar to my slaughterous thoughts,
> Cannot once start me.

Rudge is always 'starting'. He cannot even sleep — 'Heaven's gift to all its creatures.' He yearns to be punished: he returns to the scene of the crime, he gazes upon the walls of a prison 'as though even they became a refuge in his jaded eyes'. When he does lie down, 'His sleep was checkered with starts and moans, and sometimes with a muttered word or two.'[60] He has had a very unpleasant twenty years, all told. Dickens's imagination has manifestly been overset by his didactic purpose, and by memories of the theatre — of *Macbeth* indeed (the storm and the sleeplessness, for example), but more often of much inferior drama. Sikes went well on the stage, both in Dickens's own performance and in dramatic adaptations; Dickens, as everyone notes, is eminently a dramatic novelist, and both the best and the worst elements in his fiction owe much to the theatre, for which he had such a passion.[61]

Rudge belongs to the melodramatic 'Wolves tear your throats!' side of Dickens. Two examples of his rhetoric will suffice to show this:

> 'Hear me,' he replied, menacing her with his hand. 'I, that in the form of a man live the life of a hunted beast; that in the body am a spirit, a ghost upon the earth, a thing from which all creatures shrink, save those cursed beings of another world, who will not leave me — I am, in my desperation of this night, past all fear but that of the hell in which I exist from day to day. . . .'
>
> .   .   .   .
>
> 'I say begone—I say it for the last time. . . . The gallows has me in its grasp and it is a black phantom that may urge me on to something more. Begone! I curse the hour that I was born, the man I slew, and all the living world!'
>
> In a paroxysm of wrath, and terror, and the fear of death, he broke from her, and rushed into the darkness of his cell, where he cast himself jangling down upon the stone floor, and smote it with his ironed hands.[62]

Sikes and Fagin had almost, though not entirely, escaped this note: in *Oliver Twist* it had been Monks who more clearly echoed the villains of stage melodrama. Rudge is most successful, indeed, when his circumstances and reactions are closest to Sikes and Fagin — when the Bell, like Nancy's eyes, accuses him (though the passage again suggests the theatre — Irving's famous performance, years later, in *The Bells*), or when he is arrested ('Perhaps a man never sees so much at a glance as when he is in a situation of extremity') and sits in the condemned cell studying 'the cracks in the pavement, . . . the chinks in the wall'.[63] But Dickens never achieves anything with Rudge that he had not already done better in *Oliver Twist*. The interesting thing is, that he wanted to try.

It is in *Martin Chuzzlewit* that he makes a further advance. Jonas Chuzzlewit's attempts to murder his devilish tormentor Montague Tigg during their journey to Wiltshire are, to be sure, typical melodrama, as is Jonas's appearance when Montague whispers to him that he knows how Jonas killed his father.

> From red to white; from white to red again; from red to yellow; then to a cold, dull, awful, sweat-bedabbled blue. In that short

whisper all these changes fell upon the face of Jonas Chuzzlewit; and when at last he laid his hand upon the whisperer's mouth, appalled, lest any syllable of what he said should reach the ears of the third person present, it was as bloodless and as heavy as the hand of Death.

He drew his chair away, and sat a spectacle of terror, misery, and rage. He was afraid to speak, or look, or move, or sit still. Abject, crouching, and miserable, he was a greater degradation to the form he bore, than if he had been a loathsome wound from head to heel.[64]

Again the weather is heavily portentous. 'It will be a stormy night!' exclaims Montague's doctor, as the two men set out on their momentous journey — and the remark had extra emphasis for the original readers of the story, for it occurred at the end of a chapter and of an instalment. (The next two instalments ended with Montague's terrified vow, 'I shall travel home alone,' and with Jonas's arrival home after the murder, to listen for the fatal knocking at the door — 'Hush!')[65]

'It was one of those hot, silent nights, when people sit at windows listening for the thunder which they know will shortly break. . . . It was very dark; but in the murky sky there were masses of cloud which shone with a lurid light.' It is against this splendidly Grand Guignol background that the first series of attempts at murder take place. Jonas is, indeed, an artless murderer. 'Now, could you cut a man's throat with such a thing as this?' he enquires of his prospective victim's doctor, thoughtfully examining a surgical instrument before setting out on the journey: and he learns just where the jugular vein can best be severed. Three times on the way to Wiltshire he tries to do the deed.

> The lightning being very crooked and very dazzling, may have presented or assisted a curious optical illusion, which suddenly rose before the startled eyes of Montague in the carriage, and as rapidly disappeared. He thought he saw Jonas with his hand lifted, and the bottle clenched in it like a hammer, making as if he would aim a blow at his head. At the same time he observed (or so believed) an expression in his face — a combination of the unnatural excitement he had shown all day, with a wild hatred and fear — which might have rendered a wolf a less terrible companion.

He is equally unlucky and imprudent when signing Mr Pecksniff's proposal — 'he had scarcely marked the paper when he started back, in a panic. "Why, what the devil's this?" he said. "It's bloody!" He had dipped the pen, as another moment showed, into red ink.'⁶⁶ Montague certainly gets fair warning that it would be safer to 'travel home alone', and Jonas has scattered evidence against himself prodigally before at last he manages to waylay his enemy in a copse, where he leaves his body lying.

So far, Jonas's actions and reactions are mere conventional rubbish. The more original and effective part of Dickens's presentation begins with his dream, as he sleeps on the way to the scene of the murder. Dickens was always interested in dreams, about which he read and theorised with enthusiasm (and some perception). Jonas dreams of wandering through a strange city, where 'the names of the streets were written on the walls in characters quite new to him', with a companion who was 'never the same man two minutes together'. The crowds are hurrying off to the Last Judgment, when a Montague-like figure denounces Jonas 'as having appointed that direful day to happen'.⁶⁷ It is a striking flight of imagination, which foreshadows the more ambitious use of dream-allegory in *Edwin Drood*. Jonas kills Montague, and begins to make his way back to London, where his family believe him to be shut up and asleep in a room in his house, from which he has crept out in disguise. At this point Dickens shows real interest and inwardness.

And he was not sorry for what he had done. He was frightened when he thought of it — when did he not think of it! — but he was not sorry. He had had a terror and dread of the wood when he was in it; but being out of it, and having committed the crime, his fears were now diverted, strangely, to the dark room he had left shut up at home. . . . His hideous secret was shut up in the room, and all its terrors were there; to his thinking it was not in the wood at all. . . .

Dread and fear were upon him, to an extent he had never counted on, and could not manage in the least degree. He was so horribly afraid of that infernal room at home. This made him, in a gloomy, murderous, mad way, not only fearful *for* himself but *of* himself; for being, as it were, a part of the room: a something supposed to be there, yet missing from it: he invested himself with its mysterious terrors; and when he pictured in his mind the ugly chamber, false and quiet, false and quiet, through the dark hours of two nights; and the tumbled bed, and he not in it, though believed to be; he became in a manner his own ghost and phantom, and was at once the haunting spirit and the haunted man. . . .

[He arrived home.] He stole on to the door, on tiptoe, as if he dreaded to disturb his own imaginary rest.

He listened. Not a sound. As he turned the key with a trembling hand, and pushed the door softly open with his knee, a monstrous fear beset his mind.

What if the murdered man were there before him!

He cast a fearful glance all round. But there was nothing there. . . .

The morning advanced. There were footsteps in the house. . . . In his secret dread of meeting the household for the first time, after what he had done, he lingered at the door on slight pretexts, that they might see him without looking in his face; and left it ajar while he dressed; and called out to have the windows opened, and the pavement watered, that they might become accustomed to his voice. Even when he had put off the time, by one means or other, so that he had seen or spoken to them all, he could not muster courage for a long while to go in among them, but stood at his own door listening to the murmur of their distant conversation.[68]

This is a much more elaborate rendering of fear and guilt than Sikes or Rudge had occasioned. Jonas is not a professional thug like Sikes, nor a petty murderer for gain like Rudge, but a vicious and terrified little man driven to rid himself of his blackmailer. By convention, blackmailers are fair game for murderers, so Dickens can afford to enter more sympathetically into Jonas's consciousness — which is, besides, more complicated, intelligent and sensitive than his predecessors'. Moreover, while not eminently respectable, Jonas is financially prosperous and has some social standing: this increases the gap between his criminal and his usual self. This development continues: the next important murderers in the novels are the schoolmaster Bradley Headstone — who, 'in his decent black coat and waistcoat, and decent white shirt, and decent formal black tie, and decent pantaloons of pepper and salt, with his decent silver watch in his pocket and its decent hair-guard round his neck, looked a thoroughly decent young man' — and, following him, the cathedral organist John Jasper.[69]

Dr Lauriat Lane, Junior, has pointed out in an excellent essay on 'Dickens and the Double' that these three most complex of his villain-murderers are all presented as double-figures. Jonas leaves his normal and proper self 'asleep' in the locked room, and another self emerges. 'As the gloom of the evening, deepening into night, came on, another dark shade emerging from within him seemed to overspread his face, and slowly change it.' He disguises himself, and after the murder sinks his clothes in a river, from which they are fished up by Nadgett (as, in *Our Mutual Friend*, the clothes in which Bradley Headstone had disguised himself as Rogue Riderhood are retrieved, by Riderhood himself, from the pool where they had been sunk). But the dualism is not simply one of physical disguise. Jonas, it will be remembered, was 'not only fearful *for* himself, but *of* himself . . . he became in a manner his own ghost and phantom, and was at once the haunting spirit and the haunted man'. He secretly returned to the locked room 'on tiptoe, as if he dreaded to disturb his own imaginary rest'. It is mainly by this use of the double that, as Dr Lane says, 'psychological realism is introduced into an otherwise melodramatic presentation of human evil,' and in this respect as in others Jonas anticipates Dickens's later explorations of murder.[70]

Hortense in *Bleak House* (1852–3) is Dickens's next murderer. As I mentioned, she is almost certainly based on Maria Manning (there is no point in her being a Continental, except that Mrs Manning had so recently confirmed the English belief that Gallic women are passionate and violent) — though she also reminds Esther Summerson of 'some women from the streets of Paris in the reign of terror'.[71] Perhaps she suffers in being thus based upon a 'real' murderer, unlike the other murderers in the novels: certainly she never comes alive in her role as murderess. Soon after one finishes the story, one has forgotten why she killed Tulkinghorn — if, indeed, one ever quite understood. But her mental processes have, of course, been deliberately concealed from us. Her main function in the novel is to commit the murder for which other characters, closer to our sympathies, seem more likely suspects, so we must not discover that she, and not George or Lady Dedlock, has done the deed, until Inspector Bucket makes his startling revelations. He gathers together a suitable audience before he gives his dazzling display of detective expertise, recounting the extremely improbable cloak-and-dagger methods by which he and his wife solved the mystery.

Nor need the next murderer detain us long — Rigaud in *Little Dorrit* (1855–7). He has, indeed, killed a man, married his rich widow, and then killed her — '. . . but that was in another country, And besides, the wench is dead' before the story starts. During the book he merely kills a dog, and otherwise confines himself to the crime of blackmail. He suffers no remorse, guilt, or fear. He is constantly compared to, in fact he more or less is, the Devil. In his 'utter disregard of other people', his 'brute selfishness', his determination to 'subdue the society' which has, in his opinion, 'grievously wronged' him, he is entirely evil. Like the Devil, he is cosmopolitan ('I own no particular country'); and, one remembers, 'The Prince of Darkness is a gentleman,' so it is Rigaud's continual boast that 'A gentleman I am, a gentleman I'll live, and a gentleman I'll die!'[72] By gentility, he understands doing nothing, living comfortably, and being waited upon even in prison. As a gentleman-villain, he falls into the pattern of Dickens's development, but otherwise he stands apart, as a much simpler, more symbolic, creation than the other murderers.

The novels which followed *Little Dorrit* — *A Tale of Two Cities* (1859) and *Great Expectations* (1860–1) — contain murder and violence and violent death, but these are minor affairs, except when they are political rather than criminal acts. The Marquis de St Evrémonde is justly stabbed to death for his cruelty and oppression; Madame Defarge is shot dead by Miss Pross, in righteous self-defence. Orlick makes a murderous attack on Mrs Joe, out of resentment — and Humphry House's comment increases one's regret that Dickens did not devote more time to working out the implications of this character and episode:

> He is less a criminal than a turbulent, discontented underdog. . . . Orlick represents the element in English society with which Dickens never came to terms. He could assimilate the pitiable underdog; but the rash, independent, strong, turbulent, losing underdog, who became criminal more by accident than by choice, always disturbed him. Orlick is far more interesting than Compeyson or Magwitch, because his author did not put him flat and fair in the criminal department. There was an underlying fear that 'the people' in the mass might turn out to be Orlicks.[73]

Magwitch ends up under sentence of death, of course, not for killing Compeyson (though they were ready enough to kill each other, and Compeyson certainly died through trying to arrest him), but for returning from Transportation. He dies while awaiting the Recorder's Report and the result of Pip's appeals for mercy. As it happens, he need not have feared hanging, though Dickens conceals or ignores the fact that this offence had notoriously ceased to be *de facto* capital by the time when the action of the novel takes place.[74]

There had been other elements in *Little Dorrit*, however, much more akin to Dickens's studies in murder: Miss Wade's 'Diary of a Self-Tormentor', and Mrs Clennam's paralysis. The latter lives in her room, which is both cell and grave: she sits on 'her black bier-like sofa, propped up by her black angular bolster that was like a headsman's block', dressed in perpetual widow's black 'as if attired for execution'. Her son Arthur suddenly suspects that Mr Dorrit is in his 'living grave' (the Marshalsea Prison) because of some act of hers, and thus he guesses the nature of her mysterious illness—

> A swift thought shot into his mind. In that long imprisonment here, and in her own long confinement to her room, did his mother find a balance to be struck? I admit that I was accessory to that man's captivity. I have suffered for it in kind. He has decayed in his prison; I in mine. I have paid the penalty.
>
> When all the other thoughts had faded out, this one held possession of him. When he fell asleep, she came before him in her wheeled chair, warding him off with this justification. When he awoke, and sprang up causelessly frightened, the words were in his ears, as if her voice had slowly spoken them at his pillow, to break his rest: 'He withers away in his prison; I wither away in mine; inexorable justice is done; what do I owe on this score!'[75]

It is one of many fine psychological intuitions in *Little Dorrit* (Professor Trilling has discussed them well in *The Opposing Self*) — and a reminder that while, as Edmund Wilson says, Dickens's 'probing of the psychology of the murderer . . . becomes ever more convincing and intimate',[76] it is not only murderers and other criminals who exhibit this deeper understanding. Mr Dorrit is a great improvement on Mr Gradgrind, as a portrayal of an unsatisfactory father, and Mr Gradgrind had been an improvement on Mr Dombey. Similarly, Pip and Estella are a more interesting hero and heroine than David Copperfield and his Dora and Agnes had been: and there are many other examples of Dickens's more penetrating, and more internal, presentation of character in his later career. This is what one would expect, of course, but commentators intent on the darker sides of his personality have not always emphasised that his advance was general, and not confined to criminal psychology.

There had been a comparable development, for instance, in his presentation of schoolteachers. All his interesting specimens are 'bad', but it is characteristic that his first attempt — an impressive one — is Squeers, a blatant rogue and impostor, who is quite aware of his own rapacity, whereas the later 'bad' teachers are more complicated cases of educational wickedness. Mr Creakle in *David Copperfield*, admittedly, is a reversion to the old type; but Dr Blimber in *Dombey and Son*, Mr M'Choakumchild in *Hard Times*, and Mr Headstone in *Our Mutual Friend* are all competent, well-meaning, respectable and respected, though nevertheless disastrous mentors of youth. In Bradley Headstone, these two strains of his development, in writing about education and crime, come together.[77]

The vehemence of Headstone's passion for Lizzie Hexam, like Jasper's for Rosa Bud and Pip's hopeless adoration of Estella, doubtless owes something, as has often been suggested lately, to Dickens's own experiences with Ellen Ternan, whom he first met in 1857. 'I have never known a moment's peace or content, since the last night of The Frozen Deep,' he wrote to Wilkie Collins, referring to the play in which he and Ellen had performed. 'I do suppose that there never was a man so seized and rended by one spirit.'[78] Two months later, he separated from his wife. The lovers in his later novels are much more convincing than their predecessors, and it is significant that, for the first time in his fiction, the murders in *Our Mutual Friend* and *Edwin Drood* have a sexual motive. Headstone and Jasper are both trying to eliminate a favoured rival; Pip is too close to Dickens to commit a murder, so Chance rewards him without his stir — Bentley Drummle has an accident with his horse, so Estella becomes, conveniently, a widow. It is significant, too, that Dickens now chooses, after over twenty years, to return to murder as a central theme: it is prominent, indeed, only in the first eight years of his career, up to *Martin Chuzzlewit*, and in its last six years, when he produces *Our Mutual Friend*, the *Sikes and Nancy* Reading, and *Edwin Drood*. (The short-stories about murder, 'Hunted Down' and 'No Thoroughfare', belong to 1859 and 1867.) Murder, therefore, is not so frequent a theme as many recent accounts of Dickens have implied. But despite the lapse of time, and although the special direction of Headstone's and Jasper's aggression may have been influenced by Dickens's new experience of the agonies of love, they do not represent a wholly new start, but rather a resumption of the development from Sikes through Rudge to Jonas Chuzzlewit, which had been in suspense for two decades.

Headstone does not, in fact, kill Eugene Wrayburn, though he intends to do so and thinks he has been successful. He has a fit (literally) when he discovers that Lizzie has rescued Eugene, has restored him to health, and become his bride. Dickens had used this 'have your cake and eat it' plot-device before, and he was to use it again: Jonas has not in fact killed his father — Slinkton, in

'Hunted Down', finds that his 'dying' victim Beckwith has cunningly thrown away the drinks that were 'killing' him[79] — Obenreizer is flabbergasted to see Vendale, whom he had pushed over a precipice, walk in and accuse him. Some people argue that John Jasper, too, was due for a similar surprise, but I shall reject this theory. The situation is repeated elsewhere in *Our Mutual Friend* itself. Early in the story, the Harmon Murder is the mystery on everyone's lips; later we discover the complicated and improbable solution. (John Harmon has a double, George Radfoot, who murders him for gain — but Harmon, in fact, escapes, battered but alive, and Radfoot himself is soon afterwards murdered as 'Harmon'. Later Radfoot's murderers stagger and start when confronted with the 'dead' man.)[80] This is a silly and trivial mystery, but fortunately Dickens could feel that he had thus done his duty in providing the obligatory 'mystery' element for this novel. He can then treat Bradley Headstone's murderous attempt more seriously and internally, as a psychological study and not a whodunit. I shall argue that we have a similar situation in *Edwin Drood* — that Jasper has killed Edwin, and we are never intended to doubt it, and that the 'mysteries' elsewhere in the novel are of less interest than the psychology of the known murderer.

Bradley Headstone has been described as 'a notable voyage of exploration into one of the most obscure domains of psychiatry and criminology . . . a schizophrene made desperate by sexual repressions' (repressed homosexuality being 'strongly suggested'), and subject to fits (that is, 'epileptic-schizophrenic eruptions'). Maybe this is a correct diagnosis, though I would feel more confidence in it had not this commentator, just before, described Monks in *Oliver Twist* as 'a clear clinical portrait of a paranoid epileptic . . . one of the best things that Dickens has done'.[81] For Monks is emphatically not one of Dickens's successes, but a totally stagey creation: and his fits — like those of Rudge, as well as Headstone and Jasper — have little or no clinical significance. They are, rather, the occasion for striking dramatic tableaux, and vague symbols of 'a mind diseased'. Anyway, the plot requires Monks, like Hortense the murderess and like the sinister strangers hovering in the background of many of the novels, to remain largely mysterious. Dickens cannot give any close internal account of him, or of them: and they rarely emerge from the shadows for long enough even to be seen externally with any exactness.

From early in *Our Mutual Friend*, however, Bradley Headstone is seen from within: and it is characteristic that Dickens, while giving him a respectable station in society, makes him — like Jasper — a very abnormal psychological case. The fits and the nosebleeding are two signs of this: so are his violent gestures as he talks to Eugene ('breaking off to wipe the starting perspiration from his face as he shook from head to foot', with an 'errant motion of his hands as if he could have torn himself'). In his scene in the churchyard, when Lizzie rejects him and he realises that she prefers Eugene, he threatens his rival ('Then I hope that I may never kill him!' — for Dickens's murderers never learn to keep their mouths shut) and then, in a memorable moment, he 'brings his clenched hand down upon the stone with a force that laid the knuckles raw and bleeding'.[82] This is characteristic, I said — both of his attraction to extreme emotional types and situations, and of his attitude to murderers. His remark in *Edwin Drood* will be remembered, that the criminal intellect is 'a horrible wonder apart', which cannot be reconciled with 'the average intellect of average men'. It is equally characteristic that, in the novels as in his non-fictional comments on murderers, he in no way allows this recognition of their psychological abnormality to qualify his horror and reprehension of the doer as well as the deed. Headstone may be half-crazy, or half-animal, but he is nevertheless presented as very wicked, and as morally and legally responsible for his actions. Only momentarily does he appear pitiful — as in the scene when Charlie Hexam, his one remaining object of affection, finally repudiates him and leaves him 'in unutterable misery, and unrelieved by a single tear'.[83]

The nature of his abnormality — whether schizophrenic, repressed homo- or hetero-sexuality — is never, I think, explained, understood or adumbrated by Dickens; but certain phases of his mounting rage against Eugene, and of his growing determination to kill him, are depicted with great force and insight. Sexual jealousy is exacerbated by class-feeling, for Headstone is a precarious new arrival in the middle class, while Eugene is, effortlessly and insolently, a gentleman — an advantage which he takes no pains to conceal from his defeated rival. Eugene is presented with a surprising degree of condonation (partly, no doubt, to make Headstone's attack on him seem sufficiently wicked), for he goads the wretched schoolmaster, leading him on wild-goose chases, all over London. As Eugene says 'with the utmost coolness' and in his hearing, Headstone is 'undergoing grinding torments'.

It was not too strong a phrase for the occasion. Looking like the hunted, and not the hunter, baffled, worn, with the exhaustion of deferred hope and consuming hate and anger in his face, white-lipped, wild-eyed, draggle-haired, seamed with jealousy and anger, and torturing himself with the conviction that he showed it all and they exulted in it, he went by them in the dark, like a haggard head suspended in the air: so completely did the force of his expression cancel his figure. . . .

The state of the man was murderous, and he knew it. More; he irritated it, with a kind of perverse pleasure akin to that which a sick man sometimes has in irritating a wound upon his body. Tied up all day with his disciplined show upon him, subdued to the performance of his routine of educational tricks, encircled by a gabbling crowd, he broke loose at night like an ill-tamed wild animal. Under his daily restraint, it was his compensation, not his trouble, to give a glance towards his state at night, and to the freedom of its being indulged. If great criminals told the truth — which, being great criminals, they do not — they would very rarely tell of their struggles against the crime. Their struggles are towards it. They buffet with opposing waves, to gain the bloody shore, not to recede from it. This man perfectly comprehended that he hated his rival with his strongest and worst forces, and that if he tracked him to Lizzie Hexam, his so doing would never serve himself with her, or serve her. All his pains were taken, to the end that he might incense himself with the sight of the detested figure in her company and favour, in her place of concealment. And he knew as well what act of his would follow if he did, as he knew that his mother had borne him. Granted, that he may not have held it necessary to make express mention to himself of the one familiar truth any more than of the other.

He knew equally well that he fed his wrath and hatred, and that he accumulated provocation and self-justification, by being made the nightly sport of the reckless and insolent Eugene. Knowing all this, and still always going on with infinite endurance, pains, and per-serverance, could his dark soul doubt whither he went?[84]

There are reminiscences here of Miss Wade, the 'self-tormentor' in *Little Dorrit*: echoes, too, more persistently, of Jonas Chuzzlewit. But Headstone is a more interesting creation than Jonas. His passion for Lizzie and his hatred of Eugene are more deeply felt, and are more prominent in the novel: Jonas's move against Montague is one of several plots occupying the last third of the novel, but Headstone's unhappy passion runs through three-quarters of *Our Mutual Friend*. Moreover, the Jekyll-and-Hyde theme is much more fully developed — the continual contrast between Headstone's painfully 'decent' appearance and routine in his school every day, and the 'ill-tamed wild animal' that is let loose every night. This conflict had been noted on his first appearance in the book: 'Suppression of so much to make room for so much, had given him a constrained manner. . . . Yet there was enough of what was animal, and of what was fiery (though smouldering) still visible in him. . . .'[85] His torture is more prolonged, and his internal tensions are more extreme, than Jonas's; but Jonas certainly provides the pattern of murder which Headstone follows — donning a disguise, tracking down his victim in the countryside, beating him in some cowardly fashion, and then sinking the disguise in water, whence it is retrieved by his accuser. The description of his state of mind after the murder also recalls *Martin Chuzzlewit*, though it includes some new and subtler effects.

> The miserable man . . . went on towards London. Bradley was suspicious of every sound he heard, and of every face he saw, but was under a spell which very commonly falls upon the shedder of blood, and had no suspicion of the real danger that lurked in his life, and would have it yet. . . . And this is another spell against which the shedder of blood for ever strives in vain. There are fifty doors by which discovery may enter. With infinite pains and cunning, he double locks and bars forty-nine of them, and cannot see the fiftieth standing wide open.
>
> Now, too, was he cursed with a state of mind more wearing and more wearisome than remorse. He had no remorse; but the evil-doer who can hold that avenger at bay, cannot escape the slower torture of incessantly doing the evil deed again and doing it more efficiently. In the defensive declarations and pretended confessions of murderers, the pursuing shadow of this torture may be traced through every lie they tell. If I had done it as alleged, is it conceivable that I would have made this and this mistake? If I had done it as alleged, should I have left that unguarded place which that false and wicked witness against me so infamously deposed to? . . .
>
> Bradley toiled on, chained heavily to the idea of his hatred and his vengeance, and thinking how he might have satiated both in many better ways than the way he had taken. The instrument might have been better, the spot and the hour might have been better chosen. . . . Suppose this way, that way, the other way. Suppose anything but getting unchained from the one idea, for that was inexorably impossible.
>
> The school re-opened next day. The scholars saw little or no change in their master's face, for it always wore its slowly labouring expression. But, as he heard his classes, he was always doing the deed and

doing it better. As he paused with his piece of chalk at the blackboard before writing on it, he was thinking of the spot, and whether the water was not deeper and the fall straighter, a little higher up, or a little lower down. He had half a mind to draw a line or two upon the board, and show himself what he meant.[86]

As the title of this chapter has it, 'Better to be Abel than Cain.'

Like all Dickens's murderers except Rigaud, Headstone presents a salutary example of the miseries of fear and guilt. How he was 'racked and riven in his mind . . . none but he could have told. Not even he could have told, for such misery can only be felt'.[87] Fear of detection is followed by the galling discovery that he has failed to kill Eugene, that his attack has in fact brought Lizzie and Eugene together, as nothing else could have done, and that he owes his immunity to prosecution to his successful rival's forbearance. He has reckoned without Rogue Riderhood, however. (It is one of the weaknesses of the plot that Riderhood would have needed to be cretinous *not* to suspect and pursue Headstone, who, for all his higher education, is as incompetent as Jonas when it comes to devising an efficient murder.) Riderhood blackmails him, as Montague had blackmailed Jonas over the 'murder' he had committed, and Headstone, again like Jonas, is driven to end the agony by killing his tormentor. But he realises that he, too, will die. It is a nice point, as Dr Lauriat Lane remarks, that Headstone is thus accused by his 'double', that before leaving on his fatal last journey to the Weir he divests himself of the symbols of his respectability, 'his decent silver watch and its decent guard,' and that the twin-personalities — the respectable schoolmaster and the former gaolbird who 'stands for his other, lower self' — die together in each other's arms, since (as Dr Lane comments) 'the good and evil in men are inseparably mingled, and both must perish for the crimes of the one'. Headstone grapples with Rogue Riderhood as with 'an iron ring', and drags him towards the edge of the Lock.

'Let go!' said Riderhood. 'Stop! What are you trying at? You can't drown Me. Ain't I told you that the man as has come through drowning can never be drowned? I can't be drowned.'

'I can be!' returned Bradley, in a desperate, clenched voice. 'I am resolved to be. I'll hold you living, and I'll hold you dead. Come down!'

Riderhood went over into the smooth pit, backward, and Bradley Headstone upon him. When the two were found, lying under the ooze and scum behind one of the rotting gates, Riderhood's hold had relaxed, probably in falling, and his eyes were staring upward. But he was girdled still with Bradley's iron ring, and the rivets of the iron ring held tight.[88]

The corpse-laden river which had opened the novel, which had then received the bodies of George Radfoot and Gaffer Hexam, and from which John Harmon and Eugene Wrayburn had miraculously escaped alive, now claims two further victims, 'birds of prey' like the waterside men of the first chapter. 'Fear death by water' might be the epigraph of *Our Mutual Friend*:[89] and in *Edwin Drood* Cloisterham, too, has a weir.

THE MYSTERIES IN *EDWIN DROOD*

DICKENS had written only half of *The Mystery of Edwin Drood* (1870) when he died, leaving only a few hints, most of them recorded at second-hand, as to how it would develop and conclude. Many guesses have been made, but the topic has unfortunately attracted too much commentary on a level with that of 'Baconian' theories of Shakespeare — trivial and wrong-headed and uncontrolled by any real feeling for the author and his methods. Dickens's daughter Katey sensibly protested that he would have given the story an ending 'less complicated, although quite as interesting, as any that have been suggested'. Lady Pansy Pakenham's comments during a long exchange of views in *The Dickensian* are also salutary. Readers seem to forget, she remarks, that Dickens did not mean to leave his book half-finished: 'The mystery was to have titivated their curiosity for twelve months, not for eighty-five years, while a more permanent interest would have remained with the characters, who would have developed in different proportions than in the present truncated work.' It is 'not a riddle, but a labyrinth, and a correct answer to the question of Edwin's death or survival is only a first step towards the centre'.[1] Attempts to find plot-significance in every phrase of a novelist, the unmistakable mark of whose writing is, as Orwell says, 'the *unnecessary detail*,' seem to me as misguided as the common assumption that Dickens was here trying to emulate so different a novelist as Wilkie Collins, by making the solution of a mystery the central interest, instead of one of several secondary interests, in a novel.[2] Nor need we assume that everything in the fragment we have is perfect in its placing and relevance, or that Dickens was, for once, going to write a novel with a perfect plot. The completed novel might well have contained as many loose ends and imperfections as usual. Plot was, certainly, to have been more important here than usual, but Dickens rarely made the plot in itself the effective centre of interest in his fiction.

As a 'mystery', indeed, *Edwin Drood* deserves Gissing's adjectives, 'trivial' and 'paltry',[3] but it seems most improbable, both from the text as we have it and from our knowledge of Dickens's methods, that we were intended to be much mystified by the central event. Dickens's 'Postcript' to the previous novel, *Our Mutual Friend*, is suggestive here:

> When I devised this story, I foresaw the likelihood that a class of readers and commentators would suppose that I was at great pains to conceal exactly what I was at great pains to suggest: namely, that Mr John Harmon was not slain, and that Mr John Rokesmith was he. Pleasing myself with the idea that the supposition might in part arise out of some ingenuity in the story, and thinking it worth while, in the interests of art, to hint to an audience that an artist (of whatever denomination) may perhaps be trusted to know what he is about in his vocation, if they will concede him a little patience, I was not alarmed by the anticipation.
>
> To keep for a long time unsuspected, yet always working itself out, another purpose originating in that leading incident, . . . was at once the most interesting and the most difficult part of my design. Its difficulty was much enhanced by the mode of publication. . . .[4]

— and this final phrase reminds one of another apposite comment he made, in answer to the *Edinburgh Review* attack on *Little Dorrit*. Rigaud's death in the collapse of the house of Clennam, far from being a surprise or an afterthought, was, he said, 'carefully prepared' from its first introduction in the story, and no attentive reader can have failed to see 'that when Rigaud . . . first enters it (hundreds of pages before the end), he is beset by a mysterious fear and shuddering; that the rotten and crazy state of the house is laboriously kept before the reader, whenever the house is shown; that the way to the demolition of the man and the house together, is paved all through the book with a painful minuteness and re-iterated care of preparation, the necessity of which (in order that the thread may be kept in the reader's mind through nearly two years), is one of the adverse incidents of that serial form of publication.'[5] It would be a very stupid and inattentive reader who could fail to see that John Jasper is a wicked man, that he has 'cause, and will, and strength, and means' to kill Edwin, that he makes careful preparations to do so and to throw suspicion elsewhere, that Edwin disappears permanently at the climax of these preparations, and that Jasper thereafter continues to act in a fashion compatible — to say the least — with his being a reasonably prudent murderer.

Some readers may be grateful to be reminded, at this point, of the plot of the *Edwin Drood* fragment. John Jasper, the young choir-master and organist at Cloisterham Cathedral, is passion-

ately in love with a young orphan, Rosa Bud, who is at school in
his city and to whom he teaches music. Since her infancy, she has
been betrothed to another orphan, Edwin Drood, who is Jasper's
nephew (though only a few years younger than him). Edwin has
studied engineering, and is departing for Egypt: he and Rosa
decide to end the engagement their parents had wished upon them,
but, before he has time to tell anyone this, he disappears, and soon
afterwards his jewellery is recovered from a nearby Weir. Only the
unneeded engagement ring — a family heirloom — is not recovered: no-one knows that Edwin has this on him, except Rosa's
guardian, the solicitor Mr Grewgious, who has handed it over to
him shortly before. Edwin's body is not found, but everyone
assumes that he has been murdered, and suspicion falls on Neville
Landless, a young man who has recently arrived at Cloisterham
from the East, with his sister Helena, to complete their education.
Neville has manifestly fallen in love with Rosa, and has resented
Edwin's offhand manner with her; he is a passionate young man,
and quarrels between him and Edwin have occurred, which Jasper
has fomented and publicised. But Neville is clearly innocent of
murder, and Jasper is — for the reader — the obvious suspect. He
is leading a double life, as organist at the Cathedral which he hates,
and as drug-addict in low opium-dens in London. He seems to
have strange and sinister hypnotic powers; his passion for Rosa,
who abhors him, so frightens her that she flees to London; and his
conduct before the murder seems inexplicable unless he is preparing to kill Edwin and to cast suspicion for the deed on Neville. He
has shown a marked interest in the cathedral tombs, and in quicklime;[6] he persuades the stonemason Durdles to show him round the
crypt and the tower ('Surely an unaccountable sort of expedition!'
comments the narrator), and Durdles soon falls into a long drunken
or drugged sleep. Jasper is enraged to discover that his expedition
has been, in part, witnessed by a young imp nicknamed 'Deputy'.
Other facts, such as his mutterings during his opium dreams, point
towards Jasper as the murderer, and Rosa and Grewgious at least
come to suspect him. (Indeed, the wonder is that Jasper was not
quickly and universally suspected; like Dickens's other murderers,
he leaves a trail of large clues behind him.) Six months after
Edwin's disappearance, however, the mystery remains unsolved,
when a curious stranger named Datchery comes to settle in Cloisterham. Datchery is obviously trying to solve the crime; he obviously
suspects Jasper, and is collecting information about him; he is,

almost certainly, wearing a disguise, and the reader is impelled to guess that he is therefore a character already known under some other identity, and to wonder who he will turn out to be. But at this point the fragment comes to an end.

The external evidence all reinforces the obvious implications of the fragmentary story. The most important sources are, first of all, Dickens's manuscript Number-plans. These contain such phrases as 'Touch the key-note. "When the wicked man —" ', 'Murder very far off,' '*Quarrel*. (Fomented by Jasper) . . . *Jasper lays his ground*,' 'Lay the ground for the manner of the murder to come out at last', 'Jasper's artful turn.'⁷ Secondly, there is Forster's much-quoted account:

> 'I laid aside the fancy I told you of [Dickens wrote to him], and have a very curious and new idea for my new story. Not a communicable idea (or the interest of the book would be gone), but a very strong one, though difficult to work.' The story, I learnt immediately afterward, was to be that of the murder of a nephew by his uncle; the originality of which was to consist in the review of the murderer's career by himself at the close, when its temptations were to be dwelt upon as if, not he the culprit, but some other man, were the tempted. The last chapters were to be written in the condemned cell, to which his wickedness, all elaborately elicited from him as if told of another, had brought him. Discovery by the murderer of the utter needlessness of the murder for its object, was to follow hard upon commission of the deed; but all discovery of the murderer was to be baffled till towards the close, when, by means of a gold ring which had resisted the corrosive effects of the lime into which he had thrown the body, not only the person murdered was to be identified but the locality of the crime and the man who committed it. So much was told to me before any of the book was written. . . . Rosa was to marry Tartar, and Crisparkle the sister of Landless, who was himself, I think, to have perished in assisting Tartar finally to unmask and seize the murderer.⁸

Thirdly, there are the recollections of the two artists, Charles Collins who designed the front cover, and Luke Fildes who drew the illustrations. Charles Collins also, and independently of Forster, records such meagre 'general outlines' of the story as Dickens gave him: Jasper was to 'urge on the search after Edwin Drood and the pursuit of the murderer, thus endeavouring to divert suspicion from himself, the real murderer. This is indicated in the design, on the right side of the cover, of the figures hurrying up the spiral staircase, emblematical of a pursuit. They are led on by Jasper who points unconsciously to his own figure in the drawing at the head of the title'.[9] Luke Fildes, in an interview, records that Dickens intended to take him on a sketching-expedition to the condemned cell at Maidstone or some other gaol, and he reports — what he stated more categorically in a letter some years later — that Dickens gave him special instructions about Jasper's costume in one of the illustrations. 'He suddenly said, "Can you keep a secret?" I assured him he could rely on me. He then said, "I must have the double necktie! It is necessary, for Jasper strangles Edwin Drood with it." '[10]

Finally, there are the recollections of his son Charley and his daughter Katey. As she says, the family had made it a point of honour among themselves never to show their natural impatience to know how the story would end, or to tease him with questions; Aunt Georgina did ask, 'I hope you haven't really killed poor Edwin Drood?' and got the cryptic reply, 'I call my book the Mystery, not the History, of Edwin Drood.'[11] But Charley did better; during their last walk together, Dickens asked him whether he did not think that too much of the story had been let out too soon. 'I assented,' writes Charley, 'and added, "Of course, Edwin Drood was murdered?" Whereupon he turned upon me with an expression of astonishment at my having asked such an unnecessary question, and said: "Of course; what else do you suppose?" '[12] I may add that the analogues for the novel, discussed by Mr Richard M. Baker in his excellent book *The Drood Murder Case*, provide further reinforcement for the theory that Jasper murdered Drood — particularly Dickens's short-story in *Master Humphrey's Clock* (1840), 'A confession found in a prison in the time of Charles II.'[13]

These are the main items, and it is clear that they are consonant with one another (as they are with the few other items I have not mentioned), and with the story as we have it. Something must be allowed, no doubt, for slight lapses of memory, or misunderstandings of what Dickens said, and for the possibility that Dickens may have changed his mind about some of the details of his plan before he died, and might also, of course, have made further amendments had he lived to work these ideas out. The problem is further confused a little by the fact that Dickens had had to rearrange the chapter-order early in the book, and that Forster, as his executor, may have printed some of the later chapters in the wrong order: also that Forster silently retained, when printing the instalments which Dickens had left in proof, some phrases and passages which Dickens had deleted.[14] Much about the story necessarily remains obscure, but the writers who have rejected this body of evidence and maintained that Edwin Drood is alive — a theory for which *no* evidence exists — seem merely captious. Moreover, this 'Watched by the Dead' device, which Dickens had used before, would seem frivolous as the central episode in a story which has so strongly suggested that the eponymous character is dead. I cannot think that Dickens would have played so unfairly with the reader, or have thus trivialised what was certainly intended to be an ambitious study in criminal behaviour, by using a trick which had never been strong enough to bear much scrutiny. It has also been pointed out, by several writers, that there are only two young women in the story — Rosa and Helena — and that if Edwin rises from the dead this would increase the number of eligible suitors who must, by convention, receive a bride in the final chapter.

Mysteries there certainly were, by intention, but in my opinion they were to be of minor importance, bearing the same relation to the Jasper theme as the Harmon Murder, and the curious behaviour of Boffin, had borne to the Headstone theme in *Our Mutual Friend*. We are obviously meant to be intrigued by the identity of Datchery. Many suggestions have been put forward — that he is Helena Landless, Mr Grewgious, Bazzard (his clerk), Neville Landless, Tartar, Edwin Drood himself risen from the grave, or an entirely new character, maybe a member of the solicitors' firm to which Grewgious has deputed his business.[15] The keeper of the opium-den to which Jasper resorts, the 'Princess Puffer', also, it is clear, has more than a seller-client relationship to him; she is pursuing him with special ferocity, and again several possible motives have been suggested (that she is the mother of a girl Jasper has seduced, or Jasper's own mother, embittered against him by her husband's conduct, or Rosa Bud's grandmother, and so on). There are hints at other mysteries that might well have proved important — the oriental origins of the Landlesses, and the possibility that Jasper's taste for opium was picked up in the East, so that he was in some way related to them; the role that Deputy was to play in the dénouement, and again the possibility that he would turn out to be a blood-connection of Jasper's; the meaning of the scream that Durdles had heard a year before the night when Drood was killed; and several more. Above and including all these questions, of course, is the major one — given that Jasper has murdered Drood, just how and by whom will this be proved? and will Jasper be captured, tried, and executed? Here, any answer must depend heavily upon the external evidence, incomplete though it is, but there seems no reason to doubt Forster's and Fildes's account that the novel would have ended in a condemned cell.

My purposes do not require me to name my solutions to these various mysteries; nor, as it happens, do I have anything new to say on these much-discussed issues. If I were pressed to say which of the many solutions put forward seem most plausible, I would begin by stressing, more than is often done, that any solution must be tentative. For though the main lines of the story are clear, both on internal and external evidence, there are simply not enough materials to justify a conclusive decision as to whether, for instance, Helena or Grewgious is Datchery (these seem to me the most likely claimants, though there are difficulties about both candidatures). It would indeed have been a poor mystery if one could prove anything like a complete case, with only half the projected book extant. Dickens's recorded comments to Forster and the others are explicit about Jasper's having murdered Drood, but throw no light on these secondary mysteries — a fact which tends to confirm my assumption that he was relying on these 'instrumental' mysteries (about *how* Jasper was to be convicted) to provide the suspense-interest in the story, and not on any substantial doubt as to whether Jasper was in fact guilty.

As Katey Dickens points out, her father's recorded comments on the novel never suggest that 'it was upon the Mystery alone that he relied for interest and originality of his idea. The originality was to be shown, as he tells us, in . . . the psychological description the murderer gives us of his temptations, temperament, and character. . . . He was quite as deeply fascinated and absorbed in the study of the criminal Jasper, as in the dark and sinister crime that has given the book its title'.[16] I agree that this is the main interest in the novel, and certainly it is its main interest in relation to my present study.

Jasper very clearly continues the development we have traced from Sikes and Rudge to Jonas Chuzzlewit, Slinkton, and Bradley Headstone — from the member of the 'criminal classes' to the middleclass citizen apparently of the utmost propriety. Jasper is still more intelligent, more complex psychologically, more respectable, and more ambiguous in his relation to society, than his predecessors. He is a professional man — an artist, but not overtly of the Bohemian type: a teacher, but without Headstone's social insecurity. He serves a cathedral, and is thus associated with his society's highest values, in their most traditional and dignified setting. 'Strike the key-note,' Dickens had reminded himself in his Number-plan — and it was the text 'When the wicked man turneth away from his wickedness that he hath committed and doeth that which is lawful and right he shall save his soul alive'. As Dr Fielding comments, 'One thing is clear: that however closely Dickens had come to be concerned with plot, he had by no means given up the idea of having a unifying theme with a strong moral interest. In the past this morality had been a Christian one, and in several of the later novels certain key-phrases from the Bible or the Prayer-book had played an important part in the thematic structure.'[17] What relevance the 'key-note' text was to have had is one of the most fascinating and, I think, insoluble problems of the fragment: was Jasper to have turned away from his wickedness (not that one can undo or renounce a murder), and to have saved his soul alive? It seems improbable, but Dickens may have had a big surprise in store for his readers, in this respect. Whether it would have been a convincing surprise is, however, quite another matter.[18]

But the Jasper we see is wholeheartedly, though secretly, the Wicked Man. His manner is 'a little sombre', we are told when he is first described; so is his room, which is, symbolically, 'mostly in shadow.' 'A bad, bad man!' Rosa calls him, in her terrible scene with him after Edwin had disappeared and Jasper tries to take his place as her affianced: but he is quite unmoved by her accusations. His face is 'wicked and menacing', his 'features and his convulsive hands absolutely diabolical'.[19] More ambiguously, Dickens comments upon his 'one idea' after Edwin's disappearance: ambiguous because, although other interpretations are possible and more plausible, we *can* understand this is a reference to his diary-entry to discuss the mystery with no-one — 'I now swear. . . . That I will fasten the crime of the murder of my dear dead boy upon the murderer. And, That I devote myself to his destruction'[20]— words, which, as we shall see, are ambiguous enough already. Here is the comment on Jasper's 'one idea':

> Impassive, moody, solitary, resolute, so concentrated on one idea, and on its attendant fixed purpose, that he would share it with no fellow-creature, he lived apart from human life. Constantly exercising

an Art which brought him into mechanical harmony with others, and which could not have been pursued unless he and they had been in the nicest mechanical relations and unison, it is curious to consider that the spirit of the man was in moral accordance or interchange with nothing around him. This indeed he had confided to his lost nephew, before the occasion for his present inflexibility arose.[21]

The final sentence refers of course to the striking confession Jasper had made to Edwin, as early as the second chapter, completely repudiating the Christian values of the cathedral where his work lay:

'There is said to be a hidden skeleton in every house; but you thought there was none in mine, dear Ned. . . . You were going to say . . . what a quiet life mine is. No whirl and uproar around me, no distracting commerce or calculation, no risk, no change of place, myself devoted to the art I pursue, my business my pleasure.'

'I really was going to say something of the kind, Jack; but you see, you, speaking of yourself, almost necessarily leave out much that I should have put in. For instance: I should have put in the foreground your being so much respected as Lay Precentor, or Lay Clerk, or whatever you call it, of this Cathedral; your enjoying the reputation of having done such wonders with the choir. . . .'

'Yes; I saw what you were tending to. I hate it.'

'Hate it, Jack?' (Much bewildered.)

'I hate it. The cramped monotony of my existence grinds me away by the grain. How does our service sound to you?'

'Beautiful! Quite celestial!'

'If often sounds to me quite devilish. I am so weary of it. The echoes of my own voice among the arches seem to mock me with my daily drudging round. No wretched monk who droned his life away in that gloomy place, before me, can have been more tired of it than I am. He could take for relief (and did take) to carving demons out of the stalls and seats and desks. What shall I do? Must I take to carving them out of my heart?'

'I though you had so exactly found your niche in life, Jack,' Edwin Drood returns, astonished. . . .

'I know you thought so. They all think so.'[22]

This carries a stage further the tension Dickens had shown in Bradley Headstone, between the respectable schoolmaster by day and the prowling wild animal by night. Headstone had, in his dim way, believed in his little educational bag-of-tricks; but Jasper's cathedral respectability is a complete and conscious sham, a pretence which he maintains only to earn himself a living, but which

he more than resents. In several other ways, Jasper obviously inherits features from Headstone — he seeks to kill his rival for a girl
who, as he knows, finds him repugnant, and who flees from his
furious and terrifying lust; his murderous act is futile (Headstone
cements the love between Eugene and Lizzie, Jasper learns too late
that Edwin and Rosa have broken off their engagement anyhow).
The lips of both murderers go white at moments of tension, they
perspire terribly, and then fall into 'a kind of paroxysm, or fit';
both brood over the way in which they have carried out the
murder (Headstone explicitly, and Jasper allusively, in his opium-
dream). Both are compared to 'a wild beast'.

The comment on Jasper's 'living apart from human life' reminds
one, too, of earlier murderers whose deed cuts them off from their
kind — Sikes, Rudge, and Jonas — and there are other features also
which link *Edwin Drood* with its predecessors. Many readers have
noticed, for instance, how constantly this novel refers, explicitly and
implicitly, to *Macbeth*. 'When Shall These Three Meet Again?' is the
title of the chapter preceding the murder. It was 'unusually dark'
on the night of Edwin's disappearance: 'Not such power of wind
has blown for many a winter night. . . . Chimneys topple in the
streets. . . . Some stones have been displaced upon the summit of
the great tower' of the Cathedral.[23] 'Time and place are both at
hand,' says Jasper, reliving under opium the occasion of the
murder, and recalling Lady Macbeth's 'Nor time nor place, Did
then adhere'.[24] His incoherent confessions under opium obviously
recall Lady Macbeth's sleep-walking scene; the 'hoarse rooks
hovering about the Cathedral tower' may recall Macbeth's 'the
crow makes wing to th' rooky wood' and Lady Macbeth's 'The
raven himself is hoarse. . . .'[25] It is dangerous, however, to see a
special significance in these parallels: for whenever Dickens
thought about murder, echoes of *Macbeth* came into his mind. I
noted some parallels when discussing *Barnaby Rudge*, and there are
others obvious enough in *Oliver Twist*, *Martin Chuzzlewit*, and *Our
Mutual Friend*. Sikes, sleepless and haunted by Nancy's eyes, which
make him 'start' at so fateful a moment, recalls Macbeth's 'terrible
dreams' and his vision of Banquo's ghost; and when Sikes tries to
forget his terrors by fighting a fire, 'he bore a charmed life' amidst
all its dangers.[26] The weather during Jonas's murderous journey
with his victim is as extreme and ominous as on the nights when
Rudge, Jasper, and Macbeth do their evil deeds: and when Jonas
rests at an inn soon after killing Montague, 'there was a knocking

within . . . as if by some design and order of circumstances,' which continued 'like a warning echo'.[27] Similarly, Headstone cannot sleep, and is 'never off the rack', and 'Then comes my fit again' (as Macbeth says); Headstone had 'dipped his hands in blood, to mark himself a miserable tool and fool', and Macbeth likewise discovers that 'For Banquo's issue have I 'filed my mind'.[28] Some of these, and other, parallels may of course be adventitious — both Shakespeare and Dickens writing the same inevitable things about murderers. Thus, Dickens hardly needed the example of Macbeth's discovery that 'honour, love, obedience, troops of friends, I must not look to have', to suggest the idea that a murderer is likely to brood alone and to be shunned by his fellows. But it is clear that, on murder, Dickens was haunted by *Macbeth*, as, when writing about fathers and daughters, by *King Lear*. The parallels in *Edwin Drood* are more explicit and insistent than before, but I doubt whether they signify more than a fuller, because more appropriate, reminiscence of Shakespeare's most relevant, because most respectable, murderer.

So much for the links between Jasper and his predecessors: what about the differences? Some we have noticed, as extensions of trends already apparent in previous novels — the yet more 'respectable' murderer, the more extreme form of double personality. To the latter I shall return. A totally new element is opium, and the other connections with the Middle and Far East. The dream-allegory in which the murderer enacts his temptation or deed, goes back, of course, to *Martin Chuzzlewit* and earlier (with, I have suggested, a possible reminiscence of the Sleep-walking Scene), but the drug-addict who deliberately courts this sensation is a new character for Dickens. He was, certainly, using his memories of the opium-dens in Shadwell, which he had visited when he was beginning to write the novel: it would be interesting to know whether he had already decided to give Jasper his opium-habit, and had indeed gone to Shadwell because he wanted to check on the facts, or whether the visit to Shadwell suggested this as an extra trait.[29] Opium had of course played an important part in Wilkie Collins's *The Moonstone*, which had appeared under Dickens's auspices in *All the Year Round* in 1868, and opium-dens were a new feature in London.[30] Certainly Jasper's addiction to this exotic vice marks him as an unusual, and a specially wicked, villain (the 'criminal intellect' as 'a horrible wonder apart'), and the oriental visions he has, in the opening paragraphs of the book, may not simply represent his, or Dickens's, associations of opium with the East and with De Quincey's *Confessions*. The Landlesses hail from the East, and are both 'very dark, and very rich in colour; she almost of the gipsy type; something untamed about them both' — hints made more explicit in Dickens's manuscript memorandum, 'Mixture of Oriental blood — or imperfectly acquired mixture in them. *Yes.*' Jasper too is 'a dark man . . . with thick, lustrous, well-arranged black hair and whiskers', and may therefore also have come from the East as well as dream about it — though, of course, Victorian villains always do have dark lustrous hair and whiskers, and this may be the sole significance of these details.[31] Such a tame explanation would satisfy few Droodians. Howard Duffield, an eminent man in this field, has suggested that Jasper belongs to the Indian sect of Thugs, and certainly some details of his behaviour seem to fit in with the cult and observances of the goddess Kali: but this, I think, is one of the many theories about *Edwin Drood* which deserve to be cut off by a literary Occam's Razor, although so distinguished a critic as Mr Edmund Wilson has found it entirely convincing. (I am comforted by the fact that the most useful recent surveyor of the Drood controversy, Mr Richard Baker, shares my scepticism.)[32] But just what significance the East was intended to have in the novel, I regret I cannot say.

Another new feature in Jasper is his possessing hypnotic, and perhaps other para-normal, powers. When talking with Edwin in his room, which contains a picture of Rosa, 'Fixed as the look [which Edwin] meets is, there is yet in it some strange power of suddenly including the sketch over the chimneypiece,' and when later 'The younger man glances at the portrait' we are told that 'The elder sees it in him'. Jasper's 'resounding chord' on the Cathedral organ has a strange effect on Rosa, which seems more than a reminder of the man she hates, and when she is singing at the piano to his accompaniment he 'ever and again hinted the one note, as though it were a low whisper from himself', until she shrieks 'I can't bear this! I am frightened! Take me away!' She explains later that 'He terrifies me. . . . I feel as if he could pass in through the wall when he is spoken of. . . . He has forced me to understand him, without saying a word. . . . When he . . . strikes a note, or a chord, or plays a passage, he himself is in the sounds. . . .' — powers over her which he demonstrates, without the help of music, when she experiences 'the old horrible feeling of being compelled by him. . . . She cannot resist . . .' and when

'The fascination of repulsion had been upon her so long . . . that she felt as if he had power to bind her by a spell'.[33] She is not the only subject of his 'spells'; Canon Crisparkle cannot understand why he has come to the weir where he finds Edwin's jewellery, and as it is to Jasper's interest that this jewellery be found it seems likely that it is through his hypnotism that Crisparkle finds himself there.

> 'How did I come here!' was his first thought, as he stopped.
> 'Why did I come here!' was his second.
> Then, he stood intently listening to the water. A familiar passage in his reading, about airy tongues that syllable men's names, rose so unbidden to his ear, that he put it from him with his hand, as if it were tangible. . . .
> ·. . . Mr Crisparkle had a strange idea that something unusual hung about the place.
> He reasoned with himself: What was it? Where was it? Put it to the proof. Which sense did it address?
> No sense reported anything unusual there. He listened again. . . .
> Knowing very well that the mystery with which his mind was occupied, might of itself give the place this haunted air, he strained those hawk's eyes of his.

— and thus he saw something glistening, which proved to be Edwin's gold watch; and thus Cloisterham was confirmed in its belief that he had been murdered.[34]

Again, one cannot be sure just what significance these powers were to have had in the second half of the novel. Probably, as many critics have suggested, Dickens was dropping a hint when he used an unusually elaborate and otherwise otiose simile to explain how Miss Twinkleton was a starchy headmistress by day, and a romantic old maid by night — 'As, in some cases of drunkenness, and in others of animal magnetism, there are two states of consciousness which never clash, but each of which pursues its separate course as though it were continuous instead of broken (thus, if I hide my watch when I am drunk, I must be drunk again before I can remember where), so Miss Twinkleton has two distinct and separate phases of being.'[35] ('Animal magnetism' was a contemporary term for mesmerism.) Probably this notion is referred to in Forster's report of Dickens's intriguing but cryptic intention that the originality of the story was to consist in 'the review of the murderer's career by himself at the close, when its temptations were to be dwelt upon as if, not he the culprit, but some other man, were the tempted', and that his wickedness was to have been 'all elaborately elicited from him as if told of another'. Jasper's addiction to opium is not much different from a 'case of drunkenness', and he certainly indulges in 'animal magnetism'. It has often and plausibly been suggested that Helena Landless was to have hypnotised him, thus 'elaborately eliciting' his guilt from him. She has certainly been specified as not liable to be afraid of him 'under any circumstances'. She is, too, Rosa's passionate protector ('Let whomsoever it most concerned look well to it!'), and she seems to have some para-normal powers akin to his. There is 'a complete understanding' between Helena and her twin brother 'though no spoken word — hardly as much as a look — may have passed' between them.[36]

I suspect, however, that this means little more than that Jasper was to prove a hard nut to crack, except through hypnotism. Other and more complicated theories about Jasper's dual consciousness seem difficult to accept, on the evidence of the existing fragment. Jasper certainly leads a double life, but that does not mean that he has a dual consciousness. Under opium he is more loquacious — as Lady Macbeth is, when sleep-walking — but hardly more wicked than the 'respectable' cathedral organist he normally appears to be. The workaday Jasper is explicit, in his conversation with Edwin, about his hatred for the Cathedral and all it stands for, and everything that we see this ordinary Jasper do seems to be the action of a consciously wicked but careful and clever murderer — planning where to hide the body, how to prevent its identification if it is found, how to cast suspicion on someone else, and so forth. He seems to be no more a 'divided personality' (as Mr Edmund Wilson and others have called him) than any other sinner, or murderer, who takes pains not to be suspected. He has a 'second' consciousness, indeed, under opium — and thus has an 'in vino veritas' vulnerability to the Princess Puffer and anyone else who can overhear and begin to interpret his 'unintelligible' mutterings. 'I may have learned the secret how to make ye talk, deary,' she apostrophises him. 'I heard ye say once . . . , "Unintelligible!" . . . but don't ye be too sure always . . .!' — and on another occasion she makes a significant remark about opium: '. . . you always hear what can be said against it, but seldom what can be said in its praise.'[37] Certainly what she had heard was enough to make her realise what danger 'Ned' stood in, before Edwin Drood disappeared; what Jasper said during his later visit to her den further arouses her suspicions and informs us more fully, though still confusedly, about how he actually killed Edwin. Already the Princess Puffer can claim to know Jasper 'far better than all the Reverend Parsons put together know him',[38] and another opium dream should have provided further vital clues, to a listener increasingly well-informed about his background.

'If the accumulation of comment means anything, it means that we need no longer expect a solution in which all our perplexities will magically vanish.' Professor Waldock's sentence refers, not to *Edwin Drood*, but to another of the great brain-teasers of English literature — though it is, of course, much more than that — *Hamlet*; and much of what he says in his 'Study of Critical Method' about this play applies also to our novel. 'Unfortunately, it is not of the slightest consequence how very reasonably all such considerations are urged,' he remarks of some suggestions, *'if the play does not urge them.* How much *Hamlet* criticism need not have been written if this self-evident principle had been kept in mind!' He refers to A. C. Bradley's famous lectures, with their tendency to 'treat *Hamlet* as if it had actually occurred in real life, as if it were, authentically, *le cas Hamlet'*. Bradley's account, he says, is 'an exposition built up with deft skill and masterly thoroughness. His *Hamlet* stands four-square: every joint is neat, every buttress seems solid. . . . Bradley's *Hamlet* is better than Shakespeare's: it is better in the sense that it has a firmer consistency, that it hangs together with a more irresistible logic'. And he concludes: 'A play is not a mine of secret motives. We persist in digging for them; what happens usually is that our spade goes through the other side of the drama.'[39]

We are, certainly, more entitled to dig for 'secret motives' in *Edwin Drood* than in *Hamlet*, since no assessment of the novel, or of its relation to the rest of Dickens's work, is possible without our making some surmise about the unwritten second half in which Jasper's personality would have been more fully exposed. But it remains a novel (or rather, half one), as *Hamlet* is a play and not a baffling fragment from Danish history: and Dickens wrote it, not Dostoevsky or Strindberg or Wilkie Collins or any of the other ghosts who seem to have taken over in the minds of some of its commentators. Recent Droodiana, like most of the best and most of the worst Dickens-criticism of the past two decades, has been strongly influenced by Mr Edmund Wilson, whose pages on *Edwin*

Drood unfortunately are, in my opinion, among his most precipitate and questionable. He makes optimistic use of that convenient phrase 'in short'. Jasper is described by Dickens as dark, etc, 'in short, as something very much like a Hindu' — he 'has, then, "two states of consciousness;" he is, in short, what we have come to call a dual personality'.[40] Rounding some very tight bends by this handy device, Mr Wilson is able to present, with considerable confidence, an *Edwin Drood* as much 'better' than what Dickens was likely to produce as Bradley's *Hamlet* was superior to Shakespeare's: not a very difficult task, since Mr Wilson is a more intelligent critic than Bradley, and Dickens is habitually a worse craftsman and artist than Shakespeare.

Edwin Drood, he maintains, is carrying to its logical conclusion the criminal theme which had haunted Dickens all his life. 'He is to explore the deep entanglement and conflict of the bad and the good in one man. The subject of *Edwin Drood* as the subject of Poe's *William Wilson*, the subject of *Dr Jekyll and Mr Hyde*, the subject of *Dorian Gray*. It is also the subject of that greater work than any of these, Dostoevsky's *Crime and Punishment*.'[41] Mr Wilson's *Edwin Drood* is, indeed, the work of an English, and therefore a less bold and extreme, Dostoevsky: but there is a salutary comment on these fashionable parallels between Dickens and Dostoevsky or Lawrence or Joyce or Kafka — Professor G. H. Ford's reminder that, after all, 'Dickens is more like Dickens than he is like any other writer.'[42] As we have seen, throughout his fiction and journalism, Dickens regards murderers as unequivocally and entirely wicked men. Where, one wonders, does Mr Wilson detect 'the good' in John Jasper? As he admits, Jasper is 'a damned soul here and now', though he is 'a man who is both innocent and wicked'.[43] His only apparent virtue — if it is one — is his fondness for the nephew he murders. Whenever he looks towards Edwin, we are told of their first meeting in the book, his face bears 'a look of intentness and intensity — a look of hungry, exacting, watchful, and yet devoted affection'. The Dean expresses the hope that Jasper's heart may not be 'too much set upon his nephew', and Edwin himself describes his uncle's manner towards him as 'almost womanish'.[44] How genuine this affection was, and thus how much it cost Jasper to kill Edwin to gain possession of Rosa, whom he certainly loved more, we cannot tell. Necessarily, Dickens's expressions about his villain are ambiguous. It is difficult, however, to discover any other virtue even ambiguously imputed to Jasper. His association with the cathedral is, by his own confession, gross hypocrisy; his appearance of loving Edwin may well be the same.

Certainly his alleged love for his nephew does not prevent his killing him, doing the deed 'hundreds of thousands of times' in anticipation, and finding, when the decisive moment came, that 'It *was* pleasant to do'.[45] These evil thoughts, it may be objected, belong to his 'opium' self; they are expressed, certainly, during an opium session at the Princess Puffer's. Mr Wilson, adhering to the 'Thug' theory of Jasper, makes a sharp division between these two selves. Jasper, he says, is eventually to destroy himself: 'When he announces in the language of the Thugs that he "devotes" himself to the "destruction" of the murderer, he is preparing his own execution. (He is evidently quite sincere in making this entry in his diary, because he has now sobered up from the opium and resumed his ecclesiastical personality. It is exclusively of this personality that the diary is a record.)'[46] But, as we saw, when Dickens spoke of Jasper's 'ecclesiastical personality' ('exercising an Art which brought him into mechanical harmony with others'), he noted the paradox that 'the spirit of the man was in moral accordance or interchange with nothing around him'.[47] Given the conventions of the novel, he could hardly be more explicit about the wickedness of the normal 'ecclesiastical' Jasper.

The diary was, of course, to be relevant. It contained Jasper's careful record of Neville's 'demoniacal passion' against Edwin (largely induced by the drugs Jasper had put into their drinks) and his fear that Neville would murder Edwin in a fit of jealous rage. On the day of the murder he told Mr Crisparkle, to whom he had earlier shown these entries, that he would burn the diary in a few days' time, because it contained these 'exaggerative' thoughts; but Edwin's disappearance, and the subsequent suspicions against Neville, make it indispensable evidence (this, of course, was why it had been written at all), so Jasper preserved it, and showed Mr Crisparkle his further entry in it, to the effect that he would discover and destroy the murderer.[48]

Certainly it is Jasper, as the murderer, who is to suffer destruction, and doubtless this diary-entry (given additional emphasis by coming at the end of a chapter and of an instalment) was to have come true, in some sense — but not, I think, in the way Mr Wilson suggests. Jasper is no Dostoevskian character, nor a King Oedipus virtuously but blindly proving his own guilt. Dickens projected a less interesting irony, I would guess: merely that, by some miscalculation or over-reaching himself — such as, he firmly believed, all murderers made at some point in their most cunning plans[49] — Jasper would betray his own guilt through trying to convict Neville. Charles Collins, it will be remembered, noted that, in his cover-design for the novel, the pursuit of the murderer is led by Jasper, 'who points unconsciously to his own figure in the drawing at the head of the title.' It is most unlikely that he portrayed Jasper with this gesture, except under Dickens's explicit instructions; and thus it seems likely (as Lady Pansy Pakenham has suggested) that the 'very curious and new idea' which Dickens cryptically told Forster the novel would contain, was to have been 'the pursuit and destruction of Jasper *by himself*'.[50] His accidental self-incrimination would, I guess, have been followed by an obdurate refusal to confess: and thus, probably, would have ensued the ending which Dickens sketched to Forster — the murderer would review his own career 'as if, not he the culprit, but some other man, were the tempted', and his wickedness, 'all elaborately elicited from him as if told of another,' would bring him to the condemned cell.[51] His composure would be pierced, either through opium, or, more probably, through hypnosis, for in the earlier opium scenes he had not referred to himself in the third person. Helena Landless, I agree, was most likely to be the hypnotist.

Such are my hypotheses about *Edwin Drood*: not very original, I fear. They are much less exciting and ambitious than Mr Wilson's, and make a less satisfactory ending to my chapter and book than Mr Wilson was thus able to give to his notable essay on Dickens. But I think I can see why Mr Wilson was, too easily, betrayed into accepting theories which gave such a conclusive note to his final pages — and I nag at him in this way, not because I lack respect for him (on the contrary: I pore over him with continual delight and benefit), but because his very persuasive account of Dickens has become, in too many respects, the unquestioned orthodoxy of recent years.

First, the *Edwin Drood* he posits is decidedly interesting, as the Dickens he describes throughout his essay was a figure much more likely to command attention and respect in 1941 than the *bon-homme* reformist Dickens of most earlier commentators. But his accounts, both of this novel and of the whole *œuvre*, omit too much, and make claims which cannot be sustained. Dickens is, as he insists, a very great writer, whose merits had been undervalued;

but his greatness does not, I think, lie just where Mr Wilson sees it. (Another fine critic, Dr F. R. Leavis, was much less successful, a decade later, in his attempt to define Dickens's achievement; indeed, I still await a really satisfactory account of his art.) More of his greatness resides in his comedy than Mr Wilson ever recognises; his vision of capitalist society was less complete, coherent, and hostile than he claims; and the concern with crime and violence belongs more to the 'Sensation Novel', and less to the higher reaches of art, than he seeks to show.[52] The comparisons with Dostoevsky, like Macready's cry of 'two Macbeths!', only remind us that this aspect of Dickens is, at best, second-rate. That he had some insight into the psychology of guilt is shown more clearly by my quotations from *Martin Chuzzlewit*, *Little Dorrit* and *Our Mutual Friend*, than by surmises about *Edwin Drood* — at least to me, who am dubious about the notable development which Mr Wilson and others have asserted this novel would have shown. It would, indeed, be pleasant to accept Mr Wilson's claim that at last, after the disjunction of the 'two Scrooges' type, Dickens was now to have explored 'the deep entanglement and conflict of the bad and the good in one man' — but, I have argued, there is no evidence that Jasper was ever 'good' (as distinct from outwardly respectable).

I wish that Dickens had been capable of writing the novel that Mr Wilson thinks up for him. Instead, I think, he was plotting a better novel of the kind he already knew how to write — a Sensation Novel, but with a firmer plot-line, and less hackneyed sensations (hypnosis, opium, some unpredictable connection with the East). There were to be mysteries, including the enigma of Jasper's personality, but Mr V. S. Pritchett is nearer the truth, I believe, than Mr Wilson, through seeing *Edwin Drood* in the context of English fiction rather than European and American. With this novel and *The Moonstone*, he says, 'we begin the long career of murder for murder's sake, murder which illustrates nothing and is there only to stimulate our skill in detection and to distract us with mystery.'[53] Indeed, long before comparisons with Dostoevsky had become *de rigueur*, George Gissing had noted in his excellent study of Dickens both the superficial similarities and the basic differences between the two novelists. Compared with the 'indescribably powerful and finely tragic' conception of *Crime and Punishment*, he wrote, 'the murders in Dickens are too vulgar of motive greatly to impress us, and lack the touch of high imaginativeness.' *Edwin Drood* shows Jasper 'picturesquely, and little more. We discover no hint of real tragedy. The man seems to us a very vulgar assassin, and we care not at all what becomes of him.'[54]

Mr Wilson's second reason for misreading *Edwin Drood* (as I think) is equally instructive, and is suggested by these sentences, which follow his assertion that the man we are now to meet in gaol is not an innocent Pickwick, Micawber or Dorrit, and not a wicked Fagin, Rudge or Dennis, but 'a man who is both innocent and wicked'.

> The protest against the age has turned into a protest against self. In this last moment, the old hierarchy of England does enjoy a sort of triumph over the weary and debilitated Dickens, because it made him accept its ruling that he was a man irretrievably tainted; and the mercantile middle-class England has had its triumph, too. For the Victorian hypocrite has developed — from Pecksniff, through Murdstone, through Headstone, to his final transformation in Jasper — into an insoluble moral problem which is identified with Dickens's own.... Jasper is eventually to destroy himself.... So Dickens, in putting his nerves to the torture by enacting the murder of Nancy, has been invoking his own death.[55]

This passage, too, has a satisfying conclusiveness, which seems to me unwarranted by the facts.

It is part of Mr Wilson's case that 'Of all the great Victorian writers, he was probably the most antagonistic to the Victorian Age itself', that emotionally he was almost as unstable as Dostoevsky, and that he was indeed 'the victim of a manic-depressive cycle, and a very uncomfortable person'.[56] Certainly, in 1941, the popular notion of the Inimitable Boz needed correcting by a thorough immersion in the destructive elements of his character and behaviour. And certainly the Dickens who wrote *Edwin Drood* was still exciting himself by the *Sikes and Nancy* Reading, and was contravening the *mores* of his ages by sleeping with Ellen Ternan. But how deeply was he 'antagonistic to the Victorian Age itself'? and how far was Jasper a projection of his author? Of course, Dickens was exasperated by many features of his society — both what we would regard as its faults and what now seem its more benignant aspects (those penal reforms, for instance, which he deplored). But his *Child's History of England*, and all his other comments on the past, show how much better and more hopeful he thought his own age than any preceding age: and, despite his many criticisms of its institutions and social organisation, he seems to have had no expectation or desire that the future would be radically different. 'He frequently touched on political subjects,' wrote Sala of his conversation, '— always from that which was then a strong Radical point of view, but which at present [1894] I imagine would be thought more Conservative than Democratic.'[57]

It was easy, during the first flush of excitement about the newly-discovered Ellen Ternan affair, to exaggerate his moral alienation from his age, and then to blow up the more aggressive and anti-social aspects of his behaviour until a thoroughly split personality, a manic-depressive victim, emerged. One of the few pre-Ternan studies of Dickens that Mr Wilson respected, Ralph Straus's *Charles Dickens: a Portrait in Pencil* (1928), had increased the darker shades of the picture, but Dickens's surviving son Henry protested, at the time, that Straus's book, though good in many ways, presented his character and disposition 'in far too gloomy a light'. No doubt, he wrote, 'at certain periods of his life my father was intensely depressed and most unhappy. But these phases were intermittent and . . . on the whole he got a keen enjoyment out of life. Speaking of my own experience of him, although like most geniuses he was liable to moods, his general disposition was singularly bright and joyous. . . .'[58] Henry, of course, was a devoted son, and like the rest of the family, and like the official biographer Forster, he loyally suppressed some of the facts. (It was left to Katey Dickens to spill the beans about Ellen — but posthumously, through Gladys Storey's book *Dickens and Daughter*.)[59] But, granted these pious omissions, Henry's picture is juster than Straus's and Mr Wilson's, and it is confirmed by the consensus of hundreds of reminiscences of Dickens by his contemporaries.

A theory about his personality which condemns these many witnesses as white liars or imperceptive fools should have been submitted to more careful scrutiny than it got. It was welcomed, however, without too much examination, because it provided a very acceptable change from 'the jolly Dickens': also because a Freudian and left-wing age expected its literary heroes to be suitably neurotic and alienated, and because even in the 1940s there remained a special relish in every fresh discovery that the Victorians were not so inhumanly respectable as they purported to be.[60] The wrath of the more orthodox Dickensians at these imputations against their hero's character and conduct gave the iconoclasts a happy sensation of being champions of Enlightenment. Neither spirit was conducive to a quiet stock-taking. Both embattled parties were pushed into taking up positions more extreme than was wise.

Imperfections of character and temperament, as of intellect and art, Dickens certainly had. He behaved badly over the Separation business, and very strangely over the 'Murder' Reading — to mention only two obvious examples. His contemporaries had not been unaware of these defects. 'A *unique* of talents suddenly extinct, and has "eclipsed . . . the harmless gaiety of nations",' wrote Carlyle when he died. 'The good, the gentle, ever friendly noble Dickens — every inch of him an Honest Man!' A few years later, after reading Forster's *Life*, he noted that, beneath his 'sparkling, clear, and sunny utterance, . . . his bright and joyful sympathy with everything around him', there lay, 'deeper than all, if one has the eye to see deep enough, dark, fateful silent elements, tragical to look upon. . . .'[61] As the sharp-tongued Mrs Lynn Linton observed, Dickens could be very inflexible — 'his nearest and dearest friends were unable to deflect the passionate pride which suffered neither counsel nor rebuke. . . . [Although he] wrote so tenderly, so sentimentally, so gushingly, he had a strain of hardness in his nature which was like a rod of iron in his soul. . . . Nervous and arbitrary, he was of the kind to whom whims are laws, and self-control in contrary circumstances was simply an impossibility.' But, she added, he 'had very warm sympathies, too, and his true friends never found him wanting'.[62]

Sometimes Dickens recognised his own faults, generally putting them down to artistic temperament — 'the restlessness which is the penalty of an imaginative life and constitution.'[63] Thus, he lectured his wife about her jealousy of a lady he had been helping: 'You know my life . . . and character, and what has had its part in making them successful; and the more you see of me, the better perhaps you may understand that the intense pursuit of any idea that takes complete possession of me, is one of the qualities that makes me different — sometimes for good, sometimes I dare say for evil, — from other men.'[64] Late in 1857, when the Ellen Ternan infatuation had begun, he described his state of mind just after he had finished writing a story: 'It leaves me — as my Art always finds and always leaves me — the most restless of created Beings. I am the modern embodiment of the old Enchanters, whose Familiars tore them to pieces. I weary of rest, and have no satisfaction but in fatigue.'[65] A few months later, he was writing to Forster, about his marital difficulties:

You are not so tolerant as perhaps you might be of the wayward and unsettled feeling which is part (I suppose) of the tenure on which one holds an imaginative life, and which I have, as you ought to know well, often only kept down by riding over it like a dragoon — but let that go by. I make no maudlin complaint. . . . I am always deeply sensible of the wonderful exercise I have of life and its highest sensations, and have said to myself for years, and have honestly and truly felt, This is the draw-back to such a career, and is not to be complained of. . . . Nor are you to suppose that I disguise from myself what might be urged on the other side. I claim no immunity from blame. There is plenty of fault on my side, I dare say, in the way of a thousand uncertainties, caprices, and difficulties of disposition. . . .[66]

His self-accusations were rarely more specific, or more severe, than this. He was not a very self-critical, nor a self-aware, man.

In what ways, then, was he akin to John Jasper? What could Mr Wilson be meaning when he spoke of Jasper's as being 'an insoluble moral problem which was identified with Dickens's own'? The resemblances do not strike me as impressive. Unhappy though Dickens was about some aspects of his society, he was very far from being 'in moral accordance or interchange with nothing around him', a man living 'apart from human life'. He revelled in being the world's most popular novelist, and much more often spoke for his society than he questioned its assumptions. Jasper, as has often been pointed out, is a sort of artist: not a creative one, but a musical executant. He is a mesmerist, and certainly this is a feature common to him and his creator.[67] He is an opium-addict: the nearest I can find Dickens getting to this, is a reference in a letter written a month before his death to his taking laudanum for insomnia.[68] He is passionately and wickedly in love with his nephew's girl, and will stop at nothing to obtain her, though he knows that she loathes him: and Dickens had made Ellen Ternan his mistress. I agreed, in the previous chapter, that Dickens's heroines became more interesting and convincing after he knew Ellen (though they are still only passable, by quite ordinary fictional standards), and that it is only at this period that his murderers have a sexual motive. Many commentators have pointed out that the names of three of his latest heroines — Estella, Bella Wilfer, and Helena Landless — seem to echo the name of Ellen Lawless Ternan, and they have tried to deduce Ellen's character, and the course of Dickens's feelings for her, from these novels.[69] It is tempting to do so, since there is practically no other evidence about the emotions of either party in this intriguing episode. Dickens apparently confided his secret to only a very few intimate friends, and they or his executors seem to have destroyed most of the letters which contained any reference to the affair and to his feelings about Ellen. His letters to her have never been recovered, and his friends and family of course maintained a discreet silence about the matter. Ellen is reported as saying, many years later, that 'she loathed the very thought of this intimacy', but it is not clear whether this represents her feelings during the liaison, or her subsequent regrets and remorse as the respectable wife of a clergyman and headmaster.[70]

If this paucity of evidence tempts one to reconstruct Ellen and Dickens's love for her from the novels, it should also suggest that any surmises thus arrived at must be very tentative. There are too few facts, to act as controls to the imaginative hypotheses. But recent biographers have tended to repeat, at a more sophisticated level, the error of the old-style Dickensian 'duffers' they deplored or patronised: for, as in the old-style hunt after the 'originals' of Dickens's scenes and characters, so also in the pursuit of Ellen, enthusiasm has far outrun a respect for facts and probable inference. Dickens may have felt the anguish and frustration that his later heroines induce in their lovers (though Estella, Bella and Helena have little in common with one another, except the more-or-less close resemblance between their names and Ellen's). But there is no evidence either way, in the letters or reminiscences. Moreover, it is not Helena Landless that Jasper loves, of course, but Rosa Bud, whose name no more resembles Ellen Ternan's than her character resembles the other heroines'. There are other weak points in the Jasper-Dickens, Helena-Ellen, theory. Jasper, like Headstone, has a successful rival, but no-one has yet produced an Edwin Drood or a Eugene Wrayburn in the Dickens-Ellen story.[71] To this, of course, it is replied that Ellen was less forthcoming than Dickens wished (or so it is surmised — from the novels, not the facts), so he may well therefore have imagined that he had a rival, or realised how it must feel to have one. By such shifting devices one can prove almost anything.

I find it difficult, indeed, to see any 'insoluble moral problem' in Jasper or in his creator. Jasper, I have insisted, is a wicked man who murders for lust; there is no evidence in the book about his moral processes, except his opium confession that he greatly enjoyed the act of murder. As for Dickens, his life was, in general, morally unremarkable: he had his faults, and his virtues: the latter, in my judgment, predominated. The exceptional events were, of course, the Separation and the Ellen Ternan affair. About leaving

his wife, or rather casting her out, he seems to have had little compunction. His letters from this period are full of justifications of his
act, and I do not detect an uneasy tone in them — rather, a complacent self-righteousness. If later he reproached himself for the
sorrow he caused her, and the disturbance to the children's lives,
he kept remarkably silent about it.[71a]

His affair with Ellen Ternan does, I think, illustrate rather neatly
his relation to the morality of his day, and thus his attitude to
crime and its treatment. He lived with her — probably not for
some years after the beginning of his passion for her — but took
the utmost pains not to be found out. Not for him, indeed, the
almost holier-than-thou adultery of a George Eliot, nor the barely-
concealed Bohemian cohabitations of a Wilkie Collins. Dickens
was censorious of Collins, in a somewhat avuncular way. Early in
their friendship, they went on a Continental holiday, and Dickens
wrote home: 'He occasionally expounds a code of morals, taken
from modern French novels, which I instantly and with becoming
gravity smash. . . . All these absurdities are innocent enough.'[72]
His later correspondence with Collins, to be sure, often takes on a
raffish bachelor note — invitations to an evening of 'amiable dis-
sipation and unbounded license', to a 'Haroun Alraschid expedition', to 'something in the style of sybarite Rome in the days of its
culminating voluptuousness'. There are naughtier references than
are usual in his letters — aspersions on the chastity of Diana, allusions to French *lorettes* and procuresses, jokes about Collins's
'furtive and Don Giovanni purposes' contrasted with his own strict
chastity — but all these, too, are, I think, 'absurdities . . . innocent
enough.'[73] This was the agreed tone of banter between them, and
should not be taken literally; it portended little more than gay
bachelor evenings with good food and 'rosy' and perhaps, after the
theatre, a green-room rendezvous with the charming little 'peri-
winkles' of the chorus.[74] There is no evidence to suggest that
Dickens was a promiscuous man, and no-one has ever supposed
that he was.

His remark about gravely smashing Collins's fast French moral
code occurs in a letter to his wife, but it should not be written off,
I think, as a husband's adroit reassurance to his wife that he is
behaving himself while away with the boys, nor as expressing a
moral conventionality which he later outgrew. As I have said, we
know very little of what he thought about the Ellen Ternan affair
— whether it brought him happiness or otherwise, and whether or

not he felt guilty. I must guess, like the other commentators. I see no reason to believe that he found any moral justification for his conduct — neither Collins's easy amorality, nor George Eliot's new and higher morality. On this issue, as on other major issues of law and morality, he seems to have accepted the average opinions of his age. He was not much given to pondering over moral problems, insoluble or otherwise. Like most people, he was from time to time irked by the moral and legal imperatives he acknowledged: but he did not envisage, let alone proclaim, a new morality.

Of course he defied them, too — if an adulterous affair so carefully concealed warrants the name of 'defiance'. Thus there were two Dickenses, though the tension between them was not so severe as to justify talk about a split personality. The Dickens who (if my surmise is right) acknowledged the rightness as well as the respectability of monogamy corresponds to the admirer of the police, the journalist insistent on the full rigours of the law, the believer in deterrent punishment. The Dickens who, nevertheless, got rid of his wife and lived with a young actress is, no doubt, the novelist who becomes increasingly interested in criminal psychology — though remaining sufficiently guilt-ridden to punish the criminals in his novels as sternly as he demanded actual criminals should be punished. He makes no plea for sympathy or condonation on behalf of Bradley Headstone, and would (I have argued) have remained equally adamant against John Jasper. He never escaped from the moral categories of his age. This may be set down as a failure of intellectual originality, and certainly I would not claim that he chose to support current moral values after an exhaustive scrutiny of them had persuaded him that they could not be bettered. But on the whole his conventionality represents a strength rather than a weakness. Like Shakespeare in this respect, he 'keeps in the high road of life', as Coleridge wrote. 'Shakespeare has no innocent adulteries, no interesting incests, no virtuous vice; — he never renders that amiable which religion and virtue alike teach us to detest, or clothes impurity in the garb of virtue. . . .'[75]

Whatever joy or sorrow, or moral conflicts, the Ellen Ternan affair brought him, at least he conducted it with characteristic efficiency. 'Whatever I have tried to do in life, I have tried with all my heart to do well,' said David Copperfield on his behalf (though not with illicit love-affairs in mind).[76] One of the things Dickens had never done very well in his fiction, however hard he tried, was devising satisfactory mysteries, but now (as in several other respects) his life out-did his art. As he stole under an assumed name towards his love-nest (in Slough, of all places), he must have felt a certain satisfaction in so ably playing his part in a really good mystery-plot of his own invention: not written, this time, but lived.

He covered his tracks well: he was not found out. Apart from a few barely-noticed hints, no news of the affair was published until over sixty years after his death. Opinions will differ on how severely he is to be judged in this matter, nor do we yet know enough of the facts for any final judgment to be justified. 'He was intensely human,' as even his adoring son Henry acknowledged, 'and I do not suppose it could be said of him that he was freer from the faults and defects appertaining to humanity than most of us are.'[77] Most of his admirers have now reconciled themselves to accepting this more 'human' Dickens: many, indeed, have found him considerably more interesting.

His social policies and opinions, it is clear, were likewise by no means free from 'the faults and defects appertaining to humanity'. In *The Warden*, Trollope called him Mr Popular Sentiment, and we have seen how often this is a just description; but the shortcomings of his ideas on crime and criminals have been less noticed than the imperfections of his personal life. A contributor to *The Journal of the American Institute of Criminal Law and Criminology*, writing on 'Dickens as Criminologist', asserts that he was 'the champion of the oppressed . . . a reformer more powerful than any Parliamentarian', and that the criminal was, for him, 'a natural and historical phenomenon. In his unwavering adherence to this attitude, Charles Dickens marches in the vanguard of great reformers.'[78] How briefly and rarely he marches with the great reformers (and then never in the vanguard), how often he wavers, and in the wrong direction, we have seen. The author of 'Pet Prisoners' speaks less in the tones of the Howard League than in those of our bluff contemporary Sir Walter Bromley-Davenport, MP, who recently deplored the cost of keeping boys at Borstal and suggested that 'instead of paying these moronic beatniks a pension, mostly in excess of the wages received by many who have to work hard for their living, a more appropriate treatment would be a diet of bread and water, accompanied with regular doses of corporal punishment'.[79]

Sir Walter, no doubt, speaks as the Mr Popular Sentiment of 1961 on this matter. But popular sentiment, when it remembers Dickens, classes him with the great reformers, and cannot be blamed for doing so if contributors to learned journals make the same mistake. Dickens's posthumous reputation, as a man and as a reformer, has been less subject than most to the rule that 'The evil that men do lives after them, The good is oft interred with their bones'. A few years ago, *The News of the World* was protesting the wretched conditions in Pentonville, and it invoked the spirit of Dickens. Can the regime inevitable in that ancient and over-crowded prison possibly build up hope and self-respect in the prisoners? it asked. 'Or does it breed more hate, more bitterness towards society and its laws? I think Charles Dickens would have known the answer. But Dickens is dead. And Pentonville — already condemned before the war — is still allowed to live.'[80] Dickens, as we saw, resented the cost of Pentonville — and he and his generation had more right to resent the cost of prisons than has our more affluent age. In six years of the 'Hungry Forties', fifty-four new prisons on the Pentonville plan were built: by contrast, the Home Office has managed to build four since 1877, when it assumed full responsibility for prison-administration.[81] One was completed in 1958 — the first since 1910 — but now another is being built, and again, curiously enough, Dickens was invoked as its patron. For the place chosen is Blundeston, in Suffolk, the re-puted birthplace of David Copperfield, so the local opposition which is to be expected wherever a new prison is proposed was here reinforced by cries that a 'national literary shrine' was being desecrated. A local Joint Planning Committee decided to oppose the plan, but one of its members argued that Dickens would be 'the first man to be delighted to see the prison', and another maintained that 'if Dickens were alive today he would say, great humanitarian that he was, that he had no objection to the building of a new prison in any place where he lived or with which he had associa-tions'.[82] A century in the grave may of course have altered his opinions: if not, one can all too easily predict how apoplectic would have been his opinions on this proposal to spend half a million pounds on housing malefactors. It is pleasant, however, if ironical, that his reputation is still available to good causes, even those which he had never tended to support.

The irony is heightened if one holds, as I do, that he had never visited Blundeston anyway. (He stated that he took the name of this village from a signpost — nothing more.)[83] He is, in fact, one of those writers whose works have so appealed to the popular imagination that, like a popular monarch's, their memory has been honoured (and plagued) by myths. Dickens, like Queen Elizabeth I, is credited with many visits he never made — and with opinions he never held. Conan Doyle is another such: the Baker Street Irregulars lovingly reconstruct Sherlock Holmes's life at No 221B, despite his creator's confession that he had never been in Baker Street in his life, or, if he had, he had forgotten it.[84] Such activities, if sub-literary, provide much harmless pleasure, and demonstrate the very special affection which their subjects have inspired. Dickens earned this affection largely by his manifest benevolence towards the lowly, the oppressed, the sick and deformed and unfortunate. But he did not strain his readers' sympathies or understandings by asking for any unusual good-will towards criminals. Only in a few special cases, such as Nancy and Magwitch, where the offences are not heinous and the criminal proves to have a heart of gold, are we expected to forgive and forget. By the same token, however, Dickens avoids the not-uncommon literary irresponsibility of condoning crimes which, being confined within the covers of a book, can be forgiven by a very painless exercise of charity. He supports and firmly enforces the average man's sense of justice, in all its strengths and weaknesses, while at the same time providing the thrills of crime in which the average man wishes vicariously to indulge. Thus, murder remains, for him, in the first place a very wicked deed: only in the second place is it the product of an interesting abnormality of mind and circumstance: and never is this abnormality more pitiable than reprehensible.

A further illustration of the paradox of his influence occurred to me recently, when I addressed the Dickens Fellowship on the subject of this book. Aware that I was here speaking to sworn Dickens-lovers, mainly ladies of a most kindly disposition (and of a certain age), I prefaced my talk by apologising for the fact that I would be exposing some of the less worthy sides of the Master. I need not have troubled. After my lecture, my chairman — one of Her Majesty's Judges, and a very amiable old gentleman — defended hanging and flogging in decidedly forthright terms, which evoked a spontaneous warmth of applause that had greeted none of my remarks. Yet this audience would have been more sympathetic and generous than most, if appealed to on behalf of crippled children, or the many other derelicts who touched Dickens's heart. These ladies hardly deserved the description offered me by a male Dickensian in the audience — 'the Mesdames Defarge of the Dickens Fellowship' — but, in them as in Dickens, a generally charitable nature could co-exist with an unpleasantly vindictive heat towards criminals. Perhaps, indeed, one expects too much from Dickens, and from Dickensians. In his own day he had suffered, as clergymen do, from people's expecting him always to display a superhuman generosity. One of the reasons why he disliked owning land, he said, was that it 'seems to put a public man of my notoriety — with a good-natured reputation — at a disadvantage with tenants'.[85]

'Mischievous Reactionary Influences — Charles Dickens:' so runs a section-heading in a book on *Penological and Preventive Principles* (1896) by the Secretary of the Howard Association.[86] It is one of the ironies of Dickens's reputation as a penologist that he was here being attacked again for his most praiseworthy comment on prisons, the Philadelphia chapter in *American Notes*. Only a few obscure specialists, such as the Reverend John Clay and his son, perceived the respects in which he was indeed a mischievous reactionary influence. The Carlyles and Kingsleys thought him softhearted (which they deplored), while later generations of writers, in *The News of the World*, in the learned American journal, and in most textbooks of penal history, have also attributed to him (but have applauded) a measure of charity which he did not possess. His change of mind on some important issues has neither been welcomed nor regretted, for it has passed unnoticed. The presentations of the criminal mind in his novels were at first relished, or dismissed, as standard melodramatics, but have lately been highly respected — though, I have argued, the revaluation has been largely based on a misreading of the crucial and climactic specimen, John Jasper. So both the literary and the social judgments on this area of his work have, in my opinion, been a good deal mistaken: Dickens has been praised where he little deserves it, and criticised where he displays insight and good sense. Whether I am right or wrong, I have put forward the evidence, not all of it well-known, which should help other critics and historians to arrive at judgments more securely based upon the facts.

NOTES

The following abbreviations are used for the titles of books by Dickens:

AN	*American Notes*	*MC*	*Martin Chuzzlewit*
BH	*Bleak House*	*NN*	*Nicholas Nickleby*
BR	*Barnaby Rudge*	*OCS*	*The Old Curiosity Shop*
CB	*Christmas Books*	*OMF*	*Our Mutual Friend*
CS	*Christmas Stories*	*OT*	*Oliver Twist*
DC	*David Copperfield*	*PP*	*Pickwick Papers*
D & S	*Dombey and Son*	*RP*	*Reprinted Pieces*
ED	*The Mystery of Edwin Drood*	*SB*	*Sketches by Boz*
GE	*Great Expectations*	*TTC*	*A Tale of Two Cities*
HT	*Hard Times*	*UT*	*The Uncommercial Traveller*
LD	*Little Dorrit*		

All these works are cited in the *New Oxford Illustrated Dickens* edition (1947–58), and are followed by a reference to chapter and page-number, or to book, chapter and page-number. This edition does not include his letters and speeches, nor all his journalism. For these writings, the following editions have been used and are cited by these abbreviations:

AYR	*All the Year Round*, 1859–70
Coutts	*Letters from Charles Dickens to Angela Burdett-Coutts 1841–1865*, ed Edgar Johnson, 1953
CP	*Collected Papers*, Biographical Edition of the Works of Charles Dickens, 1905
HN	*The Household Narrative of Current Events*, 1850–5
HW	*Household Words*, 1850–9
MP	*Miscellaneous Papers*, Biographical Edition, 1908
Mr and Mrs	*Mr and Mrs Charles Dickens: His Letters to Her*, ed Walter Dexter, 1935
N	*The Letters of Charles Dickens*, ed Walter Dexter, 3 vols, Nonesuch Press, 1938
Speeches	*The Speeches of Charles Dickens*, ed K. J. Fielding, Oxford, 1960

For journals frequently cited, the following abbreviations are used:

Dick	*The Dickensian*
E & S	*Essays and Studies*
HLQ	*Huntington Library Quarterly*
N & Q	*Notes and Queries*
NCF	*Nineteenth Century Fiction*
PMLA	*Publications of the Modern Language Association of America*
RES	*Review of English Studies*
RSUM	*Ragged School Union Magazine*

CHAPTER I: DICKENS AND HIS AGE

1. Sala, *Things I have seen*, i, 76.
2. Wilkie Collins, 23 September 1867, *N*, iii, 542. The resultant story was *No Thoroughfare*, published in *AYR* (Christmas 1867). It proved a great hit on the stage, with Dickens's friend Fechter in the villain's role; see T. E. Pemberton, *Charles Dickens and the Stage*, 1888, 89–93, on Dickens's contribution to this dramatic version.

3. Speech at the proroguing of Parliament, 17 July 1837, quoted by Munford, *William Ewart*, 91.

4. *Parliamentary Debates*, 1810, xv, col 366, quoted by Radzinowicz, *A History of Criminal Law and its Administration from 1750*, i, 3; House of Commons, 1 April 1830, quoted by Koestler, *Reflections on Hanging*, 13.

5. Radzinowicz, i, 143–4.

6. Ibid, 152.

7. Clay, *The Prison Chaplain*, 310.

8. *Morning Herald*, 28 September 1810, quoted by Armitage, *History of the Bow Street Runners*, 177–80.

9. *OED* cites Lieber, *Essay on Criminal Law*, 1838 for 'penology' (and an English writer felt it necessary to explain Professor Lieber's new word, in 1845 — see Adshead, *Prisons and Prisoners*, vi, note). For 'criminology', *OED* cites *The Athenæum*, 6 September 1890, but Grünhut notes an English usage of it in 1885 (*Penal Reform*, 98).

10. R. and F. Hill, *The Recorder of Birmingham*, 152.

11. See S. and B. Webb, *English Prisons under Local Government*, 73–5, 53.

12. Dixon, *The London Prisons*, 390; Field, *Prison Discipline*, i, 73.

13. Reith, *British Police and the Democratic Ideal*, 18.

14. Beggs, *Juvenile Depravity*, 181, 4; David Stow, *The Training System*, 10th edn, 1854, v; Dixon, *The London Prisons*, epigraph (quoted from *The Athenæum*).

15. See Terence Morris, *The Criminal Area: a Study in Social Ecology*, 1958, Chapter iii, 'Some Ecological Studies of the 19th Century.'

16. Frederic Hill, *Crime: its Amount, Causes, and Remedies*, 34.

17. Kingsmill, *Prisons and Prisoners*, 1st edn, 1849, 153. Cf Young and Ashton, *British Social Work in the Nineteenth Century*, Chapter ix, 'The Penal Services', and Gordon Rose, *The Struggle for Penal Reform*, 1961, Chapters i and ii.

18. Savey-Casard, *Le Crime et la Peine dans l'œuvre de Victor Hugo*, 11–13; cf pp 277–85 on the penological debate and its literary products in America, France and Britain. On the rise of the detective-story in these three countries about the same period, see Murch, *The Development of the Detective Novel*. On Dickens and Dostoyevsky, see Ford, *Dickens and his Readers*, 190–8; George Katkov, 'Steerforth and Stavrogin', *Slavonic and East European Review*, xxvii (1949), 469–88; and, in controversy with Katkov, Michael H. Futrell, 'Dostoyevsky and Dickens', *English Miscellany*, vii (1956), 41–89.

19. See my essay 'The Significance of Dickens's Periodicals', *Review of English Literature*, II (1961), 55–64.

20. *Edinburgh Review*, lxxii (1843), 511–12; Forster, *Life of Dickens*, 132; *Charles Dickens' Prison Fiction*, issued by the Howard Association: a Paper prepared by the Secretary of the Howard Association, at the request of the Pennsylvania Prison Society, 1894, 1.

21. *HW*, 1 January 1853 (*MP*, 363).

22. Forster, 11.

23. Wilson, *The Wound and the Bow*, 13, 92.

24. Dickens's novels were all, of course, serialised, generally in twenty monthly instalments (the last two being published together as a double number), though some appeared weekly or over longer or shorter periods.

25. Introduction, *OT*, New Oxford Illustrated Edition, 1949, reprinted in *All in Due Time*, 196.

26. Ibid, 183, 189.

27. Orwell, *Critical Essays*, 29.

28. *GE*, xxxii, 246. See Mary Edminson, 'The Date of the Action of *Great Expectations*', *NCF*, xiii (1958), 22–35. Dickens, like many people, wavers between the two spellings, *jail* and *gaol*. I have adopted the latter throughout.

29. *HT*, I, xi, 70.
30. Forster, 25 August 1859, *N*, III, 118; 'Lying Awake', *HW*, 30 October 1852 (*RP*, 437); 'The Ruffian', *AYR*, 10 October 1868 (*UT*, 302).
31. Grünhut, *Penal Reform*, 131–2.
32. *Punch*, 16 March 1850, XVIII, 107; *Athenæum* quoted by Dodds, *The Age of Paradox*, 400; *Henry Crabb Robinson on Books and their Writers*, ed E. J. Morley, 1938, II, 695.
33. J. A. Froude, *Thomas Carlyle: a History of his Life in London*, 1884, II, 30. Cf Spielmann, *The History of 'Punch'*, 111–12: of course *Punch* made some mistakes in its early years, he says — and he adduces as an example this dismissal of 'Model Prisons'. See below, pp 76, 155–8, for further details of 'Model Prisons' and of Dickens's reaction to it.
34. Quoted by Grünhut, 49–52. D. L. Howard, *The English Prisons*, Chapters III and VI, discusses the Panopticon project, with illustrations.
35. John Morley, *Life of Cobden* (1879), 1903 edn, 90–2. Cf Dicey, *Law and Public Opinion*, 111–25, on the legislative excitement of the 1830s.
36. Fox, *English Prison and Borstal Systems*, 46; Report of the Select Committee . . . , *Parliamentary Papers*, 1863, IX, iv–vii, 41. A useful selection of extracts from this Report is reprinted in Appendix C of Fox's book.
37. Ruggles-Brise, *The English Prison System*, 42–4; Ives, *A History of Penal Methods*, 202.
38. Fox, 51.
39. Chapter XXXII of *GE*, from which this quotation comes, was first published in *AYR*, 13 April 1861. The Chatham riots — the last important prison disturbance of the century — began on 8 February (see Griffiths, *Secrets of the Prison-house*, I, 148–19, and *Illustrated London News*, 9 March 1861, XXXVIII, 218–19).
40. Griffiths, *Fifty Years of Public Service*, 175–6 (see pp 158–91 for his full account of Chatham Prison); Ives, 206; D. L. Howard, 103. Chatham, it should be added, was the most dreaded of English prisons during the next few decades (Cook, *Prisons of the World*, 38, 45, 120–3).
41. Dolby, *Dickens as I knew him*, 221–5.
42. *Parliamentary Debates*, House of Commons, 1910, XIX, col 1354.
43. Report in *The Guardian*, 12 August 1960.
44. Fielding, *Charles Dickens: a Critical Introduction*, 154.
45. Gladys Storey, *Dickens and Daughter*, 91, 219.
46. Forster, 671.
47. Dolby, 442.
48. House, *All in Due Time*, 195–6.

CHAPTER II: NEWGATE

1. Letters to Macrone, October 1835 to January 1836, *N*, I, 47, 53, 56, 61; George Hogarth's review in *Morning Chronicle*, 11 February 1836 (I owe this reference to Mr W. J. Carlton).
2. *Newgate by Charles Dickens: to which are added some Curious Facts relating to the Prison and its Prisoners*, C. H. Ross's Penny Library, ND [*c* 1880].
3. *PP*, XLV, 645.
4. On the writing of *BR*, see Butt and Tillotson, *Dickens at Work*, 76–9.
5. Forster, 808; Fildes, reported in William R. Hughes's *A Week's Tramp in Dickens-Land*, 1891, 140–1.
6. *OCS*, LXI, 545; *BH*, LII, 703; *GE*, XXXII, 246–9.
7. *The Bastille Prisoner*, a Reading from *A Tale of Two Cities*, in Three Chapters, privately printed, 1866. On the prison-image in *LD*, see Lionel Trilling's Introduction to the New Oxford Illustrated Edition (reprinted in *The Opposing Self*, 1955), and Wilson, 46–51. A. O. J. Cockshut writes well on this theme in *The Imagination of Charles Dickens*, 1961: see particularly Chapter III, 'The Expanding Prison'.

8. Teeters and Shearer, *The Prison at Philadelphia*, 114.
9. 'Crime and Education', *Daily News*, 4 February 1846 (*MP*, 18).
10. 'Perfect Felicity . . .', *HW*, 6 April 1850 (*MP*, 186–7).
11. *SB*, 202.
12. On Dickens's reading, see Chapter 1 of my *Dickens and Education*.
13. *Catalogue of the Library of Charles Dickens at Gad's-hill*, ed J. H. Stonehouse, 1935; Georgina Hogarth, 29 July 1857, *N*, 11, 864.
14. See Henry Fielding, *Joseph Andrews* (1742), IV, v; *Tom Jones* (1749), XVI, x, *et seq*; *Amelia* (1751), I, ii, *et seq*, and VIII, i, *et seq*; *Voyage to Lisbon* (1754), Introduction. Tobias Smollett, *Peregrine Pickle* (1751), XLV–XLVI, XCVII–CIV: *Humphry Clinker* (1771), letters of 12–23 June. Oliver Goldsmith, *The Vicar of Wakefield* (1766), XXV–XXXI, *Citizen of the World* (1762), LXXX.
15. Macrone, 17 June 1836, 9 December 1835, *N*, 1, 83, 56. The date 17 June 1836 is provided from the forthcoming *Pilgrim Edition of the Letters*, from which I have silently adopted datings for a few other early letters where Nonesuch gives an inexact or wrong date.
16. *NN*, IV, 29. The same perception appears in the opening paragraph of 'A Visit to Newgate' (*SB*, 201).
17. Mayhew and Binny, *The Criminal Prisons of London*, 276.
18. *GE*, XXXII, 246.
19. *BR*, XLIX, 374.
20. *TTC*, II, ii, 56.
21. Wakefield, *Facts*, iv, 16.
22. 'Report of the Select Committee of the House of Lords into the Present State of Gaols and Houses of Correction', *Parliamentary Papers*, 1835, XI, 314.
23. *Parliamentary Papers*, 1836, XXXV, 69–70, 77–80.
24. Dixon, *London Prisons*, 209–13.
25. 5 November 1835, *Mr and Mrs*, 34–5. The 'House of Correction' is Coldbath Fields Prison.
26. This and the following quotations come, unless otherwise noted, from 'A Visit to Newgate', *SB*, 201–14.
27. Butt and Tillotson, 63.
28. 'Criminal Courts', *SB*, 197; Macrone, 9 December 1835, *N*, 1, 56; cf. W. J. Carlton, 'The Third Man at Newgate', which gives interesting information on the background to the 1835 visit to Newgate. Elizabeth Fry was still alive in 1835 of course, but (as Mr Graham Storey tells me) she was in Norfolk on the day Dickens visited Newgate with Macrone.
29. Wakefield, *Facts*, 178–9, partially quoted by Dickens (*MP*, 28).
29a. G. H. Lewes, 'Dickens in Relation to Criticism', *Fortnightly Review*, NS, XI (1872), 151–2. Cf. Forster, 347, on Carlyle's influence on the early Dickens.
30. *SB*, 199–200; *OT*, XLIII, 333–6.
31. On Urania Cottage, see below, Chapter IV; and on Ragged Schools and the need for State intervention in education, see my forthcoming book *Dickens and Education*, Chapter IV.
32. Carlton, op cit, 406.
33. James Boswell, *Life of Johnson*, 19 September 1777.
34. *The Last Days of a Condemned*, from the French of M Victor Hugo, with Observations on Capital Punishment, by Sir P. Hesketh Fleetwood, MP, London, 1840, 1. (The French original was published in 1829.) George Hogarth noted in his review of *SB* (*Morning Chronicle*, 11 February 1836) the similarity of idea between this piece by Hugo and 'A Visit to Newgate', but added: '. . . there is a certain artificial and exaggerated air — a sort of French *tournure* — in Victor Hugo's description, from which that of our countryman is free; and being equally eloquent and more simple, it is even more pathetic and impressive than the celebrated passage to

which it may be compared . . .' See Walter Dexter, 'The Reception of Dickens's First Book', *Dick*, xxxii (1936), 43-50.

35. This and the following quotations come from *OT*, lii, 404-11.

36. Letters to Ainsworth and Forster, [1837], *N*, i, 131-2; Macready, *Diaries*, i, 401; Forster, 132, 453 note, 749. But see below, p 352, on the murderer in 'Hunted Down'.

37. *GE*, xxxii, 246, 250; xx, 155.

38. Wilson, 18.

39. Butt and Tillotson, 76-8.

40. Forster, 168; 'Wilkie Collins about Charles Dickens', *Pall Mall Gazette*, 20 January 1890.

41. *BR*, xxxviii, 288; Butt and Tillotson, 86; H. F. Folland, 'The Doer and the Deed: Theme and Pattern in *Barnaby Rudge*', *PMLA*, lxxiv (1959), 409.

42. Forster, 169.

43. Ollier, 3 June 1841, *N*, i, 324.

44. 'The Perils of Certain English Prisoners,' i (*CS*, 179).

45. *Coutts*, 350.

46. G. H. Ford, 'The Governor Eyre Case in England,' *University of Toronto Quarterly*, xvii (1948), 227. On Dickens's emotional patterns, political behaviour, and literary response in relation to inter-racial problems, see also K. J. Fielding, '*Edwin Drood* and Governor Eyre', *The Listener*, 25 December 1952, 1083-4, and A. A. Adrian, 'Dickens on American Slavery: a Carlylean Slant,' *PMLA*, lxvii (1952), 315-29. Professor Adrian's article shows a development in Dickens's attitude to negro slavery, from indignation to acceptance, which may usefully be compared with the hardening of his attitude towards criminals and prison-discipline.

47. *BR*, lviii, 442.

48. lxxiii, 558.

49. li, 387.

50. lxv, 499.

51. lxx, 537.

52. lxv, 503.

53. lxix, 534.

54. lxxvii, 597.

55. Folland, 407-8. I do not, however, think that Dickens works out this theme as coherently or as consciously as Dr Folland suggests.

56. lxiv, 488, 490.

57. lxiv, 491.

58. lxiv, 492.

59. lxv, 497.

60. Butt and Tillotson, 85; see *BR*, lxviii, 525-6. On this theme see Cockshut, *Imagination of Dickens*, Chapter v, 'Crowds and Justice'.

61. lx, 462.

62. Butt and Tillotson, 85.

63. *NN*, lxiv, 827.

64. *BR*, lxv, 498.

65. lxvii, 513.

66. *TTC*, iii, xii, 325.

67. *AN*, vii, 102; Teeters and Shearer, 119-21.

CHAPTER III:
THE SILENT SYSTEM — COLDBATH FIELDS PRISON

1. Macrone, 9 December 1835, *N*, i, 56. In another *Sketch* he does mention his visit to Coldbath Fields, 'to witness the operation of the silent system' ('The Last Cab-Driver', *SB*, 146).

2. Forster, 234.

3. *AN*, 1842 edn, I, 121 note (Cheap Edn, 1850, 35: omitted in most modern reprints); 'Crime and Education', *Daily News*, 4 February 1846 (*MP*, 18). Dickens sent the *AN* passage to Chesterton, for his approval (11 September 1842, *N*, I, 476): also to Tracey, on the same day (*Catalogue of the Dickens Collection at the University of Texas*, ed Sister Mary Callista Carr, 4, item A21).

4. See 'The Devil's Acre' (by Alexander Mackay), *HW*, I, 297; on Clerkenwell, see Hepworth Dixon, *The London Prisons*, 224–8.

5. On the history of these prisons, and for a full illustrated description of them in the 1850s, see Mayhew and Binny, *Criminal Prisons*, 277–486. On Coldbath Fields, see also G. L. Chesterton's *Peace, War and Adventure*, 1853, and *Revelations of Prison Life*, 1856 (henceforth cited as *PWA* and *RPL*).

6. See M. W. Patterson, *Sir Francis Burdett and his Times*, 1931, Vol I, Chapter IV.

7. Dr Lushington, *Hansard*, 28 February 1828, quoted by S. and B. Webb, 106.

8. *PWA*, II, 241–2. On Chesterton's earlier life, see *PWA* and his *Narrative of Proceedings in Venezuela . . .*, 1820, summarised more fully than here in my article 'Dickens and the Prison Governor: G. L. Chesterton', *Dick*, LVII (1961), 11–26. Much material from this article is used in the present chapter. Captain Chesterton was a forebear of G. K. Chesterton: for family memories of him, see G. K. Chesterton, *Autobiography*, 1936, 20; Maisie Ward, *G. K. Chesterton*, 1944, 8; Mrs Cecil Chesterton, *The Chestertons*, 1941, 40.

9. *RPL*, I, 23.

10. *PWA*, II, 247–50.

11. Ibid, 246.

12. Lytton, *Paul Clifford* (1830), end of Chapter VIII, footnote. Chesterton records that Lytton wrote him a very flattering letter at the time, and incorporated some information about the prison in his novel (*RPL*, I, 147).

13. Susanna Corder, *Life of Elizabeth Fry*, 1853, 216; *PWA*, II, 325. See below, pp 62–3, for an account of Elizabeth Fry's visiting Coldbath Fields in 1842.

14. *RPL*, I, 3.

15. Clay, *Prison Chaplain*, 86 note.

16. S. and B. Webb, 77.

17. *Quarterly Review*, XCII (1853), 487–8. For another classification of the 'systems', see Hepworth Dixon, 11: there were now, he said, in 1850, five main systems operated or advocated in Britain, and he named their chief exemplars — 'the City system, or no system' at Newgate and elsewhere; the Separate System (Pentonville, Reading and Wakefield); the Silent System (Coldbath Fields, Tothill Fields, and the Manchester New Bailey); the Mixed System (Millbank, Preston); and the Marks System (still existing only on paper).

18. The American and English versions of the Separate System, and Dickens's opinion of them, are described more fully below, in Chapters V and VI.

19. Quoted by H. E. Barnes, *The Evolution of Penology in Pennsylvania*, 174.

20. Ruggles-Brise, *English Prison System*, ix; Dixon, 154. Cf also the semi-Marxist interpretation of this battle of the systems, in Rusche and Kirchheimer, *Punishment and Social Structure* — their thesis being that 'Every system of production tends to discover punishments which correspond to its production relationships' (p 5, cf pp 128–31).

21. *RPL*, I, 302; II, 1, 27; Mayhew and Binny, 290.

22. Griffiths, *Millbank*, 150.

23. *Parliamentary Papers*, 1838, xxx, 37; 1837, xxxII, 1, 73. There are lengthy quotations from these Reports, on Coldbath Fields, in S. and B. Webb, 122–5, 147–8.

24. Adshead, *Prisons and Prisoners*, 1845, 193 note.

25. *RPL*, II, 27, 39.

26. *Parliamentary Papers*, 1850, xvII, question 5095.

27. *RPL*, I, 156-8.
28. *Parliamentary Papers*, 1837, XXXII, 94. A long illustrated account of the treadwheel drill at Coldbath Fields appears in Mayhew and Binny, 303-8.
29. *Punch*, 6 February 1847 (XII, 59).
30. Mayhew and Binny, 309.
31. Ibid, 282.
32. Mayhew, *London Labour and the London Poor*, IV (1862), 320-1.
33. Caroline Fox, *Memories of Old Friends*, 1883, 204.
34. *Parliamentary Papers*, 1850, XVII, questions 5077, 8529, 8537, 8547; Mayhew and Binny, 324 (and cf pp 409, 431, 469-70, on the extreme severity of the Middlesex prisons). Mayhew and Binny's book was not published until 1862, but the material for Mayhew's chapters, in which these references occur, was collected in the 1850s.
35. Ives, *Penal Methods*, 187.
36. Caroline Fox, 204.
37. *House of Correction, Cold Bath Fields: Report of the Visiting Magistrates* (henceforth cited as *CBF Reports*), Michaelmas 1847, 17. These *Reports*, and many other papers about the prison, are available at the Middlesex County Record Office.
38. This was the Rev. Edward Illingworth, Chaplain at Coldbath Fields 1839-72; see Dickens's *Letters to Angela Burdett Coutts*, passim. The editor's surmise there (p 139 note) as to Illingworth's identity is incorrect. Dickens also admired the Tothill Fields chaplain (Carr, *Texas Collection Catalogue*, 8, item A44).
39. Dixon, 243; Mayhew and Binny, 285; cf *Parliamentary Papers*, 1837, XXXII, 7, and Kingsmill, *Prisons and Prisoners*, 43-4. Dixon and Mayhew probably knew Chesterton socially, as a fellow-member of the Museum Club and of Our Club (David Masson, *Memories of London in the 'Forties*, 1908, 213, 224).
40. Dixon, 246-7. The buildings were inconvenient, in that they contained only 550 separate cells, though the official capacity of the prison was 1,250, and the actual population sometimes over 1,400. Most prisoners had to sleep, therefore, in dormitories, with officers present all night vainly trying to prevent their whispering to one another.
41. *PWA*, II, 323.
42. *RPL*, II, 127-30.
43. Carlyle, *Latter Day Pamphlets*, 1869 edn, 69-70.
44. *RPL*, II, 9-10, 26.
45. Dixon, 254-5; Mayhew and Binny, 421. For evidence of Dickens's close personal friendship with Tracey, see the letters listed and summarised by Carr, 3-11.
46. Quoted by D. L. Howard, *English Prisons*, 86.
47. See Barry, *Alexander Maconochie*, 196-207.
48. Cf Macready's *Diaries*, I, 401, and II, 76, for mentions of Dickens's visits to Coldbath Fields in 1837 and 1840.
49. See below, Chapter IV.
50. *Coutts*, 80, 26 May 1846.
51. Ibid, 89, 96.
52. Dixon, 241-2.
53. *CBF Reports* (Michaelmas 1849, 21, and Michaelmas 1850, 28) show that in these two years nine and eight Coldbath Fields girls entered the Home. Its total capacity was thirteen.
54. *RPL*, II, 184-7. See below, pp 98-9, for Chesterton's remarks on recruiting girls for Urania Cottage.
55. See below, pp 162-3.
56. For particulars of this episode, see *RPL*, II, 191-203; *CBF Reports*, January, 1847, 7, and Michaelmas 1848, 7; and Rotch's letter about the 'wicked crusade' against him, printed in Beggs, *Juvenile Depravity*, 1849, 179. A fuller assessment of

Rotch and his quarrel with Dickens appears in my article 'The Middlesex Magistrate in *David Copperfield*', *N & Q*, NS, VIII (1961), 86-91.

57. *CBF Reports*, Michaelmas 1847, 12; Benjamin Rotch, *Suggestions for the Prevention of Juvenile Depravity*, Printed for Private Distribution only, 1846. A copy of this rare pamphlet is available in the London School of Economics Library. Miss A. M. Pollard, Head of Reference Services, Middlesex County Libraries, kindly drew my attention to this pamphlet and its whereabouts.

58. *CBF Reports*, Michaelmas 1848, 7. In 1847, however, the Magistrates' vote on a motion to abolish the treadmill for females had resulted in a tie (*Times*, 28 May 1847); the old guard was still strong.

59. Mayhew and Binny, 282.

60. *CBF Reports*, Michaelmas 1849, 7.

61. *Punch*, 17 February and 10 March 1849 (XVI, 68, 97); *Times*, 2 March 1849. Shortly before this, however, *Punch* was claiming that 'We are no advocates of harshness. It only hardens criminals; sending them away from a prison much worse than when they entered it' (16 September 1848, XV, 123).

62. *CBF Reports*, Michaelmas 1849, 7; 'Pet Prisoners', *HW*, 27 April 1850 (*MP*, 235).

63. Clay, 246.

64. Quoted by W. J. Pinks, *History of Clerkenwell*, 1880, 87-8.

65. *MP*, 235, 223-4, 234.

66. Wills, 10 March 1853, *N*, II, 453; 'In and Out of Jail', *HW*, 14 May 1853 (VII, 244-5), attributed in the Contributors Book to Dickens, Wills and Morley.

67. *BH*, XXXI, 434; *OMF*, III, viii, 505-6.

68. *Times*, 21 December 1842, 19 February 1849.

69. *Punch*, 20 January 1849 (XVI, 26), 18 January 1845 (VIII, 38). *The Pauper's Song*, which attracted some notice, was by Percival Leigh (Spielmann, *History of 'Punch'*, 301).

70. Quoted by Cook, *Prisons of the World*, 34; Pearl, *Girl with the Swansdown Seat*, 57.

71. Dodds, *Age of Paradox*, 11-12; *Illustrated London News*, 16 December 1843 (III, 387); Field, *Prison Discipline*, 1848, I, 206 note.

72. This quotation comes from Morley's 'In and Out of Jail' (*HW*, VII, 244), the original draft of which Dickens had vetted and insisted on having amended.

73. *Parliamentary Papers*, 1864, XLIX, 556 *et seq*, quoted by S. and B. Webb, 137-43.

74. Ibid, 88 note.

75. *Edinburgh Review*, C (1854), 570, 574.

76. Clay, 255, 263, 259; *HN*, September 1853 and August 1854 (IV, 206-7; v, 185-6).

77. *CBF Reports*, April 1851, 10-11.

78. Radzinowicz, I, 565 note, instancing Mackintosh and Peel; see also pp 565-6 for a brief history of the treadwheel, with bibliography. See also S. and B. Webb, 96-100.

79. Mayhew and Binny, 275 (and cf pp 242-3, 300-7). Cf Rusche and Kirchheimer, 112, on why the nineteenth century should have invented these useless machines.

80. Quoted by Lionel Fox, 429.

81. S. and B. Webb, 154.

82. Clay, 98; Mill, 'Prisons and Prison Discipline', 387, 390.

83. 'Prisons', *Edinburgh Review*, XXXVI (1822), 359, 374. Cf his similar article in the *Review* (1821) under the same title. For Carlyle on the treadwheel, see 'Model Prisons', *Latter Day Pamphlets*, 70.

84. For examples of the opinions quoted above, see Lytton, *Paul Clifford*, Chapter VIII; *Times*, 20 October 1842; S. and B. Webb, 147-9; Frederic Hill, 197; Clay, 111, 133; Dixon, 246, 255.

85. Field, I, 40 note, 164. Dickens's attack on Field occurs in 'Pet Prisoners' (*HW*, 27 April 1850).

86. Wills, 10 March 1853, *N*, II, 453-4.

87. *AN*, III, 50–1. American opposition to prison-produce did increase over the years some prisons certainly having invited trouble by engaging in trade on a very extensive scale and undercutting civilian prices (Griffiths, *Secrets of the Prison-House*, I, 447–51).

88. *AN*, III, 51.

89. Edmund Wilson, 55–6. See also Barbara Hardy, 'The Change of Heart in Dickens's Novels', *Victorian Studies*, v (1961), 49–67.

90. *LD*, I, xi, 127. (A Swiss pastor was selected as the spokesman for the wrong ideas presumably because he represented both religion and the Separate System which flourished in that country.) It is interesting to contrast with this passage a report of his conversation in 1840, on the eve of the Courvoisier hanging, which he witnessed (see below, p 224). His brother Fred had defended capital punishment, on the analogy that we destroy dangerous animals and that 'human' wild animals even more deserve death. Dickens is said to have replied, 'in a musing tone, and with his far-off look' — 'If there's any truth in phrenology, if physiology is in the least an index of the inward tendencies, there are unfortunate wretches born with murderous propensities. Given a large organ of destructiveness, with little benevolence and veneration; result: murderous proclivities. Add to this predestined nature, ignorance and want, and there stalks murder unrestrained, except by fear of the gallows. Self-defense and public safety demand that the unfortunate brutes should be exterminated, but I pity the poor brutes notwithstanding' (Eleanor E. Christian, 'Recollections of Charles Dickens', *Temple Bar*, LXXXII [1888], 500). As other evidence shows, Dickens more or less believed in phrenology, which was often invoked at this period with the quasi-deterministic implication that criminals deserved pity and not punishment.

91. *ED*, XX, 225.

92. 'The Ruffian', *AYR*, 10 October 1868 (*UT*, 302); K. J. Fielding, 'Charles Dickens and "The Ruffian" ', *English*, x (1954), 89–92. Cf articles by contributors in *AYR* — 'Incorrigible Rogues', VI, 471–3; 'Small-beer Chronicles', VIII, 111–15, 296–8, 421–3; 'Injured Innocents', NS, I, 414–18.

93. Wills, 10 March 1853, *N*, II, 453.

94. *Chimes*, III (*CB*, 133); *NN*, LIII, 693; *HW*, 14 December 1850 (*MP*, 280); 'The Last Words of the Old Year', *HW*, 4 January 1851 (*MP*, 286).

95. J. C. Parkinson, reported by Griffiths, *Secrets of the Prison-House*, II, 356; Griffiths relates Dickens's many utterances on this subject to the great Reformatory Schools movement of the 1850s.

96. *OT*, XXX, 217; XIX, 139.

97. *AN*, III, 55.

98. 'Home for Homeless Women', *HW*, 23 April 1853 (*MP*, 369).

99. Thomas Adolphus Trollope, *What I remember*, 1887, II, 115–16.

100. *Charles Kingsley: his Letters and Memories of his Life*, by his Wife, 1881 edn, II, 214–15; Sir Charles Gavan Duffy, *Conversations with Carlyle*, 1892, 75.

101. House, *The Dickens World*, 201 note.

102. *Speeches*, ed K. J. Fielding, xix, xxiii.

103. *GE*, XL, 311; XLII, 328.

104. *OT*, XL, 302.

105. Dolby, *Charles Dickens as I knew him*, 68.

CHAPTER IV: THE HOME FOR HOMELESS WOMEN

1. *Amberley Papers*, ed Bertrand Russell, 1937, II, 117.

2. Cf Houghton, *Victorian Frame of Mind*, 366. Professor Houghton's pages on 'Sex' in the Victorian outlook (pp 353–72) have helped me in these introductory paragraphs; also Cyril Pearl's *The Girl with the Swansdown Seat*, 1955, a diverting

but instructive book. See also 'Fallen Women', Chapters XVI–XIX of James Green-wood's *The Seven Curses of London*, 1869, and Young and Ashton, *British Social Work in the Nineteenth Century*, Chapter XI, 'Moral Welfare'.

3. E. M. Forster, *Galsworthy Lowes Dickinson*, 1934, 28; Viola Hunt, *The Wife of Rossetti*, 1932, 12 (quoted by Patricia Thomson, *The Victorian Heroine*, 136).

4. See Peter Quennell on Holman Hunt's famous picture 'The Awakened Conscience', and the influence of 'an underlying sense of guilt' about sex and prostitution on Victorian painting and literature (Introduction to Mayhew, *London's Underworld*, ND). Some examples from fiction are listed and discussed by Patricia Thomson, *Victorian Heroine*, Chapters V and VI. An early example is the reformed prostitute Nancy Corbett in Marryat's *Snarleyyow, or the Dog Fiend* (1837). This novel may have some bearing upon *Oliver Twist*, begun in the same year (cf Walter Allen, *The English Novel*, 1954, 141–3).

5. *The Moonstone*, 1868, I, viii. Ablewhite's admirer Miss Clack clearly owes something to Mrs Jellyby and Mrs Pardiggle ('the glorious prospect of interference was opened up before me' — II, vii).

6. Acton, *Prostitution*, 175; Alvin Whitley, 'Thomas Hood and *The Times*', *TLS*, 17 May 1957. Whitley argues that Dickens's reference to the episode in his 'Threatening Letter to Thomas Hood' (*MP*, 8) suggested the poem to Hood, and notes that Dickens was 'overcome with emotion' on hearing it sung. See Dickens on the Thames as a grave for such girls ('Down with the Tide', *RP*, 169; 'Wapping Workhouse', *UT*, 19–20). Waterloo Bridge remains a favourite place for 'jumpers', mainly elderly prostitutes (*New Statesman*, 9 June 1961).

7. Acton, vi, 20, 52, 60; *London's Underworld*, 111–16; correspondence in *The Times*, 1858, quoted by Pearl, 58–66; Taine, *Notes on England*, 36.

8. The infanticide episode, in 1840, deeply moved him at the time, and was described at length, over twenty years later (Forster, 157; 'Some Recollections of Mortality', *UT*, 194–8). The New York episode was first discovered by Professor A. A. Adrian (*Georgina Hogarth and the Dickens Circle*, 1957, 114).

9. Cf House, *Dickens World*, 215–17. Professor Kathleen Tillotson, in her excellent discussion of the trammels of propriety for novelists in the 1840s, remarks that the 1867 Preface omits the phrase (*Novels of the Eighteen Forties*, 67 note). The 1850 Cheap Edition Preface had already done so. See also Mrs Tillotson's remarks on the progressive bowdlerisation of *OT*, and her comparison of Nancy to the prostitute in *SB*, 'The Pawnbroker's Shop' (*Essays and Studies*, 98–100).

10. Forster, 96; *OT*, Preface, xvii; cf *Women of the Streets*, ed C. H. Rolph, 1955, Chapter X, 'The Men they live with'.

11. *OT*, XLVI, 354; XLVII, 362; XL, 301.

12. *D & S*, LVIII, 826; LXI, 869. *Chimes* III, *Haunted Man* II (*CB*, 127, 136–7, 366). On the falsity of the 'fallen woman' theme in *D & S* see Cockshut, 105–7.

13. *DC*, XLVII, 681, 686; LI, 729.

14. Forster, 23 January 1850, 536; de Cerjat, 29 December 1849, *N*, II, 194. At least one authentic instance of the Emily episode's having 'done some good' has been recorded: a fisherman's niece, describing herself as 'a fallen one', wrote to Bransby Williams, to say that his stage-impersonation of Mr Peggotty, grief-stricken after Emily's flight, had made her decide to return to her uncle (*Dick*, I [1905], 30).

15. *Coutts*, 165, 4 February 1850; 'Appeal' reprinted, 98–100.

16. 'Home for Homeless Women', *HW*, 23 April 1853 (*MP*, 369); Chesterton, *RPL*, II, 184–6. Chesterton and Tracey had urged early in 1848 that 'some girls who have not been tried and imprisoned' be admitted to the Home (*Coutts*, 116).

17. Chesterton, *RPL*, II, 184; *Coutts*, 110, 29 December 1847. For Miss Coutts's views on dress — on which she solicited and obtained the support of the prison-governors, Chesterton and Tracey — see *A Summary Account of Prizes for Common Things offered and awarded by Miss Burdett Coutts at the Whitelands Training Institution*, 1860 edn

(with Preface by her, and Appendix containing letters from Chesterton and Tracey on 'the baneful effects resulting from an inordinate fondness or love of dress' — the feminine equivalent of the Bottle, as an agent of moral downfall, according to Tracey).

18. The chaplain was Illingworth (see above, p 63). The other clergymen were William Tennant, of St Stephen's, Westminster, and John Sinclair, Archdeacon of Middlesex. Another, unidentified, member of the Committee was William T. Dyer (*Coutts*, 329).

19. See above, p 67.

20. *Coutts*, 82, 26 May 1846. He was right about Paris. Acton, for example, had gone there for his study of prostitution and female diseases.

21. R. H. Horne, 'Charles Dickens', *A New Spirit of the Age*, 52. The next few pages of this chapter are taken from my article, 'Dickens as a Social Worker', *Social Work*, xv (1958), 525–35.

22. *Coutts*, 85, 25 July 1846; 106, 3 November 1847; House, *All in Due Time*, 235; Forster, 571.

23. *Coutts*, 118, 121–2, 140 (1848–9). Dates of letters to Miss Coutts will not be given in forthcoming references, unless they are significant.

24. Ibid, 89.

25. Chesterton, 12 April 1852, *N*, ii, 387; *MP*, 374–5.

26. *Coutts*, 104, 169.

27. Ibid, 113, 187, 214, 153–5. Sarah Hyam's disgrace is recorded in the letter to Miss Coutts of 14 April 1858 (Morgan MSS).

28. Ayledotte, 'England of Marx and Mill', 56.

29. Coutts, 98, 105, 79. For the names of such Institutions, see, e.g., *The Metropolitan Reformatories and Refuges*, 1856, and *A Classified List of Reformatories . . . and Penitentiaries*, 1859 (both published by the Reformatory and Refuge Union).

30. Ibid, 97, 133, 102; *London's Underworld*, 92.

31. Ibid, 106, 328–9.

32. *MP*, 371; *Coutts*, 133, 94, 166; on music at Urania Cottage, see letters to Hullah, 12 December 1847, 19 September 1848 (*N*, ii, 63, 120), and *Coutts*, 107.

33. *MP*, 371; *Coutts*, 97, 80, 103, 139.

34. Cf *Coutts*, 142; Professor Johnson's footnote suggestion that Dickens was referring to the *discomfort* of emigrant ships clearly misses the point. Mrs Gaskell wrote to Dickens, 8 January 1850 (*Coutts*, 161), about the notorious 'chances of corruption' on such ships. See Wills's article 'Safety for Female Emigrants' (*HW*, 31 May 1851, iii, 228), and Dickens's letter to Wills about the 'discipline' of particular ships (*N*, ii, 337, 13 August 1851).

35. *Coutts*, 80.

36. Ibid, 127, 79, 212–13; *MP*, 373. It is curious to find the establishment of an 'Honours List' at a modern Approved School for Girls, considered to be an eventful novelty (Caroline Brown, *Lost Girls*, 1955, 134). Mrs Brown's book, concerning girls who would have been strong candidates for Urania Cottage, makes interesting reading as a comparison to Dickens's methods.

37. *Coutts*, 97, 102, 81; *MP*, 375. Henry Mayhew's collaborator names the fantasies favoured by such women: they all purported to be seduced governesses or clergymen's daughters (*London's Underworld*, 38).

38. Patricia Thomson, 121: *Coutts*, 98, 100; *TTC*, i, vi, 44.

39. *MP*, 375; *OMF*, ii, i, 214. (Straw-plaiting, it must be admitted, was practised not only by Little Margery, but also by the Urania Cottage girls: cf *MP*, 371). Cf his similar comment on the alleged innocence of the staff of the New York Refuge for the Destitute: 'A suspicion crossed my mind during of my inspection of this noble charity, whether the superintendent had quite sufficient knowledge of the world and worldly characters' (*AN*, vi, 95).

40. *MP*, 369, 381: Chesterton, *RPL*, II, 186; *Coutts*, 329.
41. This view of Dickens's later relationship with Miss Coutts is argued by Dr K. J. Fielding, against the opinion held by Professor Edgar Johnson at the time when he edited the Coutts correspondence (he tells me that he now agrees with Fielding's contentions). Cf note 49 to this chapter.
42. Charles C. Osborne, editor, *Letters of Dickens to Baroness Burdett-Coutts*, 1931, 175.
43. Una Pope-Hennessy, *Charles Dickens 1812–1870*, 27.
44. *BH*, xv, 204; xxx, 423; viii, 106–7; *ED*, vi, 52. John Jarndyce had more to say against self-important philanthropists in a passage cancelled in proof from Chapter viii (*Dick*, L [1954], 189).
45. *BH*, vi, 79; Houghton, 276.
46. *UT*, 305–7 (*AYR*, 10 October 1868). The episode has been discussed (to my profit) by K. J. Fielding, 'Charles Dickens and "The Ruffian" '.
47. *DC*, LI, 730; LXIII, 869.
48. *Coutts*, 85, 25 July 1846; 164, 4 February 1850.
49. Fielding, *Charles Dickens: a Critical Introduction*, 104; 'Dickens's Novels and Miss Burdett Coutts', *Dick*, LI (1944), 31–2. See his other articles, 'A Great Friendship' (a review of the Coutts letters), *Dick*, xLIX (1953), 102–7; 'Angela Burdett Coutts and the Victorians', ibid, 153–5; 'Miss Burdett Coutts: some Misconceptions', *NCF*, viii (1954), 314–18; 'Dickens and Miss Burdett Coutts: the Last Phase', *Dick*, LVII (1961), 97–105.
50. Cf Harry Stone, 'Dickens's Use of his American Experiences in *Martin Chuzzlewit*', *PMLA*, LXXII (1957), 464–78. Dr Stone usefully contrasts Dickens's letters home from America with the books, *AN* and *MC*, which draw on the same experiences.
51. *Coutts*, 225.

CHAPTER V: THE SEPARATE SYSTEM — PHILADELPHIA AND THE BASTILLE

1. Teeters and Shearer, *The Prison at Philadelphia: Cherry Hill*, 113.
2. Tellkampf, *Essays on Law Reform*, 276; Adshead, *Prisons and Prisoners*, 93.
3. S. and B. Webb, 177; Grünhut, 30, 47; cf Ives, 198.
4. Adshead, 96–9; Richard Vaux, *A Brief Sketch of the Origin and History of the State Penitentiary*, Philadelphia, 1872, 111, quoted by Teeters and Shearer, 114. Dickens's stay in Philadelphia was indeed very short: he arrived there in the late evening of Sunday 6 March, visited the Penitentiary on Tuesday, and left on Wednesday (William Glyde Wilkins, *Charles Dickens in America*, 1911, 152–9, 304).
5. Field, *Prison Discipline*, 1846, 93–7 (I, 105–8, in the two-volume 1848 edition, which Dickens used); 'Pet Prisoners', *HW*, 27 April 1850 (*MP*, 229 note).
6. Forster, 235–6. He had told his publishers, before leaving England, that he intended to keep a note-book about his visit, for subsequent publication (Forster, 22 September 1841, *N*, I, 354). 'I have looked over my journal,' he wrote in July, 'and have decided to produce my American trip in two volumes' (Felton, 31 July 1842, *N*, I, 471).
7. *AN*, vii, 99; D. C. Colden, 10 March 1842, *N*, I, 403.
8. Edgar Johnson, *Charles Dickens*, I, 441.
9. This and the following quotations come, unless otherwise stated, from *AN*, vii, 99–111. There is a book on *Dickens in Philadelphia* (1912), by Joseph Jackson, but I have been unable to locate a copy of it.
10. See Teeters and Shearer, 62–92, on the early history of the Penitentiary.
11. Gray, *Prison Discipline in America*, 1848, 46.
12. See Adshead, 99–118, and Teeters and Shearer, 115–32; and for their comments, quoted below, on the case of the German, see pp 101–2 and 118–22 respectively.
13. Teeters and Shearer, 195–6, 121–2.

14. Ibid, 114.
15. Adshead, 118–21, 186–93.
16. Adshead, 115; Teeters and Shearer, 131–2.
17. Lord Cockburn, *Life of Lord Jeffrey*, Edinburgh, 1852, ii, 373–4, quoting Jeffrey's letter to Dickens, 16 October 1842; Forster, 174.
18. Forster, 255.
19. John Stuart Mill, *Dissertations and Discussions*, 1875, ii, 2 (reprinted from *Edinburgh Review*, October 1840).
20. *PP*, xlv, 638.
21. See Harriet Martineau, *Society in America*, 1837, iii, 181–5; Frederika Bremer, *The Homes of the New World*, translated by Mary Howitt, 1853, ii, 8–10; [Thomas Hamilton], *Men and Manners in America*, by the Author of *Cyril Thornton*, Edinburgh, 1833, i, 346–56; Captain Frederick Marryat, *A Diary in America*, 1839, ii, 262–300. See also George Combe, *Notes on the United States*, Edinburgh, 1841, ii, 3–20 and *passim*, inclining to the Auburn system, though critical of both; and Francis C. Gray, *Prison Discipline in America*, a Bostonian attack on the Separate System, reprinted in London, 1848. For a general survey of the controversy, see Teeters and Shearer, Chapter vii, 'The Rise and Fall of the Pennsylvania System', and Barnes, *Evolution of Penology in Pennsylvania*, 174–8, with a useful bibliography of this Transatlantic debate. As Dickens later pointed out, the Pennsylvania system did not spread in America (*MP*, 234–5); on the brevity of other American experiments with the system, see Barnes and Teeters, *New Horizons in Criminology*, 344.
22. Forster, 235.
23. *Times*, 25 November 1843, 27 January 1844, 29 November 1843. Cf Adshead, 13–93, 'The Fallacies of *The Times*'.
24. Forster, 396, 422, 467 note.
25. Jebb, 29 February 1848, *HLQ*, v (1941), 127.
26. Forster, 236.
27. Ibid, 236; *AN*, vii, 101, 106.
28. *TTC*, i, iii, 12, 14.
29. Zabel, *Craft and Character in Modern Fiction*, 61.
30. *TTC*, i, vi, 42–8. This episode recalls Mr Dombey's salvation by his faithful daughter Florence, which Mrs Tillotson has already compared with the reunion between Lear and Cordelia (*Novels of the Eighteen-Forties*, 170). The Dickensian treatment, especially in *TTC*, even more resembles *Pericles* — but I would not assert that Dickens was 'influenced' by either play; if he was, *Lear* is much more likely. The comparison, I hardly need add, is very damaging to Dickens.
31. *AN*, vii, 108–9.
32. Jackson, *Charles Dickens: the Progress of a Radical*, 201; Lindsay, *Charles Dickens*, 360. Lindsay, however, has some very useful hints about the sources of *TTC* (pp 360–72) — a subject on which there is, I think, no really thorough study, though the sources are much more 'documentary' than is usual in Dickens.
33. *TTC*, i, v, 33–5.
34. i, vi, 38, 46. Cf the effect of long periods of solitary confinement at Louvain, under the influence of Philadelphia: after ten years, prisoners were given the choice of Association with their fellows, but they very rarely accepted it (*Report of the Royal Commission on Capital Punishment 1949–1953*, 1953, 484).
35. ii, iv, 74.
36. ii, vi, 91.
37. ii, xviii, 188.
38. ii, xix, 190–5. Lord Brain has praised the presentation of Dr Manette as 'the most remarkable example of Dickens's psychiatric insight . . . remarkable for the accuracy of his account of a case of multiple personality and loss of memory, because it is the most comprehensive of his studies of psychological abnormality,

and because it includes an anticipation of psychotherapy' ('Dickensian Diagnoses', *Some Reflections on Genius*, 1960, 133).

39. See above, p 51.
40. *TTC*, III, xiii, 337; xv, 357.
41. *AN*, VII, 99. Cf *TTC*, II, xvii, 180–1: 'Can you follow me, Lucie?' says Manette to his daughter. 'Hardly, I think? I doubt you must have been a solitary prisoner to understand these perplexed distinctions.'
42. *LD*, II, xix, 648.
43. I, xix, 228–31.
44. II, iii, 464.

CHAPTER VI: THE PENTONVILLE EXPERIMENT

1. *Dispatch*, 17 December 1843; *Illustrated London News*, 16 December 1843 (III, 387); *Penny Satirist*, 19 December 1840; *Morning Herald*, 29 November 1842; *Illustrated London News*, 7 January 1843; *Dispatch*, 21 January 1844. These, and other relevant press-cuttings, are available in the files on Pentonville at the Islington Public Library, Holloway Road, N.7.
2. Hoyles, *Religion in Prison*, 35–7; William Eden, *Introductory Discourse on Banishment*, 1787, quoted by Barnes and Teeters, 294.
3. Clay, 188, 258, 326. The letter from Rev. John Clay to Dickens is dated March 1853; unfortunately, Dickens's letters to him seem to have been lost.
4. Clay, 620, letter to Mary Carpenter, 25 August 1854. The reference is to *HT*, I, v, 24, on the killjoys of Coketown: 'Then came the experienced chaplain of the gaol, with more tabular statements, outdoing all the previous tabular statements, and showing that the [labouring] people *would* resort to low haunts, hidden from the public eye, where they heard low singing and saw low dancing, and mayhap joined in it; and where A.B., aged twenty-four next birthday, and committed for eighteen months' solitary, had himself said (not that he had ever shown himself particularly worthy of belief) his ruin began, as he was perfectly sure and confident that otherwise he would have been a tip-top moral specimen.' Unfortunately, the archives of Preston Prison were destroyed during an air-raid, so one cannot check whether Dickens signed the Visitors' Book.
5. S. and B. Webb, 114.
6. Letter to Magistrates at Quarter Sessions and Justices of Boroughs, 1837, quoted by Burt, *Results of the System of Separate Confinement . . . at Pentonville Prison*, 279–82.
7. Quoted by Mayhew and Binny, 114.
8. Acton, *Prostitution*, 185.
9. Mayhew and Binny, 147.
10. W. L. Clay, *Our Convict Systems*, 1862, quoted by D. L. Howard, 59.
11. Fifth Report of the Commissioners, quoted by Burt, 6.
12. Kingsmill, *Prison and Prisoners*, 2nd edn, 1852, 130–7; Burt, 4, 23, 60.
13. Quoted by Gray, *Prison Discipline in America*, 167–71.
14. Clay, 192.
15. 'Perfect Felicity', *HW*, 6 April 1850 (*MP*, 186–7). This article — anonymous, like the rest of the contents — seemed striking to contemporary readers. Crabb Robinson, for instance, thought it the only pleasing item in the early numbers of *HW*. 'A capital satire', he said of its successor in the 'Raven' series (*Men and Books*, ed Morley, II, 696, 704).
16. For this and the following quotations from 'Pet Prisoners', see *HW*, 27 April 1850 (*MP*, 222–35). Dickens was, presumably, collecting materials for this article when he wrote to Wills, 'Thanks for the prison facts' (12 March 1850, *N*, II, 209).
17. Field, *Prison Discipline*, 1848 edn, I, 297. Dickens's quotations show that he used this Second Edition, not the 1846 one.

18. Ibid, I, 292–3, 330–1, 343.
19. Kingsmill, 229–31. Mayhew, I should add, heard one of Kingsmill's addresses to new convicts, and both he and they found it very moving (Mayhew and Binny, 150).
20. Burt, 64.
21. Griffiths, *Millbank*, 233–4 (see pp 150–240 on this remarkable episode); *Punch*, II (1842), 186.
22. Thomas Beard, 25 March 1861, *N*, III, 213; cf a further letter (ibid, 215), accepting Beard's article, which appeared in *AYR*, 11 May 1861 (v, 155–9), under the title 'A Dialogue concerning Convicts'. The pamphlet reviewed was *The Convict Service* (1861), by C. P. Measor, Deputy-Governor of Chatham Convict Prison; the chaplain Measor attacked most was Kingsmill, of Pentonville. For similar attacks on prison-chaplains in Dickens's periodicals, see *HW*, XIII, 194 [by Sala]; XVII, 163–4 [by Hollingshead]; *AYR*, VIII, 115; ibid, 298 ('. . . the Conductor of this Journal . . . when he took the liberty of pointing out what "Pet Prisoners" were coming to, was severely mauled at the hands of certain Reverend Ordinaries . . .'). For Dickens's own further attacks, see *HT*, I, v, 24 (quoted above, p 333, note 4); 'The Great Baby', *HW*, 4 August 1855 (*MP*, 554); 'The Murdered Person', *HW*, 11 October 1856 (*MP*, 603–4).
23. Mayhew and Binny, 219.
24. Clay, 195 note.
25. Hoyles, *Religion in Prison*, 25.
26. *Punch*, 14 December 1850 (XIX, 243); cf an item a few months earlier, 'The Convict's Gastronomic Regenerator', ironically suggesting that the present 'plan of correction by kindness' should be completed by employing Monsieur Soyer to devise an even finer system of prison cookery (20 July 1850, XIX, 33).
27. Clay, 265–6, 195 note. For contemporary expressions of this popular suspicion against the chaplains, see the pamphlet and articles cited above (Note 22) and the following specimen references — Chesterton, *RPL*, I, 88; Wakefield, *Facts*, 27; Griffiths, *Millbank*, 150–8 and *passim*; Mayhew and Binny, 169; leading articles in *Times*, 6 April 1844, 28 August 1862 ('it is part of [the criminal profession] to be well versed in the art of deceiving the Chaplain'); Sir Peter Laurie, reported as telling his fellow-magistrates that 'The chaplains were the last persons he would go to for an opinion . . . nor, if it were given, would he adopt it' (*Times*, 2 March 1849). Miss Sheila M. Smith draws my attention to a 'good' prison-chaplain in Mrs Frances Trollope's novel *Jessie Phillips*, 1843.
28. Measor, *The Convict Service*, 48.
29. Ibid, 24–6.
30. Mayhew and Binny, 169.
31. Teeters and Shearer, 155.
32. Field, II, 123.
33. Clay, 327.
34. Ibid, 231–2.
35. Grünhut, 98, 62.
36. *HW*, 8 June 1850, I, 250–3.
37. *Fraser's Magazine*, XLII (1850), 709.
38. See Mildred G. Christian, 'Carlyle's Influence upon the Social Theory of Dickens', *The Trollopian* (later *NCF*), March and June, 1947.
39. Clay, 255. Cf Tallack, *Penological and Preventive Principles*, 161, on 'Mischievous Reactionary Influences' — he, too, asserts that Dickens's influence was even greater than Carlyle's.
40. *Latter Day Pamphlets*, 1869 edn, 81, 71–2.
41. Ibid, 87, 71.
42. Tillotson, *Novels of the Eighteen Forties*, 93 note.

43. This and the following quotations come from *DC*, LXI, 846–56.
44. Sheila M. Smith, 'Propaganda and Hard Facts in Charles Reade's Didactic Novels,' *Renaissance and Modern Studies*, IV (1960), 135, 138, 140–2. The *Edinburgh Review* article to which she refers is Fitzjames Stephen's celebrated essay 'The Licence of Modern Novelists', reviewing *Little Dorrit*, *It is Never too Late to Mend*, and Mrs Gaskell's *Life of Charlotte Brontë* (July 1857, CVI, 124–56). Dickens took the unusual course of replying to it ('Curious Misprint in the Edinburgh Review', *HW*, 1 August 1857; *MP*, 628–34), and the *Edinburgh* (October 1857, 594) acknowledged his protest.
45. Reade, *It is Never too Late to Mend*, Chapter XI.
46. See, eg, Chapters XIII, XIV, and XLII.
47. Ibid, Chapters XVIII, XLII, and LXXXV.
48. John Manning, *Dickens on Education*, Toronto, 1959, 203; Joseph Arnould, *Memoir of Thomas, First Lord Denman*, 1873, II, 332. I have discussed Dickens's views on teacher-training in *Dickens and Education*, Chapter VII.
49. *Times*, 11 January 1844, article on 'Prison Discipline'.
50. For the Number-plan, see Butt and Tillotson, 172–3: 'Creakle as a Middlesex Magistrate', 'Middlesex Magistrates Separate System'. The rest of this chapter incorporates material from my article 'The Middlesex Magistrate in *David Copperfield*', *N & Q*, NS, VIII (1961), 86–91.
51. Rotch, *Juvenile Depravity*, 12, 8; Chesterton, *RPL*, II, 187; Field, I, 381 note.
52. *Coutts*, 104, 3 November 1847; 118, 22 May 1848. Chesterton's opinion of Rotch was much the same — 'a man who, to say the least, would resort to any wily expedient to attain his own ends.... No sooner had a prisoner subscribed to teetotalism, than he easily convinced Mr Rotch of his "innocence"...' (*RPL*, II, 191, 197).
53. K. J. Fielding, '*Edwin Drood* and Governor Eyre', *The Listener*, 25 December 1952, 1083. Dr Fielding produces other examples of this proclivity in 'Charles Dickens and the Department of Practical Art', *Modern Language Review*, XLVIII, 1953, 270–7, and in '*Martin Chuzzlewit* and "The Liberator"' *N & Q*, CXCVIII, 1953, 254–6. The Mr Creakle of the earlier chapters of *DC* was of course based on Dickens's own schoolmaster Mr Jones (see my *Dickens and Education*, Chapter I) — but, I have argued, there is no connection between the Creakle of Salem House and the Creakle of the Model Prison, except the name.

CHAPTER VII: THE MARKS SYSTEM

1. 'Pet Prisoners', *HW*, 27 April 1850 (*MP*, 235, 224).
2. Quoted by Barry, *Alexander Maconochie of Norfolk Island*, x. Mr Justice Barry has also written a shorter study of Maconochie, for the collection *Pioneers in Criminology*, ed Hermann Mannheim, 1960.
3. Ibid, 183–5, x. This idea of crime as a disease, and prison as a moral hospital, was becoming so prevalent among 'philanthropists' as to provoke *The Times* to protest (28 August 1862). One finds it frequently in the works of Frederic and Matthew Davenport Hill and their allies, such as Mary Carpenter. It appears in fiction in, eg, Charles Reade (prison is now 'a penal hospital for diseased and contagious souls' — *It is Never . . .*, Chapter x).
4. Barry, 211.
5. See Barry, 12, 13 (note 9). In March 1846, Dickens was arranging to introduce Maconochie to the prison-governors Tracey and Chesterton (Carr, 7, item A37).
6. *Coutts*, 78, 26 May 1846. Dickens habitually mis-spelt Maconochie's name. Professor Johnson's footnote to this letter points out that Maconochie's *Crime and Punishment* was announced as just published, in the *Publishers' Circular* of 15 July 1846, so 'Dickens must have obtained an advance copy'. This is possible: but

Maconochie was an incessant and repetitive pamphleteer, and Dickens may have obtained one or more of his earlier expositions. Maconochie produced some 46 items on penology between 1839 and 1859, those on the Marks System dating from 1845 (Barry, 182; cf his Bibliography, 263 *et seq*). The 1846 pamphlet, of 74 pages, is probably his best exposition; Dickens's Library at Gad's Hill contained, not this, but three other pamphlets by Maconochie — *General Views regarding the Social System of Convict Management* (1839: published in Hobart, Tasmania, and therefore almost certainly a presentation-copy), *Norfolk Island* (1847), *On Secondary Punishment* (undated: probably *Secondary Punishment: the Mark System*, 1848). See Stonehouse, *Catalogue*, 89. The 'paper' by Maconochie which Dickens gave Miss Coutts in August 1848 (*Coutts*, 122-3) was probably his four-page pamphlet *The Mark System* (1848).

7. *Coutts*, 97, 28 October 1847; 88, 5 October 1846.
8. Ibid, 103, 3 November 1847.
9. Letter to Miss Coutts, 10 May 1848 (Morgan MSS).
10. Barry, 59, 181.
11. *Coutts*, 127, 29 August 1848.
12. Ibid, 124-7; 'Home for Homeless Women', *HW*, 23 April 1853 (*MP*, 373).
13. Sir Walter Crofton, *Convict Systems and Transportation*, 1863, 8; Barry, 74.
14. 'The Irish Convict's Progress', *AYR*, 20 September 1862 (VIII, 31-7).
15. 'Fat Convicts', *AYR*, 25 March 1865 (XIII, 204-8).
16. Barnes and Teeters, 417-23. On Maconochie's contemporary reputation, and the Irish system, see Dixon, 11-19; Chesterton, *RPL*, II, 54; Charles Reade, *It is Never too Late to Mend*, Chapter X (where Maconochie appears as 'Captain O'Connor'); Clay, 246-55, 282, 393-8; Mary Carpenter, *Our Convicts*, Volume II, 'The Irish Convict System'; R. and F. Hill, *The Recorder of Birmingham*, 184-201; Grünhut, Chapter V, 'Individualisation of Treatment'; and, of course, Barry's *Maconochie*.
17. Macready, 22 March 1842, *N*, I, 414.
18. Henry James, *The House of Fiction*, ed Leon Edel, 1957, 257.
19. *Westminster Review*, NS, XXVI (1864), 438.
20. Forster, 637, 712.
21. Dicey, *Law and Opinion*, 418.
22. R. and F. Hill, *The Recorder of Birmingham*, 202.
23. The garotting epidemic and its aftermath are described in all histories of English penology. For some contemporary comments see Griffiths, *Millbank*, 430-6, 448-54, and *Some Articles and Letters which appeared in 'The Times' and other Papers on the Subject of the Treatment of Convicts*, collected by W. L. Clay (ND: c 1862-3). For reactions in Dickens's journal, see *AYR*, 11 October and 8 December 1862, 10 January 1863 (VIII, 111-15, 296-8, 421-3).
24. 'The Ruffian', *AYR* 10 October 1868 (*UT*, 301-8). Cf K. J. Fielding, 'Charles Dickens and "The Ruffian"'.
25. Browne, *Scotland Yard*, 148-9. These complaints occurred, as Mr Browne points out, in the closing months of Sir Richard Mayne's long career as Commissioner of the Metropolitan Police, when his energy was noticeably fading.
26. On the whole question of the relation between Dickens's 'reformism' and public opinion, see the classic discussion in Humphry House's *The Dickens World*, especially pp 41-2 and 222-3.

CHAPTER VIII: THE BENCH

1. 'The License of Modern Novelists', *Edinburgh Review*, CVI (1857), 128.
2. Collins, 6 June 1856, *N*, II, 777; Kuenzel, July 1838, *N*, I, 168; *DC*, XXIII, 342-3; XLIII, 626. Cf his earlier description in 'Doctors' Commons' (*SB*, 86-91), when the

case 'Bumple versus Sludbury' is based on one which Dickens himself had reported; his manuscript transcription of the judgment has survived (W. J. Carlton, *Charles Dickens, Shorthand Writer*, 1926, 61).

3. *OT*, LI, 399; Mrs Frederick Pollock, 2 May 1870, *N*, III, 773.
4. 'Introductory Memoir' by Blanchard Jerrold, to Douglas Jerrold, *Mrs Caudle's Curtain Lectures*, ND, xxv.
5. *MC*, XVII, 279. Cf Kit Nubbles's trial at the Old Bailey: 'Nobody knows the truth; everybody believes a falsehood; and all because of the ingenuity of Mr Brass's [legal] gentleman' (*OCS*, LXIII, 471).
6. Holdsworth, *Dickens as a Legal Historian*, 1–6, 43, 76–7.
7. *Speeches*, 98.
8. Letter to Henry Nethersole, 13 November 1834, quoted by kind permission of Messrs Speechly, Mumford & Soames, Solicitors, of Lincoln's Inn.
9. Forster, 132–3, 526; Chapman, 27 December 1839, *N*, I, 238.
10. Wills, 29 September 1854, *N*, II, 592; W. J. Carlton, 'A Companion of the Copperfield Days,' *Dick*, L (1954), 7–16.
11. Forster, 388. The member of the Government mentioned was, almost certainly, his friend Lord John Russell, who had returned to office in July 1846.
12. Madame de la Rue, 17 April 1846, *N*, I, 745.
13. Letter to Brougham, 24 September 1843, in the Brotherton Collection of the University of Leeds, quoted by kind permission of the Librarian.
14. Arthur William à Beckett, *The à Becketts of 'Punch'*, 1903, 43; T. Wemyss Reid, *Life of Richard Monckton Milnes*, 1890, I, 427–8; G. N. Ray, *Letters of Thackeray*, II, 625. On 20 February 1850, Elizabeth Barrett Browning wrote: 'Dickens and Thackeray are both, I hear, eating their terms to prepare themselves — for *commissionerships* — when their brains are worked out by novel-writing. I call it a scandalous abuse, and wrong to laborious members of the legal profession' (*Elizabeth Barrett Browning: Letters to her Sister, 1846–1859*, ed Leonard Huxley, 1929, 118). Dickens's connection with the Bar was known, indeed over-estimated: the Bodleian Library Catalogue for 1835–47, published 1851, described him as 'barrister'.
15. *Coutts*, 189, 210, 214, 222, 326; 223; 194, 285.
16. 'Some Recollections of Mortality', *AYR*, 16 May 1863 (*UT*, 194–8); 'The Paradise at Tooting', *Examiner*, 20 January 1849 (*MP*, 140); cf W. J. Carlton, 'Dickens in the Jury Box', *Dick*, LII (1956), 65–9.
17. Haines, 3 June 1837, *N*, I, 111.
18. *OT*, XI, 74 and footnote.
19. Forster, 548–9; *Figaro*, 13 January 1838 (*Dick*, XXXIV [1938], 84); Vizetelly, *Glances back*, I, 218.
20. *OT*, XI, 70–1. An attack on 'The Hatton Garden Philanthropist' in the *Monthly Magazine*, March 1834, is reprinted in *Dick*, XXXVII (1841), 167–8.
21. Ballantine, *Experiences*, 53. Mr Graham Storey points out to me that Laing was being referred to in *The Examiner*, soon after *OT*, under the name of Fang, 'as he will be known to posterity' (7 January 1838).
22. *Coutts*, 334.
23. For evidence of his friendship with these Judges, and specimens of his remarks on them, see Forster, 167, 327, 341, 529; Dolby, 28; *Speeches*, 388; *N*, III, 117, 227, 382; Ley, *Dickens Circle*, Chapter XXIX, 'Some Limbs of the Law'.
24. Forster, 341; *HW*, 13 April 1850, I, 60; and see Sir Joseph Arnould, *Memoir of Thomas, First Lord Denman*, 1873, II, 148–9, 332–4.
25. Yates, *Recollections and Experiences*, II, 132. But according to Dolby (p 28), Cockburn's presence 'made' this Reading, and Dickens addressed the salient points to him.
26. Arnould, *Denman*, I, 265; Ballantine, *Experiences*, 144. For the 'Trial' Reading, however, Dickens used the voice of his old friend, the poet Samuel Rogers.

27. *BH*, III, 30, 32.
28. *MC*, XXXI, 498; cf, in similar vein, *D & S*, XLVII, 647.
29. *Daily News*, 16 March 1846 (*MP*, 34); 'Please to leave your Umbrella', *HW*, 1 May 1858 (*MP*, 649).
30. Forster, 141.
31. *PP*, XXV, 340–2.
32. *ED*, XV, 174.
33. *BR*, LXIII, 479; 'Report of the Second Meeting of the Mudfog Association' (1838), *SB*, 661; 'Private Life of Mr Tulrumble' (1837), *SB*, 607–24.
34. *BR*, XLVII, 356–60; LXXV, 574.
35. *OCS*, LXV, 338.
36. *Chimes*, I (*CB*, 94–9).
37. *Kelso Mail*, December 1861, quoted in P. G. Laurie, *Sir Peter Laurie*, 311–12; letter from a kinsman of Laurie, cited by Fitzgerald, *Life of Dickens*, II, 129; copy of an extract from Sir Peter Laurie's Journal, 19 December 1844, quoted by kind permission of the owner, Major J. E. C. Laurie. Sir Peter was wrong about the critical reception of *The Chimes* and the success of stage-versions. He made public his chagrin about having been pilloried after entertaining Mrs Dickens at the Lord Mayor's ball (Thomas Powell, *Living Authors of Britain*, 1851, 93–4).
38. 'Ignorance and Crime', *Examiner*, 22 April 1848 (*MP*, 101).
39. *OT*, Cheap Edn Preface (*CP*, 266–7); letter to Henry Austin, 21 March 1850, quoted by K. J. Fielding in *Speeches*, 109. Jacob's Island indeed still existed in 1850, as foul as ever: there is a brilliant, but sickening, description of it by Henry Mayhew in *Meliora: or Better Times to Come*, ed Viscount Inegstre, 1852, 276–80.
40. P. G. Laurie, *Sir Peter Laurie*, 84–5, 68–71.
41. Quoted by S. and B. Webb, 106. Cf above, pp 70, 334.
42. Sir Peter Laurie, *Letter on the Disadvantages and Extravagences of the Separate System*, 1848, 4; James Grant, *Portraits of Public Characters*, 1841, I, 145 (see pp 120–53 for the 'Portrait' of Laurie). Cf Sir Peter's *Killing no Murder* (1846).
43. P. G. Laurie, 237–8, 250–5. This was one of several pronouncements by Laurie that *Punch* never forgot (eg, *Punch*, XV, 125, 156). Dickens's support for Discharged Prisoners' Aid activities continued, to his credit. An article on a pioneer in this, field, Thomas Wright of Manchester, in the *Illustrated London News* (8 January, 1853), noted that his work had been publicised, 'primarily by Mr Dickens, in his "Household Words." ' The reference is to Morley's 'An Unpaid Servant of the State', *HW*, 6 March 1852, IV, 553–5. Cf 'The De-odorisation of Crime', by Payn, on the new Discharged Prisoners' Aid Societies (27 June 1857, XV, 612–14).
44. P. G. Laurie, 204–7; cf pp 218, 233.
45. *Punch*, 5 October 1844, VII, 158.
46. Ibid, 24 July 1841, I, 21.
47. Ibid, 8 May 1847, XII, 186; 20 November 1841, I, 228; 24 June 1843, IV, 255; 30 May 1846, X, 239; 16 December 1848, XV, 260.
48. James Grant, *Portraits of Public Characters*, 1841, I, 126–9, 146; Ballantine, *Experiences*, 72; *Illustrated London News* (21 January 1843) quoted by P. G. Laurie, 217.
49. Jerrold, 3 May 1843, *N*, I, 517–18.
50. K. J. Fielding in *Speeches*, 109.
51. John Stuart Mill, *Letters*, 1910, II, 14–15; James Grant, *The Newspaper Press*, 1871, I, 281; E. B. de Fonblanque, *Life and Labours of Albany Fonblanque*, 1874, 63; R. H. Horne, 206–8. 'Hitherto,' wrote Harrison Ainsworth, dedicating his novel *The Lord Mayor of London* (1862) to a man who had twice held that office, 'Aldermen and Common-Councilmen have been a standing jest with dramatists, novelists, and comic writers, who have made them their butt, burlesqued their proceedings, and caricatured their manners.'
52. *DC*, LXI, 848.

53. House, *Dickens World*, 181–2.
54. 'Supposing!', *HW*, 20 April 1850 (*MP*, 667). Cf Dickens's 'A December Vision', *HW*, 14 December 1850 (*MP*, 282), and articles by contributors to *AYR* ('Consolidate the Statutes' and 'Patched Law', 1 and 22 August, 1863, vi, 543–9, 606–9).
55. Eg, Dickens's 'Things that cannot be done' and 'Legal and Equitable Jokes', *HW*, 8 October 1853 and 23 September 1854 (*MP*, 413–17, 445–52); 'Law at a Low Price', by Wills and Haly, urging the abolition of juries in County Court cases (*HW*, 18 May 1850, i, 176–80); 'The Duties of Witnesses and Jurymen' and 'Bringing out of the Truth', both by Matthew Davenport Hill, criticising the English rules of evidence (*HW*, 26 October 1850 and 4 October 1851, ii, 100–4, and iv, 38–40); 'Grand Jury Powers', by Morley (*HW*, 16 May 1857, xv, 457–63); on the same topic — 'Occasional Register' (*AYR*, 7 May 1859, i, 35) and 'On the Grand Jury' (*AYR*, 7 September 1861, v, 574–6).
56. 'Why?' *HW*, 1 March 1856 (*MP*, 586). Cf 'Examine the Prisoner!', *AYR*, 7 June 1862, vii, 306–8; 'The Pet of the Law', by Hollingshead, *HW*, 30 January 1858, xvii, 163–5; 'Mrs Winsor's View of the Criminal Law', *AYR*, 15 December 1866, xvi, 540–4 (Charlotte Winsor's trials for murder were a *cause célèbre* of 1865, and many people deplored her not having been hanged: see Irving, *Annals*, 696, 713).
57. *AYR*, 24 September 1859 (*MP*, 684–5). This outburst was provoked by the notorious case of the alleged poisoner Smethurst, whose reprieve shocked Dickens and others: see below, p 246.
58. 'Murderous Extremes', *HW*, 3 January 1857 (*MP*, 609–10). Cf 'The Ruffian', *AYR*, 10 October 1868 (*UT*, 308).
59. 'Things that cannot be done', *HW*, 8 October 1853 (*MP*, 416–17).
60. *Coutts*, 229–30; *MP*, 415. For an account of Dunn's activities from 1838 onwards, see *Coutts*, 45 note.
61. 'The Ruffian', *AYR*, 10 October 1868 (*UT*, 305–7); cf 'Stores for the First of April', *HW*, 7 March 1857 (*MP*, 621).
62. 'The Begging-Letter Writer', *HW*, 18 May 1850 (*RP*, 383). See Cumberland Clark, *Dickens and the Begging Letter Writer*, 1923. The episode took place in 1844. Henry Mayhew wrote in 1851 of the 'patterers' or street literature sellers: 'Mr Dickens *was* a favourite, but he has gone down sadly in the scale since his *Household Words* "came it so strong" against the begging letter department' (*London Labour and the London Poor*, i, 250). Dickens was included among the thirty 'persons known to be charitable', in the list of one professional begging-letter writer (ibid, i, 315).
63. *The Era*, 25 March 1849, reprinted in *Dick*, xiii (1917), 213–14.
64. Cf newspaper accounts reprinted in *Dick*, xxii (1926), 161, and xlvii (1951), 201. See also W. J. Carlton, 'Dickens in the Jury Box', ibid, lii (1956), 65–9, on his kindly activity over an infanticide case which he had heard, as juryman, in 1840: he recalls the episode in 'Some Recollections of Mortality', *AYR*, 16 May 1863 (*UT*, 194–8).
65. 'Things that cannot be done', *HW*, 8 October 1853 (*MP*, 413); 'Lying Awake', *HW*, 30 October 1852 (*RP*, 437); 'The Ruffian', *AYR*, 10 October 1868 (*UT*, 302).
66. 'Among the Shallows', by Pyke and Morley, *HW*, 5 November 1853, viii, 293–5.
67. See Thomson, *Scotland Yard*, 136–7; Patrick Howarth, *The Year is 1851*, 1951, 86; *Punch* (1843–8), v, 154; vi, 70; vii, 225, 245, 268; ix, 192; xi, 142, 189; xiv, 176.
68. 'A December Vision' and 'Last Words of the Old Year', *HW*, 14 December 1850 and 4 January 1851 (*MP*, 280, 286), quoted above, p 86.
69. Eg, 'Nobody's Story', *HW*, Christmas 1853 (*CS*, 63–4); 'It is not generally known',

HW, 2 September 1854 (*MP*, 440–5); 'The Great Baby', 4 August 1855 (*MP*, 552–9); 'The Worthy Magistrate', 25 August 1855 (*MP*, 559–61). Many contributors wrote on this subject: eg, 'The Great Drunkery Discovery', *AYR*, 31 July 1869, NS, II, 204–9.

70. *HT*, I, iii, 11.
71. 'Supposing', *HW*, 7 June 1851 (*MP*, 669–70).

CHAPTER IX: THE POLICE

1. Sala, *Things I have seen*, I, 95–6; Lytton, 9 May 1851, *N*, II, 307.
2. Griffiths, *Mysteries of Police and Crime*, I, 130. Cf the long quotations from the 'excellent papers in the early numbers of "Household Words" which illustrate admirably the habits of these officers', in *Quarterly Review*, XCIX (1856), 176–80.
3. Fitzjames Stephen in *Edinburgh Review*, CVI (1857), 133; House, *Dickens World*, 201; Orwell, *Critical Essays*, 23.
4. Thomson, *Story of Scotland Yard*, 112. On the development of detective work between 1829 and 1842, see Belton Cobb, *The First Detectives*, 1957, which contains accounts of some of the early exploits of the detectives Dickens knew and described in the 1850s.
5. *PP*, XXIV–XXV, 331–47.
6. On the pre-1829 police, see Radzinowicz, Volumes II and III; Gilbert Armitage, *The History of the Bow Street Runners*, ND; Patrick Pringle, *Hue and Cry: the Birth of the British Police*, 1955.
7. *BR*, XLIX, 374; XXXIX, 297; LXI, 467. On the proverbial incompetence of the watchmen, see Melville Lee, *A History of the Police in England*, 183–6, and Alwyn Solmes, *The English Policeman 1871–1935*, 1935, 117–18.
8. Dilnot, *The Story of Scotland Yard*, 53; Ballantine, *Some Experiences of a Barrister's Life*, 16–17, 21, 36, 233–4.
9. See, eg, Goddard, *Memoirs of a Bow Street Runner*, 88, 153.
10. 'The Detective Police', *HW*, 27 July 1850 (*RP*, 485).
11. Eg, Moylan, 182 — 'a few masterly sentences' from this paragraph by Dickens on the Runners may 'serve as their epitaph'; Radzinowicz, II, 263, 311.
12. Thornbury, 18 April 1862, *N*, III, 293. Thornbury was a frequent contributor to *AYR*, but I cannot find there any article written as a result of this letter.
13. Goddard, *Memoirs*, ed Pringle, Introduction, xiv–xv, xxii; cf 176–8, 153, 194. Mr Pringle, in claiming that no Runners were charged with criminal offences, seems to have forgotten the 1816 scandal, when five of them were found guilty of inciting people to commit robberies, whom they then arrested, thus obtaining a reward (Armitage, 196–200).
14. Ibid, xxi. The later scandals among the Detective Force, involving some of the officers Dickens had described, are recorded in Belton Cobb's *Critical Years at the Yard*, 1956.
15. The main exception was the case of King, a detective transported for fourteen years in 1855 for conspiring with a pickpocket (Thomson, 138).
16. Eg, Lee, 192–3, 212–13, 367; Moylan, 177–8; Armitage, 266–7; Reith, *A New Study of Police History*, 171–2; Radzinowicz, II, 263–9. Cf Bulwer Lytton's insinuations against Nabbem, the Runner, in *Paul Clifford* (1830), Chapter XXVIII.
17. For some relevant statistics on the decrease of crime, both absolutely and relatively to the size of population, see Pike, *Crime in England*, II, 457–72, and Lee, *History of Police*, 272, 336–9.
18. Wakefield, *Facts*, 2–4, 34–6.
19. *GE*, XVI, 114–16.
20. *OT*, XXXI, 222–8. Blathers and Duff are 'rewarded with a couple of guineas' for their unsuccessful expedition. They would not have been very pleased with that,

for the Runners' regular charge for provincial jobs was a guinea a day fee, fourteen shillings a day expenses, and a reward besides for a successful prosecution.

21. *PP*, II, 8; *OT*, LIII, 413; *BR*, LXXXII, 630; *TTC*, II, iii, 62–4. On the informer system, and its unpopularity, see Radzinowicz, II, 138–55.

22. *SB*, 218, 'Thoughts about People'; 377, 'The Black Veil'. The battle between the 'Charlies' and the young bloods was traditional, and often bloody; an earl and his cronies once held a watchman down and drove a cab over him (Howard, *Guardians of the Queen's Peace*, 135).

23. *OCS*, LX, 444; *Punch*, 23 February 1850 (XVIII, 77).

24. *D & S*, XXIII, 328.

25. *BH*, XI, 143–5; XIX, 264–5. Dickens only once, I think, makes the familiar joke about Bobbies and cooks (*BR* Preface, *CP*, 292). His colleagues protested (in *AYR*, XIX, 468, and NS, I, 350) against policemen's being made comic butts in Music Hall jokes and songs.

26. Murch, *The Development of the Detective Novel*, 95–6. See also the useful survey, 'Detective Fiction', in *New Paths in Book Collecting*, ed John Carter, 1934. As Mrs Murch points out, Dickens, unlike Wilkie Collins, seems not to have been influenced by Poe.

27. Dickens's articles were collected in *Reprinted Pieces* (1858), where the two originally entitled 'A Detective Police Party' are merged into one, retitled 'The Detective Police'. Wills reprinted 'Thief-Taking' and 'The Metropolitan Protectives' in *Old Leaves* (1860), but the latter article was devised and largely written by Dickens. He had told Wills to make arrangements for the expedition, with 'our friend Mr Yardley, at Scotland Yard'; he invited Wills to join him, and was sure it would make 'a wonderful good paper . . . I see a most singular and admirable chance for us in the descriptive way, not to be lost.' Later, he 'sat . . . nine hours without stirring', revising Wills's draft (Wills, 3 and 13 April 1851, *N*, II, 294–5, 296–7).

28. *RP*, 485, 502–3.

29. 'Poor Mercantile Jack', *AYR*, 10 March 1860 (*UT*, 40–51); Macready, *Diaries*, II, 228.

30. Not all his visitors were, in fact, from the Department; his party included some detectives attached to ordinary Divisions, and Inspector 'Stalker' (ie, Walker) belonged to the Statistical and Executive Branch, not the Detective Department (Cobb, *Critical Years at the Yard*, 23–5; Dilnot, *Scotland Yard*, 214).

31. *RP*, 487.

32. Percy Fitzgerald, *Life of Charles Dickens*, 1905, II, 183, 274.

33. 'The Modern Science of Thief-Taking', *HW*, 13 July 1850, I, 371.

34. Sala, *Things I have seen*, I, 95.

35. *Times*, 20 September 1853. J. W. T. Ley quotes a report in the *Daily News*, 24 January 1853, that Dickens had presented a cheque for £300 to Field, 'upon whose information he founded several articles in *Household Words* relative to the detective system' (Forster's *Life of Dickens*, 843, Note 501). I cannot find this report in the *Daily News* for, or around, that date, nor do I know of any other evidence for this improbable gift.

36. 'The Detective Police', *RP*, 486; 'On Duty with Inspector Field', *RP*, 513–23; Hon. Frederick Wellesley, *Recollections of a Soldier-Diplomat*, 1947, 74–6. On another visit to a criminal rookery, Dickens had to be rescued by the police (James Anderson, *An Actor's Life*, 1902, 86–8).

37. *Coutts*, 192–3, 13 January 1852; Lytton, 9 May 1851, *N*, II, 307.

38. *BH*, XXII, 308, 315; XLIX, 672; LVI, 763; XLIX, 678–9.

39. LIII, 712; LIV, 724; LVII, 780.

40. Browne, *Rise of Scotland Yard*, 123, 153–4. Dickens may, however, have been mistaken, in his belief (stated in his letter to Thornbury, quoted above) that Field was

a former Runner. Neither the 'Memoir of Inspector Field' (*Illustrated Times*, quoted below) nor any other record of him known to me mentions his having been one.

41. Information kindly supplied by the Commissioner of Police of the Metropolis, New Scotland Yard. Born in 1805, Field joined the Metropolitan Police as a Sergeant in September 1829, and was transferred to L Division (Lambeth) as Inspector in 1833. After service at Deptford Dockyard and at Woolwich, he became chief of the Detective Department at Scotland Yard in 1846. He retired on pension in December 1852, having been involved in many of the leading criminal cases for twenty years past.

42. *Times*, 17 September 1853. Dickens read this account, which contained the reference to his connection with Field which provoked his letter, published three days later. Did he remember from it the name of Provis, which he used as Magwitch's *alias* in *GE* (1860–1)? On Field's arrests, see below, p 344.

43. *Illustrated Times*, 2 February 1856. I owe this reference to Mr Douglas G. Browne. This 'Memoir of Inspector Field' was occasioned by his being concerned in the notorious Palmer of Rugeley case.

44. *BH*, xxiv, 348–9; for the arrest of George Rouncewell, see xlix, 672–9.

45. 'Memoir of Inspector Field', loc. cit.

46. 'Waters' [ie, William Russell], *Recollections of a Detective Police-Officer*, 1856, Preface, vii.

47. Collins, *The Moonstone*, First Period, Chapter xii. Sergeant Cuff was almost certainly based on Inspector Whicher, whom Dickens describes as 'Witchem' in 'The Detective Police'.

48. Reade, *It is Never too Late to Mend*, Chapter 1; 'Waters', 37. On the popularity of this book, see *New Paths in Book Collecting*, ed Carter, 51–3, 158.

49. *RP*, 520.

50. 'Poor Mercantile Jack', *UT*, 42.

51. *BH*, lvii, 769.

52. *OMF*, i, iii, 24; cf iv, xii, 762–3.

53. Ibid, i, xii, 158.

54. *Times Literary Supplement*, 29 July 1960, 480. Cf the aphorism by 'Nicholas Blake', that 'detective fiction is read by those with a stake in the social system, the thriller by those who have none' (quoted by Murch, 140), and Praz on 'the detective story, that positive, bourgeois type of fairy-tale' (*Hero in Eclipse*, 152).

55. Forster, 11.

56. Letters to Eytinge, 14 May 1869, and Bowring, 5 May 1870, *N*, iii, 725, 775; Forster, 844.

57. *ED*, xvi, 193; xix, 219. The period of the action of *ED* is ill-defined, but as Cloisterham is on a railway-line (even if the station is uncompleted) it clearly falls within the New Police era.

58. *MC*, xxvii, 447; xxxviii, 590–1. Another early plain-clothes detective appears in 'The Drunkard's Death' (*SB*, 490–1).

59. Forster, 636.

60. Charles Dickens, Junior, 'Reminiscences of my Father', *The Windsor Magazine*, Christmas Supplement, 1934, 24. For a fuller discussion of the roots and manifestations of Dickens's obsession for tidiness, etc, see Chapter ii of my *Dickens and Education.*.

61. House, *Dickens World*, 201–2.

62. See Radzinowicz, Volume iii, for a fuller discussion of this.

63. Wilkie Collins, 8 July 1855, *N*, ii, 678.

64. 'The Ruffian', *UT*, 304, 307–8. See above, p 173, citing Browne, 148–9.

65. My discussion here owes much to George Orwell's essay on Dickens: see his *Critical Essays*, 22–8.

66. Moylan, 33–5.

67. Cf 'Waters', who explains that he is a gentleman born, but 'adverse circumstances
... compelled me to enter the ranks of the Metropolitan Police, as the sole
means left me of procuring food and raiment' (*Recollections of a Detective Police-
Officer*, 9). The contributor of an article to *HW* (30 April 1859, XIX, 505–10) entitled 'Some Wild Ideas' included, among other 'wild' suggestions, a plan for
increasing police-efficiency by instituting an officer-class of gentlemen.
68. *MC*, LI, 788.

CHAPTER X: THE PUNISHMENT OF DEATH

1. Forster, 191–2.
2. *AN*, III, 51–2.
3. Forster, 373.
4. *BR*, XXXVII, 284. The brief mention of the Mary Jones case in the 1841 Preface
is expanded in the 1849 Preface, with a quotation from Sir William Meredith's
famous Parliamentary speech upon it (*CP*, 285, 293). Cf A. U. Ziegler, 'A *Barnaby
Rudge* Source', *Dick*, LIV (1958), 80–2. On Dickens's fictional treatment of the
penology of 'the good old times', cf *TTC*, II, ii, 56.
5. *BR*, LXXVII, 596.
6. LXXIV, 567.
7. See Bleakley, *The Hangmen of England*, Chapter VIII, 'Edward Dennis'. The
historical Dennis, by a further irony, was later presented by the Sheriffs with a
gorgeous official robe 'as a testimony to his excellent mode of performing business'.
Unable to perform it in this garb, however, he sold it to a fortune-teller (Laurence,
History of Capital Punishment, 103).
8. *BR*, LXXVI, 586.
9. LXV, 500.
10. Gilpin, 30 May 1840, *N*, I, 259.
11. Joshua Fayle, 21 January 1864, *N*, III, 378.
12. *OT*, LII, 411; IX, 59. For Fagin's use of the gallows, see XVIII, 127; XXVII, 188–9;
XLIV, 341–2.
13. *BR*, LXXVII, 590, 592.
14. Edgar Johnson, I, 299 and Note 37 (and see above, p 328, Note 90); 'Reminiscences of Henry Burnett,' in Kitton, *Dickens by Pen and Pencil*, 142–3. The following quotations are from Burnett. For a full recent account of the Courvoisier case,
see Yseult Bridges, *Two Studies in Crime*, 1959.
15. W. M. Thackeray, *Catherine and Miscellanies 1840–1* (The Oxford Thackeray,
ND), 202–5. Cf Thackeray's *Letters and Private Papers*, I, 450–4, and James Pope-
Hennessy, *Monckton Milnes: the Years of Promise*, 1949, 128–30.
16. *Daily News*, 28 February 1846. This letter has hitherto been overlooked by
Dickens's editors and biographers. Three further letters to the *Daily News*
(published on 9, 13 and 16 March 1846) were reprinted in a pamphlet with an
Introduction by the publisher (Dyson, of High Street, Shoreditch), dated 21
November 1849. Dyson was, clearly, exploiting the interest aroused by Dickens's
famous letters on hanging, published in *The Times* of 14 and 19 November, but
in his haste he did not notice the first in the series of four letters to the *Daily News*.
Later editors of Dickens's letters and miscellaneous papers seem to have followed
Dyson, and one another, though the letter of 16 March refers to this overlooked
letter of 28 February. This is the most interesting uncollected item by Dickens
that my book draws upon: it will be further quoted and discussed below. It is
reprinted in full in *The Law as Literature*, ed Louis Blom-Cooper, 1961, 382–7.
17. *Daily News*, 16 March 1846 (*MP*, 41).
18. R. H. Horne, 51.
19. Napier, 21 January 1843, *N*, I, 505.

20. On these abortive projects, see my 'Dickens and the *Edinburgh Review*', *RES*, N.S. XIV (1963), 167–72.
21. 17 October 1845, *N*, I, 709.
22. 28 July 1845, *N*, I, 688–9.
23. Henry Hocker was hanged on 28 April 1845 for murder. While a policeman was guarding the body, discovered on a footpath, Hocker came up and chatted with him and felt the corpse's pulse. For an interesting account of his demeanour, see 'Impressions of a late Trial for Murder', *Douglas Jerrold's Shilling Magazine*, May 1845, 424–36. Edward Oxford, charged with high treason, was found guilty but insane, 8 July 1840. Cf Dickens's comment at the time: 'It's a great pity they couldn't suffocate that boy, Master Oxford, and say no more about it. To have put him quietly between two feather-beds would have stopped his heroic speeches, and dulled the sound of his glory very much' (Forster, June 1840, *N*, I, 259).
24. *Daily News*, 28 February 1846; 16 March 1846 (*MP*, 36–8). Probably Napier had put him on to this New York Report; cf his letter to him, 7 August 1845 — 'Mandeville, I know. The short report, I do not. But I will make myself master of it, before I begin.' (*N*, I, 691).
25. *Daily News*, 28 February 1846.
26. *Daily News*, 9 March 1846 (*MP*, 22–3).
27. Ibid (*MP*, 23–4).
28. See Gardiner and Curtis-Raleigh, 'The Judicial Attitude to Penal Reform'.
29. *Daily News*, 16 March 1846 (*MP*, 34–5).
30. *Daily News*, 13 March 1846 (*MP*, 29–30). Spectators were always ambivalent towards the hangman: he and his victim shared the roles of villain and hero, each partaking of both roles. See anecdotes in Bleakley, *Hangmen of England*, and Laurence, *Capital Punishment*.
31. *Daily News*, 28 February 1846.
32. 'Recollections of Mrs Watson', in Kitton, *Dickens by Pen and Pencil*, 145; Una Pope-Hennessy, *Charles Dickens*, 234; Symons, *Charles Dickens*, 16.
33. *Pictures from Italy*, 'Rome', 391; *Daily News*, 13 March 1846 (*MP*, 27–8).
34. Maclise, 9 May 1845, *N*, I, 674.
35. 'The Holly Tree', First Branch (*CS*, 108–10). Before 1855, when this was published, Dickens had been in Switzerland during the winter in November 1844, October–December 1846, and October 1853. The last of these seems the most likely date for this episode.
36. A variant on this famous declaration appears in Dickens's 'Pet Prisoners' (*MP*, 228). Mrs Manning had been lady's-maid to the Duchess of Sutherland, so she is linked to Hortense by her job as well as her foreign birth: and, as Hortense was arrested by Bucket, so Mrs Manning had been arrested by Inspector Field. Mark Lemon told the *Punch* Table 'of Charley Field the detective, with his flabby hand and cool tongue, how he traced Mrs Manning to a lodging, and tapped at door "Only me — Charley Field — so just open the door quietly. Maria"' (Henry Silver's diary, 18 November 1863, quoted by permission of Messrs Bradbury, Agnew & Co).
37. *The Progress of Crime, or the Authentic Memoirs of Maria Manning*, by Robert Huish, 1849. Dickens's two letters to *The Times* are printed as an Appendix, pp 826–31. A more accessible account of the Mannings' trial and execution is in Dodds, *Age of Paradox*, 387–90.
38. Leech, 7 November 1849, *N*, II, 183; *Punch*, 24 November 1849, XVII, 210.
39. Leech, 12 November 1849, *N*, II, 183. Forster was also in the party (Forster, 533). Thomas Wright, *Life of Dickens*, 201–2, quotes from an apparently unpublished letter by Dickens about this hanging, and also from an account by a Mr Manistre of the tour through the Horsemonger Lane area which he took with Dickens and several others, during the night before the execution. Presumably this comes

from 'A Tramp with Dickens: through London by night with the Great Novelist', by State Senator Henry Manistre, *Detroit Free Press*, 7 April 1883 (listed by William Miller, *The Dickens Student and Collector*, 1946, 22). I have not seen it.

40. To *The Times*, 13 November 1849 (printed on 14 November). Not in *N*; text taken from *The Letters of Charles Dickens 1833 to 1870*, edited by his Sister-in-Law and his Eldest Daughter, 1893, 200–1.

41. *Times*, 14 November 1849. Cf *Illustrated London News*, 17 November 1849.

42. Edward Tagart, 20 November 1849, *N*, ii, 186.

43. *Times*, 19 November 1849 (*Letters*, 203–4). With the remark on Calcraft, cf the protest against the publicity given to hangmen, *BH*, xi, 147. Dickens's long quotation from Fielding comes from *An Inquiry into the Causes of the late Increase in Robbers*, 1750. This important tract is discussed at length by Radzinowicz, i, 401–15.

44. Ibid, 205.

45. *Speeches*, 103 and footnote; de Cerjat, 29 December 1849, *N*, ii, 195.

46. Beggs, *Juvenile Depravity*, 85–6; Munford, *William Ewart*, 103–4, 155–6.

47. Atholl, *Shadow of the Gallows*, 74. For dates and further discussion, see *Report of the Royal Commission on Capital Punishment*, 1953, and Koestler, 171–2.

48. Christy, 15 and 24 November 1849, *N*, ii, 184, 187; *Dick*, xiii (1917), 78.

49. Gilpin, 15 November 1849, *N*, ii, 185. At the meeting on 19 November, Dickens's proposals were attacked by Gilpin, Ewart and Jerrold, and some hard things were said about him. Letters of support from Cobden and Bright were read out. The unfortunate phraseology of some of these remarks was attacked in *The Times*, 20 and 21 November.

50. Gilpin, 16 March 1846, *N*, i, 742. Dickens did not attend, however: letters 'expressing hearty concurrence in the object of the meeting' from him, Jerrold and Cobden, were read out (*Times*, 30 April 1846).

51. 17 November 1849, *N*, ii, 185–6; Jerrold to Dickens, 20 November, in Blanchard Jerrold's *Life and Remains of Douglas Jerrold*, 1859, 286.

52. De Cerjat, 29 December 1849, *N*, ii, 195.

53. *HW*, 30 October 1852 (*RP*, 434).

54. De Cerjat, 29 December 1849, *N*, ii, 195; Forster, 533.

55. Munford, 103–4.

56. Caroline Fox, 192 (28 May 1842), on Carlyle; R. H. Horne, 205–7, on Fonblanque; Lytton's *Paul Clifford*, final paragraphs.

57. *Punch*, 17 July 1841, i, 1.

58. *Punch*, May 1842, ii, 240.

59. 17 January 1846, x, 33. This article refers to those familiar statistics of the Rev Roberts (that 164 out of 167 prisoners awaiting execution, etc), and to Lord Nugent's campaign: so do Dickens's *Daily News* letters in March (*MP*, 24, 31–2). Perhaps *Punch* was Dickens's source.

60. 30 March 1848, xiv, 127.

61. 4 January 1845, viii, 24; 1 December 1849, xvii, 220; 23 March 1850, xviii, 111; 15 August 1846, xi, 74; November–December 1849, xvii, 203, 210, 213, 214, 220; Spielmann, *History of 'Punch'*, 284–8.

62. Forster, 234; *AN*, vi, 85–6; de Cerjat, 29 December 1849, *N*, ii, 195.

63. See *The Aylesbury News* almost weekly between 26 April and 11 October 1845. Dickens's quotation (*MP*, 31–2) comes from the August 16 issue.

64. *Daily News*, 16 March 1846 (*MP*, 40).

65. Rev Alexander M'Caul, quoted in '*Inquisition for Blood*': or the Eternal Obligation on States and Governments to inflict the Penalty of Death for Wilful Murder, by A Witness for 'Judgment, Mercy, and Faith', 1847, 20; Tayler Lewis, *An Essay on the Ground and Reason of Punishment*, New York, 1846, 2.

66. See, eg, the items mentioned above, and Rev Thomas Pyne, *A Plea for the*

Abolition of Capital Punishment, c 1846; Walter Scott, *The Punishment of Death for the Crime of Murder, Rational, Scriptural and Salutary*, 1846 (Scott cites Dickens's first *Daily News* letter, pp 41-2); a reply to this, *War and Punishment opposed to Christianity*, by Ἀμφω, 1846; *Flogging, or Scourging, by Human Law, contrasted with the same Punishment by Divine Law*, anon, 1846; Alexander Campbell, *Capital Punishment sanctioned by Divine Authority*, 1846; Rev George Cheever, *A Defense of Capital Punishment*, New York, 1846; A Member of the Church of England, *Capital Punishment under the Gospel Dispensation anti-Scriptural*, 1847; A Student of St Bees College, *Letters upon Capital Punishment*, 1847; George Combe, *Thoughts on Capital Punishment*, Edinburgh, 1847. For Jerrold on the bishops, see *Punch*, 17 January 1846, x, 33.

67. See, eg, 'Death and the Hangman', *Douglas Jerrold's Shilling Magazine*, February 1846, 115-16; long series on 'The Punishment of Death', by Frederic Rowton, Secretary to the Society for the Abolition of Capital Punishment, in *Howitt's Journal*, beginning 2 October 1847, II, 218.

68. Frederic Hill, *Crime*, 168.

69. Miss Joll, 27 November 1849, *N*, II, 187.

70. Eg, in a recent article on 'Dickens on the Death Penalty', Mr C. G. L. du Cann states that Dickens never compromised on this issue (*Dick*, LII [1956], 149-51), and Miss Elizabeth Orman Tuttle says that references to his aversion to capital punishment are scattered throughout his writings (*The Crusade against Capital Punishment*, 1961, 14). Miss Tuttle's book, published after mine was completed, contains much useful historical information.

71. Fayle, 21 January 1864, *N*, III, 378. The account of an execution at Lewes, to which he refers in this letter as 'built on actual facts, but not by me', occurs in an article by Sala, 'Open-Air Entertainments', *HW*, 8 May 1852, v, 165-9. Sala demands that this 'horrible ceremony', which had occasioned some very unedifying behaviour in Lewes, be conducted in private.

72. 'The Finishing Schoolmaster,' *HW*, 17 May 1851 (*MP*, 307-12). Two contributors reverted to the old argument against capital punishment, that mistakes occur and should give us pause (*HW*, 4 August 1855, XII, 22-4, by Hepworth Dixon; and *AYR*, 23 August 1862, VII, 569-70). Generally, Dickens disliked his periodicals' containing articles about executions, unless displaying 'some very vigorous treatment' of the subject, as he told Wills when rejecting one by Alexandre Dumas (28 March 1851, *N*, II, 290-1), but he printed a bloodthirsty account of 'the impressive scene' when leaders of the Indian Mutiny were 'blown away' by being tied across the muzzle of a cannon (*HW*, 27 March 1858, XVII, 348-50). He much admired another article on an English execution, as seen by the responsible officials (*AYR*, 15 August 1868, xx, 223-5; cf letter to Wills, 31 July 1868, *N*, III, 661). Several contributors deplored the number of murderers escaping execution through pleas of 'insanity' (eg, *AYR*, 22 September 1860, III, 557-9; 22 February 1862, VI, 510-13).

73. Wills, 4 September 1860, *N*, III, 176.

74. *TTC*, II, ii, 58-9.

75. Forster, 730 note; *N*, III, 118. Nevertheless, Smethurst was reprieved, though he got twelve months for bigamy (see Irving, *Annals*, 555): the case is discussed by Leslie Hale (*Hanged in Error*, 1961, 150-60), who is severely critical of Pollock's handling of the case. For an earlier indication of a Dickens no longer believing in abolition, cf the French inn-keeper's wife (quoted above, p 83) on 'the enemies of the human race' who must be 'crushed like savage beasts and cleared out of the way' (*LD*, I, xi, 127, published in February 1856).

76. De Cerjat, 25 October 1864, *N*, III, 402. Müller did hang, before the largest and most disorderly crowd since the Mannings' execution of 1849.

77. *ED*, VI, 57-8. Cf K. J. Fielding, '*Edwin Drood* and Governor Eyre', *Listener*, 25 December 1952, 1083-4.

78. *Guardian*, 10 February 1961; *ED*, xvii, 190–5. Cf House, *Dickens World*, 87–8: 'The Jellyby episode in *Bleak House* is an excellent example of the strength and the weakness of Dickens's use of fiction as a medium of social criticism: it is prodigiously strong in personalities, but weak in arguments. The inference is that because Mrs Jellyby is ridiculous, everything she advocates is automatically ridiculous.'

79. 'Model Prisons', *Latter Day Pamphlets*, 79, 90.

80. M. St John Packe, *Life of John Stuart Mill*, 1954, 370, 465; cf Tallack, *Howard Memories*, 152. Mill spoke against abolition on 21 April 1868.

81. Spielmann, 3; George Saintsbury, *A Reconsideration of Thackeray*, 1931, 56.

82. Tallack, *Howard Memories*, 138, 143–9. In 1931, the Howard Association merged with the Penal Reform League, to become the Howard League (its Honorary Librarian, Miss W. A. Elkin, tells me). On the development and personalities of the Society for the Abolition of Capital Punishment, see Dymond, *The Law on its Trial*.

83. *Daily News*, 28 February 1846.

84. James Pope-Hennessy, *Monckton Milnes: the Years of Promise*, 1949, 130.

85. *NN*, iv, 30.

86. 'The Lazy Tour of Two Idle Apprentices,' iv, *HW*, 24 October 1857 (*CS*, 727–8).

87. *BR*, lxxvi, 583.

88. *Athenaeum*, 12 June 1875, quoted by Murch, 155 note.

89. 9 October 1867, *N*, iii, 559.

90. *OT*, l, 391. (The dog is, of course, Sikes's mongrel Bull's-eye). Sikes was originally to have been judicially hanged: sketches by Dickens's illustrator, Cruikshank, have survived showing 'Bill Sikes in the Condemned Cell' (F. G. Kitton, *Dickens and his Illustrators*, 1899, 14–15; 'Some Unpublished Sketches by George Cruikshank', *Strand Magazine*, xiv, 183–91, reproducing a specimen). Presumably, at some stage, Dickens had either not intended to have Fagin hanged, or had intended to hang them both but then decided against such a duplication.

91. *D & S*, lv, 779. On Dickens's sadism, see Praz, 137–9, 158–63, 285–6; and on Carker's death, see Cockshut, *Imagination of Dickens*, 102–3. Cockshut has an interesting comment on Sikes's death also: Sikes, as murderer, 'deserves' hanging, so the crowd howling for his death is assumed to be just, and when it sees him hang himself it enjoys 'all the satisfaction of a lynching without the material guilt of laying a finger on the man. The accident appears to provide a perfect moral loophole. But . . . [Dickens] connives at a fake lynching which is all the more distasteful for being presented as nobody's fault' (ibid, 70).

92. *OCS*, lxvii, 510.

93. Forster, 445 (and cf pp 449, 451); *Mr and Mrs*, 28 June 1850, 140–1; 'Some Recollections of Mortality', *AYR*, 16 May 1863 (*UT*, 188–94). 'Whenever I am at Paris, I am dragged by invisible force into the Morgue. I never want to go there, but am always pulled there' ('Travelling Abroad', *AYR*, 7 April 1860 [*UT*, 64]).

94. Forster, 523; cf *Mr and Mrs*, 130–3. Rush, the local farmer found guilty of this murder, did indeed receive a particularly impressive execution, under the walls of Norwich Castle (Irving, *Annals*, 265–6, 274; Dodds, *Age of Paradox*, 348–9). This case, which attracted vast interest at the time, has recently been reviewed, and Rush's guilt questioned, by Owen Chadwick, *Victorian Miniature*, 1960, 106–20.

95. Yates, ii, 104–5.

96. Collins, 12 January 1868, and Fields, 15 January 1868, *N*, iii, 599–600, 605. Dickens repeats the story to Lytton (December 1867, *N*, iii, 591). His guide on this excursion was Oliver Wendell Holmes (M. A. De Wolfe Howe, *Memories of a Hostess*, 1923, 153). An account of this famous case by Sir James Emerson Tennent, 'The Killing of Dr Parkman', appeared about this time in *AYR* (14

December 1867, xix, 9–16). Dickens had mentioned this before leaving England (Wills, October 1867, *N*, iii, 563).

97. Napier, 28 July 1845, *N*, i, 689; 'Pet Prisoners', *HW*, 27 April 1850 (*MP*, 228); 'The Demeanour of Murderers', *HW*, 14 June 1856 (*MP*, 594–8); 'The Murdered Person', *HW*, 11 October 1856 (*MP*, 603–4); 'Murderous Extremes', *HW*, 3 January 1857 (*MP*, 607–11); 'Five New Points of Criminal Law', *AYR*, 24 September 1859 (*MP*, 684–5). Cf 'Hunted Down', v (*SB*, 684–5), on murderers as calculating monsters without any conscience.

98. 'Lying Awake', *HW*, 30 October 1852 (*RP*, 437). But in 1846 he had wanted bigamists 'flogged more than once (privately)' and transported (Forster, 412 note).

99. Cf *The Times* in 1842, urging suitable punishment for a young hunchback named Bean, who had attempted to shoot Queen Victoria: 'One or more very hearty floggings in public is the kind of medicine which this disgraceful vanity best deserves. . . . Nor should we be at all sorry if his case were a precedent for some slight revival of this punishment. Englishmen are getting, not benevolent, but sentimental in such matters. Most men in the present (we must say) morbid state of public feeling would shrink from the plain and striking severity, short-lived and very trifling as it is, of the cat-o'-nine-tails, far more than the real and enduring horrors of solitary confinement' (quoted by Thomson, *Scotland Yard*, 107).

100. 'The Ruffian', *AYR*, 10 October 1868 (*UT*, 302).

CHAPTER XI:
MURDER — FROM BILL SIKES TO BRADLEY HEADSTONE

1. Forster, 43 note; Thomas Wright, 64–5. Cf 'Nurse's Stories' (*UT*, 148–58).
2. See Wilson, 9–11. The stories are 'The Stroller's Tale', 'The Convict's Return', 'A Madman's Manuscript', and 'The Old Man's Tale about the Queer Client' (*PP*, iii, vi, xi, xxi).
3. For Mrs Tillotson's argument that Dickens first conceived *OT* in 1833, see her essay in *E & S*, ns, xii, 88–90.
4. See Butt and Tillotson, 77–8; and for the early Dickens's self-identification with Scott see Forster, 306; *MP*, 75–89; *Dick*, xlvi (1950), 122–7.
5. Vizetelly, *Glances back*, i, 143. On Ainsworth's popularity, see S. M. Ellis, *William Harrison Ainsworth and his Friends*, 1911, Vol i, Chapters vii, viii, xi.
6. *Punch*, 7 August 1841, i, 39.
7. Captain Hay to a House of Lords Committee, quoted by Antrobus, *Prison and School*, 29–32. *Martha Willis* (1831) was a popular highwayman play by Jerrold; for synopsis, see Walter Jerrold, *Douglas Jerrold*, [1919], i, 181–3.
8. M. A. De Wolfe Howe, *Memories of a Hostess*, 1923, 176–7; 1841 Preface to *OT* (*CP*, 262); Dickens's diary, 13 December 1838, *N*, i, 151; and cf Ellis, *Ainsworth*, Vol i, Chapters viii and ix.
9. Butt and Tillotson, 59 and note; R. H. Horne, 1839, *N*, i, 240.
10. Probably referring to Planché's popular operetta *The Brigand* (Fitzgerald, *Dickens*, ii, 230). Dickens had made much the same point, over two years before, and in much the same words, when *OT* was still being serialised — 'A thief in fustian is a vulgar character, scarcely to be thought of by persons of refinement; but dress him in green velvet, with a high-crowned hat, and change the scene of his operations, from thickly peopled city, to a mountain road, and you shall find in him the very soul of poetry and adventure.' (*NN*, xviii, 215: in Number vi, published in September 1838.)
11. 1841, Preface to *OT* (*CP*, 261–4).
12. *E & S*, loc cit, 99–101; *The Girlhood of Queen Victoria: a Selection from Her Majesty's Diaries 1832–40*, ed Viscount Esher, 1912, ii, 86, 89, 91, 144. Mrs Tillotson aptly

cites R. H. Horne's endorsement of Dickens's policy — 'Three words — nay, three letters — would have cost him tens of thousands of readers in nearly every class of society, and they would have lost all the good and all the delight they have derived from his writings' (*Spirit of the Age*, 1844, 9). How much he lost in realism, as a result, has been noted by many recent writers: eg, House, *Dickens World*, 215–17.

13. *Rookwood*, Preface and 'L'Envoy'; Ellis, *Ainsworth*, I, 236.

14. Lytton, 1840 Prefaces to *Eugene Aram* and *Paul Clifford*; cf Paul Clifford's speeches in Court, in Chapter XXXV. On the Godwinian-criminalistic background to Lytton's early novels, see Michael Sadleir, *Bulwer: a Panorama*, 1931. Most contemporaries agreed with Dickens in preferring Lytton's moral approach to Ainsworth's; see, eg, R. H. Horne's judgments on *Paul Clifford* and *Jack Sheppard* (*Spirit of the Age*, 388, 402). But Thackeray and *Punch* were probably right in maintaining that Lytton's moral confusions and self-deceptions were no more praiseworthy than Ainsworth's frank amorality.

15. For further comments on Dickens and 'the Newgate Novel', see Ford, *Dickens and his Readers*, 38–42; Praz, *Hero in Eclipse*, 160–2; Tillotson, *Eighteen Forties*, 75–8; Lindsay, *Dickens*, 145–8; Monod, *Dickens romancier*, 104–11; and G. A. Sala, *Life and Adventures*, 1895, I, 94–104 (and cf pp 89, 209). On analogous blood-and-thunder magazine stories of this period, see Dalziel, *Popular Fiction 100 Years Ago*, and for American comparisons, Mary Noel, *Villains Galore*, New York, 1954.

16. Thackeray, *Letters*, I, 433.

17. *Catherine*, final paragraph of Chapter I, and final paragraphs of 'Another Last Chapter' (ed cit, 31–2, 185–7). Cf 'Going to see a Man hanged' (ibid, 198). Dickens replied to Thackeray's criticism of Nancy's conduct — 'IT IS TRUE' (*OT*, 1841 Preface, *CP*, 264). See also Thackeray's *Barry Lyndon* (1844) and his *Punch* parody of Lytton, 'George de Barnwell, by Sir E. L. B. L. Bart.' (*Punch*, 3 and 17 April 1847, reprinted in *Miscellaneous Contributions to 'Punch' 1843–54*, Oxford Thackeray, 84–98). This had been a favourite *Punch* item before Thackeray joined the staff: cf 'Literary Recipes', quoted above (7 August 1841, I, 39), and 'Murderers as they are, and Murderers as they ought to be' — a parallel-column comparison between *Eugene Aram* and *Jack Sheppard* and the actual facts they romanticised (early 1842, II, 82, 98).

18. Eg, Richard Ford — 'But we object *in toto* to the staple of *Oliver Twist* — a series of representations which must familiarise the rising generation with . . . the very dregs of the community. . . . Nancy is a character which all will admit is delineated with great power, however much they may differ in regard to its propriety and truth' (*Quarterly Review*, LXIV [1839], 97). Also Wilkie Collins — 'The character of "Nancy" is the finest thing he ever did. He never afterwards saw all sides of a woman's character — saw all round her.' (*Pall Mall Gazette*, 20 January 1890.)

19. *OT*, 1841 Preface (*CP*, 263–4).

20. On Solomon and pickpockets, see Goddard, *Memoirs*, 40–1; Carpenter, *Our Convicts*, I, 65–6; Reith, *British Police*, 50; Harry Stone, 'Dickens and the Jews', *Victorian Studies*, II (1959), 225–6, 233–5. On Saffron Hill 'flash-houses' like Fagin's The Three Cripples, see W. J. Pinks, *History of Clerkenwell*, 1865, 355–6, and Radzinowicz, II, 297–306. On the stolen-handkerchief industry, see Vizetelly, *Glances back*, I, 122, and T. A. Trollope, *What I remember*, 1887, I, 10–11. On all these activities, the great guide is Volume IV of Mayhew's *London Labour and the London Poor*, 1862 (selection by Peter Quennell, in *London's Underworld*); parallels to *OT* occur on every page. For an excellent history of the Fagin area, Field Lane, see *Ragged School Union Quarterly Record*, II (1877), 41–59. This magazine and its predecessor, *RSUM* (1849–75), are almost untapped mines of information on London poverty and crime.

21. R. H. Gooch, reported by Thomas Wright, *Dickens*, 118; Forster, 112–13, 475–7, and Ley, *Dickens Circle*, 18–20.

22. On these aspects of *OT*, see Kettle, *English Novel*, 123–38; Miller, *Charles Dickens*, 36–84; Graham Greene, *The Lost Childhood and other Essays*, 1951, 51–7. Dickens's personal involvement as Oliver Twist has often been noted, as has his using here the name of his companion of the blocking warehouse period, Bob Fagin (Forster, 25); see Ernest Boll, 'Charles Dickens in Oliver Twist', *Psychoanalytic Review*, xxvii (1940), 133.

23. Forster, 111; 1841 Preface — but cf the 1856 Preface where the more secular word 'incurably' replaces 'irredeemably' (*CP*, 264, 270).

24. *OT*, xiii, 86.

25. xxxix, 287.

26. Horne, *Spirit of the Age*, 26–7. Professor Monod makes the interesting observation that Dickens can afford to expend sympathy on Sikes, and later on Fagin, because by this stage of the story Oliver is safe: they replace him as victim (see his excellent Introduction to his translation *Les Aventures d'Olivier Twist*, Classiques Garnier, Paris, 1957, xxviii–xxix).

27. *OT*, xlviii, 363, 367–8, 370.

28. l, 388–90.

29. W. H. Brookfield, 24 May 1863, *N*, iii, 353; Forster, 111.

30. Macready, *Diaries*, i, 475; Frederick Yates, [29 November] 1838, *N*, i, 179; John Hollingshead, *My Lifetime*, 1895, i, 188. Hollingshead agreed with the Lord Chamberlain's decision — and, as founder of the Gaiety, he was no prude theatrically.

31. *North British Review*, iii (1845), 82.

32. Hollingshead, op cit, i, 189–90. All the 'Newgate Novels' were great stage-successes, and that is how Turpin and Sheppard and Sikes became familiar to the illiterate. Social workers particularly deplored the effects of *Jack Sheppard*, which was playing in eight London theatres simultaneously; its hero's criminal exploits always delighted the audiences (see, eg, Clay, 504, 532; Mayhew, *London's Underworld*, 274; Lindsay, *Dickens*, 147).

33. Forster, 799–800.

34. Charles Dickens, the Younger, 'Glimpses of Charles Dickens', *North American Review*, clx (1895), 680–1.

35. Kent, *Dickens as a Reader*, 259–60; Dickens to Kent, 16 November 1868, *N*, iii, 678. Kent's chapter on this Reading gives a good account of his preparations and performance. The text of *Sikes and Nancy* is reprinted with a useful Introduction by J. H. Stonehouse, 1921.

36. Mrs J. T. Fields, 16 December 1868, *N*, iii, 686–7.

37. Wilkie Collins, 8 December, and Frith, 16 November 1868, *N*, iii, 681, 678.

38. *N*, iii, 681, 700; Dolby, *Dickens as I knew him*, 386.

39. Mary Boyle, 6 January 1869; Fields, 9 April; Mary Dickens, 27 January; Fitzgerald, 15 January; Fields, 15 February (*N*, iii, 699, 718–19, 702, 700, 704).

40. Forster, 800.

41. Wilson, 61. Even at rehearsals of *The Frozen Deep* (1856–7) his realism was 'positively alarming — not to say painful', recalled his eldest son. 'In his demented condition in the last act when he had to rush off the stage, he went at it with such a will that the others had to attack him like prize-fighters' (Charles Dickens, the Younger, loc cit, 536).

42. Forster, 646.

43. Dolby, 388, 442. Dolby's book gives much interesting information about Dickens on and off the stage during the period of this Reading.

44. Wills, 23 January 1870, *N*, iii, 761.

45. Dolby, 444, 386. For his doctor's diary on the physiological effects of the 'Murder' see *Dickens to his Oldest Friend*, ed Walter Dexter, 1932, 253–4.

46. Thomas Wright of Olney, *An Autobiography*, 1936, 247; cf Forster, 804–5.

47. Kent, 87; John Hollingshead, quoted in *Sikes and Nancy*, ed Stonehouse, xi.
48. Robinson, *Wilkie Collins*, 243; W. H. Bowen, *Charles Dickens and his Family*, Cambridge, 1956, 148–59.
49. Forster, 641, 639.
50. Dolby, 435; Forster, 810.
51. *OCS*, LXII, 463; XXI, 165; LXII, 461; XLIX, 369; XI, 86; XLVIII, 356.
52. V, 40; LXII, 463; LXVII, 503; IV, 37; XLVIII, 360.
53. IV, 32. For Tom Scott, see V, 41–3, and VI, 46–7.
54. *BR*, I, 13; II, 17.
55. Quoted by Gerald G. Grubb, with great scepticism, in 'The Personal and Literary Relationships of Dickens and Poe', *NCF*, V (1950), 1–22 — *q.v.* on *BR*.
56. Poe's clever review of *BR* in *Graham's Magazine*, February 1842, which reprints part of his earlier forecast from the *Philadelphia Saturday Evening Post* of 1 May 1841, may be found in *The Book of Poe*, ed Addison Hibbard, New York, 1929, 97–115. The full text of the *Philadelphia Post* review is reprinted in *Dick*, IX (1913), 274–8; see discussion of it in William Robertson Nicoll, *Dickens's Own Story*, 1923, 221–44. Gissing also writes well on Dickens's 'inability to make skilful revelation of circumstances which, for the purpose of the story, he has kept long concealed.... Demand from him a contrived story, and he yields at once to the very rank and file of novelists' (*Charles Dickens*, 53).
57. *BR*, VI, 50.
58. XVI, 124; XVII, 128.
59. Forster, 170; Kent, 258; *The Book of Poe*, 112.
60. *BR*, XVIII, 138–9, 142.
61. See Lindsay, 146–8, and R. C. Churchill, 'Dickens, Drama and Tradition', *Scrutiny*, X (1942), 358–75.
62. *BR*, XVII, 129; LXXIII, 565. 'Don't fail to erase anything that seems to you too strong,' Dickens wrote to Forster. Some of Rudge's 'stronger' expressions, happily deleted by Forster in proof, are printed by Professor Monod (Forster, 167; *Dickens romancier*, 186–9).
63. LV, 419–20; LVIII, 442–3; LXII, 471–2.
64. *MC*, XXXVIII, 597–8.
65. XLI, 643; XLIV, 686; XLVII, 729 — the endings of the monthly Numbers XV, XVI, and XVII respectively. Chapter XLII also ends with Montague's 'I'll travel home alone!'
66. XLII, 644; XLI, 641; XLII, 646; XLIV, 685. Obenreizer, in 'No Thoroughfare', inherits Jonas's bad luck as a murderer — he makes two attempts to kill Vendale and filch an incriminating document from his pocket, but Vendale's body rolls over a precipice before he can rob it — and then, some months afterwards, Vendale suddenly confronts him, 'a man risen from the dead'. In both stories, the succession of attempts is provided, not to illustrate any theme or character, but merely to prolong the agony.
67. *MC*, XLVII, 721; cf Warrington Winters, 'Dickens and the Psychology of Dreams', *PMLA*, XLIII (1948), 984–1006.
68. XLVII, 725–9.
69. *OMF*, II, i, 217.
70. *MC*, XLVI, 717; Lane, 'Dickens and the Double', *Dick*, LV (1959) 47–55. The above paragraph owes much to Dr Lane's essay. He offers another useful comment on Dickens's preoccupation with evil in 'The Devil in *Oliver Twist*', *Dick*, LII (1956), 132–6.
71. *BH*, XXIII, 320. On Hortense and Mrs Manning, see above, p 344.
72. *LD*, I, XXX, 352; i, 9.
73. House, *All in due Time*, 218.
74. See Wakefield, *Facts*, 39; Radzinowicz, I, 624–5.

75. *LD*, II, xxx, 763; I, xxx, 353; I, viii, 89. Cf his remarks on the psychology of murder, quoted above (pp 230–1).
76. Wilson, 15.
77. On Bradley Headstone as a study in social mobility, see Chapter VII of my book *Dickens and Education*.
78. Wilkie Collins, 21 March 1858, *N*, III, 14. The facts and the significance of the Ellen Ternan effort have been much discussed lately: see, eg, Ada B. Nisbet, *Dickens and Ellen Ternan*, and Felix Aylmer, *Dickens Incognito*. Since his book was published, however, Mr Aylmer has withdrawn his conjecture about Ellen's having borne a child by Dickens, which was registered under the name of Tringham. For further discussion, see below, pp 309–16.
79. Slinkton keeps insuring his friends and relatives, whose health rapidly deteriorates thereafter. He is generally regarded as a 'portrait' of the artist-murderer Wainewright, sentenced in 1837 (when Dickens saw him in Newgate) — but several features in his presentation, and the proximity of date, suggest that Dickens was also recalling Palmer of Rugeley — another wholesale murderer of persons he had insured, sentenced in 1856, three years before 'Hunted Down'. Dickens mentions the Wainewright case in his Memorandum Book (Forster, 749, 453 note) and the Palmer case in his 'Demeanour of Murderers' (*MP*, 594; cf *N*, II, 776, 884).
80. *OMF*, II, xiii, 367–72; IV, xii, 761–5
81. Squires, 'Dickens as Criminologist', 192–9, 189.
82. *OMF*, II, vi, 292; xv, 398.
83. *ED*, xx, 225; *OMF*, IV, vii, 713.
84. *OMF*, III, x, 544; xi, 546–7.
85. II, i, 218. The *fire* and *animal* images here introduced recur throughout the presentation of Headstone — eg, II, vi, 288, 294; xi, 341, 345; xv, 396; III, xi, 546–7 (quoted above), 555.
86. IV, vii, 708–9.
87. V, xv, 791.
88. IV, xv, 802; Lane, *Dick*, LV (1959), 50–2.
89. A number of parallels, frivolous and otherwise, between *OMF* and Eliot's *The Waste Land* are noted in Lionel Trilling's *A Gathering of Fugitives*, 1957, 42–3. See also Cockshut, 175–9.

CHAPTER XII: THE MYSTERIES IN *EDWIN DROOD*

1. Kate Perugini, '*Edwin Drood* and the last days of Charles Dickens', *Pall Mall Magazine*, XXXVII (1906), 643–4; Pansy Pakenham, 'The Memorandum Book, Forster, and *Edwin Drood*', *Dick*, LI (1955), 120, and LII (1956), 96. Kate Perugini's article is reprinted in Robertson Nicoll's useful book *The Problem of 'Edwin Drood'*; so are many other basic items in the evidence, such as those (quoted below) written by Forster, Charley Dickens, Luke Fildes, and Dickens himself (the MS Number-Plans).
2. Orwell, 45; cf Professor Monod on the extensive *Droodiana* — 'Le ton général de cette littérature est alarmant. Il est effroyablement sérieux. Les auteurs semblent oublier qu'il s'agit d'un roman, de personnages imaginaires, et du plus grand humoriste, peut-être, de tous les temps . . .' (*Dickens romancier*, 467). Dr K. J. Fielding has argued — conclusively, in my opinion — that 'From first to last there is no reason to think that Dickens owed anything in his development as a novelist to Wilkie Collins' (*Dick*, XLIX [1952], 130–6). Cf A. A. Adrian, 'A Note on the Dickens-Collins friendship', *HLQ*, XVI (1953), 211–13.
3. Gissing, 69, 190. Gissing deplored Dickens's attraction to mystery and murder —

'so far from being the true material of his art' — and his final years when 'he saw murder at the end of every vista' (p 69).

4. *OMF*, 'Postscript in lieu of a Preface', 821.

5. 'Curious Misprint in the Edinburgh Review', *HW*, 1 August 1857 (*MP*, 629).

6. Quicklime does not, in fact, have the convenient properties commonly attributed to it by murderers, fictional and actual (Baker, *The Drood Murder Case*, 140–2; *Dick*, xxv [1929], 28–30). One critic suggests that Dickens, 'who lived so near the Medway Cement Works', must have known this, and therefore intended that Jasper would get caught through his ignorance (Saunders, *The Mystery in the Drood Family*, 120). But Forster's account of Dickens's intentions, quoted below, indicates that Dickens shared the common misapprehension, or at least that he expected his readers to do so. The Mannings in 1849 had buried their victim in quicklime; he was identifiable only through his false teeth (Dodds, 389). According to Forster, Edwin's body was to have been identified by the ring in his pocket; Dickens had certainly drawn attention to it very portentously — '. . . thus was one chain forged [in the vast iron-works of time and circumstance], . . . gifted with invincible force to hold and drag' (*ED*, XIII, 151).

7. Quoted by Nicoll, 58–65. The originals are in the Forster Collection, Victoria and Albert Museum.

8. Forster, 808. The 'fancy I told you of' was not entirely laid aside: it concerned 'Two people, boy and girl, . . . pledged to be married after many years . . .' (ibid, 807).

9. Joseph Francis Daly, *Augustin Daly*, New York, 1917, 107–8. The much-discussed cover design to *ED* is reproduced in most good reprints (eg, the Chiltern Library edn, with Introduction by Michael Innes, 1950, and the New Oxford Illustrated edn, with Introduction by S. C. Roberts, 1956), and in most books about *ED*.

10. W. R. Hughes, *A Week's Tramp in Dickens Land*, 1891, 140–1; letter from Fildes in *The Times*, 3 November 1905.

11. Kate Perugini, loc cit, 654.

12. Charles Dickens the Younger, Introduction to *ED*, Macmillan edn, 1923, xv. But see K. J. Fielding's criticisms of the accuracy of Charley's memory, in 'The Dramatisation of *Edwin Drood*', *Theatre Notebook*, VII (1953), 52–8. Cf Malcolm Morley, 'Stage Solutions to the Mystery', *Dick*, LIII (1957), 46–8, 93–7, 180–4.

13. Baker, 91–119, 'The Genesis of *Edwin Drood*'.

14. See Nicoll, 4–19, on the MS and proofs, and Henry Jackson, *About 'Edwin Drood'*, 35–7, on the chapter-order: also Jackson's letter withdrawing this theory, *TLS*, 7 August 1919.

15. The cases for these claimants are stated by the following authors, among others — Helena (Nicoll, 141–83; Jackson, 38–54; Walters, *Clues to 'Edwin Drood'*, 63–70); Grewgious (Baker, Chapter 1); Bazzard (Edwin Charles, *Keys to the Drood Mystery*, Birmingham, 1908; W. W. Bleifuss, *Dick*, LI [1954], 24–9); Neville (Andrew Lang, *The Puzzle of Dickens's Last Plot*, 1905); Tartar (G. F. Gadd, *Dick*, II [1906], 13; Edwin Drood (R. A. Proctor, *Watched by the Dead*, 1887); a new character (Pansy Pakenham, *Dick*, LI [1955], 121); a member of the solicitors' firm (Saunders, 81–8). Other claimants include an uncle of Edwin Drood's, long resident abroad (Mary Kavanagh, *A New Solution to the Mystery of Edwin Drood*, 1919, 29–30), an ordinary detective, and Mr Poker of the rejected 'Eight Club' chapter (Walters [1912], 230, 208). For a convenient summary, see 'Conclusions to *Edwin Drood* Tabulated' (Walters [1912], facing p 254).

16. Kate Perugini, loc cit, 643–4.

17. Fielding, *Charles Dickens*, 201–2. The text 'When the wicked man — ' occurs prominently at the end of Chapter 1, when we first see the Cathedral. The 'Resurrection and the Life' text, central in *TTC*, appears two pages from the end of the last chapter of *ED* that Dickens wrote.

18. Henry Jackson, remarking how uncertain is the function of 'When the wicked man — ', wonders whether it is significant that Dickens quotes only these four words, and stops short of the idea of repentance and salvation (*About 'Edwin Drood'*, 90).

19. XIX, 219–20. Mr Baker points out that, when last we see him, Jasper is far from repentant; he is plotting the murder of Neville, his new rival for the affections of Rosa Bud (*Drood Murder Case*, 86–7).

20. XVI, 188.

21. XXIII, 261.

22. II, 13–4. Significantly, the tension disappears on the day of the murder. He had 'never sung . . . with such skill and harmony'; it seemed that 'a false note was not within his power tonight' (XIV, 164–7).

23. XIV, 167–8. Cf *Macbeth*, II, iii, 55–64 ('The night has been unruly; where we lay Our chimneys were blown down . . .' — ' 'Twas a rough night' — 'My young remembrance cannot parallel A fellow to it'.) Also cf II, iv, 4–20, and IV, i, 52–61. See Howard Duffield, 'The Macbeth Motif in *Edwin Drood*', *Dick*, XXX (1934), 263–71, and Lindsay, 403–5. Lindsay makes some interesting suggestions about the relation between *ED* and novels by Lytton and Lady Lytton (pp 406–9, 449).

24. XXIII, 268; cf *Macbeth*, I, viii, 51–2.

25. III, 19; *Macbeth*, III, ii, 50–1, and I, v, 38.

26. *OT*, XLVIII, 369; cf *Macbeth*, V, viii, 12, 'I bear a charmed life'. For further parallels in *OT* and *BR*, see Monod, 114–15, 171.

27. *MC*, XLVII, 726; cf *Macbeth*, II, ii, 56–73.

28. *OMF*, IV, xv, 791–2; *Macbeth*, III, iv, 20, and III, i, 60–9.

29. The Shadwell excursion took place in May 1869 (*N*, III, 725, 727 and cf 775), and one of Dickens's companions records that 'In a miserable court at night, we found a haggard old woman blowing at a kind of pipe made of an old ink-bottle; and the words that Dickens puts into the mouth of this wretched creature in *Edwin Drood*, we heard her croon as we leaned over the tattered bed in which she was lying'. (Forster, 844.) Dickens was planning *ED* in July and August (Forster, 807–8; Nicoll, 57), but must have begun thinking about it in June at the latest.

30. Cf 'Lazarus Lotus-Eating', *AYR*, 12 May 1866, XV, 421–5 (by J. C. Parkinson: reprinted in his *Places and People*, 1869); 'In an Opium Den', *RSUM*, XX (1868), 199–200 (this vice has only 'recently crept into London . . .'). Frederick Wellesley describes a visit with Inspector Field to Sally the Opium Smoker: aged twenty-six, she looked eighty at least (*Recollections of a Soldier-Diplomat*, 1947, 75–6). For further, information see my 'Inspector Bucket visits the Princess Puffer', *Dick*, May 1964.

31. VI, 56, and Nicoll, 60; II, 8. Mr Lindsay asserts that the oriental references in *ED* were to embody Dickens's animadversions on imperialist exploitation (pp 392, 394, 401). I see no evidence at all for this prognostication.

32. Howard Duffield, 'John Jasper — Strangler', *The American Bookman*, February 1930; cf Wilson, 76–9, and Baker, 74–7.

33. II, 10, 14; III, 29–30; VII, 65, 68–9; XIX, 217; XX, 226.

34. XVI, 183.

35. III, 20.

36. VII, 66, 69, 64. On hypnotism, see Aubrey Boyd, 'A New Angle on the Drood Mystery', *Washinton University Studies: Humanistic Series*, IX, October 1921.

37. XXIII, 269, 273. Nicoll, 19, points out that the sentence about '. . . what can be said in its praise' was added as an afterthought in the MS.

38. XXIII, 278. This is the last item of dialogue that Dickens wrote before his death.

39. A. J. A. Waldock, *Hamlet: a Study in Critical Method*, Cambridge, 1931, Preface, 23, 34, 49, 98.

40. Wilson, 78, 83.

41. Ibid, 89.

42. Ford, 253.

43. Wilson, 92.

44. *ED*, II, 9, 7; XIII, 150. Dr Lauriat Lane goes so far as to assert that 'Jasper's love for Edwin was fully as deep as his desire for Rosa'. As over other theories, I must object that the evidence is much too slight and ambiguous to justify such categorical claims. There is no evidence whatever that Jasper is, as Dr Lane says, 'torn between his active desire for Rosa Bud and an excessive love for his nephew,' and thus 'represents a far subtler psychological problem than Dickens had ever before hinted at' (*Dick*, LV [1959], 54; and cf Baker, 44).

45. XXIII, 266.

46. Wilson, 92–3.

47. *ED*, XXIII, 261.

48. X, 109–10; XIV, 165–6; XVI, 188.

49. According to his daughter Katey, 'he often said that the most clever criminals were constantly detected through some small defect in their calculations.' This was 'the pet theory that he so frequently mentioned whenever a murder case was brought to trial' (Kate Dickens Perugini, '*Edwin Drood* and the Last Days of Charles Dickens', *Pall Mall Magazine*, XXXVII [1906], 648). Cf *OMF*, IV, vii, 708 (quoted above, p 287).

50. *Dick*, LI (1955), 119–20.

51. The idea of making the murderer speak of himself 'as of another' may have been suggested by Emily Jolly's story 'An Experience' (*AYR*, 14 and 21 August 1869, NS, II, 256–64, 280–8). F. G. Kitton reports, without quoting his authority, that this story 'suggested an alteration of plot' in *ED* (*The Novels of Charles Dickens*, 1897, 217). Certainly Dickens praised it as 'a very remarkable story indeed' in the same letter to Forster as mentioned the 'very curious and new idea' for his new novel, and many letters from this period, when he was devising *ED*, contain extravagant praise for this very mediocre tale (Forster, 807 note; *N*, III, 731–8 *passim*). His enthusiasm for it betrays his taste for crude and improbable sensation. Its only similarity to *ED* seems to be the account of the hero's delirium after illness — 'I knew all these things, but they seemed to concern some other person' (loc cit, 282). On this and other possible hints from *AYR* stories, see Baker, 95–112.

52. See the excellent criticism of the Wilsonians by William R. Clark, 'The Rationale of Dickens's Death Rate'. The high death-rate among Dickens's characters has, he argues, been taken much too seriously by those recent critics who have tried to make him a tragic figure. I have argued in similar terms, in *Dick*, LV (1959), 34–5.

53. Pritchett, *The Living Novel*, 74. Another remark in this stimulating essay suggests an approach to Dickens's criminal characters: '. . . it is really alien to Dickens's gift that his people should be made to talk to each other. . . . His natural genius is for human soliloquy not human intercourse. . . . For the distinguishing quality of Dickens's people is that they are solitaries. They are people caught living in a world of their own' (ibid, 77–8).

54. Gissing, 270, 112. Cf Symons, 82–3, on the 'terribly damaging' comparison with Dostoevsky.

55. Wilson, 92–3.

56. Ibid, 26, 56–7.

57. Sala, I, 76–7. Cf Forster, 829 — 'his old unaltered wish to better what was bad in English institutions, carried with it no desire to replace them by new ones.'

58. Henry Fielding Dickens, *Memories of my Father*, 1928, 31. Cf Dickens's remark on himself, at a period when he was suffering from heart-trouble — 'I have noticed for some time a decided change in my bouyancy and hopefulness — in other words, in my usual "tone" ' (Georgina Hogarth, 9 February 1866, *N*, III, 460).

59. Kate Dickens Perugini died in 1929, and Miss Storey's book was published in 1939.

By then the Ellen Ternan story had been told (though much remained — and remains — to be discovered about it) by Thomas Wright, in the *Daily Express* (3 April 1934), *The Life of Charles Dickens* (1935), and *Thomas Wright of Olney: an Autobiography* (1936). The first important studies of Dickens to take account of these new facts were T. A. Jackson's (1937) and Edmund Wilson's (1941). Mr Wilson's 'Two Scrooges' essay was first given in lecture-form in 1939, and parts of it appeared in *The New Republic* and *The Atlantic Monthly* in 1940.

60. As someone neatly remarked on the similar excitement caused by the discovery of Wordsworth's affair with Annette Vallon, 'The nineteenth century admired Wordsworth because he proclaimed a natural religion: the twentieth, because he begot a natural daughter.'

61. Carlyle to Forster, 11 June 1870 and 16 February 1874, quoted by Johnson, II, 1155.

62. Mrs Lynn Linton, *My Literary Life*, 1899, 61, 64, 69, 71.

63. Mrs Brown, 28 August 1857, *Coutts*, 346.

64. Catherine Dickens, 5 December 1853, *Mr and Mrs*, 227.

65. Mrs Watson, 7 December 1857, *Dick*, XXXVIII (1942), 190.

66. Forster, 640-1.

67. On Dickens as mesmerist, see Storey, 64; Wilson, 79-81; Johnson, I, 221, 409 541-59, and II, 670.

68. Georgina Hogarth, 12 May 1870, *N*, III, 776.

69. For some examples of these speculations, see Wright, 281, 284-5, 288, 298; Wilson, 62-5, 85; Lindsay, 344-8, 360-4, 372-3, 382-4, 393-402; Johnson, II, 972-3, 991-2, 1038-41, 1123; Aylmer, 82-8.

70. Wright, 356, 280; Johnson, II, 1007-8, 1104.

71. The only suggestion that Edwin Drood represents, psychologically, a rival to Dickens (though in his literary, not his amatory, life) depends upon the resemblance between his name and that of a young man, Edwin Drew, whom he advised, about this period, not to risk trying to earn a living in London literary circles (Wright, 298, 345). This may have suggested a *Master-Builder* 'youth knocking on the door' idea (Lindsay, 399-400). But it is not overtly present in *ED*, of course: Jasper, like Headstone, is a young man, not a frustrated middle-aged one.

71a. The only exception I have noticed occurs in his memorable conversation with his daughter Katey, the day before his fatal stroke. 'He wished, he said, that he had been "a better father — a better man". . .' He was referring to the Ellen Ternan affair (Storey, 134).

72. Catherine Dickens, 21 November 1853, *Mr and Mrs*, 217.

73. *N*, II, 566, 713, 848; Edgar Johnson, II, 859; *N*, III, 38.

74. Wright, 243.

75. S. T. Coleridge, *Essays and Lectures on Shakespeare*, Everyman edn, 1907, 53-4.

76. *DC*, XLII, 606.

77. Henry Fielding Dickens, *Memories of my Father*, 28.

78. Squires, 'Charles Dickens as Criminologist', 171, 201.

79. Reported in *The Guardian*, 17 February 1961.

80. *News of the World*, 7 October 1956.

81. D. L. Howard, *The English Prisons*, 86; Howard Jones, *Prison Reform Now*, 4.

82. Reported in *The Eastern Daily News*, 11 December 1958.

83. Cf letters to de Cerjat, 29 December 1849, and Mrs Watson, 27 August 1853, *N*, II, 194, 484.

84. Vincent Starrett, *The Private Life of Sherlock Holmes*, 1961, 41. By contrast, when I asked a member of the staff at Arbury Hall just where on the adjoining estate George Eliot was born, she replied that she had never heard of him.

85. Ouvry, 2 July 1862, *N*, III, 299.

86. William Tallack, *Penological and Preventive Principles*, 2nd edn, 1896, 161-5 (expanded from 1st edn, 1889, 133-4).

BIBLIOGRAPHY

Place of publication London, unless otherwise stated

Acton, William — *Prostitution, considered in its Moral, Social, and Sanitary Aspects*, 1857

Adshead, Joseph — *Prisons and Prisoners*, 1845

Antrobus, Edmund Edward — *The Prison and the School*, 1853

Armitage, Gilbert — *The History of the Bow Street Runners 1729–1829*, ND [*c* 1932]

Atholl, Justin — *The Shadow of the Gallows*, 1954

Ayledotte, William O. — 'The England of Marx and Mill as reflected in Fiction', *The Tasks of Economic History*, Supplement VIII, 1948, 42–58

Aylmer, Felix — *Dickens Incognito*, 1959

Baker, Richard M. — *The Drood Murder Case*, Berkeley and Los Angeles, 1951

Ballantine, Serjeant — *Some Experiences of a Barrister's Life*, 6th edn, 1884

Barnes, Harry Elmer — *The Evolution of Penology in Pennsylvania*, Indianapolis, 1927

Barnes, Harry Elmer, and Teeters, Negley K. — *New Horizons in Criminology*, Englewood Cliffs, New Jersey, 3rd edn, 1959

Barry, John Vincent — *Alexander Maconochie of Norfolk Island*, Melbourne, 1958

Beggs, Thomas — *An Inquiry into the Extent and Causes of Juvenile Depravity*, 1849

Bleackley, Horace — *The Hangmen of England*, 1929

Browne, Douglas G. — *The Rise of Scotland Yard*, 1956

Burt, John T. — *Results of the System of Separate Confinement . . . at Pentonville Prison*, 1852

Butt, John, and Tillotson, Kathleen — *Dickens at Work*, 1957

Buxton, Thomas Fowell — *An Inquiry, whether Crime and Misery are Produced or Prevented, by our Present System of Prison Discipline*, 1818

Carlton, W. J. — 'The Third Man at Newgate', *Review of English Studies*, NS VIII (1957), 402–7

Carlyle, Thomas — 'Model Prisons', *Latter Day Pamphlets* (1850), 1869 edn

Carpenter, Mary — *Juvenile Delinquents*, 1853
Our Convicts, 2 vols, 1864

Carr, Sister Mary Callista, edr — *Catalogue of the Dickens Collection at the University of Texas*, Austin, Texas, 1961

Carter, John, edr — *New Paths in Book Collecting*, 1934

Cavanagh, Ex-Chief-Inspector — *Scotland Yard Past and Present*, 1893

Chesterton, George Laval — *Peace, War and Adventure; an Autobiographical Memoir*, 2 vols, 1853
Revelations of Prison Life; with an Enquiry into Prison Discipline and Secondary Punishments, 2 vols, 1856

Christmas, Henry — *Capital Punishments unsanctioned by the Gospel*, 1845

Clark, William R. — 'The Rationale of Dickens's Death Rate', *Boston University Studies in English*, II (1956), 125–39

Clay, Walter Lowe — *The Prison Chaplain: a Memoir of the Reverend John Clay*, 1861

Cobb, Belton — *The First Detectives*, 1957

Cockshut, A. O. J. — *The Imagination of Charles Dickens*, 1961

Cook, Charles — *The Prisons of the World*, ND [*c* 1891]

Corder, Susanna — *Life of Elizabeth Fry*, 1853

Dalziel, Margaret — *Popular Fiction 100 Years Ago*, 1957

Dicey, A. V. — *Law and Public Opinion in England during the Nineteenth Century*, 2nd edn, 1914

Dilnot, George — *The Story of Scotland Yard*, ND [*c* 1925]

Dixon, W. Hepworth — *The London Prisons*, 1850

Dodds, John W. — *The Age of Paradox: a Biography of England 1841–1851*, 1953

Dolby, George — *Charles Dickens as I knew him* (1885), 1912 edn

Dymond, Alfred H. — *The Law on its Trial: or Personal Recollections of the Death Penalty and its Opponents*, 1865

Field, Rev. J. — *Prison Discipline: the Advantages of the Separate System*, 1846; 2nd edn, 2 vols, 1848

Fielding, K. J. — *Charles Dickens: a Critical Introduction*, 1958
'Charles Dickens and "The Ruffian" ', *English*, x (1954), 88–92

Fitzgerald, Percy — *Chronicles of Bow Street Police-Office*, 2 vols, 1888
Life of Charles Dickens, 2 vols, 1905
Memories of Charles Dickens, 1913

Ford, George H. — *Dickens and his Readers: Aspects of Novel-Criticism since 1836*, Princeton, 1955

Forster, John — *The Life of Charles Dickens* (1872–4), ed J. W. T. Ley, 1928

Fox, Caroline — *Memories of Old Friends: extracts from the Journals and Letters of Caroline Fox*, ed H. N. Pym, 1883

Fox, Lionel — *The English Prison and Borstal Systems*, 1952

Gardiner, Gerald, and Curtis-Raleigh, Nigel — 'The Judicial Attitude to Penal Reform', *The Law Quarterly Review*, LXV (1949), 196–219

Gissing, George — *Charles Dickens: a Critical Study*, 2nd edn, 1903

Goddard, Henry — *Memoirs of a Bow Street Runner*, ed Patrick Pringle, 1956

Gray, Francis C. — *Prison Discipline in America*, 1848

Griffiths, Arthur — *Fifty Years of Public Service*, ND [1904]
Memorials of Millbank, and Chapters in Prison History (1875), 1884 edn
Mysteries of Police and Crime, 2 vols, 1898
Secrets of the Prison-House, 2 vols, 1894

Grünhut, Max — *Penal Reform: a Comparative Study*, 1948

Hill, Frederic — *Crime: its Amount, Causes, and Remedies*, 1853

Hill, Rosamund and Florence — *The Recorder of Birmingham: a Memoir of Matthew Davenport Hill*, 1878

Holdsworth, William S. — *Charles Dickens as a Legal Historian*, New Haven, 1928

Hooper, W. Eden — *The History of Newgate and the Old Bailey*, 1935

Horne, R. H. — *A New Spirit of the Age* (1844), World's Classics edn, 1907

Houghton, Walter E. — *The Victorian Frame of Mind 1830–1870*, New Haven, 1957

House, Humphry — *All in Due Time*, 1955
The Dickens World, 1941

Howard, D. L. — *The English Prisons: their Past and their Future*, 1960

Howard, George — *Guardians of the Queen's Peace*, 1953

Hoyles, J. Arthur — *Religion in Prison*, 1955

Irving, Joseph, edr — *The Annals of our Times 1837–1871*, 1880

Ives, George — *A History of Penal Methods*, 1914

J[ackson], H[enry] — *About 'Edwin Drood'*, Cambridge, 1911

Jackson, T. A. — *Charles Dickens: the Progress of a Radical*, 1937

Johnson, Edgar — *Charles Dickens: his Tragedy and Triumph*, 2 vols, 1953

Jones, Howard — *Crime and the Penal System*, 1956
Prison Reform Now, 1959

Kent, Charles — *Charles Dickens as a Reader*, 1872

Kettle, Arnold — 'Oliver Twist', *An Introduction to the English Novel*, Vol I, 1951

Kingsmill, Joseph — *Prisons and Prisoners*, 1849; 2nd edn, 1852, re-titled *Chapters on Prisons and Prisoners*

Kitton, Frederic G. — *Charles Dickens by Pen and Pencil*, with Supplement, 1890

Koestler, Arthur — *Reflections on Hanging*, 1956

Laurence, John — *A History of Capital Punishment*, ND [*c* 1933]

Laurie, Peter G. — *Sir Peter Laurie: a Family Memoir*, Brentwood, 1901

Lee, W. L. Melville — *A History of Police in England*, 1901

Ley, J. W. T. — *The Dickens Circle*, 1918

Lindsay, Jack — *Charles Dickens: a Biographical and Critical Study*, 1950

Maconochie, Captain [Alexander] — *Crime and Punishment: the Mark System*, 1846

Macready, William Charles — *Diaries 1833–1851*, ed William Toynbee, 2 vols, 1912

Mayhew, Henry — *London Labour and the London Poor*, 4 vols, 1861 edn
London's Underworld, ed Peter Quennell, ND

Mayhew, Henry, and Binny, John — *The Criminal Prisons of London, and Scenes from Prison Life*, 1862

Measor, C. P. — *The Convict Service*, 1861

Mill, James — 'Prisons and Prison Discipline', *Encyclopædia Britannica*, Supplement to the 4th, 5th and 6th edns, Edinburgh, 1824, 385–95

Miller, J. Hillis — *Charles Dickens: the World of his Novels*, 1958

Monod, Sylvère — *Dickens romancier*, Paris, 1953

Morris, Terence — *The Criminal Area: a Study in Social Ecology*, 1958

Moylan, John — *Scotland Yard and the Metropolitan Police*, 1934

Munford, W. A. — *William Ewart, M.P.*, 1960

Murch, A. E. — *The Development of the Detective Novel*, 1958

Nicoll, W. Robertson — *The Problem of 'Edwin Drood'*, 1912

Nisbet, Ada B. — *Dickens and Ellen Ternan*, Berkeley, California, and Cambridge, 1952

Orwell, George	'Charles Dickens', *Critical Essays*, 1946
Pearl, Cyril	*The Girl with the Swansdown Seat: some Aspects of Mid-Victorian Morality*, 1955
Phillips, Charles	*Vacation Thoughts on Capital Punishment*, 4th edn, 1858
Phillips, Walter C.	*Dickens, Reade and Collins; Sensation Novelists*, New York, 1919
Pike, Luke Owen	*A History of Crime in England*, 2 vols, 1876
Pope-Hennessy, Una	*Charles Dickens 1812–1870*, 1945
Praz, Mario	*The Hero in Eclipse in Victorian Fiction*, translated by Angus Davidson, 1956
Pritchett, V. S.	'Edwin Drood', *The Living Novel*, 1946
Prothero, Margaret	*The History of the Criminal Investigation Department at Scotland Yard*, 1931
Radzinowicz, Leon	*A History of the English Criminal Law and Administration from 1750*, Vol I, 1948; Vols II and III, 1956
Reith, Charles	*British Police and the Democratic Ideal*, 1943
	A New Study of Police History, 1956
Robinson, Kenneth	*Wilkie Collins: a Biography*, 1951
Rotch, Benjamin	*Suggestions for the Prevention of Juvenile Depravity*, 1846
Ruggles-Brise, Evelyn	*The English Prison System*, 1921
Rusche, Georg, and Kirchheimer, Otto	*Punishment and Social Structure*, New York, 1939
Sala, George Augustus	*Things I have seen and People I have known*, 2 vols, 1894
Saunders, Montagu	*The Mystery in the Drood Family*, Cambridge, 1914
Savey-Casard, Paul	*Le Crime et la Peine dans l'œuvre de Victor Hugo*, Paris, 1956
Scott, George Riley	*The History of Capital Punishment*, 1950
Solmes, Alwyn	*The English Policeman 871–1935*, 1935
Spielmann, M. H.	*The History of 'Punch'*, 1895
Squires, Paul Chatham	'Charles Dickens as Criminologist', *Journal of the American Institute of Criminal Law and Criminology*, XXIX (1938–9), 170–201
Stonehouse, J. H., edr	*Catalogue of the Libraries of Charles Dickens and W. M. Thackeray*, 1935
	Sikes and Nancy: a Reading by Charles Dickens, 1921
Storey, Gladys	*Dickens and Daughter*, 1939
Symons, Julian	*Charles Dickens*, 1951

Taine, Hyppolite — *Notes on England*, translated by W. F. Rae, 1872

Tallack, William — *Howard Letters and Memories*, 1905
Penological and Preventive Principles, 2nd edn, 1896

Teeters, Negley K., and Shearer, John D. — *The Prison at Philadelphia: Cherry Hill*, New York, 1957

Teetgen, Ada B. — 'Dickens and some Modern Aspects of Penal Reform', *Contemporary Review*, CXXIV (1923), 501–8

Tellkampf, J. L. — *Essays on Law Reform, Commercial Policy, Banks, Penitentiaries, etc., in Great Britain and the United States*, 1859

Thackeray, William Makepeace — *Letters and Private Papers*, ed Gordon N. Ray, 4 vols, 1945–6

Thomson, Basil — *The Story of Scotland Yard*, 1935

Thomson, Patricia — *The Victorian Heroine: a Changing Ideal 1837–1873*, 1956

Tillotson, Kathleen — *Novels of the Eighteen-Forties*, Oxford, 1954
'Oliver Twist', *Essays and Studies*, NS XII (1959), 87–105

Trilling, Lionel — 'Little Dorrit', *The Opposing Self*, 1955

Trumble, Alfred — *In Jail with Dickens*, 1896

Vizetelly, Henry — *Glances back through Seventy Years*, 2 vols, 1893

Wakefield, Edward Gibbon — *Facts relating to the Punishment of Death in the Metropolis*, 1831

Walters, J. Cuming — *Clues to Dickens's 'Mystery of Edwin Drood'*, 1905
The Complete Mystery of Edwin Drood: the History, Continuations, and Solutions (1870–1912), 1912

'Waters' [pseudonym: i.e., William Russell] — *Recollections of a Detective Police-Officer*, 1856

Webb, Sidney and Beatrice — *English Prisons under Local Government*, 1922

Wilson, Edmund — 'Dickens: the two Scrooges', *The Wound and the Bow*(1941), revised edn, 1952

Wright, Thomas — *The Life of Charles Dickens*, 1935

Yates, Edmund — *Recollections and Experiences*, 2 vols, 1884

Young, A. F., and Ashton, E. T. — *British Social Work in the Nineteenth Century*, 1956

Young, G. M., edr — *Early Victorian England*, 2 vols, 1934

Zabel, Morton Dauwen — *Craft and Character in Modern Fiction*, 1957

Zilboorg, Gregory — *The Psychology of the Criminal Act and Punishment*, 1955

INDEX

Works, including Dickens's, are indexed under the name of their author. Periodicals edited by Dickens are also indexed under his name.

MIDLAND BOOKS